By the Scruff of the Neck

A suitcase of memories

By the Scruff of the Neck

A suitcase of memories

HENRI LICHT

A Personal Memoir

Published by Inge Meldgaard, Australia

Henri Licht
41 Belmont Avenue, Upwey
Victoria, Australia 3158

Australian distributor:

Digital Print Australia
135 Gilles Street, Adelaide
South Australia, Australia 5000
www.digitalprintaustralia.com
books@digitalprintaustralia.com

February 2015

Copyright © 2015 Henri Licht

National Library of Australia Cataloguing-in-Publication entry:

Author: Henri Licht
Title: By the Scruff of the Neck ~ A suitcase of memories
ISBN: 978-0-646-93301-6
Dewey Number: 304.8940492

All rights reserved. No part of this book may be used or reproduced in any manner without the written permission of the author, except for brief quotations with attribution and those contained in critical articles or reviews.

Cover and interior artwork by Inge Meldgaard
Website: ingemeldgaard.artworkfolio.com

By the Scruff of the Neck is a remarkable achievement, and I read it with mounting admiration. It is a laceratingly honest, tough minded and often very funny account of a Dutch family which lived through the Nazi occupation of the Netherlands during World War II, then migrated to Australia in 1952, first settling in Tasmania and afterwards in the Latrobe Valley, Gippsland.

Henri was born in 1942, and the main story takes us to when he was sixteen, along the way reflecting upon being Dutch, Australian, and Catholic. His account of sexual tensions within the Church and in religious schools sounds disturbingly accurate.

His story ends – so far – in 1958, but there are a few fast-forwards, including his family's move from Gippsland to Melbourne; his education at Dandenong High School from 1959; his dramatic withdrawal from the Church in 1961, to the mortification of his parents, on the issue of whether priests had the right to direct the faithful how to vote; and his study of philosophy at Monash University.

I took a keen professional interest in this book: in my own autobiography I had disposed of childhood and my family by page seventy-one, whereas he has managed two hundred and eighty-two well-written pages.

I have a cameo part in *By the Scruff of the Neck*, but only in the context of comparison with an influential earlier teacher. And yet – although I could be deluding myself – I suspect that my teaching (much of it outside the syllabus) stimulated Henri's already latent interest in cultural, historical and social issues: his references to Voltaire, Tolstoy, Stravinsky, and his detailed footnotes, remind me of somebody I hesitate to identify. The period when I taught Henri at Dandenong will presumably have to wait for the next volume.

This is an important piece of social, and personal, history, too good – if I can be frank – to be niche published. It should be taken up by bookshops, reviewed, and widely read.

Barry Jones
Companion of the Order of Australia
Member of the Victorian Legislative Assembly 1972–77
Member of the Australian House of Representatives 1977–98
Minister for Science 1983–90

TO MY PARENTS AND BROTHERS

"Happy families are all alike, every unhappy family is unhappy in its own way."

Leo Tolstoy
Anna Karenina
1877

"I think the family is the place where the most ridiculous and least respectable things in the world go on."

Ugo Betti
The Inquiry
1947

ACKNOWLEDGEMENTS

I wish to thank Pauline Clemens for her comments and corrections, as well as Des and Ruth Shiel, David McVilly, Lyn Kennedy and Gwyn Rothols, who have all made invaluable suggestions and helped me organize my material. In particular, I want to make special mention of Inge Meldgaard, whose artistic, editing and publishing skills have made this book possible, as well as Doug Macrae for proof reading the final manuscript. Nevertheless, without my parents and brothers this cavalcade of stories and memories wouldn't exist: all families have their idiosyncrasies and ours is no exception!

FOREWORD

This personal memoir describes my family's experiences during the Second World War, its immediate aftermath, and subsequent emigration to Australia in 1952. However, it's intended to be more than this. My immediate family, including members of my extended Dutch family, is the prism through which the social currents and values of that time are expressed. I also sketch my personal journey to the age of sixteen. This entails the special flavour of our neighbourhoods, Dutch and Australian, and my immersion in the Catholic world of the time. In both countries I have drawn on various personalities who were important to me during my formative years.

On the odd occasion the adult narrator skids off the young boy's narrative into reflective comments which I hope will be of some interest. I have tried to inject humour and pathos into the story and hope the various accounts are entertaining and informative. The term 'education' is used within this memoir in its broadest and narrowest sense, to include both the application of cultural values and the socio-economic forces then at play, as well as formal instruction.

I hope our immigrant experience, like so many others with their own stories to tell, throws light on what Holland and Australia were like during the 1940s and '50s. The incidents described are based on true events insofar as my brothers and I remember them. Even so, since no one can recreate the exact details of early childhood, some license must be granted when conjuring up the past. I have changed some names to avoid offence and to preserve the quasi-fictional tenor of the memoir.

Alkmaar, Holland. May 1945

My pre-memory antics about to be revealed here were conveyed to me on a number of occasions by my folks and my eldest brother, John – Jack-the-lad – and decidedly not with any intention of flattery.

As the Second World War ended in Europe, with a bang for some and a whimper for others, people danced in the streets, some even made love in alleyways, but most hung about their homes in meditative pain and quiet relief. Me, I threw a tantrum, the like of which had never before been seen in my family. My apoplexy arrived unexpectedly, like some vagabond meteor and, shaking with rage, I turned plum-coloured.

While Mother scrubbed the granite bench top in the kitchen, my little fists suddenly banged on the large window facing the paved street below, my face bursting with inexplicable anger.

'Eeeeeyow! Eeeeeyow!' I cried.

My fists became rubber hammers, my eyes narrowed, then puffed up, and my head pounded against the glass, almost shattering it. Was this the cumulative effect of years of oppression by the Germans? Hardly, I was only two and during the War often fell asleep to the soothing hum of Lancasters groaning their way to Hamburg. Hunger pangs perhaps, as the shortage of food made us irritable and our bodies weak? Or was my anger some metaphysical intimation, only divined by myself, who, being so young, was unable to give it meaningful expression?

'What's the matter with him?' asked Bill, my second-eldest brother.

'He's gone nuts. Jus' look at him! Look at him, will ya!' screamed Lex, pointing his chubby finger at me. Lex, my other brother, was a year older than me.

'His face is about to explode! What'll we do?' replied Bill, exasperated.

Meanwhile, with her flabby underarms shaking indecently, Mother pursued her fanatical cleaning, as though the parish priest was about to knock on the front door. My shrieks must have reached her though, since she abruptly stopped and rushed from the kitchen, almost colliding with Jack-the-lad sailing through the front door.

'Get out of my way, John! Herrie's lost it! Dear Jesus, what's he up to now!'

Mother stormed into the living room, shouting and slavering, gobs of spit showering the back of my neck. 'Stop it! Stop it at once or I'll slap you!' Her unruly hair and worn slippers, the heels squashed by her weight, gave her a frazzled look, made worse by having lived in constant fear of Father being arrested; now only partially relieved as she contended with the new demands of peace. I ignored her: didn't want to hear, didn't care.

I was apparently a terrible child, determined to bend the world my way through explosive anger. It had nothing to do with the family as such. It was just that I wanted to reduce the external world to bite-sized pieces and use them either for my own satisfaction or other arcane purposes. The world, which I couldn't, or wouldn't, understand, was too overpowering. It was like someone turning up the decibels on an amplifier so loudly as to damage one's hearing, or else the way colour destroyed Van Gogh. It drove him mad, just as the world threatened to do to me. I was too young and incapable of adjustment, so I just hollered, feeling sick from over-stimulation.

'No! No! Nnnooo... I won't do it. I *will* not! No! No! I *won't* do it!' I burst out angrily. What this negative statement alluded to, no one had the faintest idea. Conceivably I was rebelling, after the fact, against the daily ritual of having to swallow cod liver oil, or having to thank God for the bread crusts I was obliged to eat; or perhaps even for having to share something desirable with my older brothers.

'He's slipping... He's off again. Quick! Catch him before he falls!' yelled Bill.

Both Bill and John lurched forward to catch me as I slid down the chair on which I was standing, berating the street, just as Hitler did when he stood on his platform in Nuremberg fulminating against the universe. Yet while only my brothers listened to me, everyone listened to him, even if they couldn't understand his ludicrous tirades. Pure crowd projection! Thousands of petty and not so petty grievances channelled into an absurd torrent of words. How little Adolf manipulated people's angst! Had he spoken Volapuk or Swahili, I'm sure the people would still have cheered in mindless adulation.

Meanwhile, however, I had fainted, and without doubt, Lex secretly hoped I was dead. The idea of a dead brother appealed to him far more than a live one. The emotionality of such a scenario brought out the sadomasochism in him: the event would be different and perversely entertaining. Even so, apart from childish squabbles, Lex never really resented me. Quite decent of him really, given my outbursts.

Lex was podgy, with straight blond hair, and although overweight, was a pretty lad, with a straight nose, deep-set blue eyes and a serious expression. He always spoke of death as the most interesting phenomenon on earth. 'Hey, Pa. What's it like to be dead? What happens to ya when yer dead? Do ya leave yer body and go somewhere else, or go to someone else's body, or do ya become a baby again? Geez, it must be boring to be dead. Nothing to do underground! Does it hurt to be dead?'

Whenever he asked, 'How did he die?', referring to some pilot, politician, ancient relative or neighbour, Father answered with the stock phrase, "lack of breath". While funny, it didn't answer the question. However, on one occasion, Father chuckled and tried to coax Lex into believing that once we died, our souls floated to heaven.

'But what do ya do up there in heaven? Are there any games?'

Father usually surrendered to the absurdity of it all and turned to Mother, saying, 'I sometimes wonder where Lex gets all his nonsense from.'

Mother remained confident that in time all would be revealed and Lex's incessant questioning would cease. Little did she know that I would take over the baton, continuing the endless interrogation and, in the near future, drive everyone bonkers. Still, we all admired Lex's persistence. As third in line, I suppose it was his way of gaining attention. 'He *is* a Lijcklema,' Father would say. By this he meant his features, personality and mannerisms belonged firmly to Father's maternal side. They had been landowning barons in Friesland for centuries. My father's generation believed in lineage and all that it stood for. A wood in the southwest of the province still bears the family name.

My father, however, spoke with the *Mokum* accent, comical and strewn with Yiddish words, such as 'achenebbisj', meaning cheap, poor, vulgar; 'sjoege' – know-how; 'smoel' – gob. '*Mokum*' is an old Yiddish name for Amsterdam, meaning either 'safe haven' or 'the place'. Although not himself Jewish, he was born in the Jewish quarter, *De Jordaan*, conceivably named after the river Jordan, or perhaps derived from the French for garden, 'jardin'. *De Jordaan* was once a flower market and he had been brought up with its rich argot, not dissimilar in character to cockney English.

Father became a cheese-maker by profession, but switched to being a salesman during the Depression: odd that, when there was so little to sell. His many contacts in our province of North Holland meant he was able to do useful resistance work while the country was occupied by the Germans during the War. He knew many of the farmers around Alkmaar, some of whom provisioned him to help stave off starvation in our extended family, most of whom were town dwellers.

When home, Father would lift his knife while we ate our evening meal and use it to help paint a verbal picture of something eventful that he thought would interest us. One of his wartime stories was about a British pilot struggling out of his parachute, after having landed in a tree.

By the Scruff of the Neck

'There he was, looking stupid and uncomfortable as he dangled in the breeze, though almost smiling, can you believe... I dropped my bike, took out my cheese sample knife and climbed the willow, knowing full well that the Krauts could arrive any moment. I hacked through the cords as fast as I could, sweating like a Turk because it was only a small knife, you understand. At last he dropped onto the grass and I beckoned him to follow me.'

Silence reigned while the family hung onto every word of this gripping tale. We gazed at Father as though he was performing a vaudeville act, and then Lex piped up, 'But did he die? Was he dead? Did he hang himself?' Father ignored him and went to great lengths to once again explain how he managed to untie the young paratrooper and smuggle him to a reliable farm nearby.

Some young boys perform odd acts like sleepwalking, babbling in their sleep, or fouling their pants at inconvenient times: to Mother's great consternation, *I* plucked wool from blankets, leaving bald patches everywhere. Lex did a few of these things too, but had other quirks. He loved four things above all else: fighting, stealing sweets, luxuriating in death talk, and playing on the edge of canals – perhaps water reminds boys of happier times floating in the amniotic fluid of their mothers? What do *you* think, *Sigmund?*[1]

At one time, Lex came home with a dead sparrow, painted its eyes red to preserve the illusion of life, and cleaned its delicate feathers with a toothbrush, which he had stolen from a German officer. A 'company' of German soldiers happened to be garrisoned on the Sportpark behind our house in Newportslane:[2] to their cost, the young officers became sentimental and allowed us to roam their tents. Whether Lex's enthusiasm for thieving was due to the Krauts knocking off our food and bicycles and us stealing from them in return, I can only speculate.

Lex carefully laid the sparrow in a cardboard box, playing with the carcass day after day, until the smell became so overpowering that the usually self-absorbed older brothers curled up their noses.

'Jesus, it stinks in here! Get rid of that bird *now*, or we'll do it for you!'

'You don't understand birds like *I* do. They're thin and they aren't strong, and need looking after,' said Lex earnestly. He took the bird outside into the cold afternoon but refused to bury it, instead cleverly hiding it in our tiny backyard. A crack or fork in the lilac tree would do. Occasionally Lex tied dead birds to low-lying branches too, sometimes

---

[1] Sigmund Freud

[2] 'Nieuwpoortslaan' in Dutch

covered with snow, claiming this was what the Sioux Indians did with *their* expired young, but he was inconsolable when they were gone the next day, rats or cats being the likely culprits.

'I'll kill those cats with me slingshot!' he'd exclaim. 'Hey, Pa, how do ya kill rats? Can ya build me a rat trap?'

I've forgotten how many dead frogs he buried in the coal annex as well. We should have built a war memorial to all these dead creatures...

Once, Bill came home with an emaciated heron and tied it to one of the steel legs supporting the rabbit hutch, now vacant because the Krauts had helped themselves to our lovingly bred animals. The heron simply stood there stupidly on one leg, frozen in time, its dull blue feathers reinforcing its scrawniness. It just wouldn't move.

'Is it dead yet?' asked Lex, a peculiar smile on his face.

'No, it isn't, you dill,' spat Bill.

Lex persisted: 'I reckon it's dead. Come on, Bill! It's worthless. Give it to me! It's dead as a doornail. I can't see *any* movement.'

Lex was most disappointed when Bill proffered a wriggling worm and the bird swallowed it in a blink, before resuming its silent, moribund stance. In spite of the meal, though, it died a few days later, just to please Lex.

However, to go back to the beginning of this story, *I* wasn't dead, though had succumbed from lack of oxygen, paradoxically generated by the intensity of my fit of wrath. Even so, I still can't recall the cause of it all. If *Adolf* were around *he* might be able to explain. After all, *his* rages were legendary.

All of which reminds me of a certain Fred Winterbotham, a British spy, who visited him once and seemed impressed by his friendly manner. Noticing the man's slightly protruding eyes, he asked the *Führer* what he thought of the communists.

There was a momentary silence as Adolf's neck reddened, his eyes bulged, and he began to shudder with anger. Apparently he ranted for some time and once his tirade had come to an abrupt end, changed back to his personable self. *Sigmund* or *Carl*[3]... Please, help! Histrionic Personality Disorder, perhaps?

Whether Adolf hated the Jews more than the communists becomes a moot point. I, on the other hand, was unable to identify with such causes; the immediate, material world was more than enough for me to deal with. Maybe I suffered from premature *weltschmerz*.[4] But it doesn't

---

[3] Carl Jung, 1875–1961, a Swiss psychiatrist and psychotherapist who, together with Sigmund Freud, co-founded psychoanalysis.

[4] Sadness over the evils of the world, especially as an expression of romantic pessimism.

matter now: I have grown out of my tantrums, although the *weltschmerz* remains.

What happened next is based on the quite likely embellished account given to Father and me by John:

Mother's barking had subsided and, realizing there was little to be done while I lay prostrate, she focused instead on herself. She was about to join me in the fainting fit when John came up with the inspiring idea of carrying me over to Sister Darling,[5] the midwife, who lived diagonally opposite, across the road. It was rumoured she had special powers.

'Sister Darling will know what to do. She's a nurse and has delivered babies,' stated John confidently.

How a midwife could cure my fainting fit, only God knew, but Mother was desperate and easily persuaded. She retreated from her imminent collapse and, while everyone waited for her instructions, rolled her green eyes, affecting confusion. 'Very well then, but be gentle. He's only just come out of hospital.'

Sister Darling was a large woman with breasts like billowing spinnakers. She was a miracle worker and during both the War and its aftermath, Father made sure she had enough potatoes and turnips to eat until rationing ended. If there was a husband, none of us knew about it. Possibly carted off to a labour camp... By the end of the War, two sons had already disappeared behind Churchill's "Iron Curtain".[6] Her grief was immense but she bore her burden through kindness and helped anyone in the neighbourhood who needed her. She was not, however, religious. Quite the opposite in fact! A devout freethinker, she had belonged to the Dutch Communist Party since the First World War.

The deep cream sill of the huge bay window at the front of her house was cluttered with pots of withered flowers. Her greying hair in a bun, she immediately opened the solid, wooden front door, having already espied the encumbered clan crossing the street.

'He's passed out, Sister!' John needlessly informed her.

'Probably dead!' added Lex gleefully.

'Let me have a look at him.' It was as though she were studying a Vermeer[7] still life.

I had changed colour: bloodless, but still breathing. In the meantime, Mother's eyes had begun to dampen: this was her default position whenever her emotions were tapped, which was rather too often.

Sister Darling eventually turned to Mother and said, 'There's nothing wrong with him. He just got a little too excited about something.' With

---

[5] Not her real name.

[6] Churchill introduced his 'Iron Curtain' speech in March 1946 in Missouri, USA, to refer to the division of Europe into West and East.

[7] Johannes Vermeer, 1632–75, Dutch genre painter who specialized in domestic interior scenes.

this comforting assessment, she smacked me on the face, and, upon opening my eyes, I proceeded to bawl and bluster. Lex was surprised at her audacity but enjoyed the spectacle.

On Liberation Day, however, John wasn't overly interested in Mother's and my splutterings, since he was too excited by the ending of the War. 'At last the dirty Krauts have gone!' he exclaimed earlier that morning. 'Good riddance to bad rubbish! Bloody bastards... Bloodsuckers... Dumb squareheads... Hooray! Hooray! When's Father coming home?'

On that fateful day, John wanted to share his adventures; there was so much to tell. He had even heard the old British bulldog call it "a glorious day" on our neighbours', the De Witts, radio. Churchill remained the face of steadfastness and reassurance right to the bittersweet end. The fact that he loved a Cuban cigar enhanced Father's admiration of him, particularly since Father enjoyed a good *Schimmelpenninck*, his own preferred brand.

John was tall and skinny, with a shock of blond hair, attracting the nickname 'the whitey', although Father, with satisfaction, dubbed him 'Jack-the-lad'. He had in fact many aliases – 'the long'n' and 'the grasshopper' to name but two. It all depended on the user or circumstance. At the age of twelve he was already in long trousers and smoking with his mates, usually in front of Stockman's cigar shop. The lads met there regularly after school, discussing the fluctuations of the War, yelling vulgarities at girls passing by, and flicking cigarette butts onto the road.

'You're prettier than your sister, so how about a feel?' one shouted.

'Nice legs! Nice tits! Nice face!' yelled another.

'Drop dead, you filthy animals!' came the retort.

They dismissed her angry words like their cigarette butts.

'I heard from my father that the Russians are coming and they're not to be trifled with,' said one of the boys.

'Still, better the Commies than the Nazis,' contributed another.

They canvassed possibilities then returned to more mundane matters, like food and items for barter. Money had lost its value during the War: cigarettes were now widely used as currency on the black market. John was the go-to man in the neighbourhood for this highly sought after commodity. Five years of occupation had made John cunning, and reading him like a book, Father worried, but for the time being, said nothing.

Stealing from the Krauts was another patriotic duty, as everyone knew, even though it clashed with our upbringing, and sometimes both my older brothers and their mates even marched up and down the street

By the Scruff of the Neck

with improvised wooden guns, following a German regiment galumphing past. I didn't understand what was happening, but delighted in the street theatre.

Just before D-Day,[8] the crucial turning point for the Allies, I fell ill. Fever and a persistent sore throat left me lethargic.

'It's only a question of time,' said Father, as he, Mother and John discussed the War situation over the dinner table. 'Leenstra tells me it's all to do with finding the right location and making sure the Krauts don't twig.' Leenstra was a farmer in nearby Schagen.

But John and Mother weren't convinced. 'That Hitler isn't a fool, you know. We've already had a number of false alarms. The Krauts may be inhuman, but they're *very* smart.' John was re-stating the opinion of his mates, and since Mother hadn't detected any favourable change in the neighbourhood, she remained equally pessimistic.

In my limited way, I surmised this D-Day, or invasion day, was special, but was distracted by my illness, the tight throat having persisted for a long time; although the family was at least happy I wasn't howling.

Approaching the age of two by then, I soon had my own D-Day, when I was hermetically sealed in a large white room in the Saint Elizabeth infirmary. The room was bleak and had an enormous window looking out onto a busy corridor. It seems that I had contracted diphtheria. I couldn't read the face of the grim reaper, being too young, but according to Mother, the scythe was about to drop. I remained in hospital for a long time. Much later, with bemused pride, Mother told me all about it.

'Did you know,' she boasted to her sisters, 'Herrie hid beneath the skirt of a fat matron and somehow smuggled himself into the corridors. How clever is that! Pandemonium broke out because they couldn't find him... Rather lax though, if you ask me, considering the infectious nature of his ailment.' Her sisters just sighed.

I could talk before I could walk, but was adept at both from a young age – I can probably thank my older brothers for this, since imitation is a great teacher. My newly acquired mobility, aided by my short stature, allowed me to roam the hospital, until caught by some officious nurse and carried back to bed. Like a baboon enjoying his freedom after having hurdled the wall of his enclosure, it seems I was usually recaptured in either a ward full of recuperating soldiers or in a cupboard, sometimes having donned a *pot de chambre* as a helmet to ward off the starched linen brigade. Now and then, I was found urinating under the high, steel beds of dying patients. These people were often left alone to ponder the

---

[8] The term 'D-Day' was of course not familiar to us. It took place on the 6th June 1944.

depth of the abyss, or to distract themselves by studying the flies taxiing along pristine walls, preparing for take-off like Hurricanes before the Battle of Britain. Perhaps the patients themselves wondered when they would be 'taking off'?

In the meantime, unaware of the poor sods above me, I explored the linoleum tracks to see where they led, making sure to leave a steaming deposit freshly rolled out of my capacious shorts for some busy, unsuspecting nurse to slip on and perform a chicken dance. Father thought my early wanderlust came from our seafaring relations working the East India trade...

It never lasted long though. Alert nurses or dour doctors quickly discovered my absence.

'That Licht tyke has gone missing again,' a nurse informed the doctor on duty.

'Well, find the little bugger; you never know *what* he's up to. Last week he nearly scalded himself trying to pull a hot iron from its stand in the linen room. He's dynamite. Find him!'

Mother finished her story by saying, with pride, 'Yes! He was a nuisance, but everyone adored and fussed over him, as if he belonged to them.'

'The cherub needs a companion,' advised a nun who visited my room one day.

'Diphtheria is contagious. He can't have a friend,' replied the nurse in charge.

'But if he has been immunized and is out of danger, what's the risk?' queried the nun patiently, her large glasses obscuring her face, if not her resolve.

I was in fact in desperate need of friendship and the following day a friend of sorts materialized. He was a grownup, definitely not someone my size as I had hoped for. What could I do with a grownup? Adults, as most children know, rarely understand them. They inhabit a different universe and gabble above one's head, literally and figuratively. They also smell of tobacco, chewing gum, sweat or perfume – although the last, at least, is sometimes agreeable.

My new friend, or should I say fellow patient, was tall, dark and hairy. The D-word also applied to him. Diphtheria, however, is far more serious in adults than in children. For the first few days he just stared in front of him and sighed heavily. I had little choice but to stare back and in my childlike way study him. He ignored me and frequently turned away to face the wall next to him. At first I thought he had hidden a motorbike under his sheet, till I realized the engine was roaring through his mouth. His snoring at least demonstrated the presence of a human being.

It was after about a week that he became aware of my presence: I had climbed out of bed to stand in front of him, with my finger up my nose. 'Who are you?' I confronted him. 'What are you doing in my bedroom? Are you sick? You don't look sick. I was hoping you'd be a boy like me, so I could play with you. But you're too big.'

By this stage my fellow patient was sitting up and leaning back against his pillows. He smiled and patted me on the head. 'Well, my little clown, my name is Aaron and I'm here for the same reason you are. You don't look sick either but we both have an illness we can't see... Maybe you can tell me some stories?' When he threw back the blankets and stood up, I beheld a giant.

I had never seen Father without his white vest, which revealed only a few chest hairs popping out over the top. In contrast, this man, younger than him, was a veritable gorilla, with thick, black, worm-like hairs sprouting from his chest and arms. However, his skin was milky white and his face, though angular, was softened by large black eyes which lit up when animated. When he spoke, his generous mouth revealed stained teeth, possibly from either too much coffee, or smoking.

My hirsute hospital chum and I soon became good friends. For a few minutes he would bounce me up and down on his strong legs until he tired, then politely ask me to run along, or else lifted me back into my small bed.

Sometimes, depending on the food, we amused ourselves with farting marathons. He usually prevailed. As if his anus had ripped the sheet beneath him, his farts, *sostenuto* and *fortissimo*, dwarfed my feeble efforts. I often stood in front of his bed for a very long time just watching and listening.

Aaron's voice was gentle and calming. He spoke slowly and deliberately, as if each word cost him. 'Ah, my little tiger, did you have a pleasant dream last night, or a nightmare?' he would ask.

'I know what a mare is because Grandpa has one. Is a nightmare a horse that runs at night? I can't ride a horse, can you?'

'No. No, my little warrior. A nightmare is like a bad dream. I have them now and then. But a nice dream is rare. Do you dream a lot?'

I hadn't really given it much thought. Children ask questions but don't wish to be burdened with too much analysis. Plenty of time for that later! Nevertheless, I did want to give him an answer. 'Hmm, Heron,' as I called him, 'I *do* have lots of dreams but can't remember most of 'm. But I do remember a dream I had a while ago... I had a dream about a small beach; I don't know where. It was a funny dream 'cause I was there at night. It was dark and windy and I was frightened. A big yellow light shone onto the beach, not like the moon, but like the sun, only shining on *that* beach because the rest was inky black. No one was on the beach 'cept me. I sat on the yellow sand and peered through the darkness and as the wind became stronger, I saw a sumbarine coming straight up out of the water. I saw the lid open and out climbed a mermaid and then a giant octopus. The octopus had very long arms and tried to grab me, but the mermaid sat next to me and took me in her arms to save me. I screamed so much that even Bill woke up. I'm lucky to be alive.'

Aaron laughed quietly, then mumbled something about a job for a certain *Sigmund* and what it all meant to a youngster like me with an overcharged imagination. I didn't comprehend his weird explanation, much too difficult, and left him ruminating to himself. Instead, I crawled back to bed since I felt feverish, and began humming a nursery rhyme.

Sometimes my friend would read a book given to him by one of the nurses, newspapers being of little use under the Germans. Occasionally, when he was totally immersed, I would try to distract him.

'Hey, Heron, would you like to be able to fly?' Silence. 'I've a sore foot, can you help me?' Further silence. 'Tell me a story about whales or ephelants.' He continued to ignore me and after a long spell put the book face down onto the bed. He would then talk to himself, tapping the book distractedly. Other times, though, he sang to himself while I tried to follow the melody. Each day I grew fonder of him.

Three weeks later, northern gales attacked the infirmary, and as the small upper windows wept rivulets onto their blistering frames, I suddenly woke up, glanced over towards my companion, and discovered he wasn't there. His bed was smooth and neatly covered by a beige bedspread. I refused to believe my eyes: Aaron had disappeared into thin air! I jumped out of my island of warmth, rushed to the closed door and furiously banged my little fists against it, sobbing loudly. After a few minutes a nurse opened the door and placed me on her lap, trying to calm me down. I clawed at her and struggled to wriggle off, to little avail.

I found out much later that Aaron had died in his sleep and was taken away during the night – my sweet dreams giving me no inkling. I lay there, overwrought, watching the traffic in the corridor. Maybe the octopus I told Aaron about had strangled him?

Father informed me some years after the War that Aaron had been a resistance fighter.

'Yes! He was a Jewboy, but a lovely fellow. It's such a pity he died so young. He was very clever and studying to be a doctor. Another loss to our society! Why do so many clever people die young?' He sucked his cigar, musing reflectively. Even such tolerant Dutchmen as Father occasionally lapsed into mild anti-Semitism.

By the Scruff of the Neck

Aaron's mother, though Jewish, had married a *goy*,[9] not all that uncommon in Holland. His mother's family had belonged to the small but well integrated Jewish community in Alkmaar.

The reason he hadn't been captured was due to certain forms of Dutch recalcitrance, as well as his doctored Dutch papers. A significant number of the Dutch collaborated with the Germans but many more hated them, not only for ideological reasons, but essentially because the Dutch, especially the Hollanders from the north, are historically a no-nonsense, independent people, resenting outside interference of any sort. Yet it has to be said, most Amsterdammers were indifferent to the fate of the Jews and carried out German instructions with shameful diligence.[10] During the War, shielding Jews, communists, resistance fighters or allied pilots did occur nonetheless, despite the threat of instant reprisal. Alkmaar burghers were sometimes lined up against a wall and summarily shot.

The War often turned people into marionettes, fear and famine driving them to act strangely, with a main focus on self-interest. For example, next door to us lived an artist by the name of Pathway.[11] He specialized in still life. Towards the end of the War, unbeknown to us, his wife died of starvation. His daughter across the road had hoarded enough food to feed a battalion, yet she allowed her mother to starve. Maybe it was revenge for past misdeeds, but we suspected callousness. On the other hand, a few houses past Sister Darling lived a German woman, married to a Dutchman, who went out of her way to be kind to starving families. She detested Hitler as much as we did.

Like my cousin Han, who also died young, Aaron, with his sudden departure, took on a nebulous air, as if he hadn't really existed and instead inhabited one of my recurring dreams. Sometimes I pushed him away, other times, when lonely, I conjured him up.

I was in hospital for a number of months and noticed that just before dinnertime, the number of visitors increased. Tall men wearing bespattered raincoats, their children following close behind, strode purposefully in to visit wives giving birth to yet another child. I watched trim nurses dodging the crowd, while everyone appeared busy and preoccupied. The visitors rarely stopped by my window to wave hello to the wide-eyed little boy who had lost his boon companion. I wanted them to be sorry for me, but they couldn't care less; they were on a mission:

---

[9] Gentile – not of the Jewish faith.
[10] See Geert Mak's *A Short History of Amsterdam,* Olympus 1994, pp. 281–86
[11] Not his real name.

visit the wife and mother, exchange trivial comments, and quickly retreat.

My own family visited me in hospital once a week, usually on Sunday afternoons, although they weren't to have any direct contact with me. However, being unaware of days or dates, I was always surprised to see them. Because of the thick glass window, all I could hear were distant, muffled voices and had to rely on facial gymnastics to make sense of what they were saying.

John and Bill were always bored and turned their backs on me. Father grinned knowingly, but his mind was elsewhere, while Lex pulled down his lower eyelids or turned his eyeballs upwards to reveal their whites, a feat I always admired, then poked out his tongue. Mother just waved, smiling sadly and shaking her head in frustrated empathy, as only mothers can.

Sometimes they arrived while I was busily removing fluff from between my toes, my tongue hanging out like a dog with distemper. They all laughed their heads off. Caught unawares, I looked up by chance, screamed, and made faces at them. A nurse then rushed in, thinking I had electrocuted myself, since I was fond of stuffing power points with gunk, as all the nurses knew. Turning to my idiotic family behind the window, she threw up her arms in despair.

Even now, in my advancing years, when life's journey ought to have made me more resigned, I detest confinement. Nevertheless, the dynamics of hospitals are fascinating. For the patient, besieged by panic or apprehension, they are a necessary evil. For the very young, hospital can be a prison, pain the main distraction. Tedium casts its pall over sufferers, and time, that protean entity, marshals its hostile troops: boredom, black musings, unfamiliarity and loneliness. Life inevitably slows down – except for the hospital staff, of course – and, settled into routine, a patient may, fortunately, begin to relax, finding ways to distract themselves. Some years ago, for example, after a routine operation, I discovered a recently arrived Dutch male nurse and buzzed him rather too often with the sole aim of discussing the state of Dutch soccer and politics. He was remarkably kind and didn't mind spending a few extra minutes by my bedside, which was greatly appreciated.

I can't remember coming home but I do recall the smouldering effects of the War. Father had changed jobs. No longer a cheese salesman, he now sold confectionery to shopkeepers in North Holland. The tiny shops formed part of gigantic farmsteads created in the reclaimed polders around Alkmaar – a bit of extra money for cash-strapped farmers. Often Father went by bike, but around 1948 was given an old, grey, pre-War Ford for his travels. The samples he brought home never lasted long; Lex could sniff out a sweet through a bunker wall!

'God damn! Who knocked off my samples?' Everyone stared at Lex, who looked the picture of innocence and kept slurping his soup as if nothing were the matter.

Europe was picking up the pieces, and although our neighbourhood continued where it left off before the War, the mood had changed; life before the War had been more leisurely. However, notwithstanding the poverty, people kept their noses above water and in general treated one another like human beings.

Even so, the aftermath proved difficult, despite the best efforts of the Marshall Plan.[12] The fear of communism persuaded the American Congress to pour aid into Europe, altruism a convenient by-product. Nevertheless, without the Marshall Plan, Holland would have collapsed. The end of the War saw this little country on its knees. Food rationing continued for several years and the ravages of the Dutch famine in the winter of 1944 still rebounded. Meanwhile, war-weariness affected nearly everyone, as did concern for what the future would bring. It was all a matter of degree, location or class; the wealthy bought time by selling jewellery or other valuables and usually survived better than the poor.

There was also the usual retribution for collaborating with the enemy, though this varied markedly throughout Europe. Some countries, like the Baltic States, had willingly worked with the Germans against their Russian overlords.

A few doors up from us lived the de Kooy family,[13] a large family of three generations. It never ceased to amaze us how so many people could live in such a tiny house. Two of the blowsy daughters had entertained German personnel on a regular basis. Father, though critical, understood human frailty and ignored the collaboration. He had bigger fish to fry: feeding the family, earning enough money to buy clothes and fuel, and keeping a job.

After liberation the moral crusaders had a field day. The de Kooy girls were dragged into the street and shorn like sheep. This was common practice. But why were women humiliated more than men? Many men known to have toadied up to the Nazis either escaped punishment or were simply shunned. To be fair, some like Jan Schouten,[14] a cocky neighbour, *were* strung up. Others were pressed into clearing landmines,

---

[12] A program initiated in 1947 by George Marshall, USA Secretary of State, to rebuild postwar Europe through financial and food aid.

[13] Not their real name.

[14] Not his real name.

yet many got off lightly. In contrast, the treatment of women, some even innocent or of dubious complicity, was in itself an act of perverse abuse.

One freezing afternoon, Lex and I were returning home from school when we saw a plane flying low over the Alkmaar Wood. 'Look Herrie, they've thrown something from the plane! Wonder what it is?'

Lo and behold, a large parcel came floating down, like the spinning house from Kansas in *The Wizard Of Oz*, eventually landing on the grass just in front of 'The Four States', a set of stately homes at the end of our street. As we ran towards the parcel, one side of which was wedged into the soft earth, we were beaten to it by a nasty competitor in the form of a huge dog, its bony ribcage exposed like coils inside a worn mattress.

Animals too were starving and this cur was also frothing at the mouth. So, since rabies was common, Lex threw stones at it when it began ripping at the cardboard. 'Piss off you skinny mongrel! This is ours.' As we came closer, Lex's accuracy improved and he hit the poor mutt on the head. It yelped and took off.

Sensing a gift from heaven, Lex exclaimed, 'Wonder what's inside, Herrie!' We lifted the parcel between us and hauled it back along Newportslane. It took us quite some time to shift the heavy carton, because we had to stop several times to recover our breath. Eventually, we reached home and knocked loudly on the door.

'What the hell have you two found?' asked John, casting his expert eye over the box, wondering whether there was anything in it for him.

'You didn't knock it off did you, you morons?' Bill asked suspiciously.

We ignored the insult: 'No, we were just coming home from school when we saw an aeroplane circling The Four States and wondered why, till this came down.'

We decided to wait for Father to come home before opening it and left the parcel sitting on the dinner table. Mother had gone to visit her own mother at *The Dyke*[15] – her parents' farm. When Father arrived home, it was time to open the parcel and celebrate: our parents were well pleased to find tins of food and dry biscuits inside.

Our food intake was usually limited and basic. To have received these luxuries was indeed a gift from God...or the Americans... Perhaps God was an American? The Americans certainly seem to think so... I can't recall how long our precious gift lasted, but to this day we have a tin wrapped with a note written by Mother in neat cursive handwriting, reminding us of the grand occasion.

---

[15] An embankment to keep out the floods. Many farms built in its lee were popularly referred to as 'the dyke', or 'dike', a common Dutch topographical reference point.

By the Scruff of the Neck

The austerity of the times wasn't really apparent to us though, since we never went without, notwithstanding our meagre diet. In any case, we didn't know any better. Yet even in my childish consciousness, I felt there was an air of sadness in our neighbourhood. People were grateful to have survived the Nazi tyranny but were disoriented and didn't know what to expect from the uncertain years ahead.

During the War, Father had been detained twice and narrowly escaped deportation. The first arrest was trivial: he hadn't updated his identity papers to match his occupation as cheese salesman.

'You must understand, Herr Licht, that having false or incorrect papers should mean imprisonment. You have a week to correct the details then report here by nine o'clock... We are being very lenient with you...this time.'

The second infraction was more serious. Curfew began at eight now and Father always arrived home fairly late, never before seven at night, obliging Mother to tame their cubs by herself. On this particular night, she knew something was amiss. My brothers all grew silent, sharing her anxiety.

Father always worried about food for his tribe. Cycling furiously in the dark, the light shimmering feebly before him, he had a rendezvous with Leenstra, his farmer acquaintance, who had promised him spuds the previous week. He also carried some vital information from Piet Goudsblom, his brother-in-law, and, in addition, needed to report back to Henneman, his employer, for the daily sales tally.

Leenstra, a strict Calvinist, loathed the Germans and was active in the Resistance. His large farm had been placed under surveillance, but he was too clever to be worried by the Bavarian peasant schütze[16] stalking his property.

With difficulty, Father balanced the sack of potatoes on his handlebar and tightened his buff-coloured raincoat to prepare for the journey home. The icy wind scoured his handsome features. It was bitterly cold, but he was used to that. He knew he should be home by now, half an hour past curfew. *Hope no German soldiers are on the prowl! I'll take the back streets just to be safe. Must help my brothers with grub. I hope Alie isn't too worried. The boys will be fine. Bloody Germans! Why didn't the government offer more resistance? I wish that freezing wind would blow somewhere else!*

'Halt! Papers?' Fear surged through Father's body. 'Why are you cycling out of permitted hours? This is forbidden! Name? Occupation?'

---

[16] Marksmen, infantry.

'Herman Licht... Salesman... I'm just returning from Schagen. The wind was against me... I'm sorry; it won't happen again.'

Suspicious, the heavy-set German motioned Father to follow his motorbike to the old Cadet School, now German headquarters for the Alkmaar precinct. Father, nervous, yet composed, waited outside the commandant's office. Mother, on the other hand, would have been beside herself and fallen to her knees.

'Kommen Sie herein... Hauptmann Stenger... Setzen Sie sich!'[17]

Expecting verbal abuse, Father apprehensively sat down, although the German captain seemed at ease as he stared at Father's papers and not in the least angry.

'I understand cheese is your business, but in your travels what prevents you from contacting our enemy across the channel? If we find you are working for their side, I have little choice but to hand you over to my superiors... You will either be shot or given a vacation in one of our fine factories in Germany.' The captain briskly poked his thumb backwards over his shoulder.

Father's brow furrowed as he protested that he was merely late because of the weather, his papers already having been checked. He then changed the subject, flattering the German army on its efficiency. Father's German was tolerable and he spent a few moments on the similarities between the Dutch and the Germans, before switching to the apolitical subject of football.

The captain's face relaxed as his grey eyes scanned Father's papers, discovering they were both the same age. Then, out of the blue, he asked 'Wieviel kinder haben Sie?'[18]

'Four boys,' Father replied.

'Ich auch!'[19] the captain almost shouted. The coincidence altered his attitude and he allowed himself a tight smile. 'Hmm! Hmm! Fancy that.' He sat back and studied the ceiling as though it were the Sistine chapel.

The initial steely exchange had taken on a conversational air. After more questions, the captain almost became sentimental as he leaned over the desk, admitting to missing his wife and sons. Wistfully shaking his head, he stood up, moved closer to Father and told him to leave. 'You won't get off so lightly next time!' he said, regaining his composure. Inexplicably, Father was allowed to keep his spuds.

On other occasions, when Father was wanted by the Germans, he hid in the narrow space above the lowered ceiling separating the dining room from the front room. While not exactly a dropped ceiling, it was wide enough and long enough to conceal someone, just like a snug coffin.

---

[17] 'Enter... Captain Stenger... Sit down!'
[18] 'How many children do you have?'
[19] 'Me, too!'

By the Scruff of the Neck

Once, he shared this refuge with a neighbour in the same predicament. How they managed to squeeze in together was a miracle, obviously necessitating synchronized breathing.

Hitler and his beloved chief architect, Albert Speer, needed more manpower to work the factories. Men were indiscriminately rounded up in 'razzias' and sent to the Vaterland. Father, a strong, healthy man, was an ideal candidate, hence his disappearance when the raids were on. He became an *'onderduiker'*, or one who 'dives under'.

The grapevine was usually ahead of the Germans. Like wildfire, the rumours spread: 'Razzia! Razzia!' This frightening word derived from the Algerian variant of the Arabic for raid, 'ghaziah'. This term is not to be confused with 'pogrom', the systematic massacre of a sect, especially Jews in countries such as Russia, for example. Under Nazi rule, 'razzia' came to mean the rounding up of either Jews or other locals to be then used as forced labour and transported to what we now know were concentration camps. The Germans entered homes with bayonet at the ready, poking and stabbing through ceilings, walls and cupboards. Stupid and heavy-handed, when you consider the potential damage to one's prospective workers.

Father recounted how the sharp tip of a bayonet had once gone straight up between his legs, causing much mirth as to the possibility of him having lost his manhood. 'If they keep prodding like this I'm going to lose my old boy, I thought to myself, or else they'll skewer my heart. I've never felt so uncomfortable... I just kept hoping they'd go away... God, I hate the Germans!' Father retained his lightheartedness even under pressure.

Uncle Piet Goudsblom and Father could have been shot, just as other resistance fighters were, because of an incident one late winter's evening. Uncle Piet ran a small picturesque pub in the Alkmaar Wood called the *Café Deerpark*. On my return to Holland in 1970, I spent many twilight sessions there, drinking beer gratis and talking to the locals, who had known Father and Mother well.

'I remember your father as an affable *Mokumer* – Amsterdammer. He was a wonderful storyteller and an honest bloke,' said the local barber. 'I used to sit next to him at the football.'

'Your mother was spontaneous and good company,' recalled Arie Spijkerman, 'but boy could she talk!'

Arie, a council worker, was an old mate of John's. Ton, Uncle Piet's son and my cousin, was now the proprietor of the pub. A sense of timelessness, or rather, of suspended time, hung about the place. Much of the décor had remained the same since before the War and indeed many of the oldies who drank there were already eager imbibers before the coming of Little Adolph. They formed an interesting link between the interbellum years and the aftermath. For many of them the *Café Deerpark* was home away from home. Card games were conducted passionately amid the stench of cigar smoke and noggins of *jenever* – Dutch gin. One has only to fast forward Dirck Hals' wonderful painting, *Gentlemen Smoking and Playing Backgammon in an Interior,* 1627, to Ton's establishment and one could be forgiven for feeling as if one had been caught in a time warp; ignore the clothes.

As a child I loved this pub. The setting reminded me of a fairytale by the brothers Grimm: an inn run by an honest inn-keeper, hidden in a dark wood inhabited by goblins and plucky gnomes, and which had become a place of sadness when the wife or daughter was kidnapped and held ransom by some villain – you get the drift. The dark hues of the tall trees, amid nettles, bracken and thick bushes, allowed my imagination to supply any kind of plot.

Uncle Piet, a man of many talents, had been a baker, deliveryman, sales representative and coachman. He became well known around Alkmaar, but mainly as a publican. He would visit us on his big black bike with its huge wicker basket attached to the front, a fag hanging from his lips.

A small, dapper man, with jet-black hair, Uncle Piet had inherited a stubborn streak from his father, our maternal grandfather, Willem, and would stand up to anyone, including the Krauts. Like most good Dutchmen, he resented the occupation of his home turf, while as chairperson of our neighbourhood committee he displayed a great sense of tribal responsibility.

One bitterly cold evening, as he was cleaning up the bar, he heard a loud rattling of the front door. Due to the curfew he had to close earlier than usual and, in any case, most people wouldn't have dared venture out. Even during the day, patronage had dropped off.

'Who's there? We're closed! Come back tomorrow!' Uncle Piet called out wearily.

The cold wind snapping at the pub prompted a quick cleanup and a smart dash to the hot stove located upstairs in the living room. His wife, Aunty Trien, was already in bed and asleep.

The sound at the door now became more urgent. Piet grabbed a knife, not trusting anyone. It could be the Germans out on patrol, or any ne'er-do-well. These were uncertain times. He then heard a feeble cry for help that told him this at least wasn't a regular client: 'Please! Please! Let me in. I need to talk to you.'

Piet cautiously opened the door and a man collapsed into his arms. He looked haggard, his hair long and matted, his appearance and manner suggesting he certainly wasn't a thief.

By the Scruff of the Neck

'You must help me!' he began. 'My family is safe for the moment but the Krauts are onto me.'

Piet shouldered him into the bar and seated him on the nearest chair. 'Who are you and what have you done?' he asked.

'Nothing, absolutely nothing,' the man quickly replied. 'I am a Jew from Den Helder and a harbour town is not a good place to be. Dr van Etienne, who I have known for years through my art dealings, recommended your place.'

Dr van Etienne had been Mother's family doctor for years and a frequent visitor to our house, especially given my sickly constitution.

Piet knew concealing Jews meant almost certain death, but immediately dismissed this dreadful thought. The man was desperate and in poor shape. Delicate and pale, he had apparently been on the run for two days, safe-haven hopping southwards. He wanted to escape to Heiloo, where he had a friend who might look after him. He coughed continually and appeared quite sick. Uncle Piet himself suffered from stomach ulcers and mild pleurisy, so could easily sympathise with the man.

Piet led him behind the counter and lifted a long strip of beer-stained floor runner, the length of the bar, revealing a hatch leading to a cellar. The men descended a steep ladder into a cold airless space some three metres square. A few vats lined one wall and some garden tools lay on a bench by the other. Piet shifted the remaining contents of the cellar to one side then turned away to go upstairs, saying, 'Stay here! I'll get a spare mattress from the loft and you try to get some sleep.'

As he sat on the floor shaking, the man clutched Piet's hand and thanked him, but Piet thought, 'I have to get rid of him or it's curtains for me, especially with the Krauts around the corner.'

After making the stranger comfortable, Piet snuck out to our place, about a fifteen-minute walk away. He strode briskly through the nearby wood, which he knew backwards so could easily avoid detection. Then, after scampering along alleys and avoiding the street lamps, now beacons of gloom under German occupation, he climbed our rear fence and knocked lightly on the back door in the agreed manner. Father had already been home an hour.

'You'll have to get rid of him tonight, Piet. By morning, or even now, your place could be swarming with Krauts. You're only a stone's throw away from their headquarters. You know that! Come, I'll help you. You go first; I'll follow in five minutes. We can't be seen together.'

They took a different route back to the pub, Father going the long way along Zanderstream, on the far side of the Sportpark, and Piet taking the alleys back to the *Café Deerpark*. The wind howled around the gables and lampposts, squalls of rain lashing windows and chimney pots. Habit and the blustering weather seemed to have made the Krauts, if not complacent, then less vigilant, which suited the men just fine.

Piet arrived first, and before going inside, carefully surveyed his property. Father joined him soon afterwards. Both shook off the rain as they entered the pub.

'I'll stay here, Piet, while you check him out.'

After a short while, Piet clambered back up the ladder.

'Psst! Psst! Herman, I think he's dead. Not a sign of life.'

Together, they cautiously inspected the man. By this time, Piet had put out the upstairs lights and deadlocked the front door.

'No pulse; just look at him, stone cold – must've died just after you left. Damn, what'll we do now?' asked Father, frowning.

Piet glanced at the poor fellow and screwed up his face, saying, 'Must be terrible to be a Jew these days.'

They sat there for a while, pondering their dilemma, until Piet came up with the dangerous idea of burying him in the backyard. It was Saint Nicholas Eve, and as the saint was renowned for his generosity, Piet and Father decided a decent, if hasty, burial would be in keeping with the spirit of the day.

Towards the middle of the night a shallow grave was dug and Manheim, which was his name, was interred there for the rest of the War. Afterwards, he was dug up and received a proper burial in Den Helder. In the meantime, however, after backbreaking digging in subzero temperatures, the grave was neatly hidden with large grey pavers, which covered most of the backyard. They had previously been stolen by the Germans but somehow repossessed by Piet.

When some of the kids in the vicinity heard rumours of a buried Jew, the source possibly being Piet's own children, Aunty Trien spread the counter tale that a pig had been slaughtered there.

'My mother says you have a Jew buried in your backyard. That's not allowed,' a smug little girl from a house up the road had said. 'My mother says the Krauts will get you for this. You shouldn't have anything to do with Jews. They are nothing but trouble.'

'Well,' replied Ank and Ton – Aunty Trien's two children, a little older than our John – 'you go tell your friends it isn't true and that we've just buried the remains of a pig given to us by *Opa*.[20] Make sure you tell them, or we'll have the Krauts around here in no time.'

Not a clever ploy really, since the Germans had vetoed the killing of livestock, but in Piet's case they never tested the prohibition. Nonetheless, someone must have tipped them off that not all was aboveboard at the café. The next day, at around seven in the morning, a platoon of soldiers arrived to turn the pub upside down, a regular

---

[20] Grandpa

occurrence given its strategic location, and which naturally made Aunt Trien livid.

The stern, baby-faced soldiers trudged across the grey pavers with their heavy boots but suspected nothing and soon left. However, before they went, the platoon commander, a short squat fellow with a jutting jaw, poked Uncle Piet in the chest and said confidently, 'Wir trauen euch nicht, keine Sorge; wir kommen wieder!'[21]

Piet looked at him unflinchingly and muttered under his breath, 'And we don't trust you either, you piece of shit.'

Aunty Trien was a strong-willed woman but prone to impulsiveness; we loved her, since she spoilt us with salt liquorice diamonds and sweets. However, this time Aunty lost her self-control. A drunken German soldier had been taking pot-shots at the family dog, Puk, just for fun, although he only hit the skirting board, thank goodness. 'How dare you shoot at an innocent dog, you schwein! Dogs are God's creatures and don't know what's going on. Why pick on a small animal?'

The Kraut took this as an insult, despite Aunty Trien's justification, and returned with an order to close the place down. Uncle Piet, ever resourceful, continued serving drinks to his customers from his shed.

Meanwhile the clandestine radio became the precursor of television as the focus of family life. Newspapers were heavily censored under German occupation and therefore unreliable. The crackly news from the BBC, despite the language barrier, was précised and commented upon in hushed tones. We also listened to Radio Orange,[22] despite Nazi attempts to shut it down.

'God damn, if Montgomery doesn't get a move on in Africa, we'll be hemmed in from the south as well.' Father lived the life of the generals.

'Hey, Pa, who's 'Gomery?' asked Lex.

Father tried to explain to us urchins that Montgomery was Churchill's right-hand man in Africa. I didn't understand much, although I pretended to by nodding furiously, like Punch. What I did understand was that this 'Gomery was going to flatten a certain Rommel, which means 'rubbish' in Dutch, so I associated 'Gomery' with the removal of a pile of rubbish. I imbibed quite a bit of misinformation in this manner.

'War – warriors!'; *'Krieg – krieger!'*, much better! *'Oorlog – krijgers!'*, even better! One's native tongue bores deep through the crust of memory and yields associations that only certain sounds can make. 'WAR', what a curious word – shorthand for violence within a chronological period.

---

[21] 'We don't trust you; don't worry, we'll be back.'

[22] 'Radio Orange' was a Dutch-language radio program managed by the Dutch government-in-exile and broadcast from London, via the BBC.

Trudging boots and cracker noises! A metaphor for chaos, loss of life and liberty, visible and hidden cruelty, the latter like crimes committed in blind alleyways. Some survived the black and white photographs scrutinized so painfully post-war; others didn't outlive them.

War has many faces and remains as unpredictable as a long, drawn-out chess game. The impact of war is incalculable and can ripple throughout the ages. Historians probe, compare, measure and create narratives of sorts, appeasing the survivors. Watching documentaries or winnowing through history books, while informative, can never be the same as being there. I was there by accident of birth, but was too young to remember much. Father was in it up to his armpits. So were my uncles and family friends. Jews were in and out of it. Soldiers were in it till killed – even when maimed, captured or driven mad, they were still in it.

"Sechs Jahre genügte, um die Träume von Jahrhunderten zu erfüllen."[23] The Nazi-controlled radios and film clips resonated with the impassioned claims of Herr Hitler. The almost effeminate bringing together of the palms and the saint-like pose as he lifted his eyes in ecstasy reminded me for some reason of a picture of Saint Rochus before he was thrown into a dungeon. Gosh, Hitler had an inflated ego to think his paltry six years in power were enough to fulfill centuries of dreaming about the coming of Nazism. Bad luck Goethe, Schiller, Kant and Schopenhauer. Even Bismarck becomes irrelevant, these great men a mere sideshow to Germany's true destiny: the third empire.

For me, the War was a fragmented affair, full of derring-do and bizarre anecdotes, as well as bogeymen like Adolf Hitler and, in Italy, *Il Duce*, both demented and exulting in maniacal misdeeds. Even as children we mimicked the goosestep and, though unable to speak German, imitated the phonetic screeching of Little Adolf: maybe we subconsciously copied Charlie Chaplin's lampoons. After the War, in jingoistic comic books, I remember Hitler always siegheiling and hiding behind doors, awaiting his just deserts from the Yankees. A dull face broken by a signature toothbrush moustache, the lock of hair drooping leftwards, the iconic mask of evil. Yet, strange to say, we loved this 'mo' on comedians Charlie Chaplin and Oliver Hardy.

Joe Stalin, though a contemporary of these famous hairy-lips, emerged much later in my memory. His moustache, of different shape, suited his deceptively avuncular mien. What is it about tyrants and their hairy adornments?

Because of Hitler, no boy since his demise could be called Adolf with impunity, not even by parents with a black sense of humour. Mother saw him as an abstraction. She was far more upset by the physical presence of the Austrian, Seyss-Inquart. In the lowlands, he was seen as Hitler's

---

[23] "Six years sufficed to fulfil the dreams of centuries." From Hitler's speech to the Reichstag; Berlin, 30th January 1939.

attack dog. What a wonderful name. In fact it was a concoction, his real name being Arthur Zajtic, of Czech-Slavic origin. It was Germanized, probably for racial reasons. As a 'Germaniac' he hoped for entry into Hitler's inner sanctum.

He, alongside Anton Mussert, the founder and leader of the Dutch National Socialist movement, was despised in Holland, and as a fervent anti-Semite, played his dastardly part in sending Dutch Jews to the concentration camps dotted around Europe, including within Holland itself. He was ruthless, humourless, and plagued the Dutch psyche throughout the War.

I love the story about his imminent execution. For some perverse reason he was fatalistic about Germany's defeat yet refused to surrender meekly to the allies. His obstinacy prompted General Walter Bedell 'Beetle' Smith, Eisenhower's chief-of-staff, to drawl, 'Well, in any case, you are going to be shot.' – He was hanged as it happens. – 'That leaves me cold,' Inquart replied, to which Smith retorted, 'It will.'

Each country evokes its ogres and Holland was no exception. For some reason, while Father rarely mentioned Inquart, Mother was consumed with his persona; she considered him to be quintessentially evil. The spectacled Inquart, who had a limp, appealed to her image of the slimy Nazi. In her mind, he was reincarnated from the Duke Alva de Toledo, who lorded it over the sturdy Dutch in the sixteenth century. Or was it Napoleon, doing the same to Holland, centuries later?

Great Uncle Piet 'Lap', or Piet 'Rag', as he was known, visited shame upon us for having joined the Dutch National Socialist movement, the *Nationaal Socialistische Beweging (NSB)*, a pro-Nazi party founded in 1931. It was, however, not anti-Semitic and to begin with included Jewish members. Piet acquired his nickname from his trade as motor mechanic. However, he absconded to South Africa with the family fortune soon after the War, never to be seen again. I have only the dimmest recollection of him visiting us in his sidecar, together with his wife and daughter. He had one glass eye and, given his swarthy looks, reminded me of a pirate turned reluctant landlubber.

But Inquart remained for us the true Beelzebub. In old age, skating over Piet's treachery, Mother was still heard on occasions to utter Inquart's name with disgust. 'That Seyss-Inquart, what a horrible man!'

During and after the War, the fate of Jews was often discussed around the dinner table. They had lived and worked in Alkmaar since the early seventeenth century, many having emigrated from Portugal. They were part of the historical fabric of the town, some indeed becoming prominent councillors and businessmen. However, the close-knit Jewish community of Alkmaar was virtually wiped out by the Nazis. Nevertheless, the Baaren-Keysers, who had been close friends of ours since before the War, somehow managed to survive the Holocaust.

The Baaren-Keysers frequently visited our home. Like Father, Jo Baaren-Keyser was a salesman, and his bosom pal. A short man with beautiful, lush, wavy hair, he wore horn-rimmed glasses and sported a gold tooth. His broad head and wrinkled face gave him a comical appearance. Jo was in fact almost a caricature of the stereotypical 'Jew', both in his looks and manner. A compulsive joker and raconteur, he was always in high spirits. He rolled his r's theatrically and spoke at a phenomenal rate, rarely missing a beat.

'Hey, Herrrman, did I tell you the card joke about Samie and Mosie?' Before Father could reply, he was off. 'Samie lost a hundred guilders to Mosie playing carrrds but didn't have the cash to pay him. He told his wife Rrrachel he couldn't sleep because of migrrraine brrrought on by the debt. Rrrachel grew sick of his moaning and yelled across the strrreet, 'Hey, Mosie..!' Mosie opened the window, wearrring his nightcap. 'Yes! Rrrachel what is it?' 'I've got news for you. Samie isn't going to rrrepay you, now or ever. Now *you* can have a migrrraine.'

Jo could reel off hundreds of Samie and Mosie jokes and felt compelled to do so on every occasion. It used to drive his wife, Marie, nuts, but Father loved them and wasn't shy in coming forward with his own arsenal. We loved the banter and lay on the floor beside Father's chair, listening to the witty conversation, cigar smoke drifting to the ceiling. Jo was a funny man and none of us took him too seriously.

'Herrrman, did I tell you about the time I was locked up by the Brothers in the Saint Willibrrrord asylum in Heiloo? I was there for some business... When I wanted to leave, one of the Brrrothers thought I was an inmate and rrrefused to let me go. I was so angry and embarrassed, and it wasn't till I phoned Marrrie that he let me out. I wrote them a letter of complaint. What an insult!'

Jo sounded hurt but could see the funny side. We could too, but for quite different reasons: because of Jo's deportment and unusual head, we identified with the Brother on duty; the protestations would only have reinforced the Brother's mistrust. Of course Father never canvassed this interpretation with him.

The Baaren-Keysers were very loyal and upset when, in 1952, we decided to emigrate. They saw us off in Amsterdam and followed the ship to IJmuiden, Amsterdam's link to the North Sea. They gave our parents an ashtray as a memento of their close friendship. At the base of the ashtray was a photo of the famed Alkmaar Cheese Market. The picture was intended to remind our parents of what they were about to leave behind.

By the Scruff of the Neck

*

I can't remember hearing about Anne Frank till well after the War. Maybe our parents were waiting for an opportune time to tell us. They were familiar with her diary from its initial publication in 1947. Father, having been brought up with Jewish mates, often spoke to us about their extermination as something unimaginable, making him detest the Germans all the more.

I read *The Diary of Anne Frank* during the 1960s, in Dutch, which gave it greater intimacy. Even though Anne was born in Germany, her native tongue was Dutch. Anne's original title, *Het Achterhuis*, was altered by her father into '*The Diary of Anne Frank*', whereas the literal translation, *The Rear Premise*, is in my view the better title, or even the somewhat misleading, *The Secret Annexe*. However, no great matter... Her daily entries centred on the lives of her co-dwellers and her own reflections in that confined space on the Prinsengracht 263, Amsterdam. The location is, of course, the crucible of her reflections.

Anne Frank's irrepressible humanity was the thread that entered the eye of Hitler's destructive needle and in the end overcame him; although, sadly, she wouldn't have known this was so. Decency often wins through, though it may take a long time and at fatal cost.

Just as Joan of Arc possessed a zing factor, which made her memorable, so Anne Frank captured the world in a very special way. Primo Levi, an Italian Jew, author and chemist who survived Auschwitz, observed, "One single Anne Frank moves us more than the countless others who suffered just as she did but whose faces have remained in the shadows. Perhaps it is better that way; if we were capable of taking in all the suffering of all those people we would not be able to live." Levi's purported suicide in 1987 may well have confirmed this view, although close associates believe his death was accidental.

Most Dutch schoolchildren have heard of and studied Anne's diary. There are of course other war diaries and books, too. I have in my possession two rare memoirs published in 1945. The yellowing pages are ripped in parts and the smell of the pages somehow links me to the victims described therein. One, by K. R. van Staal, is called *Terug uit de Hel van Buchenwald*, which translates as *Back from the Hell of Buchenwald*. I've lost the front cover of the other one, by Cor Uyttenboogaard. It deals with the horrific treatment of political prisoners sent to a concentration camp in Overijssel. The drawings of the tortured are harrowing. Readers of Primo Levi and the works of Lord Russell, second Baron of Liverpool, will be familiar with such examples of Nazi bestiality, and these are just from the West. The Eastern Europeans have their own archives.

I also possess a rare copy of the collection of photographs taken when Allied soldiers liberated the death camps. Most are well known. The book, by Willem van de Poll, also published in 1945, has been an integral feature of our household. I don't know where Father acquired these books, but they underpinned our perception of the Germans as Nazi bullies, not as human beings; Germans weren't to be trusted. Fortunately, the passage of time has mellowed this assessment.

When, in 1998, Holland defeated Germany in the semi-finals of the European Cup, large orange banners were on display: one read, 'Mother, we've got your bicycle back.'[24] This, after fifty-three years!

I first visited Anne Frank House in the 1970s. A few mawkish American Jews peering at Anne's collection of film-star cards couldn't keep their mouths shut, although they had been as far removed from the European theatre of war as American *goys*. Their oohing and ahhing was so loud that I wanted to say something. But I said nothing. I wished to be left alone to reflect on the nature of Anne's strained yet somehow bearable incarceration.

As I avoided the crowd clambering over Anne's legacy, I stopped to study the old wallpaper behind her pictures. People continued to file past. The Franks' wallpaper seemed very familiar to me, like some forgotten artefact. It was in fact identical to ours as I remembered it towards the end of the War. The ordinariness of this wallpaper formed a banal yet strangely powerful bond between Anne and me. While the warplanes soared above, the small waves on our yellowed paper intrigued me as I fell asleep and in my tiny imagination I thought of them as the waves between England and Holland, where warships sailed to free us from the Krauts. Poor Anne obviously had more pressing concerns than studying wallpaper. Yet, for me, it triggered a lost link with her past: Mother claimed she served Mr van Pels,[25] when she worked for the 'Unie' – shops owned by Unilever – in the 1920s. The story remains apocryphal because the Van Pels came to Holland in 1937 from Osnabrück, Germany. It is, of course, possible, Alkmaar not being far from Amsterdam. A stray visit perhaps?

Our friends, the Baaren-Keysers, weren't practising Jews, nor did they regard themselves as ethnically different from us. They were Dutch first and foremost. Their sons didn't see themselves as particularly Jewish and mixed with all and sundry. Like Anne's varied friends this was normal for

---

[24] At the end of the War, the Krauts commandeered Dutch bicycles to make their escape back to Germany.

[25] 'van Daan' in Anne's diary. Herman van Pels worked for Otto Frank, Anne's father, before the War. He was an expert on meats.

the Dutch and heightened the tragedy that befell the Franks. Amsterdam had been a Dutch-Jewish city for centuries. We know that thousands of other Jewish girls and women were murdered or died in concentration camps, but it was Anne's diary, rescued by the indomitable Miep Gies,[26] that became the iconic account of the Holocaust.

Anne was only a few years older than our Jack-the-lad and at a stretch could even have been his playmate. Her adolescent spontaneity and astute observations have touched so many. While she was writing, I, from a purely selfish perspective, was crawling around the house shouting my disgust at the world. As I was being pushed through the Wood in my pram, she was scribbling to her imaginary Kitty. While Anne died of typhus in Bergen-Belsen, my family was privileged to breathe a different air. When, as a small boy, I stood in front of a tall horse chestnut in the middle of the Wood to marvel at its foliage and the chestnuts, Anne could only admire *her* chestnut tree through a window.

Anne's tree, like my tree, was about one hundred and fifty years old and stood behind her house, though now beset with fungus. It has become a relic of contention between a prominent Jewish holocaust survivor acting as patron of the 'Anne Frank Tree' and a careless contractor who allowed the tree and its support to be blown over. Ah, relics can bring out the best and the worst in people. Just ask Jesus Christ!

For Anne, the tree and nature were symbols of freedom and reassurance: "I was sitting on my favourite spot on the floor. The two of us [Peter van Pels and Anne] looked out at the blue sky, the bare chestnut tree glistening with dew, the seagulls and other birds glinting with silver as they swooped through the air... But I also looked out of the open window, letting my eyes roam over a large part of Amsterdam, over the rooftops and on to the horizon, a strip of blue so pale it was almost invisible.

As long as this exists," I thought, "this sunshine and this cloudless sky, and as long as I can enjoy it, how can I be sad?"[27]

But it wasn't to last. For me, having returned again and again to the Alkmaar Wood, *my* tree is still there to remind me of the feisty Jewish girl who fought so well to the bitter end. We may have been impotent to help, although Father played his minor part, but the subsequent revelations have filtered into our conscience as an elemental disturbance. The Nazis inadvertently inoculated the lucky ones with guilt. Perhaps this is no bad thing. As George Santayana, (1863–1952), the Spanish-

---

[26] At great risk, Miep Gies and her husband Jan supplied those hiding in the annexe with food and other necessities. She discovered Anna's diary and housed Otto Frank after the War.

[27] *The Diary Of A Young Girl* by Anne Frank. Edited by Otto Frank and Mirjam Pressler, Puffin 1997, pp. 196–97.

American philosopher, observed, "Those who do not remember the past are condemned to repeat it." A cliché now perhaps, but the words remain salutary to Jew and gentile alike.

While not old enough to have had first-hand recollection of the privations of war, the atmosphere of the time is still palpable in my mind. No doubt Father and Mother were the cause of these war-writ-large feelings because they often spoke about the War, mainly to do with neighbourhood atrocities and similar heart-wrenching incidents. During cold weather the family often lingered around the table discussing these things. There was something incantational about the events that occurred. They told us that the lamps often flickered due to the heavy bombing, which caused the whole house to shake. There were frequent power outages too. 'Pa, tell us who collaborated with the Krauts?' I asked, when the politics of the War became more intelligible to me.

Father was careful not to accuse anyone willy-nilly. The de Kooys were well-known collaborators and Father thought that Jan Schouten had probably been an informant too, on the strength of being seen rather too often with members of the *Wehrmacht* and also of cycling nonchalantly through Newportslane after curfew.

'The resistance hanged Schouten from the Cathill oak in the Heilooer Wood,' said Father. 'Someone must have known more about him than mere gossip. I never liked the bastard, even before the War. He was always in it for himself and joined the NSB quite early on.'

Mother claimed Schouten was an Inquart stooge as well, but couldn't prove it.

'There were many collaborators, because of the Depression, you see,' continued Father. 'Quite a few Dutch people thought Hitler was the man for the times. Hitler's economic miracle in opening factories hit the spot for many who were out of work. Mind you, they were mainly to supply Germany's military needs and the new autobahns.'

This explanation was primarily for the older brothers, while Lex and I just listened quietly, taking in snippets of information. Father went on to tell us that Cor Vlaam, a neighbour, even went to Germany to find work in the Ruhrgebiet.[28] Apparently he came back singing Hitler's praises, and as a result, soon fell under suspicion.

Father, like Lord Keynes, was convinced that it all went back to the Versailles Treaty.[29] I didn't follow the details, nevertheless vaguely surmising that the need for food and work tended to determine where

---

[28] A major industrial and cultural centre in mid-west Germany.

[29] The peace treaty of 28th June 1919, signed between Germany and the Allies on the latter's terms.

someone stood in relation to Little Adolph. In the beginning, few people were prepared for his hideous ideology, or even cared.

'Something had to give,' Mother chimed in. 'Hitler was very popular in England before the War, and by the time people woke up to him, it was too late. Many were sucked in by his rhetoric and superficial charm, too. It took a while for people, especially the grovelling politicians, to work out that what he said publicly was actually false.' Although Mother usually put an emotional spin on the facts, she was often right.

We absorbed stories about the War like mother's milk and because of their repetition and the emotions evoked, they helped shape our historical awareness from a young age. Even today, almost seventy years later, the brothers often refer to the War and the misdeeds of the Germans: *vuile Moffen* – dirty Krauts.

When I was a little older, the Alkmaar Wood became my Amazon jungle. Over four hundred years old – the oldest public park in Holland – it was full of intrigue for a boy. Shallow brooks gurgled across pebbles, water rushed beneath gnarled bridges, plovers foraged in reeds and wild pigeons warbled soothingly from lofty hiding places.

By the end of spring, when council workers had finished oiling the bridges, the sun drew out their tarry odour. The agreeable smell impelled me to slow down, to listen to the sound of birds and inhale the fragrance of all the flowers. I lay down on the green slope overlooking the Deerpark, enjoying the early spring breeze on my cheeks. Summer wasn't far away, and on the pond, cygnets were diving cheekily beneath their mothers, while peacocks wandered unconcerned amongst sheep and deer.

A cacophony washed over me as I tried to pinpoint and identify the honking and bellowing of the various animals. A wildlife park so close to home was a gift which imbued me with a lifelong love of animals, their innocence and predictability an endearing departure from the mutability of my own two-legged kind.

The Wood was situated between Newportslane and our Saint Aloysius School, giving us a chance to frequently experience its mysteries. On the periphery were three cemeteries: Saint Barbara – Catholic; the Public Cemetery, near the railway line – secular and Protestant; and the Jewish Cemetery. In the southwest was the prison, in the north a complex of hospitals, plus an old people's home called 'Westernlicht'.

These symbols of decrepitude encircled trees, streams and animals, forces of life, their very opposites. Marmots and the long green birdcage subdivided into coops for canaries, finches, exotic birds and fowls, kept us spellbound for hours. There was even a monkey cage, now closed down by animal liberationists. These days, the huge chestnuts, birches and ash trees are still among the best preserved in Holland.

During summer, the music bowl was filled with young lovers listening to jazz concerts, brass bands or Beethoven quartets. The main attraction of the Wood, however, remained the Deerpark, built in the late nineteenth century. The sheep, as well as goats, calves and pigs, were added later. Mother sometimes met her friends there, both before and after the War. As infants we hung eagerly out of our bulky prams, which were propped up by fat tyres, and watched the skittish deer grazing in the park. We squealed in delight as guinea pigs ran around amongst the grass tussocks and in and out through the hollow tree trunks.

Sometimes, though, in my imagination, the Wood became a fearful place. During cold wintry afternoons, when it grew dark by four o'clock, I quite often went there alone, my heart racing with trepidation as I imagined ghosts, or men with evil intent ready to cut my throat.

At the back of the Cadet School, vacated by the Krauts after the War and changed into a medical institute, there was a room jutting out into the Wood which had a skeleton on display. Anatomy held little interest for me, except for the prurient delights of exploring the fairer sex, but the prospect of being attacked by rattling bones that had somehow escaped the nearby cemeteries was enough to make me sprint, only stopping when I reached the large chestnut tree which heralded the end of the darkness.

By the age of seven and steeped in stories of the Wild West, I had a tendency to wander off wherever my fancy led me. Sometimes I borrowed the family scooter, the only one we had, and finished up in Bergen or Egmont, two pretty seaside villages. Along the way, I would sit beside a ditch covered with lush grass, studying the farmers bringing in the hay, as in a Van Gogh painting. Friesian cows stared vacantly at me, oblivious to the little boy scooting past or making strange noises at them.

In my imagination, I was off to California and each time I passed a field of Friesian cows, I stopped to let them in on my secret, talking to them about my dreams. They lifted their heads indifferently, sizing me up with their sad brown eyes, then went back to munching their grass. To them I wasn't worth a flick of the tail, but I loved the smell of their fresh cowpats, which reminded me of spinach pancakes.

'Hey! Hey! Hey! Hey! Ya dopey cows! What would *you* know? Go on! Keep roaring till you're hoarse in yer throats, because ya don't know anything about me and me plans. I'm going west. I'm off to America to find adventure and live with the indians. Heee! Heee! Heee! Heee! Moo! Moo! Moo!'

By the Scruff of the Neck

I sounded like an imbecile, but wanted to talk to the animals. I felt strong and powerful in yelling so freely in the open spaces, vaguely aware some farmer might hear my raving and take me to an asylum.

Buttercups and dandelions covered the fields in late summer, beckoning me to join them. I sometimes walked for kilometres into the countryside, plucking the blue and pink forget-me-nots nodding in the breeze and wondering how flowers acquired their colour. Their gift of beauty left me in awe.

I loved the sun as a huge yellow eye of hope and pleasure, and in its heat paddled in the cress-covered streams, tuning in to the bees and insects as Nature took me into her bosom. Momentarily jettisoning my petty cares, I marvelled at it all while time stood still, yet was eventually hijacked by an urge to move on.

Euphoria crept over me while I rested my back against a grassy embankment, chewing a juicy stem. Suddenly, a string of ducks rose up from a reed-infested pond, fluttering in unison and on a mission to somewhere far away. Where were they going?

'Whirr! Whirr! Whirr!', flapping as if their lives depended on it, and of course, it did. Such moments were rare and in a way never recaptured, lingering like the aftertaste of a good dinner.

'Now, my little ball of energy, what have you done today?' Mother asked cheerfully when I finally returned home. I gabbled like a lunatic, reeling off my adventures, words cascading over my tongue like a waterfall over boulders.

'I saw swans and ducks and fish and cows, all singing together under the sun... Farmers waved to me as I scooted past telling them about America... I even met an organ grinder from Haarlem who let his monkey sit on my shoulder...and an old fisherman gave me a salted herring. He explained to me what the best way is to lure worms from the soil.' Fact merged with fiction; my aim was to impress everyone around the dinner table, but they merely yawned and ignored me.

I became so carried away that my brothers told me to put a sock in it. 'Shut up you little turd; you're worse than a barking dog,' grunted Bill.

'Why does he talk so much, Ma? Did you feed him firecrackers?' added John for good measure.

'My ears are hurting, Ma. Tell him to go outside and talk to the lamppost,' suggested Lex, with fingers in his ears.

Usually they just left the table, leaving me to rabbit on by myself. Mother took it all in her stride, smiling kindly and offering me an extra serve of potatoes. It seemed she was rather amused by her *enfant terrible*. She wasn't exactly a slouch with the mouth either, as it happens.

Father hadn't yet arrived home: I would tell *him* all about my countryside adventures. He travelled in the country every day. *He* would understand...

*

In summer, Father enjoyed cycling across the extensive sand dunes near the town of Bergen aan Zee, about nine kilometres west of Alkmaar, often with Lex bouncing on the back and me in my little seat attached to the crossbar of the big black bicycle. The tyres were flesh-coloured and the endless bicycle tracks, made of neatly designed red stones, twisted and turned around the dunes like arteries around the heart. They became my 'yellow brick road' as we zoomed downhill, then, climbing the next ridge, Father began to puff from the extra weight of carrying us on board. I could smell his tobacco and mild sweat. On reaching the top, he let out a sigh of relief as, to our delight, we plunged down the next hill, the briny air tickling our noses. When would the yellow brick road end?

Then, finally, the rush of the sea, the mysterious North Sea, the mud-coloured sea, teasing the shore with its ceaseless wavelets; a pussycat in summer, a lion in winter. For hundreds of years Holland had lost many men at sea. Fishermen's wives stood at the end of piers or congregated in the weeping tower, *De Schreier's Toren*, waiting for news of their loved ones, fearing the worst.

A long stretch of wide beach ran all the way along the coast of Holland. People carved out territory on the foreshore like tomcats on heat, especially the post-war Germans, reasserting themselves with their cash. Those fortunate enough to have cars had a greater sense of entitlement because they could easily bring tents. When their work erecting them was done, they sank into flashy deckchairs, looking down on the *hoi polloi* having to make do with lying on the sand.

Father, who was only interested in swimming and conversation, couldn't care less. He would carefully roll out his towel and recline like a vizier on a magic carpet, the towel smoothing out the debris underneath. His strangely shaped ribcage, with upper ribs much wider than the lower, stood out amongst the nearby crowd. His left little toe overlapped the one beside it, too, of which he was oddly proud. The toe looked ridiculous, but we got a buzz out of flicking it back and forth.

After making himself comfortable, Father looked around, drinking in the busy scene. Swapping ribald comments with a kindred soul, he left us to our own devices. Mother had stayed home because she detested open water.

'Beautiful day, eh! And the scenery isn't bad either,' the neighbouring sun-lover said, with a laugh, referring to some shapely girls walking past.

'Ah, yes, brilliant weather, but you don't know what kind of bitches those girls might be,' Father replied, not intending to be misogynistic, but from his point of view, merely stating a possibility glossed over by the girls' attractive appearance.

By the Scruff of the Neck

Meanwhile, Lex and I splashed one another for a while, then raced back to Father and turned our backs to him to show how quickly we were tanning.

Tanning, for some peculiar reason, is often associated with good health and considered aesthetically pleasing to both genders. In those days, well before sunscreen mania turned us into clowns, nobody thought about skin cancer and everyone was happy to fry in the midday sun. It's odd, though, that many Asians regard a fair skin as desirable. Even *Sigmund* would be hard put to explain that conundrum! More the domain of Margaret Mead,[30] I suppose, or some cultural historian...

Taking little notice of us, Father scanned the horizon for ships, an engrossing interest of his. He loved to be by himself at times, away from his kids. Not surprising, given the pressure of family life. But his peace never lasted long.

'Look at me, Pa! Am I browner than Lex?'

He slowly lifted his head and declared indifferently, 'So, you think *you're* brown? Have a look in my underpants.'

Or, when the older brothers were with us as well and saw a comely girl walk past, he would take his time in assessing her and snort, 'When she farts, she smells just like the rest of us.'

While I was happy much of the time, I became gloomy when dark events arose unexpectedly, like the death of a relative or the presence of physical pain. Even back then, I thought God, always lurking in the background, lacked empathy.

Once I accidentally stumbled upon a funeral in the Wood. Much more visible than today, funerals were grand affairs, the size of the spectacle depending on the wealth of the deceased. I took up a position opposite the *Café Deerpark* and was entranced by the procession of black-lacquered horse-drawn carriages, with the main see-through coach carrying the deceased at the front. The coachmen wore black top hats, while the bridles and harnesses glinted in the sunlight when the horses shook their manes and rippling rumps. As the funeral throng waited for the formalities to begin, the horses grew restless, scraping the road and excreting scrolls of poo onto the gravel, reminding me that nature has its own way of doing things.

The men attending the funeral had pink faces and wore dark suits, while the bereaved women were covered from head to toe in black. Was the deceased a man or a woman? What did they look like? What age were they? It couldn't be a child, for children don't die, or at least, are unlikely

---

[30] Margaret Mead, 1901–78, was an American cultural anthropologist who had a significant influence upon the development of the 1960s sexual revolution.

to… What's it like to be dead? Empirically a foolish question, perhaps, yet entirely reasonable to a youngster.

I now associate parks with death, no doubt because of the Wood, but also due to another, much closer, experience.

We sometimes stayed with Aunty Gré and Uncle Wim, in the well-to-do town of Heemstede. Mother always warned us about our manners beforehand as this was another world for us. An intelligent woman, well-read and refined, Aunty Gré spoke beautiful, cultivated Dutch and seemed so elegant and sophisticated. Uncle Wim was kind, softly spoken, and a bit of a tech-head who could speak captivatingly about the intricacies of radios and crystal sets. Theirs was a refined family compared to ours, which resembled the households depicted in paintings by Jan Steen.[31] To be judged as living like the household of Jan Steen implied the height of disapproval. The fact that at times our home mirrored this famous person's proved a blind spot in our lovable parents, even though Father delighted to invoke his name when describing someone else's lawless home.

Aunty Gré took us for walks around Heemstede, taking in manicured gardens with plots of tulips, marigolds and daffodils, carefully planted in rich, weedless soil. Too perfect for reality! Her wistful nature was reflected in her remarks.

'I used to come here with Han. He was such a special child, so sweet and loving. He is now with the angels, and these flowers are a reminder of all that is beautiful and innocent…and which must perish. But one day, if the Lord permits, I shall see him again.'

Her words lingered as if she were addressing the flowers individually. Moved, I stared at them anew. 'Aunty Gré, why did God let Hantje die so soon?'

'I can't answer that, dear Herrie. He will no doubt have his reasons. Life is short, and shorter for some than others. Death is but a transition and Heaven will look after those who deserve it. Han has gone before us, preparing the way for when our time comes.'

I held onto her hand as I mulled over this beautiful answer. I imagined Han sweeping the road to the golden gates of Heaven and polishing God's throne. I thought of heaven as a special kingdom where everyone floated freely, happily holding hands and singing hymns.

My beautiful Aunty Gré, two years older than Mother, was a very religious woman, especially after she lost her son Han to pneumonia during the War. Her first son, Wil, became a priest but died of a heart attack at a relatively young age. Her husband, Uncle Wim, eventually pre-deceased her as well. As a result, she became both widow and emotional orphan.

---

[31] Jan Steen, 1626–79, a famous Dutch genre painter, renowned for his chaotic family scenes.

Much later, this sad state of affairs reminded me of the story of a poor French mother, who, as a result of the Great War, became insane with grief and often talked loudly to herself. One time, when a few young men made fun of her on the train, her husband begged them to stop. 'Please! Leave her alone! Only this morning she found out she lost her last son. We had five of them.'

My Uncle Louis, married to Mother's younger sister, Joanne, said one day, 'If women were ever to become priests, Gré would be the first female bishop.' Louis, a bon vivant and Belgian by birth, and therefore quite suspect in our northern eyes, was quite insensitive and never gauged either her emotions or her yearning for answers.

Stories of Han soon melded with my park-land walks. I half-expected to see him step out from behind one of the tall beeches darkened by the rain then take me by the hand and lead me to a field of lilies. Here, I would meet Jesus, smiling kindly. Meanwhile, Han, with his soft curly hair, would look earnestly at me, remaining silent.

I have no memory of ever actually meeting my cousin, being too young. He was Bill's age, but his aura has stayed with me for reasons I can't explain. I do, however, have one photo of him playing in a park; a beautiful curly-headed boy of about three, crouching down, picking flowers.

When revisiting Heemstede as an adult, I made for this park, now full of narcissus, ghosting through grey, slanting stones and tall monuments inscribed with gold letters commemorating the worthy citizens of Heemstede. In the centre of the park, low, overlapping, semi-circular railings surrounded flowerbeds. Shiny, black-painted steel fences with spear-shaped finials. It seemed these pristine plots were dedicated to dead souls.

No sign of Han's grave nowadays; just a few dried flowers here and there, reminding me of his evanescence. Colour and beauty forever extinguished beneath the soil; Han lying below the earth with folded hands, smiling enigmatically, as if only he knew the secret of life.

On Saint Martin of Tours' feast day my family would get up in the darkness of early morning and walk through the Wood to the town centre in order to make preparations for the Saint's festival. Lex and I joined others from our school outside the square in front of the old Weighing Tower, walking in procession, singing songs and nibbling sweets.

We made our own lanterns for this celebration and, when bitterly cold, the glow made us feel better. It was also the beginning of Advent and the last occasion to fatten up before the long fast, usually lasting five days. The feast day served to remind us of Saint Martin's generosity to a beggar, numb with cold. The good Saint cut his Roman robe in half to cover the man, or so the story goes.

One such early autumn morning, the air moist and the sky overcast, we were on our way to school and I was still rather sleepy. We were chatting away absentmindedly when we heard the loud bang of a gun resonating through the trees. We stopped and moved closer.

There, in the middle of the avenue leading to the Trotters Circuit, or Sportpark, stood a man with gun to shoulder taking aim at crows. He was wearing a heavy, dark coat and cap. His round rosy cheeks indicated someone used to the open air.

'Why are you shooting crows?' I asked cheekily.

'Well! They are scavengers you see, young fella, and because they breed too fast, force out the other birds in the Wood. All the birds have a right to be in the Wood. It's a bit like Hitler wanting to destroy people who disagreed with him. The crows are like the SS Blackshirts, intent on dominating everyone.' The friendly marksman was obviously no fan. Already he had five dead crows at his feet, black feathers strewn inside pools of blood. Most of the crows had fled by now, but the council worker, as he turned out to be, was patient as he walked from copse to copse.

I looked up at the interlocking branches, more than twenty metres high, some still with orange-brown leaves clinging precariously to them. It formed an eerie mosaic, the vast network of branches resembling the arteries of our lungs against a grey-white backdrop, as in an X-ray photo.

Filmmakers have fallen in love with this image as a metaphor for confusion, complexity, or alienation. When I returned to Holland many years later and stood there again, the Wood virtually unchanged, it was as though Ingmar Bergman[32] and his gifted cinematographer, Gunnar Fischer, were standing beside me, filming. Something, perhaps, about northern climes!

The starkness of the naked branches, a jumble of black lines as seen through a monochromatic kaleidoscope, has stayed with me as a perennial image. I'm always strangely elated when autumn comes to undo the busy work of summer. For all our scientific accomplishments, Nature's cycles, like the phases of the moon, remind us of our own stages in life. Death and renewal is all we know. We cannot reverse time, except in an Einsteinian leap of the imagination, but our often unreliable memories may now and then allow us the illusion of reinventing the past, and certainly of reliving it.

*

---

[32] Ingmar Bergman, 1918–2007, Swedish writer, director and producer of film, stage and television.

The bunker built by the Germans at the entrance to the Wood became a popular place for perverts. You know; the desperadoes whose main thrill was pathetic exposure. Others also 'played' nearby, but in a more conventional way: it was there that my hand travelled up Liesbet's dress to find a hidden treasure.

Liesbet was a tall, blonde girl, two years older than me, who went to our school and lived a few houses up from us. We frequently walked home together, discussing lessons and other topics of interest.

'Do you believe in God?' I asked her.

'Yes, I do, Henri, but my father doesn't,' she answered sweetly.

'Which would you rather be, a boy or a girl?' I asked provocatively.

'That's a *silly* question... I have no idea what it's like to think or act like a boy. Besides, there's no choice involved. You are what you are.'

I was about nine when this banal exchange took place. Even so, her explanation impressed me.

'When I'm old enough, I'm going to travel. Maybe I'll become a sailor, because sailors can visit any part of the world.' I sounded quite pleased with myself, and Liesbet remained quiet for a while.

'Yes, I'd like to travel as well,' she said eventually, 'but Mother wants me to study and do something useful, like nursing. Maybe I might even become an expert in stopping cholera or what you had, diphtheria.'

I was quite taken by this carefully considered answer and began to like her a lot. She must be brainy...

In spring, when the weather turned kinder, we dawdled in the Wood identifying wildflowers and different scents. We sometimes sat on the grass in front of the music bowl, or at a whim played hide and seek, or tried to find new tracks to school.

One beautiful afternoon as the sun filtered through the leaves, I followed her into a cluster of bushes, chasing a butterfly. It was rather small but had striking orange and brown spots on its wings and we hoped to catch it. As Liesbet gave chase she tripped over a low-lying branch and fell. Her dress shot upwards, exposing long white thighs. I was taken aback by the sight of her and dropped alongside, showing my concern, yet my eyes refused to leave her thighs, so clearly visible. I was surprised by how round and smooth they were, not at all evident by simply looking at her skirt.

I couldn't help myself as she lay there, laughing, not straightaway attempting to tidy her dress: I impulsively stroked her skin. It felt firm yet soft, like the half-pumped-up tyre of our scooter, its silkiness strange beneath my hand. Touching her like this felt as if we were doing something forbidden! Shame and desire competed for a while, the latter winning out.

'Don't touch me there! It's naughty to touch a girl.' Her voice changed, edging higher but I couldn't stop; her semi-nakedness had taken hold of me. She trembled like a newborn calf and even seemed to enjoy my clumsy pawing, puffing and purring, making no effort to get up.

Then, she unexpectedly said, 'Show me your dickie! I want to touch it. I've let you play with me, so now it's my turn.'

A bit embarrassed, I dislodged my stiff member, not yet fully grown, from my underpants and showed it to her. She was transfixed, blushing and holding it carefully, as if handling a rare specimen from an archaeological dig. It dangled and bobbed as if it had a life of its own. An inner glow tickled my stomach, while she shook and pulled it about.

'What a peculiar little sausage!' she croaked, giggling and squeezing it gently.

'Why?' I managed to ask, my voice also changing involuntarily.

'Because it's wrinkled and red, quite different from your finger.'

She obviously had no brothers. I didn't wish to comment and instinctively put my hands between her thighs, which were warm and seemed to be everywhere. As I tugged at her white panties, it seemed to take ages to lower them because they snagged along the ground, which was littered with twigs and dead leaves. She didn't seem to mind, instead gasping softly in quiet enjoyment.

I was shocked to discover a large, pink, broad bean, split down the middle. A mound of golden fur, sparse yet prominent, spread around its lips, which indicated she had still some while to go to complete puberty, although I wasn't aware of this at the time. The jolt of discovery hit me like a dentist's drill; I thought I would faint with the headiness of it all. The revelation was so intense...perhaps because of only having brothers.

All the while conscious of her musky smell, we lay there touching one another, besotted with each other's flesh, not quite sure what to do next, when she suddenly stopped, suggesting we ought to leave.

'I have to be home by 4:30 to mind my little sister; Mum has to go to work... We shouldn't be doing this you know.'

I barely listened, having for the first time unearthed the texture and contours of the female body. I was even shaking a little. Like having ingested a narcotic brew, I felt light-headed, but reluctantly agreed with her request. I folded my penis back into my pants and stood up. 'I suppose we *had* better get home,' I said ruefully.

Liesbet and I remained good friends until her family shifted south. I sometimes wonder what happened to her. What shape now, those tantalizing thighs? Is she happy? Did she become a medical researcher as she wished? Would she have changed into a fat old frump? For that matter, she might even be dead...

When I touched Liesbet that first time, my whole being tingled with pleasure. My body shuddered with a fevered rush to the head, only mildly tempered by guilt. So strange to explore a person without a penis; someone with thighs creamy as butter, wonderfully smooth and plump...

By the Scruff of the Neck

Coming from a family of boys with willies on constant display, or *slabberawatskies,* as Father called them, I found female privates utterly fascinating! And still do! The female form remains an addiction till death us do part...

All these musings are of little consequence now. What mattered was the purity and force of that first sexual encounter, deeply embedded in an unreliable memory: an event to be savoured and treasured into old age! Such are the rare pearls of youth.

That Wood, *my* Wood, had a lot to answer for. Boys lingered there, inspecting one another's willies or bums, some, no doubt, giving vent to their homoerotic fantasies. 'I'll show you mine if you show me yours.'

As an adult, the Wood, once part of me, yielded its secrets in flashes of poignant memory, perhaps in common with those others who went there to enjoy their guilty pleasures.

Sigmund, however, was onto us and the confessionals overflowed with admissions of 'indecent acts', as they were called. Contrition never lasted long though, as curiosity overcame inhibition and we returned to our 'indecent acts' with gusto.

Does it matter if we remember our first few years accurately? Probably not! As adults we cast our fishing rods back into the murky waters of our past, only, on occasion, to catch a little fish not worth having. It's illuminating to observe family members squabbling over dates, locations or wayward relatives, even leading to fights or fractured relationships. Memory is a sieve or a magnifying glass, depending upon how and why it is used.

It's also remarkable how memory lurches from total recall in youth to the shameful inability in ripe old age to name your best friend who died only a few weeks ago. To make matters even more lamentable, we learn to tell lies, to distort the past in keeping with our prejudices, to fray the edges; to sneak in wish fulfilments.

Take away the hippocampi or cerebellum and who are we? My hippopotamuses camped in my memory for years and weren't asked to leave until adulthood. Religion, guilt, and expiation, just to name a few, lodged far too long in my memory's register. In a way they never leave, but are transformed into something else, such as philosophic reflection, artistic expression, or even the accumulation of wealth. 'Ah yes, displacement,' *Sigmund* might profoundly observe.

I recall, possibly inaccurately, how my dear Uncle John, on Mother's side, and his sister Aunty Anne, who were unmarried and lived together, didn't speak to one another for days because they couldn't agree on how many times Farmer Bob van de Velde had been married...or divorced... take your pick!

'That just isn't true, John. He was first married to Magda van der Geest for about three years, then presumably filed for divorce, after which he married Hanna Brockers.' Aunty Anne raised her voice, hoping to forestall disagreement, although her brother was rarely swayed by her vehemence.

By this stage, both were becoming tipsy, having consumed half a dozen of their beloved *jenever*. Uncle John, with his long legs comfortably resting on the coffee table, turned his head to the large window overlooking the beautiful Alkmaar Wood and raised his slender hands in protest.

'Now, Annie, you know that his marriage to Brockers only lasted a few months because he was terribly unhappy. She always ordered him about, asking him to do things he didn't want to... Bob is an easygoing fellow but can't cope with being bossed around. He values his independence... Anyway, the marriage was hopeless. He ditched her as soon as he could then married that woman from Uitgeest who took him to the cleaners... Some blokes never learn. So, I reckon he was married *three* times.'

Aunty Anne refused to agree, adamantly shaking her head. 'Yes, John, but after he split up with that Uitgeest disaster he was single for a while, then married some girl from Luttik Ouddorp, and that makes it *four*.'

There was a momentary silence as Uncle John looked intently through the window, taking a deep breath. 'He didn't marry that woman at all,' he insisted. 'He'd had enough of marriage by then and they just live in sin, or so I was told by Woerdeman.' Woerdeman being the local grocer.

'Rubbish! Woerdeman is an old gossip and wouldn't know. Bob is much too respectable to cohabit with a woman, especially with the whole neighbourhood knowing about it. Anyway, his mother wouldn't have allowed it.'

Eventually they both became fed up with the subject and fell silent, then refilled their glasses again. But Aunty Anne had to have the final say: 'The trouble is, John, you don't understand women. Women from Luttik Ouddorp come from a very strict, religious upbringing and she would never just live with Bob like that.'

With this pronouncement they lifted their glasses and then ignored one another for the next few days.

Clusters of homes hemmed in by canals, woods or highways, gave birth to neighbourhoods, each with its own character. Old Alkmaar, surrounded by a moat since the Middle Ages, was granted a town charter in 1254, the name Alkmaar appearing as early as the tenth century. Now allow me a little jingoism. In 1573, against overwhelming odds, Alkmaar was the first city to repel the invading Spaniards. From then on, the tide turned against Catholic Spain in the Lowlands. The wonderfully named Dirk Duyvel, meaning 'Devil', led the Alkmaarders to victory.

Newportslane, Alkmaar, once a canal, was reclaimed as solid ground in 1910, the year of Father's birth. I was conceived there, but expelled, as it were, in the Saint Elizabeth Infirmary, just fifteen minutes walking distance from our house towards the town centre. I sort of snuck up on the family. Apparently Mother hadn't at first realised she was pregnant, until she fainted near 'The Four States'. Because of the War, Father wasn't keen to feed an extra mouth, but nature will have her way.

Our neighbourhood was situated just south of the old town, tucked away from the main road to Amsterdam. The hotchpotch of dwellings of mixed architectural merit reflected the status of their owners. There were freestanding houses belonging to the affluent but the majority were two to three storeys high, divided into rows separated by alleyways. Each particular group was different, depending upon the vogue of the day. Some had intricate crests and stepped gables; prominent Dutch architectural features. Our house, which we rented, was built just after the Great War, and appeared unprepossessing, with a small front garden and large windows. Situated within a row of houses, it was double-storeyed with a landing. Apart from our parents' bedroom, the others were tiny, and John had one to himself.

Mostly, it was John who pushed Lex and me in our ornate prams through Newportslane. He loved his little brothers and made us laugh by pulling stupid faces. He would do anything to protect us, too. I counted the stepped gables up and down either side of the houses as we passed by. 'Once you learn to walk, you can use the steps to go to heaven and meet God,' Mother gushed to me one time when she took me for an outing. As I grew older, I became aware that in December the steps were offered to Saint Nicholas to make it easier for his horse to negotiate the awkward roofs.

After many years, in 1970, I returned to this primordial nest. The young owners had converted the dining and lounge rooms into a photographer's studio, the tiny backyard now concrete. Despite the addition of an extra bedroom, I was surprised at how small and narrow the house was. How it had shrunken and buckled! Yet, as a child, it seemed large and spacious. How did we all survive there?

'Yes, it would've been different in your day,' observed the photographer 'Times change, just like fashions. Not much you can do about it.'

He implied this as favourable to the current times. I wasn't sure which fashions he had in mind but couldn't have disagreed more. Even the small front tree had been ripped out, to be replaced with dull, sand-

I sort of snuck up on the family. Alkmaar, 1942. Father, Lex, John, Bill, Mother and Henri.

coloured flagstones. The house felt tired and wounded, a sad and silent witness to the many generations who had passed through. The cracked walls didn't exist in our day, either. Our walls were kept respectable with well cared for wallpaper.

Today, Newportslane has been gentrified and, being quite close to the city centre, highly sought after. In our day, during the '30s and '40s, the houses were well established but the occupants varied greatly. Karl Marx called them petit bourgeois: tradesmen, salespeople, office workers and shop assistants. Families were large and boisterous. Respectability was worn like a shabby coat that became positively threadbare when outrageous behaviour, collusion with the Nazis, or meddling in each other's private affairs, became known.

A neighbourhood is made special by its characters, turf wars, and tribal loyalties. Loyalty was forged out of common experience: war, economic depression, festivities, and the usual marriages, births and deaths. Those from outside are regarded with suspicion, or at least, kept at a distance.

Mr Brown was the local tailor and barber. He was cheap and efficient, providing only two kinds of haircut, short and very short. All haircuts and measurements were by appointment. He and his gypsy wife presided over a brood of six, including two girls. All the Brown boys had shaven heads; not only cheap and timesaving but very handy in a fight since opponents couldn't easily lock onto them.

In many ways an admirable man, Mr Brown never appeared flustered, yet he pretended his kids didn't exist, and, of a quixotic nature, was given to romantic musings. On a daily basis, he tried to escape the drudgery of life by living mostly in his head. A man of great girth, he wandered around in pants held up by colourful braces, which were always on proud display. He rarely wore a vest or coat, even in freezing temperatures. Unfortunately, his mop of black hair and dark-rimmed glasses gave him a sinister look. He too had *that* moustache... Oh dear, not another one! But looks can be deceptive...

Gossip is the lubricant of neighbourhoods, our neighbourhood no exception, and while Mr Brown expertly cut his customers' hair, he never stopped talking, yet remained reflective throughout. He'd had a rough time of it during the War. The Germans had on several occasions locked him up. What happened to him behind closed doors no one quite knew.

Even so, Mr Brown was an innocent, with a vivid imagination and for this reason I liked him. He also enjoyed talking to Father, regaling him with absurd stories about the perfect life away from Newportslane. When he was making a crucial point he would snap his braces and finish his oration with the catch phrase, 'Now, isn't that so?'

'If *I* had been Columbus or Tasman,' he proposed to Father, '*I* wouldn't've returned to Europe, but stayed in the new continents. The natives would've provided them and their crew with women, and as long as there was water and food, they could've led a beautiful life. A man doesn't need much. Think of the freedom and opportunity!' He stared into the distance, envying those explorers fortunate to have found such a paradise. He totally ignored the hardships, the disease and the violence.

'I tell you Herman, if I had my time all over again I'd have sailed to the Pacific years ago and found myself a nice little island with plenty of water and bananas, then just laid on the beach in the sun. The missus'd be allowed to come, of course, but I don't know whether I'd take the kids...too noisy and distracting.'

I sat on the scooter and watched them closely while they aired their flights of fancy. Father put on his salesman's smile and shook his head, whether in agreement or in disbelief I wasn't sure.

Our 'Oliver Hardy', whom Mr Brown closely resembled, was at times difficult to locate. His kids, when asked where he was, simply shrugged and said, 'We haven't seen Pa since this morning. He could be over at Kramer's,' 'Kramer'[33] being the blacksmith. It was as if Mr Brown was a stranger to them. Their father's neglect, reinforced by his wife's artistic diversions, meant the family was out of control. The offspring could do as they wished, provided the cops were kept out of it and no one incurred any costs.

The family occupied a three-storey house in a row of four. The attic was a storage area but remained mostly empty. The door had been painted green and in one corner stood a tailor's dummy, together with a sewing machine. Gustav Brown, about twelve, was Bill's age and one particular Wednesday afternoon, while we were all free from school, and when I was six or seven, he invited Lex and I over for some fun. It had been raining and the neatly paved stones of the street shone with cleanliness and toy-like appeal.

'I've got an idea that'll impress you,' said Gus, with a grin. 'Let's build a swing in the attic. I'll remove the window and fix some large, round screw hooks into the frame. I've got some rope and can feed it through a plank and then Bob's your uncle... I've been planning this for a while. Pa isn't around and Mum's busy with her artwork.'

An hour later we took turns in soaring towards heaven. We were so thrilled with the marvellous swing Gustav and Bill had constructed that it never crossed our minds it could be dangerous. As far as we were concerned, the height, at least ten metres above the ground, wasn't an issue. Provided you hung onto the rope, what could go wrong? Well, quite a lot actually...

---

[33] Not his real name.

It just so happened that Father came cycling along and, looking up, saw Lex swinging merrily out of the Browns' attic...then nearly hit the milk dray coming his way.

'Come down, at once! Do you hear?' came the blunt order.

Mr Brown, predictably awol, and Mrs Brown, putting the finishing touches to her expressionist masterpiece after the style of Vlaminck, were far removed from the action.

As a child in a lively neighbourhood, it's inevitable that one interacts with the local characters and events of the day. As youngsters, we didn't need expensive amusements, unlike nowadays. Given simple moral strictures and basic social expectations, we were easily satisfied – in subverting them.

For example, a certain Mr Davo,[34] a primary school teacher, fastidious and a wet blanket, fell a cropper when Jacob de Kooy, the youngest of the family, thrust a fire poker through the front wheel of his bicycle. We loved it! Mr Davo, riding his bike sitting stiffly upright, wearing spectacles and with his hair plastered down, was the epitome of moroseness. In our neighbourhood, he was also regarded as a killjoy. Although no one liked him, he seemed oblivious to the fact.

On that particular day, Lex and I were spinning our small wooden tops to our heart's content, when Mr Davo, like clockwork, came home for lunch. Jacob knew his habits, and, given his own sadistic temperament, also knew exactly what to do.

We had grown used to pestering Mr Davo, or anyone else who took our fancy, and always enjoyed the spectacle. To observe the humiliation of such an exalted personage as this teacher was appreciated by us all, but not, of course, by him.

Once he regained his composure, Mr Davo swore to get the perpetrator: 'I'll catch you, you little beggar! Don't you worry; I'll be knocking on your father's door.' Jacob scarpered and wasn't seen again until dinnertime. Unperturbed, we resumed our play: Mr Davo knew better than to approach the de Kooy household.

Jacob de Kooy was mean. Straight brown hair crowned his heart-shaped head and his slit-eyes always twinkled with mischief. His lean, compact body made him seem older than us, yet he was the same age as Lex. Most of the time we got on well with him, though remained wary. He was always on the street looking for trouble and always planning someone's downfall. 'No one comes through this street without my say-

---

[34] Not his real name.

so. We're all mates and need to look out for one another,' he would say hypocritically. Except for Lex, we were all a little afraid of him.

At the end of our curved street was a wide road, the Regulierslaan, which intersected the Kennemer Highway, the main road out of Alkmaar to Heiloo, the next village, and then on to Amsterdam. On the other side of the Regulierslaan lay the Villa Park area, where the moneybags lived. They probably determined the width of the road separating our neighbourhood from their opulent estate...

Their houses were huge, some with tennis courts and semicircular driveways; long limousines gliding over white gravel. The properties were surrounded by woods, traversed by pretty brooks and made attractive by tall trees. Most residents were nouveau riche, some the beneficiaries of the vast wealth derived from the Dutch East Indies. They spoke differently from us. Even the girls seemed prettier, while the boys rode expensive, coloured bicycles.

Newportslane was a critical location for two types of 'intruders'. The Villa Parkers used it on occasions as a shortcut to the town centre, or to the Sportpark soccer stadia behind us. The fiercest soccer rivals in our town were *Alkmaria Victrix*, who played at the Sportpark, and *The Alkmaar Boys*, who played on their own ground further to the right opposite the tennis courts. Anything English, archaically Greek, or Latin, as the *Alkmaria Victrix* name suggests, was slavishly adopted by the Dutch, while any German reference, excluding those contained in music and literature, was avoided at all costs.

The Villa Parkers invariably supported *Alkmaria Victrix* it being older and wealthier than its breakaway club, *The Alkmaar Boys*, which we supported. In sport, typically the fans of one club hate those of another, especially if in the same league. This was certainly the case for *Victrix* and the *Boys*.

The other kind of 'intruder' belonged to the Saint Willibrord Mental Asylum. Every weekend during the soccer season, a group of about twenty patients, led by earnest-looking religious Brothers, would move through our street like a medieval procession of blind beggars.

I watched them through the spiked fence of our front garden, fascinated. Most of them seemed normal enough in appearance. However, the ill-fitting suits and drab colours alerted me to the idea that something was not quite right. Their eyes, lustreless like sick animals, were fixed as they stared in front of them, while others' were downcast, as if they were ashamed.

I was too young to understand what it meant to be mentally ill, yet could instinctively sympathise with them. A few leant forward, walking in an ungainly manner. One of them passed close by me, slobbering and neighing like a horse. Was it the sight of me that brought on this behaviour, or was it some form of misplaced enthusiasm? I became frightened and shuffled back to our front door.

One of the Asylum's best-known inmates was Silly Henk. He was allowed to roam freely, probably because he was harmless. He often paused in front of Mulder's,[35] the greengrocer, and when he poked his head inside the shop, was handed an apple or a pear, after which he retreated, punching his right fist into his left hand, his tongue flopping from his mouth. He couldn't speak but made contented grunts and by and large was treated well by the Newportslaners: except, *naturellement*, Jacob de Kooy, who followed him and aped his gestures until he was eventually castigated by an adult. I liked Silly Henk because he always seemed happy and predictable. None of us felt threatened and we spoke to him in a familiar manner, never making fun of him...except for Jacob.

Jacob's favourite victim, however, was a meek lad who foolishly used our street as the shortest route to and fro the Villa Park. He was about twelve, very tall, and with a huge head. His glasses gave him a scholarly look, yet he seemed to lack common sense. What made him such a dupe, though, was his ridiculously high-pitched voice, like a girl's. Jacob hid in wait for him.

'Right! Off yer bike, Albert,[36] or I'll put this stick through your wheel.'

'I need to get home. Mama is expecting me for lunch,' said Albert meekly.

We gathered around the hapless beanpole, wondering what Jacob would do next.

'Well, your *Mama* will have to wait a little longer, Albert.'

'If you don't let me through, I'll...I'll tell Papa!' Albert sounded nervous.

'Really! I'm shaking in my boots. I don't give a toss about your *Papa*. Now come here!'

Albert didn't move, so Jacob hit him with the stick.

'Ow! Ow! I'm going to tell the police and you'll be arrested. Papa will hear of this!' His speech, while strained, remained formal.

Jacob ignored the feeble threat and we warmed inside, eagerly anticipating the next instalment. Albert, meanwhile, just wanted to go home. He adopted Gandhi's approach and stood there passively, waiting resignedly for his punishment. He almost looked dignified. Was he a masochist?

Jacob wasn't interested in the pacifist pose, only in the ritual of belittling. 'All right, Albert. Sing the *Wilhelmus*!'

In his quavering soprano voice, Albert began the national anthem, making an immediate fool of himself. What's more, he knew all the

---

[35] Not his real name.
[36] Not his real name.

words. *No one* knows all the words to a national anthem. What a big girl's blouse! He continued singing because Jacob hadn't told him to stop. We burst out laughing and were tingling with mirth, mainly because of the pathetic voice.

'Okay! You can shut up now.'

There was a lull. Grinning faces gleefully studied Jacob's orchestration. Albert had turned pale.

'Now, the nightingale song!'

We had heard it countless times but couldn't get enough of it, especially when sung by Albert. It was a pathetic little tune for first graders.

'Oh Nightingale, Oh Nightingale, how sweet your voice to hear!'

Albert's rendition was sentimental and thin. But the absurd contrast between his size and his reedy voice sent us into a paroxysm of giggles. We were swimming in a pool of perverse pleasure and very conscious of the humiliation, yet too thick-skinned to intervene.

Right at the end of the tedious tune there was a high note, which would test Albert. He knew it and, just before the final attempt, he stopped. 'I won't sing anymore. I can't do it.'

Jacob looked at us in triumph and from his pocket emerged a small brown frog. It sat quietly in Jacob's hand, its speckled, leathery skin glistening in the midday sun, its lungs expanding and contracting evenly. We were entranced by the tiny amphibian and had a good idea what would happen next.

'Finish the song properly or I'll shove this frog down yer throat!'

When Albert began to sob, we felt uncomfortable and for the first time began to feel sorry for him; the spell was broken and our humanity returned.

'Let him go, Jacob. We've had our fun,' said Lex emphatically.

Jacob was reluctant, but Lex and I had had enough, as had my best friend, Johnny Red. Jacob sensed the change in mood.

'On yer bike, buffoon, and don't let us catch you coming through our street again.'

After a few weeks, Albert was caught again and the farce repeated. Bullying might be a singular affair for some but it usually involves an audience. After all, bullies needs someone to laud their power. Too callow to analyse the subtleties of harassment, we eagerly hopped onto the bandwagon, enjoying the sadistic thrill of humiliating someone.

We were all complicit, as were *Das Deutsche Volk* when called upon by Hitler to support the Third Reich – for example, in his famous Chancellor's speech of 1933: "The misery of our people is horrible to behold..." Slowly, Hitler's invective turned the common man, who fell prey to his beguiling rhetoric. Yet little did the ordinary German realize that "mighty oaks from little acorns grow";[37] or that their grievances, just as they may have been, would eventually result in the *Holocaust*: "All that is necessary for the triumph of evil is that good men do nothing."[38]

In contrast to Jacob, Roel van Wieringen was a local hero, who chewed tobacco and squirted the brown liquid from the side of his mouth. A scarecrow of a man, he always attracted a crowd and had been a champion sulky driver in his youth, winning a number of races. Because he lived in our street he was regarded as a minor celebrity. We all loved Roel. In actual fact he was a rather simple man who liked children and often told us stories, on some occasions even allowing us to sneak into the racing carnival.

'Quick Hanover was the best horse I ever drove,' he began enthusiastically. 'You young ones wouldn't know. I'll tell you something interesting though. Quick Hanover wasn't a large horse, but he had something extra. He always left it to the end, then took off. No horse could catch him. Quick Hanover was clever and responded to my whip in a flash. We understood one another and he wanted so much to please me that we won many times. I'll even have you know his pedigree could be traced back generations to the stables of Franz Josef, the old emperor. I still recall seeing the emperor when I was a young man visiting Vienna on horse business.' Roel leaned against his neatly bricked windowsill and ejected his tobacco juice as if to stress his point.

He always seemed to have plenty of time and never to be in a hurry. 'Hey, Lichtie. What've *you* been up to eh? Enjoying school? I hated school when I was your age. Tell me something!' Roel was gentle and took his time to talk to you.

I basked in the attention and, looking around, saw other children coming towards us: I felt *very* special. 'Well, Roel, I don't mind school at the moment because we're studying the countries of the world. I know the capitals of most places,' I said proudly.

'You must be a clever lad to remember all those difficult names. But to be a good harness racer, you have to have your wits about you. It's a different skill but just as valuable. Still, I'm impressed.'

I was taken by Roel's earlier allusion to royalty. *He* must be special too, having seen an emperor. I tried to imagine him as a young man, with his stubble and cap, standing in the middle of Vienna, gawking at the embroidered worthy.

---

[37] A.B. Johnson's *The Philosophical Emperor, a Political Experiment; or The Progress of a False Proposition* USA, 1841. Similar versions of this proverb can be found in English writing from as early as the fourteenth century.

[38] Edmund Burke, 1729–97, Irish-born British statesman, orator, and political philosopher.

Roel never changed in manner or attire. He dressed like a tramp but didn't care tuppence about his appearance. Always cheerful and upbeat, he sometimes put a coin in my palm. 'Go buy yourself an ice-cream. Don't tell your parents though.' We did, of course. Not because of the money, but because it was a gift from Roel.

Mother had known him for many years; he sometimes helped out on Opa's farm. 'He's a lovely man, but talks more than he works.'

Roel's unshaven face broke out in a broad smile whenever he saw me and he would tug his cap in recognition. I never saw him without it. He was in his nineties when he was killed by a car – modernity's insult to the ancient sport of harness racing.

We never paid to see a harness race or a football match: we had no money. Instead, we jumped the ditch west of the Sportpark, climbed up the back of the rickety public stand and slid down beneath the seats, which were attached to slabs of polished iron sheeting covering the sheds and stables underneath. The iron sheets were certainly polished after half the boys in our neighbourhood used this trick to gain entry! With a tickle of anticipation in my belly, I loved the sensation of sliding and then plopping over the edge. The local overseer, Kaandorp – his name originating from the flat-bottomed barges commonly found in Dutch waterways – was hated by everyone. There were so many illicit points of entry we knew he couldn't cover them all, but still kept an eye out for him and varied our tactics. He was officious and inept, chasing us to little effect since we were too nimble and elusive.

'Kaandorp, you silly old bugger, come and catch us if you can!' He would raise his walking stick in anger, turn pink and give chase with his wonky legs. We just laughed and took off.

Bear Stockman was another identity who seemed to have been around for millennia. He was the cousin of Stockman the tobacconist. Bear already seemed old when I was a mere whippersnapper. Yet, when I returned to Newportslane twenty years later, he was still alive and had changed little. Because of his rotundity, his blue farmer's smock, walrus moustache and signature cap, Stockman appeared stuck in time. He smelt of cream and cheese. I always saw him by himself, a wife never in evidence, although he reputedly had one.

When John returned to *his* old haunts a quarter of a century later, he happened to meet Bear Stockman in the street and was pleased to see a familiar face from the past.

'Good day Bear,' John addressed him warmly. Without batting an eyelid, Bear grunted a 'Mornin' John!' and walked straight past him, as though John had never left the neighbourhood.

I couldn't imagine Bear being young. It's as if he was born old. He was a small-time farmer, but better known as an iconic cheese-carrier. He was the photogenic face of the century-old Alkmaar Cheese Market, his bucolic features on tourist brochures for years. His congenial visage, however, concealed a calculating and rather cold personality. Brusque in manner, Bear kept to himself. He was also a skinflint. One day, he approached Lex and me as we were coming home from school. 'Boys, I've got a proposition for you.'

We were surprised at his friendliness, something he wasn't renowned for, and became suspicious.

'Would you lads like to make a bit of money?' he asked, straight to the point. Lex answered, 'Of course, Mr Stockman. What do you want us to do?'

'I'm getting a bit older now, so I'm finding it difficult to round up my cows. If you boys could help me out early in the morning and after school I'll pay you half a guilder a week. That's for both of you, mind.'

It was hard to earn or acquire money at the best of times, so we jumped at the chance.

'Thanks, Mr Stockman! There shouldn't be any problem. We'll be happy to help you. When do you want us to start?' Lex asked eagerly.

'Monday is as good a time as any. But be on time. No later than six o'clock.' Bear then quickly moved on.

Lex and I were full of excitement as we got up in the cold of early morning. It was drizzling but we had to keep our appointment. Looking outside, my enthusiasm waned considerably. But a promise is a promise, although we had kept the arrangement from our parents, anticipating strenuous objection.

Father was already up and contentedly sipping his tea, reading *De Volkskrant* – The People's Daily. He looked up as we crept past him in the passageway. Father had a sixth sense and boomed, 'Who's there? Come on, you can't fool me.'

Lex put a finger to his mouth but I began to snigger. Father rose from the table and within seconds the game was up: seeing us fully clothed, he knew something was afoot.

'Ah, gentlemen, and where are we off to then? It's a bit early for school so what are you up to?' Father wasn't angry; he rarely was. Instead, he was intrigued by the sly behaviour of his younger lads.

'Bear Stockman has offered us a job rounding up his cows,' I said, almost apologetically.

'Oh yes! What's he paying you?'

'Half a guilder...for both of us...for a week.'

'You must be joking! Rounding up cows isn't easy you know. They're stupid animals. When you have a few of them cornered, the others will bolt for sure. It's a horrible job! There's an art to rounding up cows and it takes time. *Opa* knew his cows backwards and they listened to his coaxing, but Bear has more cows than him and you'll find it very difficult to corral them all. Typical Bear! He just can't be bothered, that's all.

Anyway, you're mad to bust your guts for such a piffling amount. You'll fall asleep in class... Good old Stockman...' Father shook his head, then added, 'You're not to go through with this... Tell him on the way to school... If you have any problems, I'll have a few words with him, the old miser.'

Our naiveté wasn't dwelt on, but the disappointment was great. No lucre and therefore no new gadgets, books, comics or going to the movies. Moreover, we had to face the ignominy of Bear's castigations. Mother and Father usually insisted we clean up our own mess. No jumping in and rescuing their sons. No way! Unless desperate...

Bear opened the door and spoke first. 'You're a little late, and because of you *I'm* running late with the milking. What's your excuse?' For a man who had just hired two young workers, he showed little tact or tolerance.

'Father has forbidden us to do it, Mr Stockman. He says it's too difficult,' said Lex nervously.

'Too difficult! You aren't serious. Why, at your age I rounded up twice the number. You're a spoilt lot, you Lichties, soft as soap.'

Lex was becoming agitated, but since Bear could easily crush us with one hand tied behind his back, as far as I was concerned, it wasn't worth getting into an argument.

'Anyway, Father says you're an old miser,' Lex blurted out. 'You aren't paying us enough.'

Bear's face grew red and his eyes lit up. I got the distinct impression he was about to explode and took a few steps back, ready for a quick retreat. Lex took the same precaution. However, Bear knew his limitations and felt restrained by the repercussions if matters were to get out of hand; the social mores of the neighbourhood often acted as a brake on uncivilized behaviour. Instead, Bear just stood there for a while, then said, 'You little buggers, you can piss off. I don't ever want to see you again!' With that relatively mild rebuke he shut the door and we made our way to school, relieved, since it could have been a lot worse.

'I don't think much of Bear, the old prick. Give me Roel anytime,' I remarked, and Lex agreed.

Every neighbourhood has its curmudgeons. Near the end of our street, facing the town centre, lived a miserable grouch called Van Rietz.[39] Van Rietz, balding and cadaverous, was mainly interested in growing vegetables, judging from the inordinate amount of time spent in his garden. He despised kids.

Unfortunately for us, his large backyard abutted a hectare used by the Cubs. When Baden Powell's little workers weren't using this valued space, we used it as a football pitch; although, just after the War, no one possessed a football. Instead, during autumn, twenty-two scruffy boys

---

[39] Not his real name.

could be seen chasing a tennis ball from mid-afternoon till dusk. The winning goal was a matter of life and death, unless perchance the ball landed in Van Rietz's vegie patch. That would be the last we saw of it. Desperate pleas were intoned – all to no avail.

'Mr van Rietz, could you please return our ball?'

'No, you louts!'

'We won't kick the ball over your fence again, Mr van Rietz.'

'That's what you said last week. You're ruining my tomatoes.' An overstatement, given the size of the ball.

'Why don't you kids play somewhere else, instead of annoying me?' Van Rietz wasn't to be budged. Just as well we lived near tennis courts where tennis balls sometimes went astray...

Some time later, Johnny Red's father bought him a beautiful leather football for his birthday. A football then was like owning a Maserati. The lads of our neighbourhood were consumed with Johnny's precious gift. Being a generous soul, he was quite prepared to share the ball – which, predictably, ended up in Van Rietz's bloody garden. Van Rietz, a little greyer now, had grown even grumpier.

'Who's going to approach the old misery guts,' I asked.

'Seeing it's my ball, I'll talk to him,' Johnny offered kindly.

We all leant over Van Rietz's fence like clowns at the fair, open-mouthed and moving our heads from left to right, following the animated exchange between Johnny and Van Rietz.

'Mr van Rietz, I'm sorry my ball has landed in your backyard, but it's expensive and I only just got it for my birthday. Could you throw it back please?'

'No way! Last time it was a bloody tennis ball, now a soccer ball. What next, the Graf Zeppelin? I'm sick and tired of you whelps wrecking my garden!' He leaned on his shovel, spitting aggressively onto his cauliflowers.

A stalemate followed, then Johnny lost patience and began to threaten him. 'If you don't give me back my ball, we'll jump your fence and trample all over your veggies.' While this was not a good move, we all empathized strongly with Johnny's frustration.

Van Rietz planted his shovel in the soil and stepped forward, as if to goad us, and said, 'Oh, I see, you want to take me on. You are more than welcome to try.'

Then the unthinkable happened. With a sly grin he pulled out a large carving knife and proceeded to cut the ball in half.

Shouts of disbelief: 'That's nasty!'

'You'll cop it now, Rietz!'

'Bastard!'

'What a dirty thing to do. How low can you get!'

But the damage was done. This time, however, Van Rietz had indeed gone too far.

Johnny Red's father was a big man in the construction business. The surname had nothing to do with communism or hair colour, but everything to do with provocation. 'Red' was their real name, though, and they were respected as a hard-working family, but it was unwise to upset them. Two days later, Johnny met me with a brand new ball and Van Rietz was seen soon after sporting a black eye and a giant plaster across his nose.

My stay in hospital some years earlier left a nasty taste in my mouth. Starch, carbolic acid and iodine guaranteed a lasting revulsion towards anything medical. Death had visited me there too, through Aaron, and the suddenness of it all cast my mind to heaven and virtue. This obsession with 'goodness' lasted a long time.

Mother constantly harped on the need to be good: 'Now, darlings, try to be nice to one another, and God will reward you. Christ loves good children, children who care for others.'

I wasn't *au fait* with Mother's particular brand of wisdom at this age and took her word for it.

Goodness, in the mind of the young, is a queer concept. Its intrinsic nature isn't always understood. The fear of a thrashing, a curt rebuke, or invoking the devil's work may be sufficient to return a young boy to the path of virtue. Pavlovian virtue...superficial. Easy solutions, no questions asked. Bribery also works.

The 'whys' as to goodness, however, persisted in my tiny, restless brain. Why be good when so many others were bad and often won out? Little Adolph, Mussolini and old Joe Stalin got away with nastiness for a very long time.

Mother and Father, although the latter rarely, would on occasion use threats to force us to see the error of our ways. Normally, however, they applied common sense, best summarized thus:

"Don't hit your brother!" Lesson – pain isn't pleasant.

"Don't steal from anyone, except the Germans, which isn't really stealing, just reclaiming." Lesson – it doesn't belong to you.

"Don't swear or yell or sulk." Lesson – it upsets family harmony.

"Don't be selfish!" Usually related to food, playing marbles, not doing your fair bit, or hogging the warmth of the stove. Lesson – learn to share; it benefits everyone, even yourself.

"Don't get above yourself." Lesson – pride or conceit will distort your place in the world. Be humble, like Roel, and know your limitations.

Such precepts are well understood by wise parents. Hopefully! Only when older and more cynical do we mount an assault on these home truths and reinterpret them.

My childhood imagination was especially lit up by the mysterious world of religion. Today, cyberspace, it could be argued, has replaced the world of religion in function and symbolism – its language, rituals and content having taken on similar form, the crucial difference being that cyberspace is a technical affair. And like religion in the past, it has yet to unleash its full, ambiguous potential.

Looking back over the bumps and fissures of my life I can still smell the incense, hear the resolute *dominus vobiscums*, inhale the dust of dark confessionals, feel my sore knees and rehearse the endless Masses.

Early morning Mass, inky and dank outside, the altar lit up with slender candles. Mellow lights dangling from long chains. Brightness, brightness everywhere! The smell of wet raincoats! Watching the altar boys offering the wine to Father Pronk, who miraculously turns it into the blood of Jesus Christ. I always thought it strange for Father Pronk to imbibe blood, and hoped he would turn into a vampire then fly to the ceiling, where he would look down at us, pointing a finger and licking his lips; just as I imagined the Devil to behave, from on high.

Sitting, kneeling, watching my pals. Staring at snooty girls across the aisle. I bit into the lacquered pew in front of me, tasting its glossy veneer, and lost myself in contemplation. Standing...sitting...kneeling yet again on the hard boards, scooped hollow by many knees over generations. Just like the worn feet of cherubs in Saint Peter's in Rome: too much saliva over hundreds of years. Innocent cherubs, acid tongues.

Then, a sermon, usually about Hell. Sometimes, about the Sermon on the Mount. Rarely about love, as in *agape*.[40] Sometimes there would be a parable from the gospels. Sometimes...I drifted off.

I gazed at the Stations of the Cross, wondering what it would be like carrying the Cross. Very heavy, like carrying Lex on my back, or maybe even heavier... All made worse by copious bleeding. How does a crown of thorns feel? A bit like Jacob de Kooy digging his long, filthy fingernails into my skull. I dug my fingernails into my cranium as hard as I could, just to try the pain. The boy next to me laughed. I wanted to be a martyr, but without all the messy suffering. Closing my eyes, I pretended to be dead, and imagined myself a martyred saint. I knelt forward, only to be elbowed by the boy kneeling beside me; I ceased to be a saint and pinched his bum in return.

A shaft of blue and red sunshine flushed over me. It may have been the stained glass window of the Virgin Mary, dressed in blue and holding her son like Michelangelo's Pieta, or else the red cloaks of Jesus' disciples

---

[40] Agape: unconditional, sacrificial love.

standing at the foot of the Cross. Motes of dust swam upwards like salmon up streams. I followed their trajectory, wondering whether God would show his face at the top.

I was frightened of the Eucharist,[41] equating it with Christ's heart pulsating furiously, ready to explode. And who or what was hiding behind the altar? I thought I could hear voices and imagined the back of the altar leading to an underground burial site, full of saints' bones. The smell of incense reminded me of decay and I hoped the Mass would soon end.

'Hey Lex, I'm going to hold my breath for an hour to experience pain. Want to join me and see who lasts the longer?' I suggested one day after church.

'You're an idiot,' he replied. 'I've got better things to do.'

At other times after Mass, on the way home or to class, I challenged my mates to feats of bravery:

'I bet you wouldn't stay overnight in Saint Joseph's by yourself.'

'Yes, I would. How much?'

'I bet you wouldn't sleep in a cemetery overnight by yourself.'

'Yes, I would. More money though!'

'I bet you wouldn't sleep in a coffin at the mortuary, near dead bodies.'

'Yes, I would! Five guilders.'

I sometimes woke up at night in a cold sweat and touched my body, looking for holes. Was I Saint Sebastian? Was my head still attached to my body? Or was it doing the rounds on a platter, like Saint John the Baptist? I became Saint Alexander of Bergamo, beheaded. I was Saint Stephen, stoned to death. Did I even *dare* to be Saint Lawrence[42] and ask to be roasted on either side? I inhabited a world of fearful symbols, manipulated by priests, Brothers and Sisters, whose exhortations pushed me to new devotional heights. I would pray for an hour a day. I would let Lex have the last portion of sauerkraut.

Religion seemed as natural to me as breathing air. Sometimes I still yearn for its icons and soothing ceremonies. I felt secure, even uplifted. But one day this had to end. There were too many holes in it, like Swiss cheese. More than Saint Sebastian's punctured body. More than the rips in my tattered singlet.

---

[41] The Eucharist, or Holy Communion, re-enacts the Lord's last supper with his disciples. It is the central sacrament of Christian churches, commemorating Jesus' last instructions when taking bread and wine: "This is my body...and this is my blood."

[42] Saint Lawrence, c.225–258, martyred; condemned by the Prefect of Rome to be slowly roasted over an iron grill. When well-burnt on one side, he allegedly uttered the famous words, 'Turn me over!'

By the Scruff of the Neck

Father had his preference in priests and loved Father Pronk because he was theatrical and provocative. Father Pronk was an expert on Hell, matching Dante at every turn, his *Inferno* a veritable smorgasbord of misery and suffering; no *Purgatorio* or *Paradiso*. It was his favourite theme and people swallowed its violence with relish and shame-faced guilt.

The Krauts would be the first to enter Hell. Hitler deserved his own torture chamber, probably on a spit, or crushed by huge, boiling-hot stones. Torquemada reborn in Father Pronk; but oh, so justly this time! That'll teach Little Adolph to rough up Europe.

Father Pronk leant over the pulpit, as if to reproach each person in the congregation. His shiny pink head trembling with intent, he shook his chasuble for emphasis, or as an ostentatious prelude to his colourful oration.

'You may well think you have the answers to your desires, to your earthly dreams, but let me assure you, you are very much mistaken. Your life, brief as it is, my parishioners, is blackened by sin. Contaminated. You have become the pawns of the Devil. Avarice, pride and lust are his favourite tools. Succumb to these and you have forfeited your place in heaven. Your soul is more precious than your life. Heed the words of Christ. He will be your salvation, your bastion...your bastion against eternal torment.'

Father Pronk now adopted a hushed tone, as if privy to a state secret, the faithful succumbing to his hypnotic voice: 'Imagine, if you will, the centuries before, the thousands of event-filled years before the Romans, the Greeks, the pre-human era, going back to the beginning of time, when Adam and Eve had not yet crossed our Maker's mind. Just think about this for a moment... All these years are but a split second...a split second of the time you will spend in that infernal place, that place of wretchedness, where the gnashing of teeth will continue forever and ever, beginning with Judgment Day.' He suddenly stopped to let this inevitable prospect sink in.

Mouths wide open, eyes agog. My hands sticky from sheer terror! I felt queasy and ever so remorseful. Only yesterday I had nicked one of Johnny Red's marbles. I would have to return it straight away after Mass and pray an extra half hour.

The idea of torture for the rest of eternity was too much to bear. It was worse than sitting for a test, worse than cutting your finger, worse than fronting Saint Nicholas in December, even worse than a thrashing from Brother Fabritius,[43] my teacher. Guilt oozed over me like treacle. I needed to move quickly. Sin was my one-way entry card to Hell!

---

[43] Not his real name.

John had already yielded to the Devil; he and his mates were busy playing cards at the back of the church, unconcerned that their mortal soul was about to enter the eternal furnace so vividly described by Father Pronk. Once, John lit up a cigarette in church and was kicked out by the verger. Our parents were notified, and after a good pummelling by Father, he ran away and didn't come home for a long time.

As John became older he skipped Mass altogether, fooling us for years by correctly naming the colour of the priest's chasuble during the relevant service. His girlfriends were the informants. My little heart, however, was entirely given over to God. I still have a silver-plated spoon embossed with Christ cradling a child, both with halos, to commemorate my first communion, and a beautifully coloured print with Mother Mary staring towards Heaven, surrounded by angels and naked cherubs, my name in Gothic lettering at the bottom. Just looking at it made me feel virtuous, not yet entirely aware that good deeds were rather more important. I also won a small book with verses dedicated to the saints:

> St Anthony, who preached so well
> To the fishes, so full of fire
> That they didn't wish to miss a word
> Even if it lasted an hour,
> Also teach me to listen piously and still,
> To all that God wants me to learn.
>
> Sebastian, how you suffered!
> I see the sharp arrows cutting
> Deep into your flesh, your heart, your head
> And still you sing: your faith in God.
> Oh, may I, when struck with pain
> Stand as resolutely and gratefully.

It struck me as the height of spiritual satisfaction to be able to walk around the neighbourhood with a glowing white halo. How I envied the saints. What a sensational way to display one's holiness. I tried my very best to be righteous, walking slowly, my head ever so slightly askew in order to appear holier, and even attended two Masses per week. At night I would pray to the Virgin Mary, or Saint Joseph, after whom our church was named. As I shivered on wintry nights, just before lying down, I would punish myself by reciting the rosary for an extra five minutes. Testing myself, I imagined Saint Sebastian's arrows piercing his flesh, and kept on praying. To cave in to weakness was unthinkable. So, I prayed like a boy possessed. And in a way I was.

Fear of punishment too held my imagination. One wet afternoon, while a storm raged and the dull grey sky seemed so low as to be within reach, everyone sat cosily around the stove, exchanging gossip and drinking tea. I had a sudden urge to visit the WC, which was behind the house, next to the coal shed. I intended to do a quick poo then rush back inside. Poo paper was cut-up newspaper. Father also thought it sensible to leave some magazines out there for those who were somewhat slow of bowel movement or who wished to contemplate life in a leisurely manner.

I parked myself comfortably above the can and picked up an art magazine. Enjoying the sensation of letting go, I stumbled upon a vision of hell as depicted by some artist called Gustave Moreau: I only remembered the name when I came across his pictures many years later. Horrific images: twisted bodies with elongated heads on a reddish-brownish-purplish background, eyes pulled apart, ears on flesh belonging somewhere else and blood dribbling from strange orifices. A grotesque spectacle!

My religiosity had primed my imaginings to a heightened degree. I believed in ghosts, miracles, floating heads and evil angels. The shock of seeing this version of hell caused my mouth, in an instant, to morph into Munch's *Scream*. I began to yell, my back tingling with fear. The yells were loud enough to be heard at *The Dyke*, but became lost in the screaming gale funnelling through Newportslane.

The wind intensified, whispering death and retribution. Though I wanted to escape the loo as fast as I could, my stool refused to yield and dangled awkwardly between bum and can. I panicked and kept shouting, 'Help! Help! Please, someone get me out of here!'

The wind mocked my plea. I was very much alone.

The long tremulous moans around the house and garden continued to send shivers up my spine. Moreau had triumphed; I'd had enough. I grabbed a piece of paper, hastily wiped my bum as well as I could, pulled up my pants and ran for it – up the path, through the kitchen, and into the living room. The family ceased their activities and stared at me. With tears in my eyes, I blurted, 'I've been to Hell and seen the Devil!'

No one said anything – silence, then a chorus of laughter.

Death in its many guises has always frightened me: photos of death camps, beheadings in the Bible, Aurangzeb ordering Sikhs to be sawn in half, and emaciated old men exhaling their last gasp. Nevertheless, while playing cowboys and indians, we enacted the obligatory death throes if we were pierced by an arrow or shot. I always took longer to die than the others.

These cameos put many an actor on the path of success; yet death is no thespian matter. I break out in a sweat as I imagine myself a skeleton among skeletons, piled up in concentration camps; I become the rag-doll corpse crushed beneath the others. I become the person stood up against a wall and shot, the bullets passing airily through my body; rescued by waking up from the nightmare...in painless silence.

As a child, voodoo masks gave me the creeps. Pictures of fierce New Guinea warriors, bones through noses – code for cannibalism – inhabited my world for days, especially at night. Fear, death and religion merged imperceptibly to form a heady brew. I was determined to pray even more fervently. The Devil *was not* going to pull *my* limbs asunder!

Lex thought I was daft and a holy show pony. But as I wallowed in my ecstasy, I forgave him his uncharitable thoughts, hoping that by praying louder and longer, I could move closer to God and further away from the Devil. I knew the catechism by heart and never questioned a word. There was no need to, since the Priests and Brothers knew everything.

'Hail, Holy Queen, Mother of mercy; our life, our sweetness, our hope. To thee do we cry, poor banished children of Eve.'

It was wonderful to be so spiritual and attentive. I even gave up screaming at the world, instead speaking softly and earnestly. The rhythm of the catechism and prayers, so calming, induced a state of purity and devotion. I was too naive to analyse the incantations and ask myself what they actually meant: to question was unnecessary and disrespectful. My religiosity was like a fever: I constantly asked God for forgiveness and offered help to anyone who needed it. Not that I had much to offer...

Father remarked, 'He's getting too carried away. Soon I'll be afraid to fart in front of him.'

John tousled my hair and encouraged me to pray louder. 'Go on then, Your Holiness, tell us how to pray. You still have some nasty sins to overcome, like shitting the whole family, though there can't be that many left.' His sarcasm floated over me as I ignored his teasing. Instead, I recited the rosary from beginning to end.

Bill wasn't interested in my holy behaviour; he was training to be the sprint champion of Alkmaar. Meanwhile, Lex avoided me like the plague, finding my religious antics sickening: 'If you mention Christ once more, I'm going to crucify you myself. I've already got the nails. Ma, why can't he stop driving us crazy with his stupid praying?'

One freezing winter's morning, when we were on our way to church, it was still foggy in parts and people's icy breath could be seen from a distance. Heads down, beanies pulled over ears, scarves tied around mouths, cyclists headed to their destination, all pedalling like fury. Workmen clapped their hands to help circulation, fingers crackling with stiffness; some put their hands beneath armpits to keep them warm, others thumped cold backs. Garbos ran to keep warm, emptying the bins like zombies. Early mornings always seemed more strained than later in the day, when the frost had thawed and the sun sometimes succeeded in smiling through.

A milk dray turned a corner and struggled its way into our street, slowing down, the huge Belgian draft horse meek and obedient: immediately after the War milk was still distributed by cart. The milkman waited for his customers to emerge with their pails and once the large silver-grey milk cans ceased rocking and clanking, he jumped from his seat, taking a ladle from the can closest to him. Gijsberts, the milkman, exchanged the usual courtesies with his clientele:

'Morning!' he sang.

'Morning! Cold eh!' came the reply.

'How are the kids?' he asked sociably.

'Difficult, what do you expect?' the woman shot back.

Everyone was focused and it wasn't the time for idling – except for a thickset council worker with curly, straw-blond hair. He stood in front of Kramer's, the blacksmith, dragging on a fag, his council jacket much too short for his bulk. He seemed to have all the time in the world and thought he owned it.

As Bill, Lex and I passed behind him, he emitted a fart of enviable duration and melody. I kid you not, it sang for a minute, like a pricked balloon, and bested the virtuosity of Yehudi Menuhin. We all waited till we were some distance away, then broke into laughter and crowed:

'Must have eaten two dozen sprouts at least.'

'Strange, he didn't stink.'

'Too cold!'

'Must tell Father! He'd love that.'

When we finally arrived, the church, full of parishioners, was neither warm nor cold. We fumbled our way into the nearest empty pew. The clattering of hymnbooks and echoes of scraping feet brought a disapproving look from the verger. Father Pronk then emerged from the left hand side of the altar, as if he lived in the sacristy. He was followed by the altar boys and the mass began

Although too young to be an altar boy, I had other aspirations. Not only did I want to be the most devout boy at Saint Aloysius, but I also aimed to become a choirboy. To enter the privileged loft wasn't easy; there was a long waiting list. Choral tradition in the Lowlands had always been noteworthy, pardon the pun.

Mr Crane,[44] the choirmaster, was a stocky man with a short back and sides haircut and a broad head from which protruded unsympathetic small, brown eyes. He had a sallow face, and wore a light grey suit in which he must have slept, for it was always crumpled and seemed to be the only clothing he ever wore. But for us that didn't matter. What mattered was music.

I became a choirboy through freakish circumstance. I must have been about seven when I was thrown out of the Cubs. The Cub house was located behind the property belonging to our archenemy Van Rietz. I had gotten into a dispute with some loud-mouthed boy who challenged me to a fight. Lex, a better fighter than me, gave some clear instructions and I was doing pretty well until grabbed by the scoutmaster; both of us were immediately expelled. Strange, considering Baden-Powell wanted scouting to be a preparation for military life – self-reliance, survival, knot-tying, orienteering, amongst other martial pursuits.

Father didn't seem too fazed and suggested approaching Mr Crane for an audition: Bill and Lex were already choirboys. We were, however, expected to initiate projects ourselves. Our parents rarely intervened in our affairs, both being quick to insist:

'You'll have to sort it out yourself.'
'None of our business!'
'Don't annoy us with your problems.'

As a result, I was rather nervous as I entered the nave of the church the afternoon the choir was rehearsing. My knees shaking like maracas, I looked up to the choir loft. To my right, rays of late afternoon sunshine pierced the heart of Christ crucified, portrayed in one of the large stained glass windows. Feeling vulnerable and alone, I stopped halfway, genuflected towards the altar, crossed myself and turned around. *HE* would understand… Standing patiently in the centre of the church counting the black and white diamond flagstones as far back as the heavy oak doors, I waited for Mr Crane to notice me. My brothers weren't aware of my choral ambition.

A week before, I had visited Mr Crane to politely ask for an audition – a prerequisite for joining. His house was located in a well-established part of Alkmaar, across from Piet's Mill on the main canal encircling the old town.

Now, Mr Crane tapped the lectern, preoccupied with the nuances of the music. 'Boys, you are biting off the notes. Too brief! A bit softer and longer to bring out the dramatic impact of the *Tantum Ergo*.'[45]

---

[44] Not his real name.

[45] The Tantum Ergo Sacramentum – 'Hence so great a Sacrament.' A hymn written by Thomas Aquinas, a medieval philosopher.

His back seemed huge. Then, disaster! Bill espied me standing forlorn and alone within the cavernous church and, in the middle of a solemn *Kyrie,* yelled, 'Hey Herrie, what are *you* doing here?'

There was stunned silence as a surge of anger rippled through Mr Crane's body. The boys stared at him, then at Bill, instantly realizing he was in trouble. Mr Crane, red-ballooning, briskly turned towards Bill and in a stern voice said, 'I will not tolerate yelling in God's House... Sacrilege! Where do you think you are? I can't believe this. Bill Licht you are no longer required here. Please leave at once!'

Bill's eyes squinted in embarrassment, his quiff bobbing up and down like a cockscomb. Shamefaced, he descended the steps of the choir loft, not even looking at me as he slunk homewards. Father wouldn't be too pleased... Mother would roast him: 'How could you do such a thing? You know what Mr Crane is like!'

Thus one Licht went out and another Licht went in – or on, depending on one's stance.[46] I felt sorry for Bill, though.

Standing on his low podium, with the unsettling impassivity of Adolf Hitler, Mr Crane looked right through you if you weren't paying attention. He knew his boys and placed them strategically in front of him. If any were too loud, he moved his hand downwards as if patting a dog. If too soft, he lifted his left palm upwards in a rousing manner, his face remaining inscrutable. A boy was appointed to flip over the large sheets of black notes. No stone was left unturned; or perhaps it should be said that no note was safe until executed perfectly. The congregation might be tone deaf, but Mr Crane deemed this irrelevant to his God-given mission to raise the bar, as it were.

The choir always performed on Sundays during High Mass. On feast or holy days, such as Christmas or Easter, we were on call. Sometimes we were rewarded with small Easter eggs, but usually it was the satisfaction of having performed well that sufficed: we always rose to the occasion.

One day, Lex went missing and was discovered two hours later by Mother's sister, Aunty Anne, standing on the edge of the moat near the Friesian Bridge. His socks were dripping and he was puffing and cursing, trying to hook an old tyre floating past. You never know, it might have fish in it... Fish seem to love the inside of tyres, perhaps to hide from predators, or for breeding.

'You naughty boy, we've all been looking for you! You know you shouldn't be here.' With a half-smile, Aunty Anne waggled a finger at him.

---

[46] 'Licht' means 'light' in English.

'Thanks for picking me up, Aunty Anne. I was just making a detour along the canal.'

'I'll have to tell your Mother you've been playing near the water again...and she'll notice your socks. Water can be dangerous and you *never* seem to take any notice. She'll go berserk.'

She didn't sound angry; she was very fond of Lex, oddly enough due to his risk-taking behaviour, not unlike her own, as I am about to explain. Lex grinned and hopped onto the back seat of her bicycle.

Aunty Anne had only one leg, the result of a childhood accident. A few years after the Great War, her father, *Opa* Goudsblom was returning from market with an empty cart and lost control of his skittish horse. A sudden gust of wind from the east had frightened the animal and it bolted along the windy dyke, causing the cart to capsize. Aunty Anne, then about four, was sitting next to him. A heavy steel-rimmed wheel came off when the cart collapsed. As she slid onto the embankment, the wheel rolled on top of her, crushing her right leg.

Her disability, combined with a combative personality, could easily alienate people, especially boys her own age. She became a tomboy, swimming better than most, her stump no impediment. We were allowed to play with her stump, which resembled an arm severed at the hand. We even tried on her artificial leg and quickly realized it was heavy and cumbersome; although since she was tall, our short legs couldn't reach to the bottom of the hollow prosthesis. Later, as the art and science of prosthetics improved, her replacement legs grew lighter. Still, it must have been a tremendous physical and psychological burden, but she rarely complained.

Aunty Anne was tough and resilient and we admired her. 'No use crying over spilt milk or a lost leg,' she used to say. Nonetheless, she was not averse to punching someone who mocked her affliction:

'Hey, gammy leg, move over and let me pass.'

'Piss off, ya crippling nuisance!'

'Don't kick me with your false leg.'

Many a cheeky lad went home with a sore lip. She wasn't to be messed with! She was fearless too, and often took a gamble against the odds, including disagreeing with her employer when older.

Mother clashed with her on occasions, she being nine years older than Aunty Anne, who was the youngest of the family. Both had feisty personalities, and Aunty Anne often commented on both our strengths and our weaknesses. She had neither an axe to grind nor was she easily deceived by Mother's over-protectiveness. While Mother lapped up the compliments, she attacked anyone criticizing her kittens. Her children were sacrosanct. Father, by contrast, harboured no such delusions.

Lex's canal fetish was nothing to Aunty Anne; that's how boys behaved. Indeed, *should* behave. Mother, however, went bananas and banned him from leaving home for a week. He was, however, allowed to play in the backyard.

Two weeks earlier, I had fallen into a shallow pond in front of Westernlicht – the respite centre for old people. I leaned over too far, attempting to catch a frog or carp; a rite of passage for curious boys. I was dripping wet as I entered the front gate, water trickling down my legs.

'Oh no!' Mother exclaimed. 'What happened to you *this time?*'

Mother despised open water. She couldn't swim but hated water for other reasons as well. Holland boasts the densest network of inland waterways in the world. It therefore comes as no surprise that it also has one of the highest rates of drowning.

Wherever you are in Holland you are never far from water, and Dutch boys are besotted with it. All self-respecting clog lads develop a special relationship with their inner water-soul. Some of the great Dutch explorers and admirals cut their maritime teeth sailing the local waterways, as well as the Zuider Zee, east of our Northern Province. Forget about the Dutch boy who put his finger in the dyke; a fabrication anyway.

I love all seasons, though winter is a treacherous time of year; despite its initial cover of fresh snow, like an endless ermine coat, luxurious and beautiful. Snow quickly turns to sleet, or with a drop in temperature becomes black ice, turning surfaces into glass-smooth death-traps. Winters and wars are often synonymous with disaster, too, to wit Napoleon's Moscow venture and Hitler's Stalingrad fiasco.

In Holland, as winter draws to a close, canals, ditches, duck ponds and lakes begin to melt and entice young lads to ice-hop from one side to the other. For all of us, shortcuts were there to be taken. One sunny afternoon Hubert Koopman thought he would try his luck. He had been meaning to do it for a while. The ice seemed strong enough, as it always does, ensuring the ruin of many an impatient youth.

Hubert was in my class, a shy slow boy, who gawped a lot and rarely said anything of note. Living near the Horse Market, he reckoned the bridge between the Bergerway and the inner town was too far away, and decided to skip across the pack ice.

Hubert thought the embankment close enough to chance a few more floes, the verdant shoulder, so near, pushing up the purple and yellow crocus buds. Despite warning shouts from an elderly gentleman walking his dog, he ventured on, oblivious to the fact that halfway across the moat the current had changed, forcing the ice sheets to thin out.

Cyclists and cars sped past, ignoring him, as they had seen hundreds of lads and even some girls, attempt this foolhardy practice. Hubert, staring into the sun, misjudged a floating piece of ice and, as he stepped onto it, it flipped. Frantically waving his arms, he lost balance and splashed into the icy water.

The freezing cold quickly took hold of his slight frame and he went under. A few wood pigeons fluttered over the poor boy, heedless of his predicament. He surfaced briefly, only to be sucked under again by the swift current. In a last desperate attempt to grab hold of the ice, his hands clawing wildly, his left arm went up into the air, then sank again, like a retracting periscope. After a few hours or so he re-emerged as a blue bundle of clothing snagged on one of the pylons of the Berger Bridge, and spotted by an idler leaning over the railings. Earlier, the elderly gentleman had desperately shouted for help but no one heard him – the sound of traffic drowned out his feeble cries.

When Hubert's funeral was held, the school was ushered into Saint Joseph's, a long procession of glum boys and girls, their eyes fixed on the small white coffin in front of the altar. Fastidious Brothers gently herded them into the long pews. Some of the girls were crying quietly, others held hands. The boys were silent for once, casting cursory glances at the coffin. Meanwhile, the organist trod a delicate path between solemnity and virtuosity, the stops pushed in and the low notes murmuring grief.

As a classmate, I was permitted to sit up front and could almost touch the coffin. I sat there for some time, eventually dozing off. Pale Hubert was as silent in death as he was in life. Why did our merciful Lord let him die? He was an innocent and couldn't imagine evil.

"Only the good die young", however, is meant to convey the good fortune of those entering heaven before the rest of us, who, it is stressed time and again by our spiritual minders, need to first crawl through "the valley of the shadow of death" – a biblical metaphor for our miserable and unpredictable lives. But a comfort of sorts remains at hand: have faith in the Lord, since through His intercession we can avoid evil and cope with suffering. Yet shouldn't it really be that boisterous and difficult boys ought to die first?

And why evil and suffering in the first place?' I asked myself much later. Why the existential hassle of it all? Maybe God, a supernatural chess player, for motives not vouchsafed to us mere mortals, deigns to emerge from some black hole, like a lion king from his lair, to enjoy a wager with Himself and direct His Christ to make His moves. Bobby Fischer and Magnus Carlsen,[47] eat your heart out... Or maybe God was

---

[47] Both world chess champions.

caught off-guard when he created us. Was it God's 'oops' moment, or Darwinian bad luck, that we turned out so flawed? Flaws, like fleas in our daily lives. Oh yes, 'free will', that elusive engine of our misfortune – or perhaps the *diabolus ex machina*.[48]

Yet God is omniscient, so why not a pre-emptive strike on this unreliable will which gets us into so much trouble? *Dominus vobiscum*,[49] indeed! Only when it suits! Now you see Him, now you don't. A marvellous cosmic game that only He can play, even though the rules remain obscure! Winners and losers! Perhaps we are Ayn Rand's[50] children after all. So, was Hubert a loser through accident, or just sheer carelessness on the part of our Creator?

Much later in life I learnt from the historian Johan Huizinga, another victim of the Third Reich, that people of the Middle Ages, certainly in France and the Lowlands, loved the idea of death. Death was so common that medieval peasants took it in their stride. Apparently Father Pronk's predecessors revelled in it. Death became an obsession premised on a sublime afterlife. Bergman's *Seventh Seal*[51] wasn't created in a vacuum. How things have changed... Science, skepticism and atheism have challenged the acquiescence in a religious justification of death.

Right up until the 1960s, the medieval canvas of Death prevailed for many of us. Everything is perishable and fleeting, so bring on death, whatever its guise. Don't despair; heaven is awaiting the good and just. Just be patient; it will all soon be over.

Yet even then, as I silently watched the grand little coffin staring back at me, I suspected that Hubert would have preferred to stay on *this* side of life. I felt a sudden urge to leap out of my pew, rush to his white box, and open the lid; to yell, 'Get out Hubert! Before it's too late. Wake up and try again! I shall be your best friend for life. You shouldn't be in there!'

But it was too late. All I would see, I knew, would be a shrunken, waxen face peering out from some ridiculous satin material, Hubert's hands folded in obeisance... The spiritual masseurs knew their job and temptation passed.

We all stood up as the parents, siblings, family and close friends filed past, Mrs Koopman sobbing uncontrollably and leaning on her husband's

---

[48] 'Demon from the machine', meaning the introduction of an unexpected event or force that makes matters worse.

[49] 'The Lord be with you.'

[50] Ayn Rand, 1905–81, proposed the morality of rational self-interest: egoism is the "virtue of selfishness". Hence, heroes are those who ruthlessly pursue self-interest or are the winners, as opposed to the losers, in society.

[51] This film was set in Sweden during the Black Death, where a medieval knight takes on Death, or The Grim Reaper, in a game of chess.

shoulder; their children weeping as well, red-faced, slightly confused, not used to such public display and looking a trifle absurd and ugly.

Father Pronk, tailor-made for the task, then took over the reins. He waited impatiently for all to be seated. The shuffling and snivelling came to an abrupt end when his authoritative voice stemmed the tide.

'My dear parishioners...the Koopman family...we are here in the most unfortunate circumstances imaginable, to farewell our beloved Hubert and return him to the bosom of Christ. His unblemished soul will yield an early passage to the life hereafter, where God and His angels will comfort him forever. At a time of such great sorrow let us remember that we are not here to question God's will. We are not alone in carrying this heavy burden, so deeply felt by all of us here today.'

Yes, we are indeed alone, and why shouldn't I, in my juvenile way, question Him?

All grief is personal and solitary, the sharing of pain perhaps easing the burden of grief. At the same time as we experience the loss of a loved one, we weep secretly for our own impending demise. Sharp memories can hurt, while loss of memory in advanced years may be a blessing for some.

'Our hearts go out to the family Koopman...
May the Lord embrace our sorrow!
Death comes like a thief in the night...
Dominus vobiscum.'

We all play with death, some more seriously than others, but children see death as sleep transfigured. It's their myth of transubstantiation; a child's view of death is softened by the imagination. For them, death remains ephemeral.

I have a collection of Catholic illustrations from 1887-8. One painting shows a trio of young gypsies frozen to death in the Austrian Alps. The victims are arranged as though posing for a death scene, the older boy, covered with a thin blanket, is sitting in front of a tree, leaning forward, as if reflecting, while the younger boy is resting peacefully against his sister, seemingly asleep in the snow. All appear at peace, as though recovering from an arduous journey. Yet they are stone dead.

Leo Tolstoy's visceral portrayal of his tubercular brother Nikolai and his own experience in Arzamas[52] was meant to capture the horror of death, not sanitize it. On the other hand, Goya's heroic defender of

---

[52] Leo Tolstoy, 1828–1910, Russian novelist, claimed to have been visited by 'death' in 1869 in an inn in a small village named Arzamas.

Madrid[53] takes on martyrdom as a response to death, while nineteenth and early twentieth-century Irish poet William Butler Yeats, saw death as a human construct and haughtily dismissed it:

> A great man in his pride
> Confronting murderous men
> Casts derision upon
> Supersession of breath;
> He knows death to the bone –
> Man has created death.

In my own view, death remains the greatest insult to mankind. Life, that most wonderful noun in delicate parenthesis, infinity on either side, snuffed out in a nanosecond – or in Hubert's case, probably much longer. Did he have a Pincher Martin[54] moment, or like Peyton Farquhar in *An Occurrence at Owl Creek,* compress his short life into a one-minute dream? We will never know till our own death arrives. If there is a God, He is poker-faced.

Jan Licht, Father's father, died in 1946. I was three years old and have only a blurred memory of him. Just before he died of cancer, he stole out one morning to revisit some of his haunts, unable to stomach the grim surroundings of the hospital he was in. He didn't make it very far, since he was too weak, and was soon found sitting quietly on a park bench in the Wood near the hospital.

'Father, why are you sitting here?' asked his eldest son, our father.

Opa Licht, recognizing his son's voice, didn't look up, but whispered, 'I know I'm going to die, but I just had a sudden urge to go out here in the open air where I can still smell the trees and see the clouds. I hate it in there.'

'But you'll catch a death of cold.'

'If only, son.'

Opa Licht was an emotional man who hated Alkmaar, which he regarded as a provincial backwater. Born and bred in Amsterdam, he missed his brothers. On Fridays he came home early from his commercial rounds, and after a smooth shave and selecting a good suit, emerged from his bedroom, well satisfied. Tapping his wife on the shoulder, he

---

[53] In 1814, Francisco Goya, 1746–1828, painted *The Third Of May 1808*, to capture the heroic defence of Madrid against Napoleon.

[54] Both *Pincher Martin* by William Golding, 1911–93, and *An Occurrence at Owl Creek* by Ambrose Bierce, 1842–1913, capture the last moments before death when the victims' lives unfold in an impressionistically short time.

said, 'Now, Wiep, I hope the little monsters behave themselves! I'm off to Amsterdam on the fiver' – the five o'clock train – 'and I'll see you Sunday night.'

His wife survived the mayhem of each weekend by either visiting Mother's family at *The Dyke*, as the Goudsblom farm was called, or playing off Father's siblings one against the other. It was sheer madness. Bart,[55] the fourth son, was difficult, and made more so by an obdurate mother who played favourites.

One cold Saturday night, Bart and his younger sister Rita[56] had an altercation. Rita had been plaguing him about his laziness. Bart became so incensed that he seized a fork and planted it unceremoniously in Rita's buttock.

'Take that, you bitch! I hate you and hope you and your prissy boyfriend die in hell.'

Rita's screams reached the neighbours, who knocked on the door, thinking someone had been killed.

'Pardon our interrupting, Mrs Licht, but we thought something terrible had happened.' Which it had, but they were quickly fobbed off and assured it was only a friendly tiff. Mother Wiep then grabbed hold of Bart and ordered younger brother Guido,[57] who was in the process of gluing together some wood for a toy boat, to belt the crap out of Bart.

As Bart bellowed, Rita managed to extricate the fork and stem the bleeding. The neighbours, now resigned to the noise of the mad family next door, took little notice.

Swift and violent justice was meted out and the family hummed along just fine. For a while at least! It was only when fed and everyone settled down in front of the stove, farting and belching with gay abandon, that the family at last took on a semblance of normality. Contented murmurings, like purring cats, could be heard from the various corners of the living room.

Fffffft! Prrrr! Hmmmm! Aaroomph!

Ah, Jan Steen would have felt right at home. It's not entirely surprising that some of the younger members of the family turned out a little odd.

John and Uncle Guido were about the same age and sometimes invited girls home. Lex and I were either bribed to say nothing to the oldies or threatened with a fate worse than that of the victims of the Inquisition.

---

[55] Not his real name.

[56] Not her real name.

[57] Not his real name.

'If you don't keep your traps shut, we'll electrocute you with a trillion volts,' Bill warned. When it came to girls he uncompromisingly colluded with John and Guido.

Lex was smart enough to ignore the threats and to wheedle favours out of the older boys, which they regarded as a small price to pay for the privilege of kissing and cuddling. I supported Lex in his argy-bargying because he usually drove a better bargain; Lex was cunning.

'A guilder this week and a guilder next week,' Lex demanded. 'Herrie is my witness. No money and we'll squeal.'

Where did he learn to bargain so deftly? I just went with the flow; girls of John's age were far too old for me, as well as stuck-up and uninteresting. Anyway, I had little to gain by blabbing to the old folks, but a great deal by remaining silent.

Uncle Guido was a ladies' man, as we discovered in the fullness of time. We regarded him more as an older brother and comic-strip hero. He had been in the marines, was very handsome, and like Lex, loved a good stoush. He joined the merchant navy in 1952, where he worked for three years as ship's carpenter on the *Johan van Oldenbarnevelt*, built in 1929.

In 1953, we boarded this beautiful ship to meet up with Guido. Despite its old hull, the marvellous interior, with its artwork, exquisite chandeliers and rich tapestries, reminded me of Rembrandt's gigantic dark paintings, and the wonderful colours compared favourably with those of the famous dining room of the Krasnapolsky restaurant in Amsterdam. Unfortunately, the *Johan*, renamed the *Lakonia*, perished in 1963, in a fire near Madeira, with great loss of life.

While still living with his family, Guido often visited us, his wonderful carpentry skills turning out sleek sailing boats, table-tennis bats, nodding parrots on sticks, and a state-of-the-art chicken run. We thought him larger than life. However, after the early death of *Opa* Licht, in 1946, as Father's youngest brother, he became a loose canon; *Oma*[58] Licht couldn't control him. Our father, being the eldest, attempted to rein him in, but failed, and as a result, Guido gained quite a sullied reputation around Alkmaar. Yet for us, he was Olympian and unimpeachable. He and John remained bosom pals for many years.

Opa Licht loved motorbikes, and although he was versatile, wasn't temperamentally suited to being a mechanic. One day, when he encountered a particularly difficult problem with a chain, he spent a considerable amount of time trying to sort it out, all to no avail.

---

[58] Grandmother

'God dammit, why won't the fucker go onto the sprockets!' he muttered to himself. 'Either the chain is too big, in which case I'm going to kill Johan,' – the supplier – 'or, there's a link missing.'

A mechanic's soliloquy is fairly predictable. Either something works or it doesn't and when it's the latter, blasphemy follows as naturally as night follows day. Swearing acts as a circuit breaker...for a little while! Inside *Opa* Licht, the anger brewing finally erupted like Vesuvius. A big man, he lifted the entire bike and hurled it through his sizeable shop window, almost killing an old lady passing by.

'Oh my loving God, you almost killed me, you stupid man!' she howled. 'One second later and a *very* expensive funeral for *you*, Mr Licht!'

Ignoring her, he stalked off in a huff, incapable of apologizing.

Just before the Great War, when already married, with two sons, *Opa* Licht took on the dignified profession of undertaker. Amsterdam is made up of canals centrifugally moving away from the Dam Square, the beautiful homes of the wealthy lining the waterways. Because of the narrowness of the streets abutting the canals and the height of the gabled houses, the best way to transfer furniture and the like was by using a pulley system attached to a steel hook jutting out from the top of the facade, a method which goes back centuries. Dutch architects of the seventeenth century and onwards designed the top gables to lean forward slightly, in order to facilitate the hauling up of objects and so minimize damage to the buildings.

Opa, then a young man, was given the job of collecting a male corpse from the Leidsegracht. He and his companion went about their business and lowered the rough, temporary wooden coffin in the manner described, the sealed unfortunate being shaken around like a rag doll. The coffin was eventually manoeuvred onto a handcart and off they went, back to the mortuary where the corpse would be prettied up for the family.

It had been snowing and bitterly cold. On most corners of the canal hub could be found a pub, some reaching back to the seventeenth century.

'I've had enough, Dirk; I'm rattling in my harness. I need a drink.' By which *Opa* meant not only *jenever,* but also to thaw out and to play a round of billiards.

'I couldn't agree more. My fingers are about to drop off and *I* need a leak,' replied Dirk.

The coffin was unloaded and placed underneath the billiard table. To leave it outside was to invite pranksters; besides which it would of course look out of place. The game went on for some time, till interrupted by a muffled knocking: 'Cathump! Cathump!'

Taking little notice, the men continued playing until disturbed once again by the sound, which came from beneath the table. 'Cathump! Cathump!' They stuck their heads down to look, then pulled out the coffin. When they removed the wooden lid, a very flustered corpse emerged, cursing and understandably irate.

'Damn it, I'm not dead yet, you morons! What are you up to? Who told you I was dead? Can't you see I'm still alive?'

This was patently obvious. Whether the bumpy descent had shot some oxygen into the deceased, or whether he had been fatally misdiagnosed – which, it seems, was not entirely uncommon in those days – was never established. Perhaps in today's age of instant litigation, he could have made a tidy sum and used it to pay for a better diagnosis...as well as a more sumptuous funeral at a later date!

Opa Goudsblom's funeral was a far more dignified affair. He also died of cancer, though at home on the farm. Aunty Anne led us to the bed where he lay. The room was dark except for four large candles tied to the bedposts. The candles flickered gently and threw up huge shadows on the smoky wallpaper, adding to the solemnity of the occasion. The *chiaroscuro* created by the closed curtains and the candles reminded me of a passage to hell. My heart beat faster as I approached. *Opa* was the first dead person I had ever seen.

He seemed asleep and looked peaceful enough, with his drooping moustache carefully brushed, his familiar deep-set eyes now closed. He was clutching a rosary, his hands lying on the white sheet neatly folded back over the blanket covering him. Dressed in his best suit and tie, with a Windsor knot neatly manoeuvred around his neck... I wondered who had tied it?

We bowed our heads, and when we knelt down next to him, Lex inexplicably touched his cold hand. I was too afraid and moved back a little, wondering what *Opa* was thinking, yet at the same time realizing full well that dead people can't think. He looked so wooden and introspective, as if we weren't there. And indeed, to him, we weren't.

Opa Goudsblom had been conscientious and righteous. He, like so many of his generation, tackled a great variety of jobs. Before the Great War a person didn't choose a job, the job chose the person. He had been stationmaster, milk hawker, coach driver, vendor – in the busy, seasonal seed market – and cheese carrier. He finally finished up doing what he'd always wanted to do: farming, albeit on a small scale, with just ten cows in summer and fewer in winter. This was supplemented by some market gardening.

Tall and round-shouldered, he could be seen hoeing the large vegetable garden at the back of the farm, or milking a cow in the shed, always in his blue smock, sitting awkwardly on a tiny, three-legged stool.

We were warned off the farm's manure pit because of its rickety cover.

'You are not allowed anywhere near the pit. If you fall in, you'll be dragged under like quicksand,' Aunty Anne told us.

Instead, we built forts and castles with the wooden crates lying around the place. Our grandparents were easygoing, even indulgent.

After finishing work for the day, *Opa* often sat in his corner chair in the living room smoking a meerschaum, pontificating about the state of the world. 'Yes, Herman, if people only minded their own business all would be well with the world.'

When Father suggested that resisting the invasion of Holland by Hitler's troops was, for example, justifiable, *Opa* frowned in disapproval, so Father changed the subject.

Stubborn and opinionated, *Opa* was also tight-fisted, but scrupulously honest. It was *Oma* who had hollow hands, giving us ten cents to buy a croquette or a ticket to the movies. Whenever we visited *The Dyke,* she insisted on giving us cakes or sweets.

A young farmer, and keen athlete, who lived a few hundred metres further up the road from *The Dyke*, could often be seen jogging conscientiously up and down the narrow road. His diligence paid off when he won a few local events. *Opa* would study him closely, noticing the lad wore the latest white gym runners.

'If I had runners as good as his,' he said, 'I could also be a champion.' The logic was ridiculous and raised a good laugh. But he meant it. Once he made up his mind about something he was difficult to budge.

I began school not long before *Opa* Goudsblom died and to begin with, I hated it. My first day at kindergarten was a disaster. A boy dubbed the Biter attacked me mercilessly in the playground. He was a year older than me and hailed from the Red Village, so named because it was considered communist, some having been lucky enough to survive Hitler's 'holiday camps'. Most of these red-raggers were unemployed. They and other Dutch prisoners-of-war were still returning in dribs and drabs from the Soviet Union, right up until the mid-fifties.

The Red Village was feared because of its tough folk. At times, gangs invaded the Newportslane for a showdown, usually to do with either the cigarette trade; macho assertiveness, which John was keen to exhibit;

My first day at kindergarten was a disaster. Alkmaar, 1947. Henri: top row, middle.

girls, or simply to settle old scores. Testosterone-fuelled confrontation; so often the case!

However, to return to my first day at school, the Biter couldn't or wouldn't talk. Instead, he resorted to biting all and sundry. In the absence of authority, he attacked anyone who annoyed him. My swagger and overactive gob soon attracted his attention.

His monstrous mouth, filled with jagged teeth, contrasted with his pleasant, dark complexion and large, sad brown eyes. As I walked through the front gate, prattling away, he took an instant dislike to me and without a qualm ran towards me, sinking his considerable ivories into my left calf. I was completely taken by surprise. I didn't know what to do. My squeals only urged him on, and the playground came to a standstill, everyone staring at us.

'Owww! Owww! Owww! Piss off! Leave me alone, ya turd! You're hurting me,' I screamed.

The Biter didn't let go, instead gnawing deeper into my flesh. I was going to lose a leg. I punched him in the face, but my fists bounced off like ping-pong balls. He was obviously concrete from the neck up.

'Let go! Let go, or I'll kill you!' A pathetic threat falling on deaf ears. I was oscillating between despair and anger: it was the Biter who was doing the killing.

His teeth felt like clamps with serrated edges. He wouldn't let go, the mute brute. Blood began to trickle down his teeth. My blood! Pain went up a notch. Dracula would have been impressed. While the Biter clung to me like a leech, I was beginning to feel dizzy and the agony continued unabated. Then, out of nowhere, Lex pushed through the crowd of young onlookers and without wasting time proceeded to boot him in the head. Our heavy Bata shoes, meant to last forever, made useful weapons in a fight.

The Biter and Lex were in fact old adversaries. Lex wasn't afraid of anyone and the Biter knew it. Without hesitating, Lex gave him another kick, this time under the rear, all the while belting him around the ears with clenched fists. At last the Biter extricated his teeth, slinking off with a hideous grin.

That was my introduction to kindergarten, supposedly an idyllic garden of peace and harmony for children to enjoy... From my initial experience, kindergarten seemed more like a tiergarten full of wild animals, where the gnashing of teeth acquired a whole new meaning: the scars took weeks to heal.

At least my kindergarten teacher, a tall bony woman with glasses and a kind face, never failed to be good-humoured.

'Now, little ones, look at me and when I clap my hands I want you to stop at once and listen to what I have to say.' She was wonderfully patient and smiled continually, even when we made mistakes or weren't listening. She taught us to tie our shoelaces, paper weaving – which I considered pointless – counting and singing; the last I did enjoy. She sang sweet ditties of the 'Oh sweet red robin up so high, why not join us and please don't cry,' kind. Innocence and eagerness made us putty in her hands.

She held us by the hand as we skipped along in the cramped concrete playground. We always had to be busy doing something, just for the sake of it, whereas all I wanted to do was sit in class and pursue my fantasies, or go to sleep.

There was a large carpeted room in our kindergarten, backing onto a canal. Totally empty, it was used as a gym. Here we played games such as rolling around on the floor and doing exercises. I would sometimes rest and look out onto the water as small barges passed by. The oily darkness of the canal gave me the shivers. I loved this short stretch of water, though, because it never stayed the same. Its banks, lined with thick timber sleepers, disappeared with the tides. Why weren't the houses flooded, I wondered? When it rained, thousands of pockmarked circles spread across the water, while ducks sailed back and forth, impervious to the columns of water thrown at them from the heavens. In winter, older boys and girls wearing bright clothes could be seen skating past.

On the other side of the canal, a line of small houses followed its contours. Rows of red and pink begonias festooned the windowsills, mostly painted green or black. Some of the houses had large bay windows which overhung the waterway and in one of them I could sometimes see a man reading a newspaper, pipe smoke hovering above the pages. Next door, a lean young man played the piano, his head following the tender phrasing. A large woman in a floral dress entered the living room, carrying two cups. For her husband, son, or daughter perhaps? Maybe a neighbour or a friend? Not important, really... All were absorbed in their daily routine, as was I; I could have sat there for hours, but the pedagogues wouldn't let me. They were employed to keep me occupied with all sorts of tedious challenges.

In the corner of a thin strip of concrete playground to the left of the kindergarten, which was named after Saint Teresa of Avila, I often sat on a bench just looking at everyone, even in winter. A girl called Mieke always played by herself. Her clothes were ragged and much too big for her. Obviously hand-me-downs from one of her sisters. She had a runny nose, which sometimes became an unsightly mess, the yellow mucus forming a moustache. The other pupils either avoided or teased her.

'Hey, snotty nose, when are you going to clean yourself?' yelled a lanky boy.

'Just look at her! She must have a terrible family to let her come to school looking like that.' Three girls were in a huddle, pointing at Mieke.

'Mieke, Mieke, what a dirty girl! Do you live in a dustbin?' asked some dimwit.

Cruelty begins at a young age and is often rewarded by the encouragement of others. It took me a long time to gain her confidence, but one day she broke her silence. 'Mother is sick,' she volunteered.

'What's wrong with her?' I asked.

'She coughs blood all the time.' Mieke sounded surprised and helpless.

'Does your father look after her?'

'I don't have a father. My oldest sister looks after us,' she stated matter-of-factly.

I fell silent for a moment as a wave of sympathy overcame me, then said, *'I'll* be your friend.' Trying to be helpful, I added, 'I'll give you a handkerchief too, because no one likes a girl with a snotty nose.'

I shouldn't have said that. She stepped back as if hurt, saying, 'I don't want your handkerchief...but you can play with me.'

We became good friends after that, though she always stayed on the periphery, seemingly indifferent to the jibes. I felt sorry for her. Towards the end of spring, she left her usual corner and began to join in the games. Even so, she remained aloof.

Across the road from Saint Teresa's was Saint Aloysius Primary, which we all eventually attended and which we had looked forward to with anticipation. In my first year, I had the displeasure of having Brother Fabritius as a teacher.

Brother Fabritius was 'neurotic', even though I didn't at the time know or understand the term. His pasty skin made him appear sickly and fragile, yet he exuded energy and alertness. Of slight build, he had a sharp, studious face and wore thin-framed glasses that gave him a devout look. He never smiled and his slightly hooked nose flared up at the least disturbance in class. We were afraid of him. His vigilance got on our nerves. We hated him.

Sigmund, and his senior and contemporary, Baron von Krafft-Ebing (1840–1902), an Austro-German psychiatrist and the author of *Sexual Psychopathy: A Clinical-Forensic Study*, loved to talk of sadism as sexual perversion. They maintained that men were prone to sadism while women enjoyed masochism. Interesting, but sexist rubbish, I daresay. However, Fabritius was definitely sadistic...or at least, certainly not normal, that's for sure. As a seven-year-old I was of course too immature to understand the effects of sexual repression, but from an adult perspective, I suspect he suffered from acute sexual anxiety... Whatever the explanation, Brother Fabritius certainly enjoyed humiliating his students.

By the Scruff of the Neck

Kees Mulder, the greengrocer's son, was big and somewhat stupid, and Brother Fabritius always picked on him. He should have known by now that you can lead a horse to water, as they say, but... Big Kees couldn't even be led. He couldn't remember the distance to Amsterdam, couldn't spell 'rhythm', didn't even know his seven-times table. Big Kees didn't know *anything* except how to eat.

A thick tapered rod about a metre and a half in length was the standard tool for inflicting punishment. The rod was normally used as a map pointer. Not to know one's capital cities or times tables meant shuffling to the front of the classroom, bending over and copping a teeth-rattling whack. Brother Fabritius must have used the rod for his daily exercise because boys were regularly hauled to the front. In hindsight, he spent more time walloping pupils than teaching them, me included. Nowadays, whenever I see a large map anywhere, I subconsciously insert a pointer...

One late Friday afternoon, Big Kees trudged to the front for his unjust desserts...yet again. 'Kees Mulder, when will you learn that milk comes from cows and not from factories!' Fabritius was just going through the motions.

'Sorry, Brother, but I thought...'

'I am becoming sick and tired of this, you big oaf. Do you know anything? Come on! Bend over!'

We didn't even look up, so used to this tedious ritual were we. But then the unexpected happened.

'No! *No!* I am no longer bending over!' Big Kees had had enough.

Heads shot up, eyes alert. What was this? Insubordination? Appetite truly whetted, Reet Gerrits poked me in the shoulder; I was still nutting out a fraction and hence a bit slow in sensing the changed atmosphere.

'No!' insisted Big Kees. 'Why, goddamit, do I always have to please *you*? Why don't you pick on someone else for a change?' Which Brother Fabritius frequently did, as a matter of fact; it was just that Big Kees was his favourite patsy. Nevertheless, the *sans-culottes*, in the shape of Big Kees, were manning the barricades. Revolution in the classroom! Big Kees then turned around, ignored Fabritius, and, with a grimace, sat down.

This was theatre of the highest quality. What would Fabritius do next? The nostrils began to arch, the blue eyes lit up. His head, with its thinning hair, began to shake with rage. We all sat in silence, waiting for something to happen. Brother Fabritius almost ran to Big Kees, then began trouncing him – on the head, the shoulders, and on the arms. This was unprecedented.

Fabritius didn't let up. 'Who do you think you are? How dare you question me! I have never met such an insolent fellow as you. I won't put up with it, do you hear! *Apologize!* Apologize at once!'

We all looked on, stunned. By the end of the tirade, Big Kees began to bawl, slowly at first, then more loudly. However, Brother Fabritius' vicious attack came to an abrupt end when the bell intervened, heralding the end of both the school day and the week. Big Kees wailed a little longer then suddenly stood up and ran out of the classroom. Brother Fabritius let him go; what else could he do? We collected our belongings and strode home, nattering about Big Kees' revolt and little else.

Monday morning, while Brother Fabritius sat snugly behind his desk and everyone was working quietly on a set of sums, the door opened without a sound, not even preceded by the usual polite knock which alerted the class that someone was outside. We all looked up, bewildered at the break in routine, and saw Big Kees entering the classroom, followed by his older brother, Gerard. Gerard was studying at the local technical school to become a plumber.

Big Kees was about Fabritius' height and still growing, and if he acquired his name because of his size, Gerard Mulder was even more of a fearsome sight. The Dutch are amongst the tallest people on the globe and Gerard's genes did him proud. This veritable giant casually approached Brother Fabritius.

Meanwhile, Brother Fabritius had been deep in concentration, underlining passages from his missal. We all put down our pens and waited as his ratty head slowly lifted. Then, as he became aware of the huge figure before him, he said something remarkably foolish. He thought his status as Brother and teacher was enough to deter anyone. Given the times, this was a reasonably safe assumption, but on this occasion, he was mistaken.

'*Excuse me*, who are *you* and what gives you the right to come into *my* classroom without knocking? Would you kindly leave at once, before I report you to Brother Superior for trespassing.'

Like watching an international soccer match, the whole class was glued to the ball, in the shape of Gerard, Big Kees having taken a back seat, so to speak.

'And what gives *you* the right to smash *my* little brother, eh? Damn you! Why don't you pick on someone your own age instead of him?'

Little? Hardly! Still, size is relative.

As Fabritius began to look uncomfortable, we thoroughly enjoyed the change in the power relationship. It was wonderful to see Fabritius in a pickle of his own making, though he manfully kept up a front: 'I don't wish to discuss this with you. If you have any complaints, I suggest you speak to Brother Dominicus.[59] So, would you please go?'

It didn't sound very convincing; more like a plea.

---

[59] Not his real name.

By the Scruff of the Neck

Gerard, following a family trait, was a lad of few words. He glanced around the room, studying the pictures on the back wall, then suddenly picked up Brother Fabritius by the throat and lifted him high up against the blackboard. Fabritius looked absurd dangling there like a puppet, his composure utterly shattered.

'I'll teach you to pick on my little brother!'

Fear etched itself on Fabritius' scrawny face; a frightened little man emerged, who began to splutter, 'P...put...put me down at once! I order you to put me down. Your brother disobeyed me. Put...put me down!' Fabritius then began to screech: 'Stop it! Stop it!'

With one arm, thick as a leg of ham, Gerard lifted the skinny rodent away from the wall and, with all his might, hurled him against the blackboard. The force of the thrust was so powerful the blackboard split down the middle. The whole school must have heard it.

As a thoroughly shaken Brother Fabritius collected himself, Gerard hit him in the stomach, then, for good measure, rammed his head through the cracked blackboard. Brother Fabritius' rear end waggled as he tried to extricate himself. Eventually he slid to the floor and fell in a heap, exhausted, blood trickling down the side of his mouth.

Although Charlie Chaplin was one of our heroes, Gerard quickly replaced him. What a tremendous sight! He slapped his hands together in triumph, pulled his jumper down over his pants and, taking his younger brother by the hand, jauntily left the classroom.

Brother Fabritius' authority was never the same again. We also noticed the number of birchings declined markedly. I found it puzzling, though, that this orgy of delectable violence never drew a response from the other Brothers in the school.

I can't recall my teacher in grade two very well, but in grade three I had Mr de Rieu[60] as teacher. He was short and always wore a light-brown suit. His triangular-shaped head tilted to one side as he listened to us. While distant, he was gentle, and we loved it best when he read stories to us about pirates, or the adventures of the great Dutch admirals. But reading to the class was a luxury. Most of our time was given over to arithmetic or the pedantry of Dutch grammar.

In spring, Mr de Rieu opened the windows to let in the fragrance from the Brothers' garden. The Brothers lived behind a wall separating the school from the priory. A few non-teaching Brothers were gardeners, or cooks, such as my Uncle Rinus; or Brother Eymard, as he was known. The garden boasted beds of roses, violets, scarlet pimpernels, tulips, and

---

[60] Not his real name.

Father's most beloved flower, dahlias. Whenever we were sent on an errand to the priory, which was rare, we would linger to admire the patchwork of blooms. Unfortunately, I was stung by a bee one afternoon and carried on as if I was about to cark it. I rubbed the spot, with little improvement, but Mr de Rieu wasn't too concerned.

'Mr de Rieu! Mr de Rieu, I've just been stung! How long will the pain last, Mr de Rieu? Do I need to go to hospital? It hurts... It's killing me, Mr de Rieu!'

'You're fine. Just fine. Keep it under control. It isn't the end of the world. We've all been stung by a bee before. Don't fret so much. Yes, yes, I know it hurts, but we'll treat it. No need to carry on.'

He inspected the pierced skin and took me to Brother Superior, leaving the class in the charge of a trusty lieutenant – who presided over a rabble one moment and a chorus of angels the next: on Mr De Rieu's return.

Brother Superior, Dominicus, took great care of me. 'Fancy meeting another member of the Licht family,' he said, smiling, and folding his hands. 'I only spoke to your brother Bill a few days ago. Apparently he and Brother Gregory[61] didn't see eye to eye about some homework, but we sorted it out, as I'm sure we'll fix your little mishap. What's your name, boy?'

'H..Henri Licht,' I stammered.

'I was only after your Christian name, my lad. I read somewhere that boys stung by bees grow up to be happy and famous, so consider yourself fortunate.' He hummed to himself and stood up.

The thought of future success lightened my misery and the pain eased as he applied tartar oil and gabbled away to put me at ease. Bee stings were common and Brother Dominicus had a handy supply of medicines in a small wooden cupboard next to his stuffed wildlife collection. He was a big, happy man, always singing. What a contrast to that martinet Fabritius!

By now, however, school was getting on my nerves, so I decided to play truant. The world outside was far more interesting. In Holland, the midday break was two hours and sometimes I would lag behind my older brothers in the Wood, even when they were running late for their afternoon class and despite knowing lateness wasn't tolerated. Eventually I decided to take afternoons off completely. The Wood was cool even in summer, and mottled with beautiful bursts of green and yellow. I could see pigeons and thrushes fussing about in the dense foliage and couldn't resist hiding in the bushes. I sat down, avoiding the stinging nettles, and inhaled the scents, watching the sunlight play on the green leaves swaying in the breeze. Sometimes I caught young lovers kissing and felt a

---

[61] Not his real name.

tingle in my groin as they groped and laughed, their dalliances a great source of amusement. The dappled greenery provided cover as I fondled my penis, not quite sure what my inchoate sexual feelings meant. I only knew that I enjoyed them, and a kind of pleasurable narcissism took hold of me.

Later, after loitering near the monkey's cage, I headed for the Kennemer Highway. Here I sat by the gutter, sometimes lucky enough to stumble across carbide, or calcium carbide, to be precise. Maybe the white lumps were remnants from a few days earlier, when pranksters, out to impress girlfriends, lit it to enjoy the resulting explosion? Fire and explosions were all grist to a boy's mill, and with matches being easily found, turmoil was guaranteed.

I loved the smell of carbide and took pieces home to show Lex, who was impressed and wanted to set fire to them straight away. He was the better scavenger though, and sometimes arrived home not only with chunks of carbide, but other exotic finds, like a fancy clog to be made into a boat; car bits; dog's teeth; a rabbit's foot, which he dangled around his neck; or nails to be used in pipes or bullet shells to detonate phosphorus – a very popular pastime.

My absences from school were duly recorded, then sent home when a pattern emerged. As a result, I played cat-and-mouse with my parents, claiming to have been too frightened to go to school because of boys bullying me. Since Mother instantly became angry and upset at the idea of her darling being picked on, I was given a reprieve, but Father remained suspicious. Nevertheless, I quickly discovered that at roll call a student's absence would rarely be queried if a note was produced, and these were easily forged. I became cunning and would attend school for a while, then take a day off. I always made sure the weather was pleasant; no good absconding when it was pouring with rain! One such day, I hitched a ride on a cart carrying vegetables, the driver never asking why I wasn't at school. I felt very important sitting beside him while the draught horse clomped away, its rump glistening with sweat, the strong smell of vegetables inviting me to be part of Mother Earth.

From this great height, the leisurely pace allowed me to revel in and absorb the sights and atmosphere of the streets, the traffic, the shoppers walking along the footpaths. The driver and I talked about football and the price of potatoes, too. He asked me what I wanted to be when I grew up: 'Okay, my young friend, what job would you like to do when you leave school?'

'Oh, I'd like to be a fighter pilot or a captain of an ocean liner.'

'Hm! You have to be smart for that. It would require many years of study, you realize... What does your father do? Oh, yes! 'Uncle John' Goudsblom is your uncle,' he stated, tautologically and with knowing surprise. He seemed an amiable fellow and I suspected he too played truant while at school: honour amongst truants, past and present, I imagine.

If my truanting day was Friday, I explored the old Cheese Market. Barges unloaded their round, yellow cheeses onto trays carried by sturdy men. The covered stalls on the market boundaries did a brisk trade with the tourists, mainly Americans and Germans. Commerce is very forgiving of wartime foes... Standing in front of the ancient weighing tower, I waited for the chimes on the hour, followed by the charge of miniature horsemen beneath the belfry: I loved the bright colours as they zipped around. I knew that the tower was converted to its current use in 1582, serving as a guesthouse for weary travellers during the previous two centuries. Wouldn't it be fantastic to climb this ancient building, mount the horses and overlook so much of North Holland!

On cold days, I sometimes cadged fairy floss or an apple dumpling from a generous stall keeper. 'Hey, boss, can you spare a dumpling? I have no money and I'm starving. I'll pay you next week.'

The stall keeper looked me over and said, 'Oh yes! Pull the other one. Anyway, here... I've got one for you. But don't bullshit me next time.'

I made sure to avoid him in future.

In winter, the smell of dumplings baked in boiling oil and the strong reek of fish surpassed all the other smells, as they wound their way around alleys and busy stalls, starting from the fish banks. These odours are forever chiselled into my memory – for some, memory's larder remains remarkably well stocked.

At other times, whenever I earned or found some silver coins, I would be off to the movies. To go to the movies was the height of luxury. In our household, Laurel and Hardy reigned supreme. They were more popular than Chaplin or Keaton and were always referred to as 'Fat' and 'Skinny'. Neighbourhood buffs would put on screenings in a garage, charging half the price of theatres...and it was closer to home.

Laurel and Hardy were stereotypes, but as vaudevillians, could milk an audience with comical expressions perfected during the days of the silent movie. Like Chaplin, they also represented the working classes, inverting its structure. They were the antiheroes, deflating the rich and powerful, who were invariably portrayed as snobs or charlatans.

Buster Keaton's deadpan expression and triumphs against ludicrous odds wore a bit thin after a while, but Laurel and Hardy somehow remained credible, despite the formulaic repetitions and slapstick. Laurel, the dreamy innocent, rolled through life unaware of impending doom, or made inconsequential observations that either infuriated Hardy or baffled him as he stared into the camera with his piggy eyes and quivering double chin. Elegant buffoonery... The flabby face, the scratching of the skull, the deliberate enunciation and the improbable plot all meshed for a good afternoon's entertainment. I used to experiment with my cap just as Hardy did with his bowler hat.

My truanting, unfortunately, came to an abrupt end one day when I was caught at the scene of an accident. Opposite the Wood, on the Kennemer Highway, a cyclist had collided with a car and a young boy was lying in a pool of blood. Curious onlookers emerged like cockroaches, gaping at the victim, motivated by a mixture of sympathy and the allure of street theatre.

The crowd was keen to find out whether he was still alive. 'Poor boy, what happened? Didn't he look?' a man asked.

'I reckon it was the car's fault,' declared a stout woman.

'No! No! No! The boy was talking to his friend and wasn't watching,' contradicted another.

'Yes, but bicycles have right of way and the car should've stopped,' offered a more knowledgeable chap. Cyclists were frequently knocked over by cars.

I was one of the cockroaches who couldn't resist the spectacle... but I found myself in unexpected company.

'Herrie, why aren't you in school?'

A familiar voice struck me like a thunderbolt. Aunty Anne was standing on the footpath next to her bicycle. The shock was almost greater than seeing the broken body on the road, now covered by a blanket. Lex, notwithstanding the tragedy, would have appreciated all this: the mangled body, and especially me getting caught.

'Er! We were let out of school early,' I improvised.

'But it's only three o'clock. School doesn't finish till four,' she asserted incredulously.

'Must be something special happening for the Brothers,' I said, latching onto the first thing that entered my head.

But Aunty Anne was no fool and threatened to take me back to school. My usual evasiveness wasn't working and I couldn't very well plead illness this time, so I played my last desperate card.

'I'm frightened of school because...because of certain boys at playtime.' The bullying excuse had worked so far.

'In that case, your parents will have to speak to Brother Superior.'

Aunty Anne knew I was fibbing and ordered me onto the back seat of her bicycle. She wasn't very keen on me, as I well knew, considering me spoilt.

A stickler for rules, she entered our front door triumphantly and quickly informed Mother of my misdeeds. 'Ali, guess who's been wagging school!'

I went red in the face and mentally prepared myself for a tongue-lashing.

'I don't believe it! So, you've been lying to us. God will punish you for this. I don't know what to make of you! What will become of you when you grow up?' Mother verbally threw everything at me, but at least didn't slap me.

I escaped into a surreal world and pretended I was in a coma. I heard Mother's words but none of them registered. It was Father who posed the greater threat. His rebuke could be far more painful. He was more creative with his punishments and regarded truanting as indicative of weak character, something to be snuffed out, pronto.

I was confined to my room outside school hours for seven days. Students in my time still went to school on Wednesday and Saturday mornings, so the otherwise free afternoons of those two days became part of my incarceration. Father disliked violence, but punishment must be given...

At first I thought the confinement wouldn't be too bad, but boredom and the limited space soon began to nag at me. So little to keep me occupied! What misery! All I could do was ponder and read a bit. However, incarceration hones the imagination. I had to organize my time in such a way as not to go mad or become 'combustible' again, as in my first few years on earth; I had quickly learnt that temper tantrums didn't work: I was simply ignored or mocked.

What does an eight-year-old do in his bedroom, shared at night, I should add, with Lex and Bill? All bundled up in one double bed, sinking like a 'V' in the middle. I being the smallest was restricted in more ways than one – plonked right in between my older brothers.

I stood on a chair, trying to peer over the edge of the small square window, flush with the angled roof. It was my only view of the outside. Oscar Wilde talked about his "little tent of blue" and while I had never heard of him at the time, I now know what he meant. To be cooped up was a far more sinister punishment than a cuff around the ears.

A flotilla of clouds sailed past, the occasional bird in search of food dived to the ground, and here I was gazing at the Sportpark, now empty and forlorn. The backyard wasn't worth dwelling on. Not much to see at all. This dull view for a whole after-school week! Despondent, I began to think of a way out. Maybe I could run away? Maybe I could become a cabin boy like de Ruyter, who grew up to be the most famous seventeenth-century Dutch admiral. Hiding on a ship or an aeroplane would be better than this! Maybe I could burn the house down... But I hadn't any matches.

I looked at the row of books beneath the window and pulled out a copy of *Eagle Eye* by J. Nowee, a popular Dutch 'Wild West' writer. I had already read it, so moved on to his *The Smugglers Of The Rio Malo*, a gripping yarn about rustlers, featuring my Indian hero, White Feather, but it had also been accounted for, in less than two days.

By the Scruff of the Neck

Nowee, however, wasn't in the same league as Karl May, my favourite Western writer.[62] Ironically, I shared this enthusiasm with Adolf Hitler, who met him in 1912 at a public lecture, before the Great War. It's ironic that Hitler modelled himself on Old Shatterhand, one of May's enduring heroes, because May was, in fact, a pacifist. But then, Herr Hitler was rather selective and superficial in his reading.

I lay on the sagging bed with my hands behind my head, ruminating, then looked at the dull yellow wallpaper and dwelt on the idyllic little painting of a country garden hanging opposite, with children playing and a dog jumping alongside them. Who were these children? I wanted to play with them.

I imagined myself an ant crawling up the wall and having circumnavigated the picture frame, I found an entrance to that lush garden belonging to some wealthy English family.

No doubt due to Churchill's role in Holland's liberation, the Dutch were for a time besotted with anything English. In 1948, Uncle John went on a soccer exchange to Bath, now a sister city of Alkmaar, and returned victorious. He gave us dinky toys that drew the envy of the neighbourhood: a London taxi and a Morris Oxford, as I recall.

This was the only time Uncle John travelled overseas. Boats held no interest for him and he was absolutely petrified of flying. He even weakened at the knees if he couldn't hear the reassuring sounds of the Weighing Tower; although, with trepidation, he did cross the border into Germany for soccer engagements. His German was good, but he understandably viewed the Krauts with suspicion, as well as tribal wariness.

However, *my* English friends were waiting for me. In my mind's eye I zigzagged, then crawled underneath the frame, and as I pushed upwards, my feelers hit a small brown door the size of a wide splinter. When I tapped it with one of my long legs at first nothing happened, but then, slowly and creakily, the door swung open, just a little. With my bulbous head I pushed it even further ajar. There in front of me I beheld a thick bough, inviting me to slide down its smooth, curving arm. It shook up and down, as if daring me to stand on its broad back. The bright green foliage, the blue sky and the mild weather indicated summer. I felt giddy looking over the sides of the bough, yet remained determined, so stepped forward, making sure not to lose my balance, my ant-legs gripping the bough's slippery bark. When I let go, my belly tingled with excitement as I hurtled downwards, twisting around corners like a bobsled pilot, the

---

[62] Karl May, 1842–1912, dominated the *zeitgeist* of pre-war and post-war youth in Germany and Holland. A German writer of travel and adventure, he wrote about the old West and the desert Arabs without any firsthand knowledge of them. He did visit these places, but late in life. His romanticized view of 'the noble savage' and the quest for racial tolerance influenced Albert Einstein and Albert Schweitzer.

leaves fanning my antennae, my huge eyes focused on the descent. What incredible speed! The bough eventually evened out and I came to rest on a carpet of thick grass. There, I found my new friends leaning over me, laughing, as if they expected me, like a distinguished guest. They gently picked me up and began talking to me.

'Oh, little ant, you're lost and lonesome. Come and share our lemonade. You're so different, in your little white coat.' They had never seen a 'white' ant before.

They found me a tiny straw, smaller than a pin, the thickness of a strand of hair. But my voice, well versed in ant-speak, was surprisingly loud, and I demanded the tastiest of food.

'I'm famished and would love something sweet, preferably cream cakes and large chocolate letters, but only the best and most delicious will do...otherwise, I shall crawl back up the branch, at once, and you'll never see me again.'

They laughed at my bravado and the pretty girl in the middle lifted me onto her bare arm, where I crawled up and up, till I reached her large, ruby lips. I kissed her and she kissed me in return, even though she knew I could bite her. She had fallen in love with me and I with her.

How ridiculous! An ant and a girl. How sublime, though, to be so appreciated and made the centre of attention. Meanwhile, the dog was going berserk, as dogs often do.

After all the lovely food was eaten, I grew languid and wanted to stay, to sleep in that magical garden forever. I was ever so sleepy and nodded off...zzz...zzz...half dreaming of cream cakes and half immersed in the soft, couched grass, dreaming of the English country garden with its trimmed lawns and happy children...

My slumber was rudely interrupted by Lex hollering something from the other side of the door. *Why won't he go away and leave me be?*

'Mother said you can come down now, ya duffer!' yelled Lex, thumping on the door.

I slowly emerged from my dream, resenting the intrusion, but the prospect of being released, on this my seventh day, quickly displaced my fantasies. Once outside, I slid down the banister. 'What's for tea? I'm starving!'

As usual, everyone ignored me. Lex had just returned from the Hareland, a grass-covered opening in the Wood, behind the Villa Park. He had been playing cowboys and indians and was telling Bill about a new gang trying to take over our turf.

Bill wasn't all that interested, boasting he had finally joined the athletics club and wasn't going to be the champion long distance runner of just Alkmaar, but of the whole world.

John was in a good mood and shook his hunched shoulders in self-satisfaction. He had acquired a rare *La Corona* cigar band from a family contact called Mr Jutjes, a tobacco trader, who had just returned from Cuba. 'Must be worth at least ten guilders... He's only interested in cigars, not their bands, and gave me a few common ones plus the corona. How lucky can you get?'

Father told us some distant uncles from America would visit soon, but only John was listening. Mother was too preoccupied with 'Jan in de zak', or 'John in the sack', sometimes referred to as 'Brother in the sack', a tasty, rich pudding made from flour, raisins, lemon peel and yeast, cooked in a damp cloth and doused in syrup. Cheap and ideal winter fodder for hardworking farmers and large families.

Seeing no one was paying me any attention, I yelled over the hubbub: 'None of you care! I'm going to run away and never come back!'

Bill ceased his athletic self-promotion and replied, 'I'll give you a sovereign if you stay away for ever. Then we can all have some peace.'

I began to sulk and planned a horrible death for all my brothers. When Lex grabbed the largest slice of 'Jan' I suddenly realized I had better get a move on or there wouldn't be any left.

At various times, class photos of students and their teachers were taken. Sibling photos were also taken. One such photo was of Lex and Bill with me on the left, all of us looking bright-eyed and bushy-tailed; although I thought I looked stupid – gap-toothed and with an artificial smile, sitting in front of a stuffed weasel.

Soon after this annual event I was concussed while playing soccer in the playground. Some idiot pushed me and I fell over and hit my head on the concrete pavers. I managed to crawl away on all fours, but with lasagne-like squares spinning before me. Each image had fuzzy rings around it and I wasn't sure where I was. I felt drowsy, but somehow remained awake. A kind of fog descended upon me; not unlike the shimmering air above bitumen in summer. It was almost like being in a parallel universe. Altogether, a very odd experience! I still have a vivid memory of the sensations, which resembled a migraine, with a wavy curtain overhanging one's eyelids.

Later, when I thought about it all, I wondered whether death would be like this, a transition from reality to 'teichopsia',[63] to darkness? But darkness is still a visual sensation... Maybe! At the time, I knew I was alive because of the horrible feelings, but perhaps I was slipping into a death-like delirium?

Anyway, I fainted, and eventually woke up in bed. It was a strange kind of consciousness, where everything seemed shut out, yet incoherent

---

[63] A transient visual sensation of bright shimmering colours, similar to that preceding a migraine.

Looking bright-eyed and bushy-tailed. St Aloysius, Alkmaar, 1951. Henri, Bill and Lex.

By the Scruff of the Neck

images kept squirming about in my head: Mieke's snot, deflated soccer balls, Father Pronk arm-wrestling the Devil, and Mother screaming at me from the Weighing Tower – the brain is a mystifying organ! Who knows, conceivably God and the brain are the same. I would tell my friend Johnny Red all about it, as soon as I got better.

Inseparable, Johnny Red and I would scooter everywhere together. He went to another school and we usually met up afterwards, in front of Woerdeman's, the grocer. Johnny had a squarish head and a large forehead with a curl falling over it. His thick lips and ash-grey eyes gave him a melancholic look. Thoughtful and generous, he was good at sums and knew the height of all the local churches. Where he obtained this information, I hadn't the faintest.

Once, on the way to Heiloo, we passed a rickety shed on top of which stood a boy hurling abuse at us. He was our age.

'Look at the idiots, can't even scooter properly. Scrotum heads! Cock-suckers!' He was enjoying himself from the safety of his position. We stopped and returned the verbal fire.

'What a hero from up there! Why don't you come down, you coward, and repeat what you just said to our faces?'

The lad responded by throwing a brick at Johnny's head, almost cracking his skull. Blood oozed all over Johnny's clothes and at first I didn't know what to do, then put my handkerchief over the wound to soak up the blood and stop the bleeding. While the boy fled, I told Johnny to stay still and wait for the blood to dry. He looked very pale, just sitting there, not speaking; not even so much as a moan – just cursing under his breath. I didn't know what the term meant then, but he was the first stoic I ever knew.

After a while, he stopped bleeding and we returned home. Nothing was done about it though: apparently cutting up a soccer ball was far more serious than inflicting a deep cut. Luckily, the wound healed up nicely and in the meantime was admired by all the lads. Mrs Red cut the hair from around the gash, which was about four centimetres long, with a dark-red crust. While it healed, Johnny had the look of a saint about him.

On beautiful days, we explored the Heilooer Wood together, which was wilder and much bigger than my Alkmaar Wood. It straddled the railway line and we spent hours train spotting. We edged up close to the railway tracks and lay on the quartzite rocks used for ballast, watching as the heavy trains, both passenger and goods, thundered past, their whistles shrieking angrily. We paid particular attention to the locomotives, ignoring the carriages.

Johnny Red and I were inseparable. Newpoortslane, Alkmaar, 195-. Lex, in black jacket, Johnny to right, then Henri.

'Clickety-clack, clickety-clack, barroom, barroom,' then the shrill 'iiiihhhhiiii!' of the steam whistle. I hadn't heard of the Doppler effect, but in my mind the agonizing wail of the train conjured up the cries of the slaughtered innocents in the Bible, the association strangely brought on by my spiritual yearning for moral perfection and assiduous reading of the catechism. Sometimes the wailing augured danger, or profound sorrow, the pitch varying with the speed and weather. The shrieks burrowed into my very marrow and lifted me to a fresh state of consciousness, as if some new event was about to happen, unleashing death and destruction. Much later, I associated the grunts of slow-moving trains with the Nazi transports carrying worn-out Jews, who were beyond complaint, like dulled cattle, and destined for the death camps, somewhere in the east.

Boys occasionally placed stones on the tracks, soon crushed or flicked sideways. They had the potential to derail the trains, but the anticipated thrill of witnessing a crash made the tykes impervious to any other considerations.

In the heart of the Heilooer Wood, a mound called the Cathill became the rallying point for gangs, as well as a must-kiss venue for lovers, especially in summer. The Cathill had most likely been formed by the soil dug from in front of the stately home 'Nijenburg', though it may also have originated in medieval times. The mound, already slightly raised above sea level even then, was alleged to have been the place for executing witches. The huge hole in front of the stately home was converted into a landscaped pond.

In the early eighteenth century the estate originally belonged to the Van Egmond barons. Now, a huge oak tree stood on top of the mound. It was hundreds of years old. Its trunk and boughs had borne thousands: highwaymen, *plein air* artists, starving children and courting couples, all the way back to the eighteenth century. We climbed towards its canopy, hoping to emulate the birds roosting there and to see the rest of the world. The low, thick limbs were ideal for stepping on. In winter, too, we sometimes visited this 'old man', now clothed in patches of snow. The fierce winds at that time of year snapped off some of its dead branches, leaving scars on the ancient trunk.

Sometimes, Uncle John took us to the old forest halfway between Alkmaar and Heiloo and told us stories about its past. He would stop at the base of a tall beech and tap the bald spots where branches had been, beckoning us to come closer. He whispered to gain our attention: 'Now listen carefully. You see these circles?' We crowded around the tree, intrigued. 'These,' he told us in dark tones, 'are the secret doors to the underworld, used by gnomes at night. These little openings lead to a spiral staircase all the way down to below the tree roots. The gnomes relax there in their rough wooden chairs, smoking long pipes in front of a blazing fire, recounting tales to the animals of the wood, each one very comfortable and listening attentively to the adventures of their hosts.

'Because it's too cold to remain on the open, snow-covered ground, the animals bunker down here for the winter in the lap of luxury. I know you mightn't believe me, but that's what happens down there. *Opa* actually saw them once, a long time ago when he was hunting for rabbits. He told me that the gnomes ate and sang and discussed the life of the forest to their hearts' content, not unlike our own family after a good nosh-up. You have to tap the wood very gently and hope someone will come to the door.'

Lex, Johnny and I were transfixed, and young enough to entertain the possibility. After all, we couldn't see inside the trunks so the conceivability, not to say the desirability, of finding our friendly gnomes at home played on our minds. I didn't know about Lex or Johnny, but I couldn't wait to meet them. In fact I became so excited that I would run between the larger trees, wading through the snow, knocking ever so carefully on the smooth portals, begging for a response.

'Please, open up! I want to come down and talk to you. Open up little gnome and take me to meet your furry friends.' My mind running amok, my tiny knuckles rapped the heart-shaped entrances hooded by thick bark, and I waited impatiently for some small red-faced fellow to open the door. In my imagination, he, always a he, would politely invite me in for a cup of tea, all the while stroking his pet squirrel, and would tell me how, a long time ago, the lowest branches were used to dispatch thieves and murderers, and, more recently, during Hitler's war, when traitors and German soldiers met with a sticky end. Father had seen the stretched necks of some of them... I shuddered in my gumboots.

The gracious gnome gave me a bag full of chestnuts, acorns and beechnuts. 'And don't forget to give some to your family and friends and neighbours and your poor cousins and...' He prattled on as he walked me to the front door, puffing on his pipe. 'Don't tell anyone I live here, or they'll all come expecting nuts and the like, which would be very insulting to my squirrel guests staying for the winter. It's not easy hanging on to your nuts in winter!'

I promised, and told him I'd return next week to give him dark chocolate letters and cinnamon cookies for Saint Nicholas Day...

But first I had to make contact!

*

December and April were the busiest months for Confession: Saint Nicholas Day, the birth of our Saviour, his gruesome death, all sparked a rush of guilt and priests did a roaring trade in indulgences. Martin Luther must have turned in his grave!

Nevertheless, December was my favourite month. Johnny Red and I usually had a wow of a time throwing snowballs through bedroom windows left open by mistake or by some health fanatic. The temperature at this time of year was often at least minus ten Celsius.

'See that window on the second floor of Harteveld's, I bet you can't land a snowball in there.'

Johnny proved me wrong with a sizable snowball deftly squeezed through the opening. I followed suit but failed the first time, so had another go, this time more successfully. The Harteveld's bedroom floor would be awash by morning and they wouldn't have a clue how the water got there. Brilliant!

My birthday came two days before Saint Nicholas Day; and, would you believe, Lex was born on John's birthday, while nature conspired to eject me on Bill's? If this wasn't bad enough, having to share presents, the arrival of the Saint from Spain meant even fewer gifts. Very thin pickings indeed! Mother and Father had either been careless or very, very clever. My folks, nonetheless, always managed to deliver something to make me smile.

Uncle Piet, as neighbourhood commander-in-chief, believed in authenticity and brought in a professional Saint Nicholas, or *Sinterklaas*, for our celebrations. The saint's imminent arrival was enough to keep me awake the night before. Tall, mitred, carrying an elegant crosier, the saint projected a well-modulated voice and was accompanied by two Black Petes,[64] whose faces, in truth, were too dark to capture the genuine Moorish hue. However, the appearance of Saint Nicholas without his horse disappointed me.

Picture books usually portray the white-bearded Saint as galloping fast and furious across the rooftops, carrying heavy bags of gifts, ginger nuts and marzipan, with the Petes in hot pursuit. Children rarely questioned the credibility of this magical feat...but I did, up to a point. After his departure, I asked, 'Hey Pa, why the clog filled with hay and a glass of water for his horse, when there isn't a horse?'

'Well, son, sometimes he rides his horse, other times he just walks.'

Father was good at explanations, but I didn't quite believe him. It was all very disconcerting to a seven-year-old. Still, I suppose if Christians, and particularly Catholics, can perform miracles, a moonlight canter

---

[64] Black Petes were originally Moors who helped the Saint with his duties. Since Saint Nicholas came from Spain, or possibly Turkey, the dark hues of his helpers are associated with the Mediterranean region.

across gabled roofs was a mere bagatelle. He probably lost his horse somewhere, or lent it to one of his Petes. But I was troubled nevertheless.

Much more worrying were the large sacks carried by the Black Petes. Sometimes they threatened to open them for some naughty child to be shoved inside and sent back to Spain, obviously a ghastly place of torture, which, of course, it had been during the Inquisition. I was an obvious candidate and my palms felt tight and clammy. My behaviour report card was abysmal. Bosch's seven deadly sins in varying degrees all applied to me. My stomach churned as I imagined the list of heinous misdeeds being read aloud from a weighty scroll. Yet how did Saint Nicholas know about all these crimes? He must have forensic powers, and as God's earthly emissary, could obviously divine the souls of wicked boys. I tried to feel contrite, but also knew I couldn't control my impulses.

For about five years I was scared out of my wits by this supposed saint. Mercifully, he always found some saving grace in me, and provided I mended my ways, I would be given one more chance: 'Your wonderful parents' *Are they really?* 'and your fine teachers' *Open to question, that one!* 'might let you move up to the next grade if you change your annoying habits, such as plucking blankets, teasing your brother Lex,' *What about his pranks on me?* 'truanting, telling fibs, having evil thoughts,' *Not clear on what they're supposed to be.* 'disobeying your parents, and sometimes taking what isn't yours. However, the Lord is very forgiving, so here is a present for you, but first, you must promise...'

Ah, an ocean liner made of cardboard and filled with toffees, bonbons and sugar candy cigarettes. Hallelujah! I just made it! I wonder what Lex got...Bill...John?

Lex received a toy rifle and a book on Apaches: their customs and language, with special cut-outs. For the next fortnight he would only communicate in Apache or Navaho, which were, apparently, more or less the same. He practised his sign language, too, which none of us understood, and didn't want to.

'Me, Apache, me, fighting man. Akoo! I will hunt buffalo on prairie with new gun. Pshaw!' As it happens, 'Apache' means warrior.

He drove everyone nuts, except for Bill, who encouraged him and often stuck two fingers above Lex's head – feathers, or fool fingers? Father periodically told him to shut up, while John just spoke over the top of him...

The whole charade fell apart one Saint Nicholas Eve when I caught Jack-the-lad emerging from the coal shed with a black face, his voice unmistakable. The next day I wouldn't let up. 'I saw John last night pretending to be Black Pete. Why did he do that, Father?'

'Er! One of the Petes fell off the roof and Saint Nick needed urgent help, so John volunteered.'

'But John isn't black! And anyway, if he's a real Black Pete, why did he have to use boot polish?'

'Otherwise the rest of the neighbourhood kids mightn't believe...' Father looked distinctly uncomfortable and changed the subject.

It was the beginning of the end, not helped by Johnny Red's observation that Saint Nicholas existed hundreds of years ago, so how could he still be alive? I remained practical, though, figuring that to give up belief in the Saint could jeopardize my haul of presents... So, the fiction continued for purely selfish reasons. Lex's hunger for presents also saw Saint Nicholas as a means towards an end: *he* wasn't overly impressed with the Saint and his entourage, either.

Our hunting ground, as it were, was the Hareland, which, as the name suggests, was once home to a large population of hares. That was a long time ago, in the nineteenth century, when it belonged to the local baron. The rich kids couldn't be bothered with this wonderful slice of woodland, but of late, a group of interlopers from the Overdie, a district to the southeast of Alkmaar, was staking their claim. We virtually lived next door and weren't going to tolerate these newcomers on OUR land. It wasn't our land, of course, but its proximity to Newportslane bestowed a sense of entitlement.

A meeting of all the local lads was held in front of the pub next door to our place. Girls weren't included because they had other interests. Jacob de Kooy and Lex were the ringleaders and came up with a number of proposals.

'We'll dig a hole in the ground and cover it over with sturdy saplings and sheets of iron, then camouflage it with sods and branches strong enough to jump on.' Lex was effusive.

Jacob was always in the know. 'There's a pile of metal sheets near the railway on the other side of the Western Road... Bertus, you and a few others go get them, before they're knocked off by someone else.'

'In the meantime,' Lex continued gravely, 'we'll build a secret entrance and dig two deep pits, on either side of the hideout, and cover them over to conceal our whereabouts. They have to be very deep though. So, when the Overdiers fall into the traps, we'll have them at our mercy.'

Lex claimed this was how the Apaches sometimes caught their prey. It was undoubtedly a brilliant plan. Fortunately, the soil in North Holland is sandy and easy to dig. We all went home full of resolve.

About ten lads raided their parents' toolshed for spades of different sizes and arrived at the Hareland, ready for action. We only had Saturday afternoon and Sunday to finish the task, so enthusiastically tackled the laborious job of digging, then shovelling the soil into a big heap, which would need to be dispersed later on to avoid warning our adversaries. We then used clear bottles for windows, pushed through to reach the concealed hideout. A couple of discarded motorbike exhaust pipes were used as ventilators, strategically placed so as not to attract attention.

Sweating and swearing, we imagined we had entered the world of Karl May and viewed the Overdiers as hostile Indians. A backup plan was for five of us to hide in the bushes, in case the Overdiers managed to foil our first plan; we would attack them with sturdy sticks and belt the crap out of them.

Each day after school we rushed to the Hareland to see if the dugouts had been tampered with. The piece of tin covering the secret entrance was concealed by innocuous-looking clumps of grass. When we crawled inside, inhaling the smell of wet loam, it felt like bivouacking with Old Shatterhand and Winnetou, another of Karl May's wonderful characters. Occasionally we found a worm and put it in a jar to be used later for fishing. Ah...nature was the most beautiful theatre in the world!

'This must be how hares feel when they hide in their burrows.'

'If an atom bomb went off, we could hide down here.'

'You wouldn't have time to get away. It'd be all over in seconds. You'd be burnt to a crisp.'

'We're like dead people buried underground but still alive.'

'No, just moles in human form!'

The following Wednesday afternoon, a few of us waited in the pit while five chosen lads skulked around in the bushes waiting for the Overdiers. Wednesday afternoon, our free time, seemed an obvious opportunity for their invasion. We didn't have to wait long.

About twelve boys of varying sizes, wielding sticks and clubs and talking loudly, entered the clearing looking for trouble. We could hear them from below the ground.

'Those Newportslaners are a bunch of nancies. When we find them we'll tear 'em apart and take over their land!' Their confidence, judging by the loud laughter and boastful remarks, meant tough business. One tall lad, swinging a motorbike chain, lifted up a hand and said, 'It's all very quiet around here... I don't trust it.'

They had crossed the middle of the patch a few times when two smaller boys, who must have been twins from their size and looks, walked over our sturdy pit and, not watching where they were going, fell through the thin cover into the hole to our left, the branches used to cover it following after. The other boys rushed forward to peer over the edge, while their two comrades yelled for help. They hadn't hurt themselves too badly but were shaken by the fall. 'Bloody Newportslaners fooled us and knew we were coming. Ouch! I've hurt my ankle...and my ribs too. God damn it, get us out of here!'

By the Scruff of the Neck

Two of the bigger boys stretched out their hands – just as Jacob gave the signal to attack. The ambuscade was well timed; we raced towards the Overdiers shouting, 'Bastards! What do you think you're doing on our land? Scram!'

On seeing us, they bunched together and quickly moved back to whence they came, swinging their weapons as the enemy dashed towards them. We kept a safe distance, while Jacob let his slingshot do the talking, hitting one of them. The poor wretch cried out and rubbed his face in agony. They might have had superior numbers, but two members of their gang were still in the pit, and as they stood there, not sure what to do, the ground in front of them moved as one boy after another emerged from our dugout, giving the impression there might be even more of us hiding in the bowels of the earth.

Outwitted, the Overdiers decided to take the line of least resistance; they fled, leaving the twins stewing in the pit. We pulled the blubbering boys out of the hole, gave them a swift kick up the backside, and warned them never to set foot on *our* land again.

'If you come back, next time we'll string you up by that tree!' yelled Jacob, pointing to a nearby oak.

Victory was ours, and as we congratulated each other, asserting how tough and clever we were, it began to rain heavily, quickly turning cold. It had never occurred to us that continuous rain would soon fill our hideout. The rain kept pelting down and the floor of our beloved pit was soon awash, water seeping in from all directions. The walls became so wet and greasy it was quite clear that the hideout was not the place to be. So much for our hard work! Maybe a tree-hut would have been better... Once the holes had filled with water and we were sure the enemy had retreated, we lost interest and decided to go home. It struck me that the process of digging and scheming was far more rewarding than the end result!

When the excitement of Saint Nicholas Day had ebbed, we turned our attention towards the end of term and the solemn beauty of Christmas.

The winter term was the mid-stage of the school year. Fabritius had been spirited away some time ago and was now remembered only as a nightmare. By grade three, my curiosity had taken off like a jet plane. Mr de Rieu encouraged us to ask questions and spurred us on even further by setting us a list of intriguing projects, sparking a chain reaction. I added a few questions of my own: What is the deepest part of the ocean? Why doesn't our planet fall to the bottom of the universe? Why do we grow so slowly? Are plants really animals? Do they cry when we step on them? How far is the furthest star? If God loves us why does He allow pain? Why are there only two genders and not three or four? Why are our eyes where they are and not in our foreheads or on the sides? Why can't worms see?

I pumped my classmates for information, who in turn grilled their families. I also pestered my long-suffering parents, uncles, aunts, grandmothers, brothers and visitors. All in all, an exciting venture! My brothers sometimes replied properly, other times, derisively, but usually told me to bugger off, whereas Father listened patiently and answered to the best of his ability. Mother, however, lost her cool, regarding my relentless interrogation as reminiscent of Nazi methods. 'Why don't you ask Mr de Rieu? I'm too busy to answer all your stupid questions!'

Uncle Louis, my mother's brother-in-law, who lived in Hoorn, some distance away, made the mistake at one of our many family gatherings at *The Dyke* to suggest that on Koninginnedag – Queen's Day,[65] the celebratory orange balloons rising to the heavens represented unborn babies. He said that when a balloon burst and landed somewhere in the vicinity, a baby would be born.

'If you can find an orange balloon,' Uncle Louis promised, 'I'll give you a guilder.' His artistic mane of curly hair shook with mirth, since he expected my search to be futile.

I couldn't see the connection between balloons and babies, but Uncle Louis claimed storks flying by punctured the balloons, causing them to drop the babies. He was confident that the balloons would blow sufficiently far away for this to be an unlikely event. He was wrong. I scoured the neighbourhood for days and eventually found two orange balloons, one in the Wood in front of the statue of Dr van Dam, a renowned local surgeon, now deceased, and the other snagged on a branch near the birdcage. The jangle of coins already rang in my ears.

When Uncle Louis and Aunty Joanne arrived at *The Dyke* some weeks later, our family were also visiting; we sometimes stayed there overnight. Since Uncle Louis and Aunty Joanne weren't able to have children of their own, they had recently adopted two baby girls, Loes and Pam. The new babies were manna from heaven; I triumphantly pulled the two trophies from my pocket and shoved the orange balloons under Uncle Louis' nose.

'Damn! I'd forgotten about them. Tsk! Tsk! Still, a promise is a promise,' and he opened his leather purse and placed two guilders on my upturned palm. Uncle Louis, as it turned out, wasn't such a bad egg after all, which he was perceived as by some members of the extended family. I felt like a millionaire and with great glee polished the wonderful silver

---

[65] Queen's Day, and now King's Day, began with the accession of Queen Wilhelmina in 1890. Dates have been altered for various reasons. Today it marks a holiday where 'orange madness' allows the normally staid Dutch to thoroughly enjoy themselves.

coins. When I held them up to Lex, whose chagrin was clearly visible, he threatened to murder me if I continued to show off!

The birth of Christ was a time for celebration and taking stock, Christmas itself a reflective affair, without presents. Instead, mouth-watering pastries, such as *kerstkrans, kerststollen* and *tulband* – made from raisins, almonds, orange peel, icing sugar and spices, baked in butter and formed into symbolic shapes – were the reward for waking up in the middle of the night to attend midnight Mass.

Our northern winters allowed for some innovation to the biblical tale, just as other nations have adapted it to their own cultures. We brought the large wooden crib down from the loft, then the various statuettes representing characters from the Bible.[66] After dusting them off, the statuettes were placed reverently around the crib, after which Lex and I ventured into the snow-decked countryside to search for pagan reminders of another tradition. We were instructed to return from the Heilooer Wood with the greenest moss, springy and moist; mistletoe, and red-berried branches of holly.

Still under the spell of Uncle John's story, I knocked on the door of my friendly gnome, but he wasn't home; possibly out chopping wood or visiting friends. Instead, flushed with excitement, we left the tree and searched around the Cathill for everything we needed, then whooped and rolled around in the virgin snow, hoping to catch sight of the hare whose dainty footprints tracked to the underbrush: over the years, we rarely did.

Another time, one cold afternoon, I did spot a hare, painstakingly cleaning its whiskers with its paws; I was transfixed, watching while the animal, except for its ablutions, sat quite still, seemingly without a care in the world. With my heart thumping and my fingers limbering up in thick woollen gloves, I stood there, too afraid to disturb its gentle motions: the sanctity of silence forbade it. In spring, when its vulnerable young darted hither and thither, the hare would protect its leverets from vulpine predators by simulating boxing, and even ward off a frisky buck if it came too close. 'Mad as a March hare' may well have derived from these pugilistic antics, used both to shield the littluns and to reject any persistent and unwanted beau.

---

[66] Saint Francis of Assisi popularized the nativity scene in 1223 at Greccio in Italy. He introduced live animals and shepherds into his pantomimes, staged inside a cave. His aim was not only to promote animal welfare, but also to wean people off the expectation of lavish gifts: gift-bearing derived from the Magi, yet obscured the point of Christmas. In this quest to refocus on Christ, Saint Francis was, in some countries, remarkably unsuccessful. However, nativity scenes spread throughout Europe and, for practical reasons, figurines replaced humans and live animals.

*

Evergreen trees, usually fir, were a pagan import used during winter celebrations. Although they were at one time forgotten, it is said that either Saint Boniface or Martin Luther, or perhaps even both, revived the idea of a tree as a symbol of rejuvenation, a negation of harsh winters. Also, aromatic young fir or pine trees quickly dispelled the stale smells of cooking and sweaty bodies, showers not existing then, or even in our day. A fir tree was given pride of place somewhere near the nativity scene crib, to remind us of crop renewal and warmer seasons. The illusion of spring warmed our hearts, and when decorated, the tree, with its dazzling display of colours, was transformed into a symbol of hope. I loved to sit beneath it, snug and secure, looking up at the winged angel atop, protecting us from evil, and the colourful balls twirling in the draught. White candles threw out flickering shadows from their dancing flames, and later, the soothing smell of snuffed wicks reminded me of holiness and death. I fell into a trance as fierce winds from the North Sea shook our house and gripped our souls, reminding us that the pale green horseman of the apocalypse was never far away. Holy! Holy! Holy! My prayer tally went up markedly around this time.

The crib's manger occupied the centre of the shepherd's hut and the statuette of the Virgin Mary was dressed in cobalt blue, while Jesus, swaddled in beige, pointed a didactic finger at the shepherds. Joseph, with dark beard, stood aloof in a coffee-brown robe, looking a little confused at having to play second fiddle to mother and child. The shepherds, in their short, olive tunics, somehow managed to look surprised, standing with long, outstretched fingers, anxiously welcoming the Christ child. The Magi, burdened by thick brocade and outlandish headgear, knelt stiffly, proffering their gifts of gold, frankincense and myrrh, hidden in ornate oblong boxes. I shall forever associate the delicious fragrance of fir and pine with the gifts of the Magi, whatever the elusive scent of the intriguingly named frankincense and myrrh might be, never having personally come across it.

The brown ox, grey ass, and white sheep all stood motionless on the freshly gathered moss, almost as if they didn't want to be there. Perhaps they were embarrassed by the size and opulence of the camel, with its haughty bearing and plush saddle placed over a blue velvet rug. I ignored the flying angels; too showy and unbelievable. My nose, well tutored in the smells of *The Dyke*, where the cattle were kept indoors during winter, supplied the smells unwittingly and I wondered how the holy family could have abided the noise and stink of these animals. And where would they find a loo? The humans, that is! Yet the peaceful scene filled me with a euphoria bordering on substance abuse and I wanted to linger, to watch the figures forever. The Gospels in diorama! School and Church, however, inevitably intervened.

Christ's humble beginnings were impressed upon us as the antidote to any airs and graces. Our Christianity was understated; not much fanfare, Father Pronk's dramatic efforts the nearest concession to entertainment. I took the advice of the priests without question and tried to be the good boy Mother wanted me to be. God was the Maker, the shadow of our daily lives, religion a dour affair. Guilt and the mortal-venial sin dichotomy were the drivers of our conscience. Like dog's fleas, they were difficult to get rid of.

I hadn't heard of Yuletide at that age. This English term is first known from around 1475. Yule was originally a winter solstice festival celebrated by the Germanic and Nordic peoples, absorbed over time during their Christianization into festivities surrounding Christmas. Amongst scholars, Yule is thought to be the modern representation of the Old English words ġeol and ġeola, with the former indicating the midwinter festival of 'Yule' and the latter indicating the month of 'Yule', around December or January. Both words are considered to be derived from Common Germanic, and are related to the Gothic, jiuleis, and Old Norse, jól. Among many others, the long-bearded Norse god Odin bears the names jólfaðr, meaning 'Yule father', and jólnir, 'the Yule one'. In Old Norse poetry, jólnar is often employed as a synonym for 'feast', or the Norse gods in general.

In ancient times, in Persia, festivities were meant to coax Mithras, the sun god, from his hiding place, to turn darkness into light. The Babylonians celebrated *their* feast of the son of Isis, or nature, on the twenty-fifth of December. Gluttony, drinking and the exchanging of gifts were their associated rituals. The Romans, whose winter solstice was named after Saturn, the god of agriculture, began their celebrations a little earlier, around the seventeenth. Saturnalia was the yearly festival when slaves were freed and citizens ate too much and drank themselves into oblivion. Delicate feathers were snaked down gullets until sufficient irritation yielded half-digested scallops, venison and other delicacies, burped into special receptacles. A discreet intermission and then a renewed assault on the flanks of a well-cooked deer or some other exotic dish, the conversation never waning. The cycle was repeated until exhaustion dragged them to their beds. Ah, the ancient Romans certainly knew how to do it!

In Rome at that time, 'mummers', so beloved in Belgium and Germany centuries later, strutted their stuff, singing and dancing through narrow streets, performing their colourful pageants. It was from this street theatre, amongst other things, and not only the medieval miracle plays, that Christmas pageantry arose; mummers from medieval times simply continued the old pagan frolics, adding scenes from the Bible as they saw fit.

Christianity and paganism danced a pas de deux throughout the centuries. Christmas, it can scarcely be denied, was originally based upon pagan events, modified according to the needs of the new religion; the birth of Christ often blended in beautifully. *When* Christ was actually born, however, remains conjecture, and Jesus, it seems, received far more attention after his demise than he did in his own lifetime, mainly due to the efforts and writings of the Roman Jew, Paul, his disciple.

'Give me a bit of your blanket, dickhead! I'm cold!' Post-war poverty meant we couldn't afford thick blankets. Bill yanked the thin orange-flowered fabric over his shoulders, leaving Lex exposed, his bony knees touching the chilly wall, his teeth rattling as he wheezed and mumbled to himself. Lex instinctively pulled the blanket back and the tug-of-war continued for a while. As a compromise, both brothers snuggled closer to the centre to draw some heat from me. Thankfully, I was fast asleep, dreaming of soccer stardom.

Our bedroom was like a morgue in Siberia, the only heat emanating from our bodies. It was minus twenty and Holland had become a block of ice. Sometimes the full moon attempted to penetrate the thick, swirled ice covering the tiny, four-panelled window of our bedroom, our frosted eye to the sky. The light cast blurred yet elegant designs onto the pale yellow wall, reminiscent of hastily sketched Japanese figures: a swan or a cherry tree.

In the living room, the chugging stove was always hungry for fuel and we took turns during the day to fetch the anthracite from the coal shed; the coal bin seemed constantly empty.

'Your turn, Herrie, and don't whinge,' Mother ordered.

We stuck to the stove like limpets and dirty underpants clung to us for days. Skid marks and urine stains were simply ignored by our fraught mother, who was too cold and far too busy with other more essential tasks to wash them regularly. Shivering ribcages, stentorian yells, Tarzan poses and crumpled socks; we slithered over one another like elvers in a tub, anything to escape the cold. The localized warmth didn't travel very far up the staircase, so at night we changed into our frayed pyjamas in front of the stove, now the heart of the house. During the daytime, our warm clothes became second skins, until Mother deemed it necessary to pay a visit to the communal washhouse, depending upon who or what stank the most.

By the Scruff of the Neck

One morning, I distinctly remember Father railing against the two-metre wall of snow blocking the front door: 'I feel like a bloody Eskimo leaving his igloo. I'll be late and the car probably won't start. Dammit! Hey, Jack-the-lad! Get out of your nest and start digging us out...and get Bill to help. I need to have some grub before I go...'

An hour later, John and Bill, moaning and shouting, had dug a narrow tunnel. Two piles reaching the top of our large front window became the avenue of honour onto the street. We younger ones were too busy keeping warm, but soon joined them, not to help, but to take in the enchanting streetscape. Newportslane, a street paved with dark red, narrow bricks interspersed with cream-coloured ones, reflecting warmth and familiarity, had been transformed as if by magic into a wonderland of soft snow, the glaring whiteness hurting our eyes.

It was still snowing gently as we ventured out in our thick coats and clogs, our fingers crackling like dry twigs. The snowflakes descended as tiny crystal parachutes, only to melt on contact, the heaviest snow having fallen during the night. A stray dog, emitting puffs of vapour, trotted across the fluffy surface, leaving well-defined paw marks. It sniffed the base of a partly hidden telephone pole and lifted its leg, leaving a yellow stain on the snow.

The verandah of Liefting's[67] pub next to us was completely covered with lush snow, dripping water onto the pavement, while the power cables above the street drooped under the weight of their ribbons of ice. In the 1940s there were few cars to be seen and those parked on the sides of the street were now dressed in snowy jumpers. It was ever so quiet and muted. A few of the neighbours' kids were already off to school but couldn't resist hurling snowballs at one another as they went. Once they saw us, we attracted friendly fire, but no harm was intended.

When I returned many years later and walked the same street, visiting our home, now a photographer's studio, I saw myself, the little blond boy, slightly obsessive, sliding down the banister, and wondered who and where I had been, trying to remember it all. I recalled standing in the middle of a row of boys, arms crossed, wearing a worsted jacket and with a cheeky grin. Alongside me were Johnny Red and the others, now dispersed to other paths.

What became of them all? Are they still alive? We were once in one another's pockets, smelt one another's hair as we broke bread in our dugout on the Hareland. Can one be reincarnated in reverse and go through everything again?

---

[67] Not its real name.

The aura of war was still with me in 1970 and images of prisoners tied to stakes by Nazi bullies appeared before me as in a dream. For insolence, or stealing a crust of bread, concentration camp inmates were forced to undress and yield to the elements. They were left to freeze in the bitter cold, to be slowly dragged to an agonizing death by glacial winds, tearing at flesh, so delicate and spare. Eyes turning inward and lost; speech, a luxury. Golgotha revisited. Too weak even to think of Christ or any other God!

These contemporaneous realities had eluded me in 1943, being so young: a new arrival, loved and cared for, dressed in crude but sensible clothes, chortling in the snow as, unknown to me, these emaciated wretches met their deaths amid silent trees, the sparrows darting between frozen limbs.

Was this meant to be part of the grand design? Could *I* have been hanging there but for a bit of spermal ducking and weaving? Cosmic cruelty... Unanswerable questions! Imponderable... Stalin's gulags screaming similar refrains.

We couldn't wait to leave for school, hoping for solid ice on the canals. A ripple of exhilaration surged through my body; the early morning promised excitement. We held snow-clog competitions on the way. The idea was to walk daintily, like ballerinas, across fresh snow, trying to attach as much of it as possible to our wooden soles. We were competing to see how high we could go. When about six to eight centimetres thick, the snow would collapse and we began anew. The laughter and repartee would wind us up as we tried to outdo one another:

'Look at me! I'm taller than you.' – *Disintegration!*
'Now I know what it's like to be as tall as Father or Uncle John.'
'You walk like a girl, ya nancy!'
'Shit! I've fallen over again. I feel as if I've got a carrot stuck up my bum. Bum, bum, rumble-bum, bubble gum and tumble dumb.'
'Well I won't eat it then!' – *Hoots of laughter.*
'My dick's frozen off!'
'*My* snow is thicker than *yours!*'
'There's better snow on the footpaths.'
'Morning, Bear!'
'Morning, boys!'

Racing through the Wood, we stopped to extol the beauty of the trees, draped in snow, pristine sugar-coating bulking the skeletal branches, my mind composing fanciful rhymes:

By the Scruff of the Neck

Minky stoats,
Furry coats,
Elms on moats,
All in their winter's best.

High up in the branches a crow squawked. Flapping lazily, it took off, searching for a stray mouse not in its house in this bitter season.

We feigned death by lying down on the billowy snow, or improvised building a snowman, using black stones for eyes...and suddenly realized we were running late for school. Trickles of water followed us into the corridor as we lined up for class.

I felt secure and comfortable in my desk. 'Hello books, hello pens, hello pencils, hello dear inkwell, hello dear desk.' My fingers still tingled; my nose still dribbled from the cold.

Mr de Rieu tapped his desk and we paid attention. 'How tall is the Eiffel Tower?'

The lesson sailed away.

On our Wednesday afternoons off from school, we delighted in skating the many waterways, or tried our luck on the town moat, pushing and pulling our sleds as fast as we could, avoiding screaming girls and smug adults skating by at a leisurely pace, singing or whistling. The clear skies and cold air didn't bother us; our energy kept us warm. Sometimes I stopped to look at the others enjoying themselves and reflected on my own good fortune in being there. Soon I was off again, trying my best to beat Lex and Johnny Red.

'Come on, Boys!' *The Alkmaar Boys*, our local football team, were struggling. A momentary silence and I homed in on Father's unmistakable voice, urging the players on from somewhere in the middle of the main wooden stand of the Sportpark. We were allowed in at half-time and were waiting impatiently at the gate. Even though all the tickets had already been sold, the management thought it reasonable to let people in at halftime, most of whom were youngsters. 'Come on Boys, get rid of that ball!' Father's loud baritone admonished them, winning approval from the partisan crowd, but the advice was totally ignored. Of course Father was simply continuing the tradition of the Roman coliseum; blood sports may have given way to more civilized physical encounters, but the passions remained the same. On various occasions, he and Uncle Louis came home sporting black eyes and torn raincoats. Mother and Aunty Joanne both scolded them, pointing out the cost of their soccer enthusiasm. Only a fortnight ago, Uncle Louis had even broken his umbrella by clocking an opposition supporter over the head. A gift from a kind uncle in Ghent, the expensive and heavy *parapluie* became a useful weapon in the melee over a disputed 'offside'. Aunty Joanne seethed and Uncle Louis withdrew to his *atelier* like a cur to its kennel.

Theirs was a barren relationship, temporarily relieved by the adoption of the two girls, Loes and Pam. Divorce? Inconceivable, given the morality of the time. Whenever they had an altercation – usually every few days – Uncle Louis retired to his workshop. Here he spent hours painting tranquil country scenes from North Holland in poor imitation of Hobbema.[68] As he grew older, he escaped to a good fishing spot on the IJsselmeer – formerly known as the Zuider Zee.

Uncle Louis, alleged Jack-the-lad, also found solace in booze and bordellos, the best of which were to be found in the *Oudezijds Voorburgwal* in Amsterdam, known locally as the *Walletjes*, or little walls, referring to the fortifications dating back to medieval times. Apparently our Uncle was a fine pillock of society: waltzing with the barmaids; firing off crude jokes, his soft southern lilt bursting into a paroxysm of laughter; laying bets, and merrily downing one *jenever* after another.

The ancient canal east of the Dam Square, just south of the *Oude Kerk*, the oldest church in Amsterdam, was once divided between mistresses and molls on the northern side, and the remnants of monasteries and stately homes on the southern side, an apt mirror of contradictory endeavours throughout the ages.

Amsterdam's comical juxtapositions reinforced its reputation as a fun city. My old spiritual friend, the historian, Huizinga, coined the term *homo ludens*, or 'playful man', as integral to history, and invested time in unravelling the role of 'play' as it relates to culture. He obviously had Amsterdam in mind as the fulcrum of playfulness, with its *ludieke* innovations, or 'happenings', as some Amsterdam youths called them. Whichever outrageous event occurred in Amsterdam, the rest of the nation was apt to follow.

One only has to look at the work of the Brueghels, Bosch, or Gerrit Dou, and indeed our family's patron saint, Jan Steen, to connect the dots of playfulness in Dutch history. Amsterdammers, *par excellence*, have always approached life through the prism of jocularity, no doubt enhanced by the bustle of polyglot traders and canny Jewish business people. Amsterdam, as no other city, is synonymous with the bearable lightness of being, its culture so very easy to enjoy.

Father donned the garb of the Amsterdam wag with consummate flair, while Amsterdam's Yiddish deflationary humour was part of his emotional being. He had a wonderful companion in Uncle Louis, who

---

[68] Meindert Hobbema, 1638–1709. A Dutch 'Golden Age' landscape painter.

was, of course, an honorary Amsterdammer by virtue of his participation in the quirks of the noble city.

Amsterdam blossomed in the seventeenth century – the golden century – and Father inherited its pollen. He opted for humour and gentle cynicism, the Amsterdam *modus operandi* for coping with life. This humour suffused our daily lives and also became our currency.

Later, during the 1970s, when I meandered through the maze of canals, crossed quaint narrow bridges, and admired the haughty streetscapes, I became an unwitting agent of Amsterdam's divine purpose, which was to provide the perfect setting for free and creative expression. My return involved my writing a thesis on the Dutch *Provos*, or provocateurs. They were a group of anarchists who continued the tradition of the crazies, eccentrics and syndicalists of the past who had existed in this city for a long time, now merely transmuted into modern guise.[69] Their creed of non-violence, absurdism, and opposition to bureaucratic fascism, came as natural to me as eating herrings at fish stalls. I was genetically programmed to bear witness to the unique madness of Amsterdam.

After the *Provos* faded into irrelevance, their mantle, albeit much more political, passed on to the harmless *Orange Gnomes*, who carried on the good work of fighting capitalism by subversive means. They were brave but largely unsuccessful. Nevertheless, in 1964, the squatters of Amsterdam, of similar political persuasion, became, throughout the western world, the template for invading unoccupied buildings, leaving a lasting legacy; although squatting has of course been with us since biblical times.

At night, taverns, whose entrances had been crossed by geniuses and simpletons for centuries, became ad hoc theatres. Publicans shed their humdrum daylight roles and instead balanced kegs of beer on their chin or jumped onto counters to offer a respectable rendition of *O sole mio*, or Rossini's *Largo al Factotum*,[70] giving the Neapolitans and celebrity baritones a run for their money. Academics, artists, imbeciles, musicians, poets, philosophers, touts and transvestites milled around their favourite bar to discuss intricate subjects or to give public performances of their wares. I have even seen dwarfs somersaulting onto the ample bosoms of barmaids, or that of the frothy wife of the publican.

In the background, one could espy a modern pupil of Vermeer or den Hoogh, sketching away happily, only interrupting his or her

---

[69] Over the centuries, Amsterdam was often the centre of political and artistic rebellion. In the 17th century there were many riots in the city, which, as political protest, were directed against heavy-handed authority. It is a tradition reasserted in the anarcho-syndicalist popularity of Domela Nieuwenhuis, Bart De Ligt and Christian Cornelissen of the late-Victorian period.

[70] An aria from *The Barber of Seville*, sung at the first entrance of the title character, Figaro.

concentration by lifting a glass of ale. On Friday nights in particular, I observed students re-enacting the antics of their forebears by vomiting onto the pubs' massive wooden steps, hollowed out by centuries of human traffic. In summer, during the 1960s and early '70s, Amsterdam youth also assembled near the statue of *Het Lieverdje*, 'The Little Darling', in the Spui, a popular square for reciting vulgar or witty poems, parodying politicians, or lampooning living conditions in the capital. To give a few examples of the period:

REHEARSE FOR THE APOCALYPSE

"Yes, folks! Now you can be the first on your block to experience ecological disaster. Why wait until 1980? Don't let the future take you by surprise. Prepare now for the end of civilization. Rehearse for the apocalypse." *etcetera*

Given our preoccupation with global warming during the late twentieth and early twenty-first centuries, this was remarkably prescient.

OR

"I have no device and I don't carry a banner; I struggle for life in my own way. My shield is love, my weapon my word; I sing against smear, I sing against murder."

It was Amsterdam's take on 'flower power' and everyone was invited to join in. I loved the raillery. To immerse oneself in Amsterdam nightlife was to become part actor in a grand municipal comedy. Anarchy and inanity are the weapons of Amsterdammers, who must make fools of themselves, and others, or relinquish their birthright as free citizens. This was well understood by the police, most of whom were genuine Amsterdammers themselves.

In one of the city's squares or nooks, Descartes and Spinoza, despite the latter's youth, could easily have yarned together in some coffee house, just a stone's throw away from Rembrandt, sweating away at his huge canvasses. After a hard day's work at roughly-hewn desks, they may even have let their hair down – long hair then being the fashion – to perform clog dances, or to recite Catullus, in a manner not too dissimilar to intellectuals quoting Vondel, Holland's 'Shakespeare', and gyrating to the Beatles in the *Paradiso* in more recent times. Descartes' resounding maxim of *cogito ergo sum* ought to have continued with *'especially in Amsterdam, where I have produced my best work'*.

In many respects, notwithstanding modernity, cyber intrusion, and the influx of outsiders, Amsterdam has remained the same: frivolity and artistry the dominant traditions passed from one generation to the next. These days, where else in the Western world can one smoke a joint in a café with impunity? Perhaps only Christiania in Denmark and certain American states... Father knew most of this and in his youth had been a typical flâneur[71] of the old city, soaking up its ancient secrets, and, just like his father, sometimes sought to escape Alkmaar's provincialism by immersing himself in the cultural abundance of Amsterdam; although he differed from his père in not wishing to escape his family. Father loved and protected his family like a mountain gorilla its young. He was a sensitive man in many respects and tolerated Mother's theatrics because he understood her frailties. Despite them, and despite post-war austerity and low profit margins, only rarely did he explode in the manner of his own father.

Father used to refer to his tolerance limit as 'crossing the red line'. If Bill became unbearable – usually through pestering us younger brothers by dangling smelly socks in front of our noses, farting into our faces, and the like – Father lost his cool completely. He must have read Karl May's books, since on one particular occasion, just like Winnetou, he threw a knife, straight as an arrow, which, but for Bill's instinctive ducking, could easily have scalped him. The knife went crashing through the front window...and Dutch windows are unusually large, reflecting either the business smarts of Dutch glaziers or the showy honesty of Dutch family life.

'You could have killed him!' screamed Mother.

'That's right... The little shit... Pity I missed!'

Sixty years later, I am still the proud owner of the carving knife, affectionately referred to as 'Herm'.

Sometimes, Mother, whose melodramatic inventiveness knew no bounds, harried the poor man about the appalling behaviour of Jack-the-lad, even after a ten-hour stint on his bike in the rain. Father was in fact frequently nagged about Jack-the-lad's peccadilloes: not turning up to dinner on time, his swearing, and his general misbehaviour. She would go on and on like a dripping tap: 'Where *is* that boy, Herman? Probably drinking somewhere with his horrible friends... He can't be trusted... It's only a question of time before the police will be knocking on the door again. You *have* to do something about him or we'll all suffer.'

In reality, none of us suffered. Instead, we all lived contentedly in our own bubble. We couldn't give a hoot. The only one who really suffered was Father. He had become restless, torn between Mother's relentless hounding and his need to relax a little before dinner. But Mother wouldn't let up, her large green eyes moistening with intent.

---

[71] An aimless idler; a loafer.

'I'm really not well. Why is John so difficult? What have we done wrong to deserve his ingratitude... Herman, I can't take it any more! Where is he?'

Quite easy to surmise! Jack-the-lad was probably having a good time in one of Alkmaar's many pubs boasting to some girl about his soccer skills, or some deal he could arrange, predictably with the aim of luring her into the cot; whereas Mother always gave the impression that he had become lost up the Orinoco and was tied to a tree in the middle of the jungle, about to be carved up by natives.

Father was hungry and, instead of replying, said he could eat the arse out of a dead rat, but Mother ignored him and kept harping on about Jack-the-lad, as if the world would end unless he was brought into line.

'Herman, we *have* to do something. Only last week, Father Pronk ticked him off for swearing in front of some kids. He's our punishment, our curse. Why can't you straighten him out? You're the man of the house. Do something!'

Father rustled the newspaper more vigorously, while she moaned on and on. Mother wasn't a psychologist, but should have known better than to burden a man on an empty stomach: nevertheless, she was unrelenting.

Having finally reached boiling point, Father threw down the newspaper and looked up. We knew he would do one of two things: he would either counter Mother's fevered ravings by warning her to back off, or state matter-of-factly that he had had enough: 'Alie, you're going too far. Don't push me over the red line!' he'd say, his voice going up a notch. Or, he would stand up and race to the front door, shaking with rage. 'I'll kill him, the skinny little prick... That's it! I'm going to kill him. I've had enough of everybody!'

While we hovered near the stove during winter, exaggerating our day's triumphs, it wasn't uncommon to hear the front door banging against the passage wall that ran from front to back of the house and into the small kitchen, then Jack-the-lad racing past, hoping to straddle the concrete rear wall and flee into the Sportpark, Father in hot pursuit!

'I'm going to get you, you miserable worm! And when I do, I'm going to unscrew your arms and *kill* you...slowly.'

But Jack-the-lad was fleet of foot and usually managed to escape. From my recollection, Father only caught him the once, when Jack-the-lad tripped. The yammering that ensued was at the same time both amusing and frightening. We could hear the physical blows and violent threats.

'I'll never do it again! Don't hit me! I swear I'll be on time from now on.'

'Come here, you bastard! I'll teach you to give Mother a hard time.'

The irony was that Mother placed herself between John and Father, pleading that he leave him alone.

'Don't hurt him! Don't hit him too hard or you'll break his arm! He'll finish up in hospital.'

But Father was on a rampage, his emotions unleashed and impervious to reason. How do you stop a runaway bull? Father was a tall, sinewy man, with big hands and he knew how to use them. When he was in overdrive nothing could stop him. Yet he wasn't normally a violent man. It's just that common sense left him when he felt cornered; when he thought there was no choice but to attack whoever was in his way.

While Jack-the-lad bore the brunt of Father's ire, we received our fair share throughout the year, but deservedly so. When Father was tired, which was nearly always, and Mother began to complain about us, he would try to deflect her fault-finding by simply pointing out that that's what boys do: 'What do you expect, Alie?'

At times we were our own worst enemy. On hot summer nights, for example, boredom and irritability made an unstable combination. Bill often became aggressive and made unreasonable demands. 'Tell me some rude jokes, or I'll pummel you,' he threatened, already smacking my face, although gently.

'No! I don't want to, and anyway, I don't know any. Stop hitting me, or I'll tell Pa!' I replied sulkily. Lex pretended to be asleep.

'I bet you can't stand on your head and clap at the same time. I'll leave you alone, if you can.' Bill was in one of his sadistic moods.

A racket followed, with Father soon standing at the bottom of the stairs yelling, 'If you aren't quiet in two minutes, I'll come upstairs and sort you out!' Silence for a few seconds, then resumption of our oafish behaviour. 'I've warned you once and this is absolutely the last time,' he boomed. Peace for a few moments and off we went again. Lambs to the slaughter!

Thump! Thump! Thump! Father's temper had broken the barrier and up he came, fast as a train, to open the door and grab Bill, then leave an imprint of his huge mitt on his buttocks. Next Lex, and finally me!

Clouts around the ears and a Niagara of tears, amid promises not to do it again and accusations that it was Bill, or Lex, or me, who started it, all sobbing loudly after the prodigious whacks...before finally finding the words to describe our revenge when we grew up!

'I'll be bigger than him and I'll garrotte him with my bare hands,' Bill boasted, although not quite sure what garrotting meant.

'I'll drag him to Kramer and put his head on the anvil, then hit him with a sledge hammer so hard that his brains will *ooze* out,' said Lex, drawing out the word "ooze".

'I'll keelhaul him under the biggest ship in the world,' I added feebly.

The next day, walking awkwardly to school and still sulking, we met up with our mates to discuss the latest soccer results. That night around the dinner table, Father promised to take us to Amsterdam to see a film: Father, reborn a hero, last night's smacks almost forgotten. We would visit the zoo to meet members of our extended family and have lunch at Krasnapolsky's. It couldn't get better than that!

Our Father, which art in Alkmaar,
Hallowed be thy Name.
Thy Kingdom come,
Thy will be done in Amsterdam,
As it is in Alkmaar.

During the late 1940s, we had previously enjoyed a cheap dinner at Krasnapolsky's, which was just recovering from the effects of the War and the German occupation; although it had managed to remain open to all comers. Did *Der Führer* stay there, or that snake-in-the-grass, Inquart? Conceivably! We admired the dark, wooden panelling and the art deco lampshades, and although I have no memory of the menu, it must have been good because it was at the Krasnapolsky, the acme of good taste.

Wilhelm Adolf Krasnapolsky, a German of Polish origin, followed his father to Amsterdam in 1856 to, at first, join the tailoring business. His commercial acumen, however, soon rested on the New Polish Coffeehouse, which he bought and converted into the now famous and eponymous restaurant, situated between the Damrak, Amsterdam's main thoroughfare, and the Warmoestraat, the start of the red light district. For over a century, business and sex, like a happily married couple, dominated this area of prime real estate. Even James Joyce stayed at the 'Kras', incorporating the fictive colour, 'Krasnapolsky red', into his novel, *Finnegan's Wake*.

Four of us sitting on a donkey! I, in the front, in a multi-coloured, ring patterned, woollen jumper, putting on a fake smile for the brownie camera; the donkey standing in resignation, puffy eyes downcast, musing: *Not another insufferable family on my back!*

Exhausted, having dipped our toes in the delights of Amsterdam, we turned north, homeward bound in the old grey Ford, all feeling sleepy. Father slowed down to point out the *Dyke* belonging to his grandmother Rens, in the village of *Sloterdijk* in Amsterdam's northwest. She owned three houses there, nowadays classified by the national trust. Part of Great Uncle Piet Lap's undeserved inheritance perhaps!

We visited old Rens in a retirement home in 1949, when she was ninety-seven. She had raised Father during his adolescent years and he always spoke very highly of her. Rens belonged to the Lijcklema clan, and as the granddame of the family, was treated with reverence. Lex and I were given slices of honey cake when we visited her.

Rens was a big woman, strong in mind and body. She owned a number of barges used to transport flour. When in her seventies, she could still be seen with heavy flour bag on shoulder, walking the plank between barge and *terra firma*.

She was also a generous woman. On Saint Nicholas Day she organized treats and presents for everyone. Sometimes, however, one of the children was given the wrong or an inferior present. The father of the child quickly nipped any protest in the bud, saying, in restrained tones, 'If you complain, I'll slaughter you when we get home. Get rid of that scowl, now! Take your present and go to *Oma,* thank her properly, and no muttering; read your poem to her and be grateful.'

'Thank you, *Oma,* for your lovely present and here's my poem...' The children curtsied and received nods of approval from *Oma* and the elder uncles, no matter how grating the poem or poorly recited it might have been.

Now, though, the grey Ford purred away happily and Lex was already asleep. From my cosy position on the back seat, I felt pleasantly rosy. Studying the twilight sky brewing up a storm, I followed the last vestiges of the crimson clouds, while Father hummed a tune from some opera, his head in its familiar slightly slanted posture. Meanwhile, Mother quacked into his ear about buying some rug beaters for spring.

Mother was the third child of six. Because of her theatrical personality her parents dubbed her 'The Star'. She left school at age twelve and had been considered a diligent and able student. Those were the times of having to support one's family, higher education being a luxury, only for the rich. Father also left school at a young age and always regretted his lack of education. Nevertheless, both were avid readers, Father becoming an autodidact of sorts. He had a good memory, stuffed with quaint facts.

Our parents came from highly-strung families, which didn't augur well for us. Father's family expressed their nervous energy through cynicism and drollery, rarely taking matters seriously, whereas Mother's took itself much too gravely. The Lichts were funny, the Goudsbloms pallbearers. Expressions like "He tried to make me happy with a dead sparrow" or "Oh, so you think *he's* ugly! Have you looked in the mirror

The Star: Alida Licht, Alkmaar, 1929

lately?" peppered Father's conversations, whereas *Opa* Goudsblom was laborious and much too serious. For instance, while in dispute with his younger brother, Great Uncle Jack, he gave a long and dreary, convoluted rationale for why farmers were superior to railway workers... Soon everyone fell asleep.

Even so, Mother was probably the most light-hearted of her tribe. She had an easy touch, laughed a lot and tended to look on the bright side. Father and Mother were great dancers, too, the Charleston their signature gig. Also, while not exactly slovenly, she cut corners. If a neighbour dropped by, for example, she would quite literally sweep the rubbish under the carpet, wink at her visitor, and put the coffee on; she loved a natter. Yet, when the mood seized her, which was rare, she could become overzealous in cleaning the house. Mother, to say the least, was unpredictable.

On long summer nights, our parents occasionally entertained business acquaintances and close friends. Their younger contacts wore smart clothes and the women were pretty and confident. Nearly everyone smoked then and the living room soon resembled a gambler's den. Before being sent upstairs, out of the way of the adults, we were allowed to mingle with the guests for a short while. Mother solicited our best behaviour, promising to send up a plate of goodies – but only if we behaved ourselves! Ah, bribery can be relied upon; corruption begins at home.

Once the guests were seated, Lex and I would crawl under the chairs occupied by the attractive women, hoping for a peek beneath their skirts. The guests ignored our antics as something restless little boys unselfconsciously did. I remember looking up at the pale flesh extending beyond their stockings, which were held up by suspenders. Fascinated, I was responding to my impulse to fathom the mystery of a young woman's thighs, unblemished and firm like early summer plums. Much later, Lex told me that he had done the same, our peckers quivering with delight as we re-lived the tantalizing experience.

In 1946, Mother gave birth to yet another boy, Frank, nicknamed Flozzie because of his long curls. Another mouth to feed and Mother disappointed again: she had wanted a girl. If Jack-the-lad had been a girl she might have gained a true helpmeet. How that would have changed the family dynamics!

Shrugging his shoulders, Father philosophically accepted his latest bundle, saying, 'Drat, another boy! Mother and I were hoping to have a girl at long last... There's nothing any of *us* can do about it, though,' as if we were somehow partly responsible. As innocent bystanders, we were a bit peeved by Father's odd attribution. 'What's it got to do with us?' asked Jack-the-lad, puzzled. Father just shook his head and smiled.

The new lad was formally baptized Franklin Delano, after President Franklin Delano Roosevelt, who had died recently. At least the great man's name would be carried on in our family... Ours, however, wasn't the only one. Whereas girls' names were usually confined to royals and saints, it was considered patriotic to name boys after political and military heroes associated with the War. But for the Allied victory, who knows how many Adolphs, Benitos, Erwins, Hermans, Heinrichs, Josephs, or indeed Evas, would have been trotting around Europe!

As Flozzie grew up, he played with the girl next door; same long, blonde hair and similar laugh. Strangers couldn't tell them apart. Twin sisters? Mother was perverse, hoping beyond hope that Flozzie would turn into a girl. Praying for a miracle... Even *Oma* got into the act, calling him *wollemeintje*, 'my little woollen one', after a picture book character, which was enough to give anyone a complex. Not a good start for a robust male. Moreover, Flozzie had four unruly brothers to order him about. He didn't stand a chance.

Despite such impedimenta he turned out to be not only normal, but also a lovable younger brother: gentle, considerate and dreamy. Like Mr Brown, the tailor, he too survived by living mainly in his head. He pursued such harmless activities as racing his girlfriend on a tricycle, building sandcastles in the front yard or at the beach, and singing *Goodnight Irene* till late into the night to lull himself to sleep. Flozzie built up a huge collection of lead soldiers, model farms and an assortment of other miniatures. His hobbies became his quiet friends and his way of telling the rest of the world to leave him alone. The real world was harsh and cruel; he didn't know how to deal with its 'slings and arrows'. For example, by creating his *Madurodam* – a miniature city of famous Dutch landmarks – he felt safe, useful, and aesthetically satisfied. Later in life he also became a pigeon fancier, or pigeon *milker,* to use a Dutch colloquialism.

Mother adored Flozzie and protected him from the older brothers, who, as it turned out, always kept an eye out for him. They treated him like an ornament, a doll, appealing to their softer side. Picking him up, they tickled and kissed him, made ridiculous noises to elicit gurgles or smiles, yet soon tired of this daily ritual and returned to their usual pursuits. Perhaps that's the ambiguous fate of being born the *Benjamin*[72] of the family.

*

---

[72] In the Bible, out of twelve children, Benjamin was Jacob's youngest and favourite son, hence the idiom.

Post-war Holland remained stagnant and drab, with few luxuries. Mother, hemmed in by a volatile brood, felt frustrated, with an unsatisfied yearning to express herself. During the late twenties, she had been in charge of a recently established *Unilever* shop in Alkmaar and by all accounts was a hard-working and efficient manager. Then, marriage came along, and with it, her pups, torpedoing any further ambitions. Under different circumstances she could have been an actor, or perhaps a chorus girl. Before she married, she often came home late after work, having spent her spare time learning how to dance or else meeting up with friends, when, instead, she should have been home helping.

Her lot, however, was shaped by the Depression and both wars, which meant we became the captive audience of her moods. She was a good woman at heart, but had a rebellious streak and liked to have her own way. If her demands weren't met she wasn't afraid of smacking us or showering us with verbal abuse, although as we grew older, stronger and smarter, she resorted to more ingenious stratagems to bend us to her will. To be fair, bringing up a family of boys was a Herculean task, especially with Jack-the-lad running riot.

Father, for all his hard work, at least got out and about. Sometimes he took us with him in his grey Ford; which, however, didn't always turn out to be a positive for us. He could be holed up in a shop or barn for hours while we waited impatiently for his face to appear. As a good-looking man with comic flair, he knew how to entertain his customers.

That winter, Holland's weather was in a bad temper; torrential rain turned into sleet and grabbed people by the throat with gale-force winds. The open polders, flat landscape and sparse tree cover conspired to make life difficult for your average Hollander cycling along the narrow *dykes*. It wasn't uncommon for cyclists or motorists to finish up in the drink. Father's boss ignored all this and expected him to perform, which he invariably did.

Meanwhile, Mother became a homebody. She had little choice and snuggled up to the stove, her fat legs exposed to the heat as she sewed buttons on shirts or peeled potatoes. Her legs would turn red and form huge scarlet circles below the knee, as if someone had branded her with a red-hot poker.

One wet, lazy afternoon, our behaviour had become intolerable. John was arguing with Mother: 'What would you know about it, Ma? I refuse to wear that lousy suit to the birthday party! It's old and has holes in the back.'

Mother persisted: 'But John, it's the only one you have and it still looks respectable.'

'Yes, Ma, I believe what you're saying but I can't handle looking like a dud. I'm off to meet me mates. Ta-ta!' He slammed the door and took off on his bike.

Bill wasn't home, since he had just gained a job as a delivery boy with a reputable patisserie, but Lex and I were stirring each other over *Snakes and Ladders*. By now Mother was truly nettled. Our shouting, John's offhandedness and the dismal weather pushed her over the edge.

'I can't stand this house any longer; I've had enough! I can't do it any more!' she screamed. She fell to her knees and began praying, her hands trembling. 'Oh, Blessed Virgin Mary, please, please, I beg you, strike me down at once and take me to heaven. I can't cope. I want to die!'

We stopped our niggling, stared at her in amazement and apologized as best we could. 'Sorry, Ma... We didn't mean to upset you... We won't yell any more... Honest!'

Mother's dramatic display had curbed our grizzling, but she wasn't going to let us off the hook that easily. She stood up, gripped the chair like an invalid, eyes rolling, then turned towards us and in a quavering voice worthy of Bette Davis, croaked, 'You have no idea what suffering you cause your mother, day in, day out. I've made up my mind. I'm leaving this family and will never come back.'

We looked at her in disbelief.

'Your cruelty has made me think very carefully. I have someone in Hoorn who'll look after me. She's my childhood friend and I'll shift in with her and start my life over again... I ask myself, why did I ever get married...why did I have children? Especially monsters like you! No mother deserves such horrible children!' She spat out the words 'monsters' and 'horrible' as if she had just swallowed poison.

Our fragile sensibilities gave over to loud sobs as we implored her not to go. Who would do the cooking? Who would do the washing? How would Father react to her absence? It was our fault and we were now paying the price for our selfishness. Lex and I hugged Mother and we promised to become angels; to do whatever she asked. As boys of around six and seven we weren't savvy enough to realize she was playing her violin to perfection.

'I'll catch the four o'clock train and that's the last you'll see of me.' Mother almost sounded triumphant as she dropped into her chair in front of the sympathetic stove. I felt devastated. We had gone too far.

Miraculously, about a quarter to four, Mother fell asleep. I nudged Lex and whispered, 'Should we wake her up at four?' Lex turned crimson, trying to suppress his anger at my stupidity.

In the meantime, Flozzie was quietly strangling his golliwog. Half an hour later, our little brother was getting hungry and began to rattle his cage. Mother remained asleep, or affected to. I lifted Flozzie from his cot and took him out the back to the kitchen, where Lex shoved a peanut butter sandwich into his gob to shut him up. We stayed there until Bill came home.

By the Scruff of the Neck

Mother at last opened her eyes. 'Ah, Bill, my darling, you're home. Look at the time. I've missed the train. Goodness, how time flies. I'd better feed Frankie. He must be starving.'

Flozzie, his mouth covered in peanut butter, was being rocked on Lex's lap and thoroughly enjoying himself. On seeing Mother, he cackled, 'Nnnnice! Nice!'

Mother had exacted her revenge. We remained ever so quiet.

One afternoon, in 1949, Jack-the-lad finished up in the Schagen lockup, and not for the first time. Sometimes it would be for 'affray', legalese for a dust up with the farmer lads at a country fair, and other times for breaking and entry, usually for booze or cigarettes. There were even occasions when he was caught stealing cars, Father's included: John enlisted his younger brothers, including me, to push Father's Ford past the house of some relatives we were visiting in Breda and go for a joy-ride around this ancient town of the Brabant region. We were on an extended holiday for the first time since the War and visited places like Limburg and *de Veluwe,* a large wooded reserve in the province of Gelderland.

'Well boys, I'm bored witless listening to those holy Joes inside. Let's visit the town and enjoy ourselves,' said John, with a grin.

Father was occupied in earnest conversation with his host, while Mother bragged in her affected upper-class voice about the academic prowess of her younger sons. She exaggerated her rolling r's and imitated the more clipped vowels of the educated Dutch, a habit which annoyed the shit out of Father and the rest of us too. Had she taken lessons from Jo Baaren-Keyser?

'Indeed, Mrs Brrraad, Lex and Herrie did very well in their tests and will stay on until the final year then hopefully go on to university.' Mother ignored Father's open-mouthed surprise.

Father, however, had stopped mid-sentence when he saw his precious car roll past. He knew instantly it was Jack-the-lad, not aware, though, that we were aiding and abetting. Nevertheless, he couldn't just leave his hosts to chase the car... He would deal with Jack-the-lad later!

Breaking the law became almost the norm for disaffected post-war youngsters. Social frustration, few job prospects, and being constantly broke, encouraged them to misbehave. Finally, yet another transgression, the theft of someone else's car, was piled onto John's list of previous convictions and it began to look grim. Once again, Father had to put up bail, and neither his threats nor Mother's hissyfits had any effect. The impending charge *did* bother him, though, but not much; in the eyes of his mates John was a hero.

Fortunately for him, on this occasion, Uncle John, Mother's brother, became the knight in shining armour pressed to rescue him. Uncle John was a civil servant, well regarded by the provincial establishment in North Holland. He had been a first-rate footballer and as he grew older took a keen interest in the welfare of wayward teenagers. His committee work and civic duties were well known around Alkmaar. A confirmed bachelor, he always found time to help others. As a result, everyone referred to him as Uncle John. It was he and Aunty Anne who looked after *Oma* Goudsblom in her old age.

Having had a love affair with the Dutch language since birth, Uncle John saw himself as a moral crusader, using figurative speech as either his shield or his weapon, depending upon the matter in hand. Also, having worked for the Department of Labour for many years, and therefore being a consummate bureaucrat, his use of language was a wonder to hear.

Though not a trained lawyer, he could teach barristers a trick or two. 'Ah, leave it to Uncle John. He'll fix it,' was the common advice to parents whose sons had fallen foul of the law. His euphemisms toyed with the seriousness of the offence, while long meandering sentences fused officialese with poetic imagery. The fact that in this case Jack-the-lad was his nephew was mere coincidence. Uncle John came across as a man totally trustworthy and morally unassailable. To doubt him was to doubt the Pope. Many aberrant young footballers slept soundly because of Uncle John.

Tall, thin, upright, with his hair lacquered and parted down the middle, Uncle John stepped forward as the key character witness in Jack-the-lad's court appearance. He was immaculately dressed yet feigned indifference to the judicial niceties around him. He had a job to do. He always began with a broad canvas, gradually and painstakingly narrowing his defence to the point of the charge.

'Within the field of possibilities,' he said, luring the old magistrate into his fantastical trap, 'it's a miracle that this young man is standing here at all. The Krauts took away his precious youth for almost five years. We at least had ours, despite the Depression. We had the freedom to pursue our interests, Your Honour. No curfews; no soldiers breathing down *our* necks. I ask you, in all seriousness, how could *anyone* have coped as a teenager under the tyranny of the Germans?'

Their eyes fixed on Uncle John, everyone present nodded their head in tacit agreement.

'This troublesome period in our lives, Your Honour, only comes once. Our youth is full of ideals on the one hand and nagging self-doubt on the other. Adolescence is most certainly a mixed blessing, while following one's mates is virtually unavoidable. All of you, cast your minds back to this turbulent and remarkable period of your own lives. If I may use a maritime example... To understand modern youth properly one has to dive below the surface and study the wonders of the deep. The adolescent psyche is like the Atlantic Ocean, full of mystery and creatures yet to be discovered.'

The magistrate was becoming restless, yet remained intrigued, slowly yielding to the magnetic personality before him.

Uncle John paused in his oration and, with his sad, hooded eyes, looked around the courtroom, assuming everyone present of a certain age would, in wistful approbation, remember.

'*You* will understand what this means, Your Honour. We are all vulnerable at the best of times, and given the distractions of youth and the scars left by this horrible war, what chance did this lad, or any of his generation, have?'

Here, the good magistrate raised an eyebrow. However, it became plain to everyone that Jack-the-lad was pure as driven snow and had only gone off the rails because of the Krauts. Rather a long bow perhaps, but not entirely implausible.

Uncle John lifted his head, his earnest gaze resting on the impassive magistrate, waiting for a sign of encouragement. Depending upon which magistrate heard the case, a tremble or a shake of the head would be enough for Uncle John to infer he was on or off the right track.

Father, though present, was peeved. A day in court meant loss of earnings. Worse, he suspected that Jack-the-lad's persistent bad form wouldn't go away, despite his brother-in-law's efforts. Another solution *must* be found.

One day soon, the answer would come from relatives visiting Holland from America.

The day's soccer match ended in a draw and Father was reasonably happy, given the superiority of the opposition. 'All right! A quick visit to Aunty Trien and then we must be home by six. We're expecting some visitors from America.' *Martians about to invade Holland, far more likely...*

Bill had landed a job with Uncle Piet Goudsblom, parking bicycles beside the pub. Apart from walking or driving in the few cars belonging to the nobs, everyone came to the football on bike. Quite a nice little earner! Bill loved the job because of the tips, but only if *The Alkmaar Boys* won. A drubbing not only meant there'd be little extra, but guaranteed abuse by the hotheads, who couldn't abide defeat.

However, despite his immediate concerns, Bill was curious about the relatives from Chicago. Father had described them as very wealthy and an important link with the past. Bill, for once, was therefore keen to finish up early, while Jack-the-lad had told his girlfriend he couldn't take her to the movies that evening because important visitors were coming. Lex and I were also intrigued and the fact they were Americans added spice to our interest. Father often spoke of Hoite – pronounced 'Huite' – and Ate, two of his great uncles on his mother's side, who had migrated with their parents from Friesland to Chicago towards the end of the nineteenth century. Hoite's and Ate's parents had produced ten children.

The Lijcklemas became interested in emigration due partly to the stagnation of the Dutch economy at the time. Like their forebears, they looked to America as the Promised Land. Emigration, however, was a serious disruption to one's life and cost a lot of money. It was a decision not to be taken lightly.

The family remained close, however, and crossed the deep now and again. They retained their native tongue, too, and, like many other wealthy Dutch Americans, hankered after the old country, just like the Italians and so many others did. A high proportion of emigrant Dutch were either strict Calvinist – members of the Dutch Reformed Church – or Catholic. The Lijcklemas were Calvinists. Other Dutch links went back to the Mennonites, who, with their Swiss-German brethren, fled religious persecution in sixteenth-century Catholic Europe and settled in either America or Russia.

Father's grandfather, Jan Lijcklema à Nijeholt, third eldest, was one of the few who preferred to remain in Holland, settling in Amsterdam and marrying our resolute great-grandmother, Rens Sannes. They set up a profitable transport business, mainly barge traffic. Regrettably, Jan, like his son and grandson our Father – died too young. Coincidence, genetic programming, or plain bad luck? Either way, all three were heavy smokers.

To my juvenile ears, emigration sounded like a curious disease, and figuratively it was: many caught the emigration virus at some stage but not all emigrated. Just as well!

Nevertheless, coming back to the present and to the end of the football match, Father was keen to get home and help Mother prepare for our guests. He pedalled faster than usual.

'I wonder what Americans look like?' asked Lex.

'I reckon they're tougher and smarter than Hollanders,' I said, forgetting that the American Lijcklemas had spent a considerable part of their earlier life in Holland. My rather rash judgment was based on cowboy and gangster movies.

'Yeah, I reckon you're right,' agreed Lex. 'They can ride horses, play cards fantastically well and shoot straight. I read somewhere they can hit a nickel from a hundred paces. I bet they can even fight better than anybody else.'

By the Scruff of the Neck

I took his word for it, he being an expert on American Indians, guns and fighting. Father ignored us and kept pedalling.

'Maybe these Americans have brought guns with them. If I could borrow one, I'd love to shoot Van Rietz through the head and watch his blood splatter all over his tomatoes!' Lex could be quite bloodthirsty and vengeful at times.

'Same colour, Lex. You wouldn't be able to tell the difference,' I yelled over Father's shoulder.

We didn't know what to expect but at least knew Americans spoke and behaved differently from the English, even though they spoke the same language. While the British remained popular in Holland, the Americans were beginning to dominate through films, comic books and music. Americans had panache; Americans were superheroes and very special. After all, hadn't they liberated us and cornered that arch-rat, Adolf Hitler? No matter that it was the Soviets who reached Berlin first and the Canadians who set us Northerners free...

Once home, we washed our hands in the small kitchen sink and walked into the sitting room, having been forewarned to be polite and modest. 'No big mouths or smart comments, do you hear?' Mother had insisted.

The late afternoon sun cast slatted shadows on the maize-coloured wallpaper of the sitting room. Clouds of smoke rose from around Father's chair, but the men opposite him weren't smoking.

I scurried over to Father and sat next to him on the floor. Lex followed and sat on the other side. John and Bill had yet to arrive. Mother, in the meantime, was busy in the kitchen preparing a late afternoon tea.

Great-great-uncles Hoite and Ate were three generations older than Father, who was in his late thirties; the uncles were in their eighties, although you couldn't tell by just looking at them. Father was the eldest in his family, as his father had been. This had a direct bearing on their visit to us: it was customary to visit the eldest in family hierarchies first.

It was the old patriarch Lubertus Lijcklema à Nijeholt who decided to leave the mother country in around 1880 and try his luck in Chicago. He was accompanied by his wife Ijsbrandje and six of their ten children. They had been farmers in Friesland and knew about livestock.

During the great fire of Chicago in 1871, which destroyed a third of the city, the rail network managed to survive pretty well intact. Its infrastructure was also unharmed. The city's' location made it the ideal link between the eastern and western states, and since the Chicago commercial establishment was crying out for labour to rebuild and expand, immigration was the answer. Lubertus began his American life working in the meat works. Upon reaching adulthood, his children soon found their own vocations. Hoite became a successful builder, while Ate purchased a Chevrolet franchise, taking advantage of the growth in the car industry. They both became wealthy in a comparatively short time, yet remained emotionally tied to their country of birth.

Hoite and Ate had typical Lijcklema features: deep-set eyes and taut, pale skin drawn over fine facial musculature. Hoite still retained a full mop of silver hair, while Ate, somewhat darker in complexion, had lost most of his, with only a few wisps left, dangling awkwardly over his forehead. Both men were tall and slim, and wore grey woollen suits of expensive cut, which I, rightly or wrongly, interpreted as indicative of immense wealth. I was taken by their smart appearance, perhaps unconsciously comparing their attire with Father's shabby outfit, and was particularly impressed by Hoite's bow tie, wishing I owned one. I'd never seen any before, except in movies.

I had half expected these ancient relatives to speak American English as in the movies, so was pleasantly surprised they spoke Dutch. The grown-ups were in deep discussion and ignored us. As children, we knew our place. We could watch and listen, but never dared interrupt. I noticed that despite their age, the uncles were alert and listened closely to what Father had to say.

'Herman, what hope have you got? Holland is broken and bureaucracy has gone mad here. You have to move with the times,' said the old man to Father's left, exuding authority and rectitude.

Hoite, being the elder of the two brothers and more talkative by nature, leaned forward, stressing his point by repeatedly shaking his right hand. An odd gesture, I thought, and wondered if he had met Karl May's Old Shatterhand or Winnetou? Entirely possible in the Wild West!

'True, Uncle, but I have a good job here with the Eagle soap company and to uproot one's family is difficult. Our mothers would be devastated if we left for another country. Don't forget, we are the largest of the immediate family. My brothers-in-law, John and Louis, and our friends don't wish us to go. We've discussed emigration so many times I've lost count.'

'I understand that, Herman, but you have to look ahead – look to the future.' Hoite almost seemed impatient with Father. 'Europe is finished and it will take years to rebuild. The future belongs to new countries like America...Canada...Australia. Even South Africa is looking good. They are big countries and haven't been ruined by invasion, or the likes of Hitler and Stalin.'

'And there's plenty of land and resources to share around. Think of your boys,' chipped in Uncle Ate. It was the first time he had spoken and his Dutch had a peculiarly slow drawl that hinted at an American accent. Hoite was easier to understand, having left Holland at an older age.

The brothers momentarily interrupted the lively exchange and nodded in our direction, finally acknowledging our presence, but didn't talk to us. Meanwhile, Mother beamed and served tea and cinnamon biscuits, followed by other tasty treats. Our normal dinner had been postponed, but for once we didn't mind at all.

'Who are these confident old men?' I mused. 'They probably live in huge houses with large gardens and garages big enough for two cars. Maybe they even own ranches, with herds of cattle and horses. Their cars might well have wooden panelling inside and out, like those long, sleek limousines in the pictures. The grandkids would have everything: bikes, ponies, new clothes, and even guns. Some kids are ever so lucky!' Not that I was particularly envious or unhappy in not having much. Freedom to move around where and when I wanted made *me* happy. Still, America seemed tantalizingly alluring and I wished Father would emigrate tomorrow; though I knew I would miss Johnny Red and my other mates.

'Our generation is spent, Herman; and well spent, I might add,' Hoite continued emphatically. 'Our father was a practical man and worried about his family, just like you. He realized at the time, and it was a very long time ago, there was little future in Friesland, with famine and unemployment in the rural provinces. So, he opted for new possibilities. He felt he had little choice. The fact he left it so late was because of Mother, who didn't at first wish to go. Our Aunt Anna, however, followed him to Chicago. Father Lubertus and she were very close and took to Illinois like ducks to water.

'It took us a little while to get used to the language and easy-going ways of the Yanks, but we fitted in quickly enough. English is difficult, but you soon learn if you have to. Don't worry about the language. Worry about food and a roof over your head, Herman. The rest will follow. Necessity is the mother of invention... You know what I mean!'

Once his elder brother had finished making his point, Ate took over. Ate's voice was soothing. He spoke slowly and earnestly, whereas Hoite seemed a little intense. Ate seemed at peace with himself and the whole wide world. I took a shine to his easy manner.

'Some of us stayed behind, Herman. This hurt Mother especially, as you'd expect. But Father said that as soon he had some spare dollars he would go back and try to persuade the rest to come over. This kept her going for a very long time. Unfortunately, he wasn't successful. John was already engaged to Rens and the others were also starting their family lives. Our brothers and sisters were too well established by then and wrapt up in their daily lives. Strange to say, they never expressed much desire to visit us, either. Of course, the Great War intervened and the fluctuations of the economy in Europe kept their noses to the grindstone. It was easier for us.

'That's why we're here now. A pity though that most of our brothers and sisters are no longer with us. We kind of drifted apart: different interests you see, Herman. Besides, our own children and grandchildren shifted centre stage. That's what happens in life. But we haven't neglected our brothers and sisters. Hoite and I love travelling now that we're single again. The Lijcklemas are a sturdy bunch... We still miss the women though.' Ate paused to collect his thoughts, staring vacantly ahead.

I was fascinated by his euphonious voice and tried to understand the sweep of the family references. I couldn't follow it all but gathered their wives had died. Even so, they hadn't retired into their shells like some of our elderly relatives. Both men seemed vigorous and it seemed to me they could go on for another million years. Their resilience had something to do with living in America, I supposed. I kept secretly hoping Father would take us all there. The grand-uncles' vitality suggested that people over there led far more colourful and healthy lives.

I could tell Father was keenly interested in all they had to say, but began to wonder how Mother would react. She loved *The Dyke*, her brothers and sisters, and especially *Oma*. 'Grandmother Anna', as Father sometimes called *Oma*, would be shattered if we left for another country.

Ate resumed, in his gentle voice, 'We've visited Yellowstone, Yosemite and the Everglades on a regular basis ever since we returned from fighting the Boche. Before the First World War we didn't have time to visit these places. They're our favourite scenic spots now. All large cities are the same, but Mother Nature always surprises. Yes, Herman, as you might know, America is bigger than Europe, and because everyone speaks the same language, more or less, people move freely and feel this great country running through their veins. Other than for the negroes and the native indians, perhaps, it's an easy place to be, with wonderful scenery, great food, and buildings going up everywhere. America hums along just like my Chevy, with great power and acceleration. You'd love the place, Herman. People there, as opposed to your narrow-minded Hollanders, assess you by your efforts and achievements and don't care about class and pretty speeches. You are what you make of yourself.'

As Ate painted the American dream, I imagined Chevrolets zooming all over America, and inside those magnificent machines, happy children eating popcorn and hugging large dogs. Ah, what a life! It seemed life there was one long holiday. Much later, I discovered that our American uncles had somewhat oversimplified their take on the country. But their homage to America was meant to compare, and indeed contrast, the vibrant ways of a new country with the sclerotic institutions and habits of old Europe.

Father absorbed this information as eagerly as drinking his *jenever*, happy to listen and to be wooed by the magical qualities of this American utopia, a mere fortnight's sailing away! He lit up another cigar and crossed his legs, a sure sign he was enjoying himself. Smoke circles drifted towards the ceiling and I thought of Winnetou sending smoke signals to his tribe, warning of nasty fur traders about to attack his people.

By the Scruff of the Neck

Hoite resumed the reins and headed in a different direction. 'Your situation, Herman, is vastly different from ours. For a start, you can fly nowadays, much quicker and far cheaper than the ships of our day. And ships today are faster and more pleasant, if you did choose to come that way. We were steerage passengers and spent as much time hanging over the railings feeding the fishes as sleeping. The food was inedible, but we knew the voyage would only last a fortnight, not like centuries ago when passengers suffered for much longer. Also, the fact you have boys will be welcomed in the States, provided they're prepared to work hard.'

Uncle Hoite's history lesson was interrupted by the noisy banter of John and Bill. When they entered the sitting room, to discover two sprightly old men in animated conversation with Father, they immediately fell silent. The two elderly men looked at the new arrivals and almost stood up at the same time, extending their hands to my brothers. I winked at Lex, as if to say, 'John and Bill ought not to be treated with such grace and deference.'

As John and Bill moved to the two empty chairs near the front window, Father did the formalities.

'Wonderful boys you have here, Herman. They look quite healthy, despite the war. Tall, too!' Hoite seemed impressed.

I held quite a different view of my elder brothers. As far as I was concerned, Jack-the-lad was shady, though admittedly good to us younger ones most of the time, while Bill was all right but a serial pest. Clearly, the ancient uncles were just being polite.

Hoite continued his glowing account of America. It became obvious to me that the American Lijcklemas struck gold by emigrating. They had established themselves well and made their families comfortable.

Mother now joined us and began to question them about household costs. The comparisons were embarrassing. The Yanks were living in the lap of luxury while we wrestled with coupons, rations, and long queues. We felt inadequate and envious: I had a sudden urge to run all the way to either Amsterdam or Rotterdam and catch the first ship to New York! Mother, despite a brave effort to impress the uncles, surrendered to their superior knowledge and worldly experience.

'Yes, Alie, I agree fish and cheese are better here, but that's about it. The food in America is cheaper and just as tasty. We eat great quantities of beef and pork. Young men like John drive their own cars and many go to college. Work is assured, especially now that we have to catch up with pre-war production. I suppose the War did at least put an end to the Depression, but Holland still hasn't recovered from either the War or the Depression. That's why it's a good time to consider moving overseas, Herman.'

The evening ended with a few *jenevers* and coffee. *We* were given orange cordial, a rare treat. The relatives took their leave and I went to bed dreaming of strange lands and adventures. My mind shut out the dreary routine of going to school and performing the domestic chores expected of us and instead focused on the offerings of a new continent so enticingly described.

Great-great-Uncles Hoite and Ate were later to remind me of Uncle Ben in *Death Of A Salesman*. It so happened that Hoite and Ate visited our home in the same year Miller's play was staged for the first time on Broadway, in 1949. But whereas Uncle Ben was dead, serving as Willy Loman's aspirational role model, Hoite and Ate were very much alive, performing a similar function for our father: of the 'Go West Young Man' variety, as popularized by Horace Greeley in 1865. For them, emigration, like the various gold rushes of the past, was equated with wealth and vast opportunities. All that was needed was a bit of courage.

Everyone eagerly waited for the order that would release us from class. It was lunchtime. Our stomachs were serenading our brains, and several boys were scraping the polished wooden floor with their shoes, like cattle pawing the earth before a stampede.

'You may go! *You* Lichtie and *you* Balkens are the last to leave, for wasting time.'

The class streamed through the door into the corridor. Ah, freedom for a while! Amid shouts of bravado to our mates, I caught up with Lex as we headed for the Beggars Lane, the only way out of Saint Aloysius to our place. As we neared the end of the lane, we were surprised to see Father standing patiently next to his bicycle. Something must have happened. We ran towards him.

'Eh, Pa, what are *you* doing here? Why aren't you at work? Is Ma sick? Is something wrong with Flozzie?' The questions tumbled out. Father never took time off, let alone to pick up his sons from school. As my mates filed past, they looked at Father, as if to say, 'Shit, what's your old man doing here?'

'No! No! Nothing's wrong. I just happened to be nearby and thought I'd meet you and give you a lift to save time.' I clambered onto the crossbar and Lex straddled the back seat. Off we went.

Enjoying the easy spinning of the wheels on the bicycle track, I watched the periphery of the Wood whiz by, then as we turned into Newportslane, Father broke the silence: 'Tell me, boys, what do you think of going to another country?'

'Whaddya mean, Pa; for holidays or something?' asked Lex.

'No, a new country, forever; for the rest of your lives. I mean emigrate to a whole new place, far from here.' Father seemed a little put out by having to broach this delicate subject. 'Mother and I have been talking about leaving Holland for quite some time. Things aren't brilliant here and I happen to know of many families applying to migrate. It isn't as easy as it sounds, but I just wanted to know what you two think of the idea.'

We weren't aware that our parents had already spoken to John and Bill about this new venture. Nor had we noticed that our parents had been going out during weeknights rather frequently of late: maybe something to do with Father's work; Mother had recently gained a part-time job in Father's business and both attended meetings and fairs promoting their goods. John was entrusted to mind us while they were gone, which we liked, since he allowed us to do what we pleased.

It turned out that Father and Mother had been attending migrant information nights. Father had caught the migration fever and managed to infect Mother, who hated to be left behind by current trends. She could be an immovable object once she had made up her mind, but Father's charm and passion percolated her resistance. Without her support, his dreams of geographical conquest would be dashed.

For reasons never made clear to me, America, Canada and New Zealand dropped off the radar. Yet why Australia, which apparently was their dreamed-of destination, I hadn't a clue. More Dutch people emigrated to Canada than elsewhere, largely because of proximity, and partly because of the close bonds forged between Ottawa and The Hague during the War. Indeed, the Dutch royal family had decamped to Ottawa during that time. Must be nice to be born royal...

Mother was aware that friends and relatives were taking wing to new destinations. Moreover, her introduction to a vast, wheat-coloured continent inhabited by laughing jackasses and hopping marsupials, seen on a scrappy film screen, appealed to her, oddly enough. Still, while she loathed water, she venerated the sun, and this new country had buckets-full of bright light. Mother may have earned the nickname 'The Star', but Father, when affectionate, called her 'my little vitamin', *mijn vitamintje*, since she swore by cod liver oil and the sun as the panacea for all ills. Vitamins A and D were the new health cures for post-war mothers. Whether the experience of the hunger winter of 1944 conditioned her health preoccupation or the oblique influence of America's famous paediatrician, Dr Spock, had anything to do with her vitamin obsession, I can't recall, but for Mother, Australia and good health became synonymous.

Father saw it differently. His projections, influenced by Hoite and Ate, were more spatial and fertile. A continent roughly the same size as America and with fewer inhabitants, however dry, conjured up the *voortrekkers*, or 'forerunners', of South Africa. The indigenous people of Australia, with their flat noses and primitive weaponry, struck him as exotic and challenging. He saw himself as a pioneer.

There must be valleys with rivers untamed, awaiting an industrious family to turn them into veritable gardens of Eden. He gathered that most Australians lived in a few large cities, but this was probably because they were either afraid of the interior or simply for convenience. With five sturdy lads Father thought he could easily cope with the outback, set up a camp near some watering hole and begin constructing a log cabin to accommodate his family.

Mr Brown, the tailor, had already suggested this virtual *El Dorado* some time before Father watched these glorious possibilities on the screen, shown at migrant promotion nights. He vaguely knew he had to find work and earn money, but his heart was with the outback and the natives. Why, his mouth-organ prowess wasn't far removed from the strange instrument called the 'didgeridoo'... If the natives could play this sublime piece of wood, so could he.

Father, more than Mother, saw the need to learn English and both enrolled in English classes. Although Father easily remembered the new words, he mangled them with his *Mokum* accent. He fought on valiantly, but his accent stood out like his beloved cigar.

Mother, however, had neither the patience nor the interest to master the strange new language and its difficult pronunciation. Dutch was phonetic, English pathetic; vowels jumped in all directions, or when uniform, lead to all kinds of meanings and therefore couldn't be trusted. For Mother, 'th' remained a hard 't', so that 'thought' became 'taught', 'taut', 'tort' or 'torte', all with entirely different meanings, and she quickly tired of this Anglo-Saxon curse.

Their aim was to get an assisted passage, largely paid for by the Australian government, since full payment for the whole family was unaffordable. How long it would take to meet the financial requirements, Lex and I never understood. The organizational side of emigration neither interested us, nor should it have. We were too young and instead were immersed in the imagined world of this other country, the voyage to be enjoyed as a spirited overture to the opera of *Australia Felix*. Lex and I took each day as it came in the lead-up to the departure. We weren't sure when it would be, since Father and Mother didn't let on, but discovered later that there were various delays and only when some other family cancelled their emigration plans did we make the shortlist.

Mother initially felt an explanation of the emigration idea would be best coming from Father. On the day he collected us from school, he had expected protest: leaving one's mates behind, closeness to family members – not least *Oma* Goudsblom – disruption to schooling, fear of sudden change, and the closing of a chapter in our lives that had been relatively comfortable. He needn't have worried. Children are addicted to the world of adventure and fanciful escapes. Lex and I made it clear straightaway that we looked forward to the idea of travelling to a foreign land: we were simply carrying on the fine and wild tradition of Old Shatterhand and Ironfist, another of May's characters.

'Which country are we moving to, Pa? America or Canada? I prefer Canada; I can join the Mounties when I grow up,' I said confidently.

'Nah, America is much better. I'd love to live with the Apaches and smoke a peace pipe with them then go buffalo hunting. What a life that would be!' Lex trotted out excitedly.

'Well! Have I got news for you! We aren't going to Canada *or* America, but to a country called Australia.' Father's announcement left us speechless. 'Yes, I know you're surprised, but Mother and I have weighed up all the reasons for going to this faraway place. Mainly it's because there aren't many people there and it's so huge it'll allow us to build a fresh future. There's so much room and timber we'll live like kings of the frontier.' Karl May had waved his magic wand over Father as well it seemed.

After a long pause, Lex was the first to respond. '*Auw-stra-li-é,* what sort of place is that?'

'I've seen it on a map at school,' I blurted out. 'It's somewhere near the bottom, not far from the South Pole. I know it's big and looks like a huge dog's head or a bit like a fat star.'

'Are there any Indians in this funny land?' asked Lex hopefully.

'I'm sorry to say no, Lex. There *are* natives but they look more like African blacks, though more primitive,' replied Father, trying to reassure him.

'Cannibals! I don't like cannibals. I don't want to go to a country full of cannibals who tear you limb from limb and put you in a pot for their evening meal. I'd rather stay in Holland,' stated Lex, pouting.

Auw-stra-li-é. What did the word mean? We knew nothing about this land. I associated America and Canada with plains, New York, Chicago, Ottawa, deciduous forests, oil wells, Laurel and Hardy. *Auw-stra-li-é* was a blank, and remained so, till Father and Mother began to sketch in the details...as they saw them from promotion nights, friends and officialdom. They also arrived home with glossy brochures. *Auwstralié* was a hot continent surrounded by lots of water and endless beaches. Despising the long cold winters in Holland, this image lifted our spirits. There must be *some* civilization, judging by a massive spanned bridge joining hills full of houses. They even had cars and boats. All this made attractive sense.

The animals, however, were most peculiar: dogs on huge legs bouncing around in grass, funny flat-nosed bears munching away in high trees, large birds scampering across dry fields, and birds with colourful feathers, far bigger than our feeble pigeons and wood-birds.

But what really grabbed Lex were the reptiles, spiders and insects: poisonous, vicious and lurking – crocodiles, snakes, ugly lizards, and horrible, biting ants. 'Do these creatures kill ya? If they're everywhere, I'm not going. I'll stay with *Oma*, if you don't mind. Uncle John'll look after me. I'm not gonna have my insides sucked out by some monster, or finish up in the guts of some crocodile.' Lex was imagining the worst.

I couldn't but agree. *Auwstralië* made the Amazon rainforest seem like an expanse of tranquility. Even Africa was safer. You *could* see tigers and lions, and a gun would do the job. Elephants might trample and trumpet all over you, too, but they were big and could be seen miles away. You just had to have your wits about you. But creatures slithering around your feet in thick grass and spiders hiding in trees ready to pounce and inflict a horrible death gave us the heebie-jeebies. This *Auwstralië* was obviously a treacherous place. No wonder so few people lived there.

What was Father suggesting! Father and Mother had clearly lost their marbles. Lex and I had definitely changed our minds. *We* weren't leaving! Flozzie, of course, didn't know what day it was and only cared about his golliwog and food, so he didn't count. John and Bill, however, did have something to say about this fearful continent.

'I don't want to leave my mates, Pa. Besides, I'm in love with Ina Karstens.[73] What kind of girls do they have in Australia? Dutch girls are the best... And I only know a few words of English. How am I going to meet Australian girls? So, no sex for *me* in that stupid country.' John felt short-changed.

Mother scolded him: 'Watch your filthy language. All you care about is girls and having a good time. When will you learn you're part of a family? You're the oldest. Show some care.'

Bill on the other hand was ecstatic. He hated Holland: his patisserie boss exploited him. He loathed school: his teachers hit and humiliated him. Jack-the-lad couldn't be entirely trusted, either, one moment supporting him and the next making fun of him; Bill was tired of the persistent rivalry. Even Mother neglected him somewhat, since she had too much on her plate.

Bill was happiest on the athletics track, helping on *Opa's* farm, visiting cattle yards around Alkmaar, or helping Uncle Piet. Farming was in his blood and farming he intended to do, and do it well. He loved the land, and he understood cows and horses. In turn, they understood him. Bill was wary of people though, and wanted to shape his own future, just as *Opa* Goudsblom had done.

As a result, *Auwstralië* loomed large in his imagination. The idea of flocks of sheep and tough cattlemen guiding herds through the scrub inspired him. He dreamt of droving and rounding up sheep, or milking thousands of cows. Right in the middle of this strange bushland he would

---

[73] Not her real name.

build an enormous farmhouse with a large vegetable garden, sheds and fences, and with a pack of well-trained dogs by his side. Bill thought this *Auwstralië* could be his Shangri-la. He believed in hard work, a simple life, plenty of land and a bit of luck. Bill couldn't wait to set sail.

Father did his best to change Lex's mind and also mine. 'You two, you've got it all wrong. Yes, there are venomous snakes and crocodiles, but only far away from houses and only in certain parts of Australia. Nothing to worry about! You'll learn to live with them, just like the natives.' Father himself didn't really know much about this strange country and relied on common sense and dangling carrots in front of his sceptical sons. 'Imagine the open spaces. You'll be able to swim every day – after school, of course. You'll have your own horse, and a gun too. Think of the adventures you'll have!'

He gradually won us over. The idea of riding a horse seemed better than driving a car: galloping in the wild towards the sun was as good as going to heaven. Certainly more exciting! As for those terrible slimy beasties, well, we'd better be on our mettle. We'd train our dogs to be on the lookout for them. The brochures showed drovers with wide-brimmed hats always accompanied by dogs. Yeah! Dogs were the answer. They could hear and smell those creatures a mile off, alerting us to any potential danger. Moreover, didn't Ironfist down a grizzly bear with one well-aimed shot? We just had to practise shooting and hope to split those snakes in half.

Uncle John wasn't at all happy, though. Whenever we visited *The Dyke,* he tried to dissuade Father from leaving. 'You've got a good job here, Herman. Why do you want to risk it by going to some godforsaken country where you may not make it. Emigration is hard, Herman.'

But Father was too consumed by his idealized prospects – and had other reasons as well. 'I tell you something, John. I'm sick and tired of the petty-mindedness and crushing officialdom in this rotten country. Yes Sir, no Sir, three bags full, Sir. You can't move without some bureaucrat breathing down your neck, poking his nose into everything. Not only that, selling is difficult. A few of my colleagues are rogues and have taken shortcuts by stealing my customers. They lie and bluster and put me down. I'm sick of it! I've had Holland up to here.' Father levelled his hand across his throat. He wasn't usually demonstrative but disgust with Holland had been welling inside him for some time.

'There are new opportunities in this country. We've got a chance to change our lives and build something new. In Australia they aren't big on ceremony, I've been told, and bosses even call you by your first name... No, John, I understand where you're coming from, but my family needs fresh air and room to move.' Then, echoing the sentiments of his great-uncles, he finished with the clincher: 'Holland's economy is stuffed anyway and we're just pedalling on the spot. I owe it to my boys to move to Australia.'

Uncle John shook his head in dismay, but realized Father couldn't be swayed. For all their differing opinions, they respected each other and knew when to change the subject.

It never occurred to us young'ns that Uncle John and Aunty Anne were so integrated into *our* family that emigration would leave a huge hole in their emotional life. It would be even more difficult for *Oma*. Her other children had either left Alkmaar entirely or moved some distance away. Uncle Piet's children had grown up too and were no longer living in Alkmaar. We only lived down the road and saw her regularly, so had become her main focus. To sever this link would hurt her badly, and Mother too. Father's family were more distant and relatively uninvolved.

The preparation for our departure seemed to take forever. Father and Mother, like most Dutch emigrants, wanted to keep their furniture, their beloved paintings – originals and copies – the kitchenware, knick-knacks, books and clothes. Apart from sentimental value, these items could be indispensable since none of us knew what to expect in *Auwstralië*. Better to be safe and bring along as much as possible.

Father ordered a large, custom-built, rectangular pinewood crate the size of a small garage. Whether the size of the crate was determined by one's bank book, the size of the family, or simply by choice, remains a mystery to me, but we regarded the crate as a little home for us when we arrived.

Some immigrants in the 1950s either lived in their sizeable wooden boxes for a while or used the timber for building. Waste not, want not, and don't forget the War. It was quite a sight to see hundreds of wooden crates stacked on the wharves in Fremantle and Melbourne, and undoubtedly the same in Sydney.

Lex and I quickly told all our mates that we were emigrating to a country called *Auwstralië*. I straightaway detected a change in our status. Johnny Red said, 'Gee, you *are* lucky! You won't have to go to school for a while and travelling on an ocean liner must be fun, just like a moveable hotel where the scenery changes all the time.' Johnny had a vivid imagination.

The whole neighbourhood was stirred up by our plans. The Browns were envious and Gus wanted to come with us, but, of course, wasn't allowed. Mr Brown advised us to take a few cows and goats, just in case. Even Jacob de Kooy was moved. 'It won't be the same without you and Lex. Dammit, who am I going to have fun with?'

For the first time, I was sorry for Jacob. We knew he had a troubled home life and found solace and camaraderie in us. Given the age gap between Jacob and his sisters, he felt like an only child and rarely received much affection from either his parents or his sisters. It was as if

The Dyke 1951. Pam, Aunty Anne, Henri, Aunty Gré, Will, Father, John, Mother, *Oma*, Loes, Bill, Frank, Uncle John, Lex.

he were a nuisance to them. He was always on the street, forgotten by his family, who were still recovering from the shame inflicted on them at the end of the War. As former collaborators, they were ostracized and still talked about around the dinner table. The de Kooys were strange people...

The finer points of our departure were left to our parents. 'We have to go to Amsterdam for a medical check-up,' said Father. 'The migration authorities don't want disease-ridden weaklings coming to Australia.'

We were told to disrobe in a cold room annexed to some hideous hospital in Amsterdam. Cream, green and brown were the standard hospital colours; it seemed as if the architects had never seen a rainbow or experienced the birth of spring.

There were others waiting their turn to be x-rayed and prodded. We were almost being treated like cattle, but Lex and I laughed through chattering teeth as we stepped behind a leaden shield meant to protect us from radiation. Later, when studying our stick-like bones, we thought it hilarious. It felt odd to see our skeletons on a smoky screen, the brothers making up stories about strange objects dancing around my thorax.

'Look... Look, John, Herrie's swallowed electric wire!' shouted Bill, enjoying himself.

'No! No! That isn't wire. It's fish bones,' insisted John, grinning.

'You're all wrong. Look at his guts; full of rubber bands!' yelled Lex.

Father looked on, bemused, although he loved all this idiocy. Mother was holding Flozzie, who kept reaching out to an attractive nurse sauntering past. I, however, wasn't amused. Mortality was just around the corner: take away the flesh and all that was left was a pile of bones; which reminded me of the skeleton in the Alkmaar Wood, except that he or she was three-dimensional and therefore far more frightening.

The nurses ignored our loud exclamations, well accustomed to silly families crashing through their corridors; tuberculosis, pneumonia and other respiratory illnesses were still common in the 1950s, legacies of the War, hence the frequent use of x-rays. A percentage of people, it was claimed, developed cancer because of over-exposure to radiation, but our family knew nothing about these dangers.

For some reason, we visited the hospital several times, but passed all the mysterious tests dreamt up by the doctors and bureaucrats. As youngsters, these shenanigans were taken with a grain of salt. I simply assumed they formed the irritating minutiae of emigration, and perhaps the lives of refugees too. It didn't bother us, as long as there was no pain and we had plenty of laughs. Anyway, you just did what you were told; complaints never arose. Besides, no school on those days!

*

By the Scruff of the Neck

Our departure date had been set for the seventeenth of June 1952. Everything was settled, our household goods sent ahead in our pine crate. We would stay at *The Dyke* for the final week, where Lex and I were to be given *Oma*'s double bed, off the living room.

School suddenly ceased to be of any great importance. I knew, however, that I needed to learn a new language and my curiosity was aroused, so I sought to take this challenge in my stride. In fact, I was looking forward to learning English. After all, it was the language spoken by our liberators.

Even though I understood only about half a dozen words in English, I considered Dutch rather insipid by comparison. By adulthood I had changed my mind and reverted, having found English rather too elastic, and capable of meaning all things to all men. Dutch resurfaced as more elemental and gutsy, notwithstanding its pompous tendency to borrow heavily from English.

The relief after having sat the final examinations was wonderful and I looked forward to having no further school demands, particularly now that we were leaving for overseas. Summer holidays weren't far away now, either, and although discipline was still maintained, it was rarely applied. Even Mr Rieu became a little casual and said, 'Yes, boys, we are about to lose another scholar to a foreign country. Soon there won't be anyone left in Holland.'

I couldn't concentrate and adopted a devil-may-care attitude towards lessons. As far as I was concerned, the authorities could jump. Instead, I tried to imagine the excitement of sailing on an ocean liner, and to visualize this great new country, thousands of times bigger than Holland. Gosh, it must be huge! I wondered what *Auwstraliers* looked like; a bit like Americans, I supposed. Would I make new friends, not knowing the language? I was used to my classmates and felt comfortable with them, and even thought the girls in my class were all right. But Australian boys and girls might be different...more difficult. Did Australians play soccer, or some other code? I wasn't sure. Time would tell.

Auwstralié took on new connotations: a vast, flat country, unimpeded by manmade structures, stretching out as far as the eye could see. A stupendous natural setting for new activities, with exotic odours; trees and flowers of different shape, hue and smell; undulating hills, and weird animals. It had to have a bigger sun, surely! Why? Because it was closer to the equator, or so my limited geographical knowledge led me to believe. Therefore the sun must also be brighter. A bigger and brighter sun!

*

Just before we left, Father and Mother were told by some fool that there were no dentists in Australia, or at any rate, inferior ones. Their teeth weren't healthy, so they decided to kill two birds with one comprehensive extraction. Despite being only in their early forties, they both left the dental surgery with arrangements made for pairs of glittering new choppers. Later, on one of Father's rounds, he chatted up a farmer's attractive wife as they stood talking in her little shop – some farmers kept a grocery shop to supplement their income. Unfortunately, he became rather excited and accidentally coughed his upper denture out onto the counter. What a conversation stopper! Any romantic progress came to an abrupt halt. Father went red and the wife giggled awkwardly. He quickly retrieved his clacker and turned tail.

'I have never been so embarrassed in my life!' he told us, while we sat around the dinner table.

Mother gave him a contemptuous stare. 'Serves you right, flirting with that woman.'

Because of the severe winters in Holland, farmers often constructed a small bedroom the size of a double bed that was totally enclosed, with a tiny window, high up, being the only source of light. A double door formed the entrance and, when closed, served as part of the living room wall. Our little room at *The Dyke*, with its wooden walls painted grey, had a few pictures of rustic themes on its walls, which kept us company. We were used to this room; we had slept there many times, even during summer, when the heat was oppressive. Just as we were about to leave Holland, it was already warming up.

In winter, whenever we stayed at the farm, Aunty Anne took us to the back of the farmhouse, where she inflicted a brutal cleansing in a large tub filled with near-boiling water. The sweet milky smell of the housed cattle mingled with the steam. After Aunty Anne finished rubbing us down with a coarse towel, our skin gleamed and a sense of wellbeing enveloped us. We laughed at the cows shitting unselfconsciously onto the concrete floor.

'Would you like some hot poo with your dinner?' I asked Lex.

'Of course. I could mash it up with me spuds. How delicious!'

Aunty Anne warned us to behave ourselves, or else! She could be quite menacing, so we shut up.

This beloved ritual would now come to an end. We didn't realize this at the time, being too easily distracted by the moment, but *she* did.

*

By the Scruff of the Neck

Early on the morning of the seventeenth, Lex and I put on our khaki uniforms, khaki being fashionable, and waited for a large black car to arrive. The familiar rank, yet agreeable, aroma wafted from the back of the farmhouse as I opened the back door for the last time. *Oma* was already stoking the stove, as it was chilly this particular morning. I could hear Father and Mother talking quietly in their bedroom. John and Bill were still asleep, recovering from their late evening's farewells. Flozzie, a little older now, was singing to himself. I looked around the friendly living room, studying the furnishings, the etchings, the bric-a-brac, and realized my first nine years in Holland were almost over. A fleeting sadness, even fear, about embarking upon an opaque future overcame me. I could feel but not articulate the sudden dread of leaving, a sense of free-fall, the abrupt estrangement of everything familiar. The paintings on the wall, the red-flowered rug, the copper ornaments, the Delft-blue ceramics, photographs of *Oma*'s sisters, of her own children, and of some I wasn't sure about; all had shed their intimacy. They now belonged to the past: stiff, frozen, foreign, as if everyone in the photos had died, even though most were still very much alive.

Even the large sepia photo of *Opa* seemed different. He had been dead these past five years, and although he and *Oma* were contemporaries of Queen Wilhelmina, *Opa* appeared to belong to a previous century, the century of Queens Victoria and Emma.[74] Yet, as I glanced towards the corner window facing the driveway and inhaled the remnants of last night's cigarette and cigar smoke, I saw *Opa* sitting there. I heard his voice and saw his moustache twitch as his brother took him to task over some matter of the day.

The feeling of having to let go was gradually overtaken by the prospect of the next few days. A boy of nine has too much energy, too many dreams of the future, to reflect morbidly on a brief past. The younger the person, the easier it is to adapt!

Father and Mother were more measured. They had to think about organizing their sons and having all the right papers. They went through tedious lists and re-examined the second-hand suitcases for the umpteenth time. *Their* memories had deeper roots and their allegiances were stronger. Father was quiet and purposeful, while Mother prepared us for our journey amid tears and promises. We were used to her teary manner and didn't bother to unearth her true emotions, yet her mood must have been dark and heavy. Our departure, like so many others in Europe, was heart-rending for relatives and friends alike. The War had cast a long shadow over the future, emigration being but one consequence.

---

[74] Queen Emma of the Netherlands, 1858–1934.

Emigration means dramatic change. *The Dyke*, Alkmaar, 1952. Father, Mother, Frank, John, Henri, Bill and Lex.

Filled to the brim with our belongings and the younger boys, the sleek black limousine slowly drove away along the dirt driveway. Mother stayed with us, while Jo Baaren-Keyser had offered to drive Father and the older boys to Amsterdam in his car.

I still see my old, gummy *Oma* dressed in black, her shoulders covered with a beige lace shawl, lurching forward, tears running down her wrinkled cheeks, hands raised as if wanting to pull us back to *The Dyke*. She chased us on her bowed legs but couldn't keep up. *Oma*, the frail kindly matriarch, was about to lose a large chunk of her life. We would never see her again.

I still imagine her stretching her aching back as she makes her way to the tiny kitchen. Rooted in the soil, she spoke the local West Friesian dialect and doted on her large brood. For her, a village ten kilometres away was foreign territory, let alone a strange continent on the other side of the globe. Born in 1879, she straddled the old and the new in scientific discovery, but, like so many others, the anguish of losing family would always remain. Emigration, by its very nature, means dramatic change for all involved, and for *Oma*, it was difficult to comprehend and to accept. At least she had Uncle John and Aunty Anne to soften the blow, although they themselves were stung by our departure.

Mouldy streets, a final nod to Central Station, a furtive glance at Amsterdam's rundown waterfront and lonely storage sheds. Lex and I were silent as we fed off the scenery, heading towards our destination. I gazed up at the gantries supporting cranes that rose high over the shipments like giant vultures. Lex cried, 'Look how high they are! Will the cable snap? Who drives those machines?'

We weren't yet aware of how small our world in Alkmaar had been. Our lives had revolved around our neighbourhood, school, church, and *The Dyke*. We rarely visited the Alkmaar town centre or any other city, or even went shopping in the modern sense: we were too skint. Our daily lives, while happy enough, were curtailed by the aftershocks of the War: austerity, bleakness and routine. We took the certainties of Alkmaar for granted, such as the Wood, the Cheese Market, the Deerpark and the imposing late-Gothic church of Saint Lawrence. Limited contact with outsiders meant our provincial life resembled Swift's Lilliput. Now, emigration would put us in touch with Gulliver. Suddenly the world had become a whole lot bigger, and for the first time, we were hurled into its vastness. We didn't know what to expect, but excitement was guaranteed.

Our ship was moored at the west wharf. Amsterdam and Rotterdam, huge ports – the latter, the largest in Europe – breathed naval history. Amsterdam had carried the East and West Indies trade for centuries and its quays were old and ramshackle, the War having prevented renovations. The long quayside brought to mind the adventures of seafarers I had read about in popular books of the time. I wondered how many men-o'-war and merchantmen had anchored there. Dutch clippers, herring boats, polar-explorers, all would have left from these quays, and from the historic ports dotted around the Zuider Zee. Nowadays, the docks have long since been modernized to accommodate the bulky passenger liners and long container ships, which now bear the names of continents and former colonies. Even Australia acquired a berth: The Australia Dock.

In my enthusiasm to take in the view, I briefly mounted a bollard and surveyed the scene, skimming over the heads of the throng standing along the quay. I imagined the behemoths of the seventeenth century lying at anchor, three or four deep, the scalloped sails lowered by brave sailors dangling precariously from topgallant masts during a hurricane; as well as the sturdy lookout, lurching from left to right on the masthead during a storm, scanning the horizon for possible signs of danger. On other days, when calm had returned, this same lookout might be on the alert for whales.

For a young boy to step from a car and catch his first glimpse of an ocean liner, previously seen only in movies and postcards, was mind-numbingly impressive. It was mid-afternoon and the sun smiled kindly. A festive air had set in and the ugliness of the harbour was alleviated by a brass band in black and red attire, belting out folk tunes to give us a jolly good send-off.

The *Fairsea*, buttressed by cocky tugboats, bobbed gently alongside. Behind her lay a dark liner called the *Orontes*. She had sailed from England and like the *Fairsea* awaited passengers for either Australia or America. Reminiscent of contented cows, the moored liners waited patiently, piddling dirty water into the harbour, while cranky seagulls scooped up vegetable dross tossed from the orlop deck.

I scanned the length of the *Fairsea* and counted fourteen lifeboats, then doubled them, since presumably it would be the same for the other side. The masts lent a certain grandeur and elegance to the ship. The many portholes suggested cabins, but as I later discovered, there *were* no cabins, just large dormitories with bunks. It wasn't a huge ship but it was the largest I had seen, till much later, when I sailed on bigger vessels, including the *Australis,* another migrant ship.

However, with emigration abuzz around the globe, the sight of ocean liners became common during the 1950s. Today we have surrendered to jumbo jets; ships, in my opinion, are more varied and interesting, albeit considerably slower. While aeroplanes enclose, ships open up, especially near land, and steer their course through many varied and fascinating geographical and climatic features.

The *Fairsea* bobbed gently. Amsterdam, 1952

'That black ship is bigger than ours,' said Lex, somewhat proprietarily. At this stage we hadn't yet boarded the *Fairsea*, but Lex had already adopted the ship as ours. I did the same.

'Maybe so, but I reckon ours is more streamlined and has better-shaped anchors. I prefer our hull to that filthy black one, and our single funnel, with its 'V for Victory' sign, to their old-fashioned two. Ours looks really neat, don't you think?' The *Orontes* looks dirty and rusty, so much older and decrepit, I thought smugly.

The quayside was thrumming with activity. The wharfies responsible for preparing the huge ship for its next trip ignored the bustle of curious visitors and were busy off-loading supplies through a large, open metal door in the middle of the hull. Some were testing the security of the gangway. Yelling to each other to make themselves heard, their voices competed with those of the boisterous crowd spread out along the quay. Most of the men had a cigarette dangling from the corner of their mouth.

The noise and commotion overtook our worries as we boarded the rickety gangway. I could smell the water. Looking down over the side then along the ship, I suddenly felt afraid and hesitated momentarily before glancing back at the crowd, some of whom were waving goodbye, others showing off by mouthing jokes or gratuitous advice. Our family and friends stood in a cluster towards the back. Uncle Louis and Uncle John were in earnest discussion, while Jo Baaren-Keyser puffed on his cigar, staring dolefully at us, as if to say, 'It was nice knowing you; I wonderrr how you'll all finish up?' He stood out in his dun raincoat with no rain in sight. His large head tilted back, he shouted something funny to Father, who was the last of our family to step onto the gangway. Jo's wife, Marie, daintily waved her handkerchief, while Aunty Anne and Aunty Joanne looked rather sombre. Aunty Gré blew her nose and leaned against the shoulder of her son Will, who wore a black cassock, still a few years away from completing his studies for the priesthood. He kept taking photos and occasionally spoke to his father, Uncle Wim, who stood unmoved, seemingly unimpressed by all the kerfuffle.

I wondered when we would see them again. Their familiarity had been a constant in our lives. Holland, being small, lent itself to regular visits. Now, they were soon to become strangers, receding eerily into the mists of time. By moving into an unknown future we were the *voortrekkers*; we, or rather, Father and Mother, were the risk-takers: it could all go pear-shaped. But this never occurred to us as children, since we had implicit faith in our parents.

Once onboard, we left the discovery of our sleeping quarters till later. I split from my family and found myself standing next to a girl of my own age, leaning over the rails. She was waving furiously to the folks below.

'Are you happy to be leaving Holland?' I asked her.

By the Scruff of the Neck

She looked at me in disgust, her red eyes clearly suggesting otherwise. Feeling a bit foolish, I added, 'It's hard to leave your friends, but you'll soon make new ones and you still have your parents.'

I was chuffed when her sad face softened and she almost smiled. 'I suppose so,' she said quietly, 'but I don't know whether I can live happily without my girlfriends. They are so important to me.'

'Write to them. Send them postcards. That way you'll keep in touch and maybe one day they can come over and visit you.' This also seemed to make her a little happier.

By now, the wharfies had completed the loading on and off and were waiting for further instructions from their supervisor. Prior to departure visitors were usually allowed onboard to take a squiz at the ship from the inside. For some unknown reason, though, this time, they weren't. Perhaps the ship was behind schedule...

Once the last passengers had boarded, the gangway was removed and the wharfies resumed their usual tasks. The thick hawsers were lifted from the bollards and I could hear the creaking of the rusty capstans drawing up the ropes, almost like Lex slurping his noodles. The eye-spliced endings of the ropes thudded on the oily seawater before being hauled in, dripping wet – or perhaps shedding tears for the sad occasion. The umbilical cord had been severed. We had become an island.

I suddenly felt trapped and hoped the ship was strong enough to withstand the gales and mountainous seas Father had forewarned us about. On the other hand, I knew there was nothing I could do. I noticed that the girl I had spoken to earlier held her father's hand and appeared more at ease, so made a conscious effort to enjoy myself.

The frantic waving and shouting of the crowd was interrupted by the joyous toot of a tugboat, heralding action, and then, as if to obliterate the sound of the valiant band, the horn of our ship burst forth three times. The tugboats attacked the hull like bull terriers, two pulling and one pushing at the back. I soon saw the gap widen between the pier and us. We were moving! The tugboats flexed their muscles and the *Fairsea* reversed into the channel that led to the North Sea Canal, which in turn finished up in the IJ,[75] the large, enclosed pond that served as the water epicentre of Amsterdam.

It almost seemed as if we were sailing backwards. The seagulls floating on the wind emitted plaintive farewells, almost as if wishing us an ominous journey. Then, at a suitable point, the ship rotated until the bow drew parallel with the pier, now dotted with tiny people. The colossus began to grumble. It had woken up and lumbered into life, the engines beginning to tremble and the ship to creak and strain. The iron railings, the expansive steel hull, vibrated as if kick-started by an electric

---

[75] The IJ is the lake forming Amsterdam's waterfront. The word is derived from the West Friesian word *ie*, meaning stream or little river.

current. The funnel exhaled smoke from her diesels and we were finally on our way. With a final derisive hoot, the *Fairsea* slid forward into a comfortable speed to enter the North Sea Canal, heading westwards and towards IJmuiden, the 'mouth of the IJ', and the town at the end of the canal, our last link with Holland.

Starboard faced Alkmaar some distance further north, but thoughts of my beloved hometown were temporarily superseded by the romance of this new ship. I followed the other passengers to the taffrail to bid a final adieu to those on shore. As the afternoon sun hung low in a patchy sky, I had a fine view of the green fields safe behind their dykes, although lying below sea level. I was determined to stay near the front of the upper deck, not only to welcome the North Sea but also to experience the exhilaration of sailing on a boat in such a grand manner. High up, with a tolerable breeze and a wide view in front of me, I imagined myself to be an admiral in the Dutch navy orchestrating his fleet for the very first time

Nevertheless, I was getting hungry, but knew dinnertime hadn't quite yet arrived. I didn't have a clue where the others were, nor cared. The ship gliding through the thirty-kilometre canal seemed like Moses parting the Red Sea. To my right, the steel works, belching smoke, appeared somehow surreal in the flat, marshy landscape. To my left were lush fields inhabited by fat Friesian cows and farmhouses; in the distance, a dapper windmill, a feature so typical and unsurprising that I merely noted it. It would be a long time before sighting one again.

Because of the flatness of the land and the height of the *Fairsea,* we seemed to be hovering like a low-flying aeroplane. Then, my attention reverted to the front of the ship and I couldn't keep my eyes off the prow, slicing through the water. I wanted to watch the mechanics of the giant sluices, too. Once we entered the open sea, with no land in sight, I would go below deck for the first time to find my parents and have a bite to eat.

Most of the passengers had already gone inside, no doubt to check their sleeping quarters, the dining room, and the recreation facilities. I wanted to call out to them, 'Why are you going inside, when there's so much to see out here in the open?' Their retreat made me feel special and resolute. The convergence of nature and the engineering feats of man were spectacular, and I sensed this harmony in my own, personal way. Here I was, a nine-year-old boy in awe of the elements and man's cleverness.

The canal was wide enough to allow traffic both ways, which was essential, of course. Fishing trawlers; huge freight ships; long, flat barges; and pleasure craft surged happily along to their destinations. The coloured vessels of differing shapes and sizes, with their proud flags flapping cockily in the light breeze, enlivened the canal. The occasional seagull swooped by, squawking its approval.

By the Scruff of the Neck

Cyclists raced the boats and a few 'buzzers' – motorized bikes – even managed to go faster, while cars easily overtook us. Heavy lorries thundered by in either direction, transporting goodness knows what. Holland was such a busy little country, it all seemed a bit of a contest. The sheer majesty of our ocean liner, however, outshone all the other modes of transport. While the captain may have been in charge, I considered myself a most fortunate boy to be standing on the deck without a care in the world. What a sight! This new adventure was to last five weeks, a very long time for a young lad. This was better than anything I had ever experienced, save perhaps for that unforgettable fleshly encounter with Liesbet, only a few months earlier.

The ship slowed as we approached the giant locks, which at one time were the largest in the world. Despite IJmuiden being a young city, only coming into existence with the construction of the North Sea Canal between 1865 and 1876, its strategic importance to the Dutch and the Germans during the War meant the town had been heavily bombed by the Allies. What is not so well known is that like the Suez Canal built a few years earlier, and the Panama Canal somewhat later, the North Sea Canal was built under terrible conditions. The workers lived in straw huts, were paid dirt wages by the English company used for its construction, and many succumbed to disease and alcohol abuse. Years later, upon my learning this, it all sounded very familiar. To have passed through these great man-made canals dug by cheap or conscripted labour gave me at least some small idea of the woes involved. 'Progress' always seems to come at a price, I being the pampered beneficiary.

Waiting for the docks to change water levels prompted the passengers to re-emerge and the deck was soon crowded again. But I wasn't interested in the people. I stood on the extreme end of the upper deck and had a box seat view of our grand procession. The ship marked time and waited until the water level was the same as the ocean on the other side and we then moved forward. The giant steel gates, black and rusty, opened and shut at a snail's pace, yet given the amount of water to be hefted around, they were remarkably efficient.

As we waited for the locks to do their work, I spotted Jo Baaren-Keyser and my Heemstede relatives standing on the embankment, waving to us for the very last time. What a surprise! They must have known about the hold-up at the locks. I waved to them and hoped Father and Mother were nearby to witness this final goodwill gesture. Then the ship moved forward again and soon the friends and family faded, perhaps forever.

Once the locks had been crossed, the crowd went inside, but I and a few other boys and girls stayed, staring expectantly in front of us at an endless dark green sea. Ah, at last the open sea, linked to every corner of the world! After half an hour or so, I went to the rear of the upper deck for one last look at the country of my birth. It took some time for the coastline to disappear – that low thin line behind which I had been so happy and so well looked after by my parents, family, and trusty neighbours. The pangs of regret didn't last though, as the ship began to ride the waves. Although my stomach remained unaffected, my appetite wasn't. Must be the sea air... The boundless seascape eventually made me feel lonely and insignificant, too, so, after quite some time, once I'd had my fill of sea air, I decided to go below deck.

'Where have you been?' asked Lex. 'Ma's been looking for you. We haven't started dinner yet, thank goodness. You're just in time. I know where we're sleeping. I'll take you there after the grub.' Lex was rather bumptious because he had already explored most of the ship below deck.

The thrill of exploring all the nooks and crannies of a ship is a bit like exploring a museum, except you're always conscious of the ship's movement, as well as the ubiquitous water pipes and electrical wires, all coated in thick cream paint, snaking around decks, passageways, dormitories and urinals. As it turned out, the *Fairsea* was rather rudimentary, but we weren't to know otherwise.

I followed Lex into the dining room. Long tables, each covered by a clean, starched tablecloth, were set up to run all the way to the other side of the room. Cursively written menus, which, together with the ship's news, were printed daily, had been placed near the cutlery.

'Shit, I never expected the royal treatment,' muttered Lex.

The waiters were Italian and we, not being used to Italian cuisine and service, were a little taken aback by their lavish hospitality and *savoir-faire*. They spoke a mixture of bad English and Italian.

Here I remind the reader of our primitive social habits, in the spirit of Steen's household. Good table manners had completely passed us by, but we were willing to learn, since none of us wanted to make fools of ourselves. Like acting in a new play, we closely followed the movements of our more sophisticated elders. Some of the passengers even prayed before lifting a spoon. It seemed out of place, but I, being religious, thought this effort brave and admirable.

'Excuse me, little boy, could you please pass me the salt and pepper?' a grey-bearded gentleman asked in a friendly way. At home, we either demanded, yelled, or reached across the dinner table. This was now absolutely *verboten*.

'Er, waiter, where is the butter, please?' an attractive blonde woman asked, making a scraping gesture.

The polite request came as a revelation to Lex and Bill, so used to screaming at one another with sarcasm or threats: 'Hey, dickhead, pass's the butter... If you take *one* more of my spuds, I'll ram this fork down yer throat!... Take your time, I'm only *starving* to death.'

By the Scruff of the Neck

As I studied the courteous give and take of my fellow passengers, it was obvious that in teaching proper table manners, Father and Mother had been seriously deficient. However, at home, if we became too boorish even for our parents, Father, without stopping the flow of his conversation, would simply say, 'Would you like me to put your finger in the boiling gravy?' or, 'When's the last time you had a hot spoon against your cheek?' These 'witty' threats were enough to make us behave. In this public setting, however, we needed to be very watchful of errant behaviour.

The immediate problem now, though, was one of comprehension. Our delightful waiters couldn't speak Dutch, so improvisation was inevitable. Pointing to condiments, making shaking gestures to suggest the need for salt and pepper, or the lifting of glasses or cups to request a fill-up, all made up the sign language of the migrant.

Father, meanwhile, was in great spirits, cracking jokes, while Mother exercised her affectations by talking with some chap about her past, full of self-importance and exaggerating somewhat.

'Oh yes, when I was working at the 'Unie'…Unilever, that is…I told my girls to treat each customer with the utmost respect. Being in charge was quite a responsibility, you know.'

It was enough to make John and Bill choke on their pasta, but Lex and I were too busy eating, and stirring Flozzie, to notice Mother's conceit.

A bald, portly waiter was assigned to us. He was quick and attentive and always smiling. '*Buona sera signore e signori*,' he said to the adults, as he waited for them to be seated.

For some reason he took a shine to us. We were fair and full of life, which appealed to his Mediterranean nature. He exchanged some words with his colleagues then turned to us and said jovially, '*Benvenuti cari ragazzi, vi auguro buon appetito,* very gooda boys.' This was his standard greeting – welcome and hope you enjoy your meal.

Strange to say, it was Jack-the-lad who exhibited exemplary manners. Our family, being Neanderthal, clearly couldn't be the source of his accomplishments. It seemed that he had learnt his graces elsewhere. But where? It couldn't be *The Dyke*, even though Aunty Anne had tried to raise standards, with little success. Possibly Uncle Louis and Aunty Joanne had taught him the basics; he often stayed with them and they insisted on proper manners. But as we observed Jack-the-lad's studied politeness, it suddenly occurred to me: *Of course, his girlfriends!*

To illustrate this discovery, a few months prior to our departure, I, as Jack-the-lad's cute little brother, was invited to the upper-crust household of his latest flame, Ina Karstens, and soon discovered our family's social habits did indeed originate in the Dark Ages. The Karstens family spoke ever so politely to one another and arranged the dinner table in the same way as on board this ship; that is to say, working the cutlery from the outside in, beginning with the soup spoon.

I nearly creamed my underwear when, in response to his mother's inquiry concerning the quality of the meal, one of Ina's brothers declared, 'Mother, this isn't just delicious, but over-delicious.' I had never heard this superlative before and from then on we all invoked it ironically whenever Mother excelled herself, which, however, was rarely.

If nothing else, John had mastered etiquette to an enviable degree. He knew on which side his bread was buttered and always tried to impress the ladies. One pertinent anecdote begs to be told. On the same day as I was introduced to high society at the Karstens', Jack-the-lad took Ina and me to the beach in his battered Volkswagen. All the brothers are able to swim, except for John, who, like Mother, also disliked water; but naturally he had to be macho in front of Ina.

When I dived into the feeble ripples, Jack-the-lad took me to task over my dismal execution. With one eye on Ina and the other on the shallow, placid water, he sought to demonstrate how to do it properly. 'This is how a dive should be done,' he said bombastically. Ina sniggered politely because the belly-whacker that followed was loud enough to be heard across the English Channel.

I was about to shout, 'What a pathetic effort!', but managed to restrain myself, acutely aware of Jack-the-lad's howler in front of the love of his life. Despite a red-raw streak across his torso, he composed himself and manfully strode up the beach as if nothing had happened. Needless to say, I spilt the beans around the dinner table. It was a roaring story on which we have feasted for decades, although John always looked daggers at me whenever the subject came up and vowed never to take me *anywhere*, ever again!

To return to the *Fairsea*, because we were allocated seats, it took rather a long time for everyone to be served. The headwaiter served up the soup or dish and the passenger nearest him passed the bowl or plate along to the end of the table. One day, the man doing the passing had had enough and protested indignantly: 'I keep passing on, I keep passing on, and I can't get a decent feed myself!' The waiters stopped, milled around the headwaiter and began an animated discussion, hands flying everywhere, smacking foreheads in amazement and assailing us with a torrent of Italian. We all stared at them in astonishment. From then on, with the aim of being more equitable, the headwaiter ordered his underlings to vary the distribution from either end of the table. Such sensitivity was appreciated by the adults, if not by the children, who were still determined to get in first.

We rarely saw our parents throughout the day. Mother's self-promotion didn't go unnoticed by the captain and she was often invited to sit at his table. From his point of view, Mother was an attractive and sociable guest. Despite the language barrier, she had a knack of making herself understood and also of ingratiating herself. Father, on the other hand, was more interested in playing cards and smoking his cigars.

I soon got to know the different decks, hideaways and forbidden areas; our new home for the next five weeks offered a treasure trove of surprises. So much to see, so much to do...and so much to avoid, as I found out in due time, like seasickness and bad food. Luckily, Lex and I were hardly ever seasick; maybe one or two days at the most. Seasickness was for others, especially for older people only used to land. Mother and Father did suffer from *mal de mer*, and John suffered from toothache, but had to manage as best he could because there was no dentist onboard. Bill also got seasick, as well as succumbing to a fever, which confined him to bed for days.

Lex and I were like youngsters let loose in a lolly shop. The greatest thrill came from the ship's height. Vantage points could be changed at will, to look down on the ocean, other decks, people and, when in port, on the myriad activities around a harbour. The occasional bouts of solitude, while staring at endless waves crashing their white combs against the hull, was easily compensated for by entertainment onboard or studying the extraordinary effects of the weather. The restless ocean is never the same and its relentless wooooosh is its way of conversing with us, to let us know there are secrets below rarely divulged from within its vast green belly.

There was another family, the Kogers, who had three boys about the same age as we younger ones, and their time, like ours, was largely spent on deck. They were already known to our parents and also came from Alkmaar. We became close friends and despite having pursued different careers, are still in touch, more than sixty years later.

Too excited and distracted by my new surroundings, I couldn't get to sleep easily on the first night, but must have done eventually as the next day arrived quickly. Our open quarters, as I remember, consisted of triple-tiered bunks in rows of four. Some of the boys kept whispering but were quickly told to shut up, which they did. It was rather crowded, although that didn't bother *us*, so used to sharing beds and having one's privacy invaded. The sheets were changed once a week, the acrid smell of bleach lingering for days, and the grey woollen blankets were dispensed with once we reached hotter climes. I can't recall much animosity among the lads who shared our open room. Pillow fights were a regular feature, until, at a set time, the lights went off. Before long, weariness and an unstated rule not to disturb anyone, meant easy sleeping. Not much different from boarding school, I suppose... Bunks were for sleeping not malingering, except when one was forced to remain there due to illness. Meanwhile, Flozzie kept a close watch on Mother and shared her sleeping quarters; the sexes were separated except for the very young. Father remained with the older boys. My bunk was comfortable enough and felt protective in its design, and after a deep sleep, I awoke and made for the nearest deck, past the lifeboats and davits. Despite a veil of mist, I could make out the white cliffs of Dover. The chalky bluffs unlocked my memory, releasing all that I associated with England: beefeaters, cars, castles, football...and the War.

England was my first foreign country. The insularity of my little Holland saw other countries as alien and even a little hostile. The *Fairsea* drew closer, seagulls yammering and swirling, and then, as if wanting to keep a safe distance, the ship veered away and sailed south. We kept gazing at the spectral headlands, as if seeing the planet Venus close up for the very first time.

On the third day we entered the Bay of Biscay, which for me became the Bay of Biscuits. It was renowned for its unruly weather and we were told that dry biscuits were the ideal antidotes to seasickness. However, it being summer, or perhaps because the winds couldn't be bothered, nothing much happened there.

It wasn't until we passed through the Strait of Gibraltar that the Mediterranean decided to put on a show. I had heard about the Pillars of Hercules from Father but was disappointed by the Gibraltar promontory; I had expected it to be higher and couldn't make out Monte Hacho on the other side, the northern coast of Africa. Still, sailing so close to the famous Rock, arid and craggy, introduced me to a geological feature quite different from flat Holland. My new sense of space marvelled at this famous landmark.

'It makes the Cathill look puny,' I said to Lex.

'It sure does!' he replied. 'I'd love to climb that rock. Imagine the view!' Always looking for a challenge, Lex deemed the Rock worthy of the attempt.

As we entered the ancient waters of the Mediterranean, encircled by so many different countries, I recalled that this hallowed sea had given birth to the Greek and Roman civilizations, as told in the simple but telling words of Mr de Rieu: 'Children,' he said in his quiet way, 'if it weren't for the ancient Greeks, you may well not have been here, for they were the inventors of modern medicine. We have so many cures for illness today and it all began with them.' While perhaps a rather grand sweep, it nonetheless made us listen.

My historical reflections were quickly abandoned when the weather turned. Dark, brooding clouds swept towards us from the southeast, blackening the sky. The air was warm, so to see the clouds being chased by rumbling thunderstorms was both unexpected and fascinating. I went inside to visit one of the toilets nearby, intending to race back to the foredeck to study this change in the elements. As the arc of my urine hit the porcelain, my feet began to shift, and so, unfortunately, did the trajectory. My head caught the swell and I began to feel woozy, but managed to make my way back and catch up with Lex. 'I think the boat's rolling,' he called out, as I reached for the security of a nearby storage box.

A large man stood in the middle of the deck, enjoying the weather. I decided to join him. 'Isn't this wonderful!' I shouted to him.

'Yes, my little friend, but this is only the beginning. Wait till the storm grabs hold of the waves properly... You won't be standing here much longer.'

He was right. Lex and I moved against the swell, the steel floor beneath our feet beginning to creak, and we knew we were in for a rough spell. It wasn't at all like being on a roller coaster or carnival ride, where you could get off after a set time: once a ship decides to roll, or worse still, pitch, you're in its grip and have to go along regardless.

We were a long way out of the narrow strait by this time and the sight of land was fast diminishing. The sea was acting like a boxer limbering up and the *Fairsea* became its reluctant sparring partner. We enjoyed the rolling for a while, but when it began to rain, the ship decided to protest by moving every-which-way.

'I'm going inside. See you later!' shouted Lex.

I decided to remain a little longer, but a heavy sensation welled up inside me, as if having overeaten. The big man tipped his head to bid me farewell and he too disappeared. I was the only person left: self-flagellation to the point of foolhardiness maybe, yet I was enjoying this eruption of the elements. The light rain didn't bother me. I staggered my way to the handrails to have a closer look at the angry water rearing up and crashing over the sides then running along the grooves lining the edges of the deck and disappearing down drainage holes placed at intervals. When I looked up at the funnel, I saw the smoke streaking backwards. The gale made the wire rigging sing, and I shuffled further forward towards the bow. The huge waves rose and fell majestically, breaking loudly against the hull, the swells larger than a football pitch. I imagined myself falling overboard, a mere pink speck swallowed up by the surging water, while the waves marched on like a well-drilled regiment.

I couldn't keep my eyes off the white-green soup below, and as I leant further out, someone grabbed me from behind. I tightened my grip on the rails and slowly turned around. It was one of the crew, who screamed at me in Italian: '*Che ragazzo sciocco, sei troppo vicino all'acqua. Un passo indietro, un passo indietro!*'[76] I hadn't a clue what he was on about but gathered he didn't want me so close to the water. I held his hand as he dragged me away from the rails and ushered me to a safer area between some storage boxes. His stern demeanour then changed into an understanding smile and he kept rattling away in Italian.

The sailor entrusted with my salvation was in his early twenties, with regular features, olive skin and a healthy row of teeth. He wore a black beanie that didn't completely cover his mop of curly hair. Someone on the bridge must have seen me lean over the side and ordered a quick intervention. *I* couldn't see the danger, provided one held on firmly to the railing. It never occurred to me that a rogue wave or sudden roll of the ship could have lifted me overboard.

When he pulled me towards him, one feature struck me as unusual: he was missing his left thumb, although the handicap obviously didn't prevent him from working. I found out later that my rescuer was given the moniker 'Knobby', the word working well in both English and Dutch. He escorted me to the purser's desk then left me to my own devices. His final word was '*ciao*' and mine was 'thanks', one of the first English words I had managed to learn.

Knobby must have missed his own family, because he sought us out, either talking to us in Italian, all the while gesticulating like some opera singer, or trying to help with our games on the foredeck. Sometimes he emerged with some discarded timber or rope and loved it when we patted his back and exaggerated our *grazies*. He didn't seem to take much notice of his superiors while he dawdled and laughed with us at our silly antics. He simply enjoyed our company.

After the storm subsided and people were recovering from the joys of seasickness, the passengers began to mingle and become more animated. At night, the adults went to the main lounge to play games or perform for the others. Father taught me the mouth organ and like a serial pest I kept practising till everyone within earshot became thoroughly annoyed. 'If you play one more note, little fella,' some grumpy old fool said to me, 'I'll shove it down your throat!' Here I was, the emerging Larry Adler,[77] and all he could do was threaten violence. What a killjoy. Nevertheless, I managed to become sufficiently proficient to chance my mouth at public entertainment. With the confidence of ignorance, I gave a rendition of the Boer War folk tune, *Sarie Marais,* to polite acclaim. In Australia, I intended to join a harmonica club.

English lessons were popular, with diligent parents urging their children to attend, but true to Mark Twain's famous saw that school wasn't going to interfere with *his* education, our parents left us alone.

---

[76] 'You silly boy, you're too close to the water. Step back, step back!'

[77] Lawrence – Larry – Adler, 1914–2001, an American, was known worldwide as a highly accomplished harmonica player.

By the Scruff of the Neck

And I'm glad they did. Nine-year-old boys, as a general rule, shut out the world and other human beings, unless relevant to their own small universe. As a result, I took little notice of my family, other than Lex, assuming they were finding their own amusements. In fact, Father and Mother were enjoying themselves and interacted blithely with their fellow passengers whenever they felt the need for company.

The foredeck of the *Fairsea* became a stage for make-believe, the officers standing on the bridge no doubt smiling at our ridiculous pantomimes. We pretended to be pirates and swashbuckled our way across the oceans, jumping from storage boxes, hiding behind windlasses and lifeboats, despite the latter being in an out-of-bounds area. We even used the deckchairs as boats, relying on the wind to push the canvas outwards. It didn't occur to us that a sudden gust could send us overboard.

The deck contained winches, toolboxes, housing for thick ropes, steel cables, and tarpaulins for use during bad weather. The crew were remarkably tolerant when, while playing there, we constructed a cubby-hole right by the bow of the ship. Taking some spare tarpaulin, we could cover ourselves snugly and look out onto the waves through a slit in the bow's iron sides. For some unknown reason, few boys and girls, other than us, visited the front of the ship.

I spent hours looking through the opening at the front of the ship, the bow cutting determinedly through the ever-changing sea, lifting and thumping on the angry waves, sometimes reeling, followed by a large boom when the ship hit a wave at the wrong angle. When the weather turned nasty, why didn't this huge ship, groaning and baulking, fall apart, I wondered? It must have been far more frightening in the wooden boats of the past, or for the ancient Egyptians sailing in their fragile papyrus vessels. With my face ruddy from the sun and the sea air, and the salt spray prickling my nose, the vast space all around lifted my spirits, the horizon becoming a magical line, the elusive skyline hiding strange countries and people. *Treasure Island* was just over the horizon!

Sometimes dolphins accompanied the ship, diving and jumping out of the sea at a tremendous speed. These clever animals moved so gracefully, their glistening coats and elegant curves dashing through the water like quicksilver. The sleek creatures loved showing off and swam in schools of five to twelve. I envied their speed and freedom and wished to be one of them, never tiring of watching these acrobats. They were so nimble and resolute. How clumsy were we by comparison. Whenever they appeared, usually in shallower waters, not far from the coast, so did the couch potatoes. Once we out-sped the dolphins, or they tired and fell behind, we returned to our games on the foredeck.

*

Rudyard Kipling once said, "If you truly wish to find someone you have known and who travels, there are two points on the globe where you have but to sit and wait; sooner or later, your man will come there: the docks of London and Port Said."

While this is a dated boast, the 1950s, in terms of their innocence, enthusiasms and travel routes, still belonged to the first half of the twentieth century. All ships from Europe to the East had to pass through the Suez Canal, the 'highway to India', which meant Kipling was partly right. Before we entered the Canal, we berthed at Port Said, northern gateway to the Red Sea; which, by the way, is named either after its seasonal russet algal bloom,[78] or conceivably, after the kingdom of Edom abutting it, 'edom' meaning 'red' in Hebrew. We docked not far from the imposing monument of Ferdinand de Lesseps standing regally on the tourist jetty.

'Who's the statue of?' I asked Father, standing next to me.

'Oh, that's the man who dug the canal, or rather who organized the digging. He was an engineer.'

I imagined hundreds of swarthy men digging furiously in the heat, day in day out. What a job, I thought. Still, someone had to do it. It was the pinnacle of de Lesseps' achievement before he was accused of fraud and died a ruined man. I didn't know that at the time so stared at the memorial in awe. I wasn't aware either that cutting a channel through the desert had been attempted many times since the days of the pharaohs, without lasting success.

Our migrant days were a constant surprise. We didn't see ourselves so much as emigrants as adventurers sailing the globe and I suspect the other passengers felt the same. A rickshaw ride was talked about for days, and to visit a bazaar was an event inviting outrageous haggling, the shopkeepers too clever by far for their naive buyers. Unused to so much variety, we eagerly accepted anything different. Lex, holding Flozzie by the hand, walked towards me and pointed to the activity around the pier. 'I've never *seen* so many boats! What do they use them for?'

A flotilla of open boats, or dories, moved towards us, rowed by boys and old men. A few larger boats, weighed down by oblong green melons the size of footballs, manoeuvred towards the steel door of our hull. They were obviously supplying us with exotic fruit. But why were the smaller boats heading for our ship?

'Look at them; look at them go! Gee, they're fast. They'll be here soon,' I said excitedly.

---

[78] The Biblical Book of Exodus tells the story of the Israelites' crossing a body of water during their escape from slavery in Egypt. This body of water is called *Yam Suph* in the Hebrew text. *Yam Suph* was traditionally identified as the Red Sea, however *Yam Suph* can also been translated as Sea of Reeds.

By the Scruff of the Neck

'And whoever arrives first will get the cream of what they're after,' replied Father. And he was spot-on. As soon as the boats rocked against our hull, a thin, brown-skinned, buck-toothed lad of about twelve called out in broken English, 'Hello, nice friends! Hello! You give money and me dive for you.'

His clumsy English wasn't understood straight away by the Dutch passengers, but the diving by his peers soon got the message across. Before long, he was joined by other slender youths, all yelling, 'Money please, misters. We dive for you. Thank you! Thank you!'

Another boy kept hitting his chest in gorilla fashion, hoping to attract attention and thereby payment. Sure enough, as the first coins were tossed overboard, like seasoned pearl divers, three or four boys dove into the water, their rear ends covered by what looked like tea-towels. We could see their slim bodies slice through the thick green water in pursuit of lucre. They stayed down for a very long time, indicating both considerable depth *and* strong lungs. Eventually they emerged, smiling broadly, eyes gleaming, sometimes with a coin between their teeth. Each time a boy came up trumps, Flozzie laughed and cheered: 'See, Pa, all wet, all wet. Ha, ha! I like the boys going down. Good, eh?'

Father and Mother loved the display too, but Father was puzzled: 'I don't know how they can stay under for so long.'

'They must be specially trained,' Mother astutely observed.

John and Bill were too busy elsewhere with more mundane matters, such as girls or swapping cigarettes for money. What currency did we use onboard? English, Dutch or Italian, or a combination of these? I suspect the coins thrown into the water were a mixture of denominations. Some of the passengers may even have thought the diving performance gave them a chance to get rid of their spare shrapnel. The divers didn't seem too fussy.

I was introduced to English money by curious happenstance. After watching the diving for a while, I went to the other side of the ship. Here another remarkable feat was being enacted. A number of Arabs, dressed in sheets, or so it appeared to me, gathered around the hawsers below. Some were toothless and some wore elaborate headgear. They latched onto the thick ropes emerging from the front and aft decks of the *Fairsea* then swiftly clambered up, agile as monkeys, the ropes swaying under the weight of their dark sinewy bodies. If they slipped, death or serious injury awaited them. What they were supposed to do once onboard, I didn't know. Perhaps they were employed by the Port authorities to help with the loading of food, water and fuel, and the unloading of waste?

After a few minutes, six of them stepped onto the deck and disappeared below. I returned to the diving lads, still spruiking for money and diving merrily. After I tired of watching them, I wandered back to the portside, hoping to catch some new excitement there. I expected the

Arabs to have gone by now, only to discover them sitting cross-legged beneath the lifeboats. They grinned, as if to say, 'Don't worry, dear boy, we mean you no harm,' then pointed at me, cackling in their own lingo and tearing round loaves of flat bread into pieces, which they dipped into some kind of sauce or relish. One of them beckoned me to come closer.

Earlier, Knobby had warned me about them. *'Ehi, bel ragazzo! Attento ai borsaiuoli.'*[79] As it turned out, he was wrong; pickpocketing wasn't at all on their agenda.

I jumped the railings and sat down next to the beckoner. He laughed and proffered a slice of one of the green melons I had seen earlier. I shyly reached out to accept the fruit. Watermelon: what a treat for an innocent palate! Soon my mouth turned red, like a clown's, and the Arabs chuckled with delight. They then offered me the strange bread, dipped in relish, which tasted tangy yet agreeable.

It was from these happy men that I learnt a number of new English words. They took their time, gesturing elegantly and pointing at simple objects, laughing as they did so. 'This – a boat.' The word sounded like our 'boot', so was easy to remember. 'You – a boy, this – money,' and would you believe it, they gave me some English coins!

After sharing their food, they rolled out a rug, got down on their knees, all facing the same direction, and began to pray. I had assumed they were going to have a well-deserved kip after their labours in the heat, but I was mistaken. I found out later from Knobby that these men were praying to their own God, rather than ours, and would stay aboard until we reached Port Tawfik, in the city of Suez, at the other end of the canal. Knobby used a piece of timber and a pencil to show the distance between Port Said and Port Tawfik, relative to the lengths of the Mediterranean and the Red Sea.

What to do with the money the Arabs had given me? In a moment of inspired altruism I decided to surprise Father with a box of cigars. The shop near the bursar's office carried a good range and once I worked out the value of the coins, it turned out I had just enough to buy a small box of White Owl cigars. I loved looking at the lid, which had an owl perched on a cigar, and hoped Father would be impressed. He was, but seemed a little perplexed. Perhaps it was an American brand unfamiliar to him, or perhaps not to his liking? He didn't say much, instead hugging me and nibbling my ear, as was his affectionate wont. When the ship left Port Said late that night, we could see the city's lights flickering in a vault of darkness. I got up early the next morning hoping to catch further new activities before the ship entered the Red Sea. I wasn't disappointed.

Film aficionados of *Lawrence of Arabia* may recall Lawrence stumbling upon the canal after sighting a huge funnel and ship's masts

---

[79] 'Hey, pretty boy! Watch out for pickpockets.'

sailing past the crest of the last sand dunes. T.E. Lawrence[80] himself does not provide any evidence for this fictive apparition in his autobiography, *Seven Pillars of Wisdom*, although it makes for dramatic cinematic effect.

As Lawrence put it, "By midday we were through the dunes, after a happy switchback ride up and down their waves...Suez was to be guessed at, as a frise of indeterminate points mowing and bobbing in the mirage of the canal-hollow far in front."[81] In the hope of finding solace in a good bath and fresh food, Lawrence rode onwards to the outpost of Shatt, where he had great difficulty gaining access to a boat to cross the canal. But why allow a stunning image to get in the way of the truth...

My truth was different. The sky was almost blindingly blue, without a wisp of cloud to be seen. I parked myself atop a toolbox at the front of the ship and took in the desert dunes either side of me. A gentle breeze made sitting there in the growing heat bearable. The ship carved its way through the narrow canal, which allowed only one vessel at a time in any given direction, with bypasses at El Ballah and the Great Bitter Lake. A new world of relentless sun and endless sand greeted me, inhabited by pockets of people who were reliant on local trade and their domestic animals. Periodically, I saw Bedouins walking their caravans of camels and their herds of goats alongside the canal. Who were these mortals, invariably dressed in *djellabas,* or long-sleeved loose robes? The women's faces were covered; this and their unhurried gait bespoke decorum, as well as harmony with their trying surroundings. As the ship sailed on, I, however, was becoming sunburnt, yet couldn't keep my eyes off these vivid cameos.

Lex joined me and we pointed in all directions, chattering to each other as we saw quaint buildings; a collection of tents on a strip of desert; a cluster of mud-brick houses surrounded by palm trees; or a long, flat, brick structure with a spherical dome – at the time, I didn't know what a mosque was. The sparseness and lack of bustle came as a surprise to us. Holland, punctuated by waterways, lush pastures and busy transport, was its opposite. Poverty and hardship were evident here, but in what way did they impinge upon the Arab's apparent sense of wellbeing and contentment?

To a young lad, comparisons present themselves readily and people's livelihood and possessions quickly emerge as something to be

---

[80] Thomas Edward Lawrence, 1888–1935, British scholar, military strategist, and author. He learned Arabic on an archaeological expedition and during World War I conceived the plan of supporting an Arab rebellion against the Ottoman Empire as a way of undermining Germany's eastern ally. He subsequently led Arab forces in a guerrilla campaign against Ottoman troops.

[81] *Seven Pillars Of Wisdom*, T. E. Lawrence, Penguin 1964, p.325

commented on. 'What kind of beds do they sleep in?' Lex wanted to know.

'I have no idea; possibly something made from thick carpet,' I suggested. 'Look at the soil, dry as a bone. How do they grow vegetables?' I naively assumed that our northern vegetables were necessary for all of mankind.

Lex was better informed and said, 'No, they must eat different food, like dates and camel meat, or even goat meat. You can't grow spuds here. Not enough water.'

The *Fairsea* stopped several times in the bypasses, waiting its turn to go ahead. Ships promenaded patiently: oil tankers, freighters, other ocean liners, and gas tankers with white cupolas like the domes of mosques transferred by some sorcerer: by now, I had learnt from Father about a strange religion called Islam, with its architecture of domes and minarets.

No small craft were to be seen on the canal, not until we reached the various lakes along the way. I wasn't sure what was happening when we entered a large expanse called the Great Bitter Lake, so-named because of its salty water. At first I thought we had reached the Red Sea, but Father said that couldn't be because we hadn't yet reached Suez, and also, it seemed, the journey from Port Said to Suez would take about fifteen hours or so.

The large, peaceful, saltwater lake was surrounded by desert, although this didn't register with us, since the shores soon shrank away into the distance. After a few hours we re-entered the canal and resumed our journey southward, arriving at Port Tawfiq mid-afternoon. I was unaware that we were only an hour's drive from Cairo and the land of the pharaohs. Once we had passed the port, the ships in front fanned out into the open water of the Red Sea. The shores began to fade from view and the ship seemed to go faster.

Having been on the deck for most of the day, as the late afternoon sun sank towards the horizon, I realised I was sunburnt, but took little notice. More importantly, I began to feel hungry and wanted to go below to the dining room. A number of times I had spotted the Italian waiters, chefs and kitchen hands sipping wine in a corner there. It didn't usually seem to bother them to see a fair-haired lad wander through the aisles then go out again through the far door. The *Fairsea* was an easy ship to move around in, and on the whole, the kitchen crew were blasé about our peregrinations. Perhaps it had something to do with Italian family life.

Doors on ships are heavy due to the variability of the weather. Some are made of steel, others of heavy timber and brass bracing, depending on the aesthetics of the various decks. I tried to open the door to the main deck, but it wouldn't give. I tried again and, with much difficulty, managed to shift it ajar. When I put my foot between the door and the jamb and pulled with all my strength, I encountered a boy my own age who had deliberately tried to prevent me from opening the door. It must have been his idea of a joke.

'What the bloody hell do you think you're doing, you twerp! I want to get inside.'

He just laughed and said, 'If you think you're so tough, why don't you fight me?'

Being hungry and rather annoyed, I didn't think too much about his challenge and just punched him in the mouth. He immediately stepped onto the outside deck and grabbed me around the neck. Unlike Lex, I'm not a fighter by inclination, preferring to settle differences verbally. On this occasion, however, my anger got the better of me. I was up for it! I ribbed him with my elbow and he let go. I then grabbed him in turn, threw him onto the deck and sat on top of him, pummelling his gob till he begged me to get off. A man walking past dragged me away and told me to bugger off.

A few days later, I caught up with the same boy, who said, 'So, you're the little fighter. I'm sorry I stopped you from coming inside.'

I was surprised at his generosity. To call me "the little fighter" was an exaggeration and to apologise must have been galling for him. Still, I took on the soubriquet with a certain pride and ran with it for the rest of the journey. While not close, I got on well with him for the remainder of our voyage. Many years later, he visited us in Morwell, Victoria, and recounted this piffling event. I think it made a greater impression on him than me.

The white light and scorching sun plagued our fair skin as we headed for Aden, in Yemen, a mysterious country I got to know better much later in life. We nevertheless ignored the sunburn and, despite the pain, kept inventing new games. Sometimes we went for a dip in the small swimming pool, but it was often so crowded we didn't bother to use it. Usually, we just kept up our playful antics on the main deck as we sailed down the Gulf of Suez and eventually out into the Red Sea, working our way south past Jeddah on the coast, not far from Mecca, to the Mandab Strait, between Djibouti and Yemen.

One hot mid-afternoon Knobby led me to the dining room where the waiters and kitchen staff were relaxing with a glass of wine. I sat down with them and Knobby offered me some. I had never tasted wine before and as a virtuous young lad at first shook my head. A few of the men cheered and laughed, then insisted: 'Good for you *ragazzo*. *Bello! Bello! Fantastico!* Enjoy, enjoy.' It never occurred to them it was anything out of the ordinary, but for me it was. I gulped down the liquid, thinking it similar to lemonade or orange juice, even though it tasted sharp, like vinegar. They laughed again, while Knobby said quietly, '*Bevi lentamente, ometto mio*'.[82] He lifted his glass and sipped the red wine slowly and deliberately, then put the glass down. I understood. My glass was filled a second time, and after a few more mouthfuls, the wine began to grow on me. Enjoying all the attention, I slowly began to also enjoy the sensation flowing through my body, even though my head spun a little. I savoured the wine more cautiously, in the meantime trying to follow the expressive gestures of the men, eventually realizing they were having a great time sharing their wine and companionship, yet at the same time, were amused by my inexperience.

One of the chefs, fat and hairy, with a smile as wide as a Neapolitan pizza, began to sing *Torna a Surriento* in a surprisingly good voice. The others joined in, shedding tears of sentimentality. The notes allowed for easy sharing, so I too followed the melody, although my lyrics were only an approximation to the Italian. At least my choir experience enabled me to sing in tune.

After they finished, I pulled out my mouth organ, always at the ready for a surprise concert, and having just mastered the song *Funiculi*, took off in full flight, with the men clapping to my rhythm. A few passengers, hearing the lively music, looked in and sat down at the far end of the room. My boisterous rendition was duly applauded and the bulky chef ruffled my hair, loudly saying, '*Che spettacolo meraviglioso. Per favore, suona di nuovo, biondino.*'[83] I duly obliged and even the shyest passengers joined in. Despite feeling tipsy, but also bolstered by it, I played several more sentimental songs, such as *La Paloma* and *Over the Rainbow*. The men then returned to their work in the kitchen to prepare for the evening meal.

The afternoon had turned out unexpectedly well. Unbeknown to my parents, I occasionally had a few more wines with the crew and almost began to like it. Many years later, on the Isle of Samos, I got plastered on *retsina*. At first I thought that particular wine rough and better used as a disinfectant, but after a few more glasses it took on a life of its own and improved in proportion to my declining articulation.

At the time, Aden was still a British protectorate and a strategic port for ships travelling south or east, not dissimilar to the entrepôt of Singapore. With a backdrop of volcanic mountains, it's a magnificent city, going back to biblical times. Some Biblical historians have suggested Aden may have

---

[82] 'Drink slowly, my little man.'
[83] 'What a wonderful performance. Please, play it again, blondie.'

been the final resting place of Cain and Abel. Once the ship arrived there, Father, Mother, John and Bill joined the adult Kogers in visiting this ancient port. The rest of us hung over the railings watching them leave, since we were considered too young to be allowed to go ashore, or perhaps even a nuisance.

On their return, we found out some big fat Arab had offered a considerable sum of money to buy Mother. Not only was Mother attractive but also a little plump, which apparently appealed to the merchant. We younger boys weren't particularly aware of Mother's physical attractions, but the generous amount of money on offer prompted us to urge Father to sell Mother at once: No! We weren't serious, of course, and in any case, Father loved her too much.

Unfortunately, John finished up in the infirmary, this time from something he caught when he drank the water.

Crossing the Indian Ocean was the longest stretch of water without visible land. I have no recollection of the tropical islands we passed, if indeed we did, but do recall fun and games when we crossed the equator into the southern hemisphere. Lex and I won a three-legged race and were given a certificate with a picture of Neptune holding his trident above a blue sea. Later, our names were written on the bottom.

I can't recall the voyage ever being boring, which some people consider such a long journey to be. The weather was indulgent and didn't shift, staying hot and clammy. The ocean minded its own business, with gentle swells and the occasional flying fish putting on an aquatic chase. These fish abound in the tropics and propel themselves out of the water using their powerful and fast-moving tails. Their wide fins then allow them to fly through the air for up to fifty metres. They're fast, but not fast enough to elude dolphins and porpoises, usually nearby. I often leant over the railings for a long time studying these silvery creatures, until cramp or another diversion sent me elsewhere.

The final week before reaching Fremantle, in Western Australia, was memorable due to squalls and huge seas. My first experience of a sea storm, the Mediterranean tempest, came and went quickly, but this was in quite a different league. The rain and wind blustered for days and passengers often remained below deck due to seasickness. The waves loomed like a mountain range one moment, pushing the ship to dizzying heights, then collapsed into a vast hollow. Momentary respite, and then the *Fairsea* rose again like a plucky warrior, thrusting into a new group of waves as if jousting, each wave unpredictable and seething with intent. The ship rolled around like a grain of rice in a spoon. The noise of the

Fairsea hitting the water sounded like someone walloping the surface with a giant spoon, followed by the emptying of a large bucket.

It was difficult to work out the direction being taken by the ship, since visibility was poor, with runnels of water spreading across the windows and portholes exposed to the battering rain. How the captain and his officers on the bridge saw through all this porridge baffled me. I suppose they had their instruments and, apart from dangerous reefs, were relatively safe in this seemingly limitless expanse.

Meals became a balancing act, with crockery sliding all over the place. The waiters, however, remained stoical and kept serving. *Why didn't they get seasick?* The bowls, however, were only half-filled and seesawed to the brim, yet remained miraculously below spilling point. Half of the passengers didn't turn up for meals, though, and even I doubted my stomach, but Lex and I weren't to be denied; our bellies hung onto our food. Just as well, since vomiting is never a pleasant experience!

One early morning, having lain awake for hours listening to the creaking and griping of the ship, I decided to gauge the strength of the storm holding us captive. Lurching from side to side, I climbed the stairs to the middle deck and stepped outside. There wasn't another soul to be seen. It seemed to me as if the wind was conducting a complex orchestra, snarling as it pushed successive sheets of rain across the vast ocean, which growled in anger, its surging green waters contrasting with the strange, piercing light of the white-grey sky. Maybe somewhere out there lurked the *Flying Dutchman*, foreboding disaster... The unfortunate captain of this doomed galleon, featured in so many stories of the sea, was very real to me; I sensed ghosts everywhere.

I ventured to the front deck, only to discover it to be wet and slippery. The wind frightened me, and despite barely noticing the cold, I shivered as the howling gusts shook me to the marrow. They conjured up the souls of lost sailors. How many men had drowned over the years? So many, all with distinct faces, all of varying stature, with different voices, their own gifts, and all dying in the line of duty, leaving families guessing their fate. Sucked beneath the inscrutable water, ripped apart by sharks and other creatures of the deep. What a dreadful end!

While the wind raced across the canopy of the ship, the funnel, the rigging and the masts silently stood witness as I saw myself in the sea, clutching wildly at useless waves, gulping gallons of deadly brine, eventually surrendering to the ocean currents and the inevitable journey downwards, never to see daylight again.

The *Fairsea* trembled like a wild animal as the waves pounded the ship. Fear seized me by the throat, my forehead filmed with perspiration, and I fled inside. There was ghostly silence in the corridors and no one to be seen in the lounge rooms, until I noticed the girl I had spoken to on our departure from Amsterdam. She was sitting near a window reading. I walked towards her like a drunken sailor and plopped onto a seat opposite her.

'Isn't it quiet; nobody here,' I began.

She looked up and said, 'My parents are *dying* from seasickness. The smell in our room is repulsive, so I decided to leave. I'm not very well myself, but I'd rather suffer here, more in the open. Is that why you're here?'

'Not really... I just wanted to see how rough the weather was. It's chaos out there! I hope we make it.'

I wasn't going to let her know about my earlier terror. As I spoke, the ship shuddered and seemed to move sideways. My heart surged, but outwardly I remained calm. 'What are you reading?' I asked. 'And...and by the way, what's your name and where are you from?'

'Well, well, you *are* a boy in a hurry! You want to know everything... Now! Typical... My younger brother is the same. No patience and always on the go. Anyway, if you *must* know the answers, since it won't do any harm, my name is Karla. We are from Saint Pancras. Papa is a teacher and Mama, a nurse, if that's your next question.'

For a girl expressing grief not long ago in Amsterdam, she had certainly recovered her composure and made me feel a little inadequate.

'I didn't mean to be rude,' I replied. 'I just wanted to know, that's all. We're almost neighbours. Saint Pancras is just near Alkmaar, where *we* come from.' Now that she was happy again, I wasn't about to remind her of the loss of her girlfriends back in Holland.

Her face was pale, probably because she felt queasy, but her bearing and thick blonde hair gave her a look of strength. She also spoke very well and was probably smarter than me, although she may have been a little older; I couldn't quite tell. She continued eagerly, now that I'd set her off: 'I simply *adore* Enid Blyton and am reading my sixth book by her, *Five Get Into Trouble*. I can read English reasonably well but still prefer reading them in Dutch. Have you heard of her?'

'Hmm... No! Must be a girl's book... Have you heard of Nowee or Karl May or Captain Rob?' I asked, hoping she hadn't and determined not to be outdone by her superior knowledge.

'Of course I have. My brothers read them all the time. Anyway, you're wrong, you know. Enid Blyton's books are about boys as well, and both the boys and girls are cleverer than the police. I like that. I *adore* Julian!' Her eyes sparkled and she shook her head with delight. I got the sinking feeling I couldn't compete with her, neither with this Julian fellow. A shameful sense of ignorance overcame me and I changed the subject.

'It's three more days and we'll reach *Auwstralië*. Where are you getting off?'

I sounded a trifle offhand, but she ignored this and said, 'Our family has friends in Melbourne and they will put us up until Papa and Mama find work. Our friends have been there for two years and seem to be doing well. Father teaches mathematics and can speak a few different languages, which might help. Still, I hope my parents can make themselves understood. Their English is good, even if they speak with our Dutch accent. Australians speak a funny kind of English; nothing like the wonderful characters in Blyton's books, or the young English Princesses... And what is your family going to do?'

Karla spoke of mathematics as a subject familiar to everyone. I hadn't progressed beyond arithmetic so was impressed by the ease with which she spoke of such a sophisticated subject.

'I'm not sure. Father said something about a camp. But I haven't a clue. I just want to travel in this new country and help find a good piece of land where we can build a house and grow vegetables.'

She seemed amused and fell silent for a while. 'Well! I hope your family won't have to stay too long in this camp. Papa was in a camp during the War. Camps were meant for holidays once, but not in *my* experience. All I know is that camps have strict rules and can be nasty. I hope you're fed properly. Papa was in one in Germany and he returned all rags and bones.'

I knew what she was referring to. As for this migrant camp, I hadn't given it much thought and resolved to find out more from Father.

As the ship leapt about and performed its violent theatrics, more people emerged through the barricaded doors and shuffled, with difficulty, to the safety of fixed tables and chairs. Down below, the *Fairsea* smelt like a cesspool. Some of the passengers were too weak to shift themselves and kept retching; a vicious cycle since the stench brought on more bouts of shouting hello into buckets. Seasickness can render a farmer, usually strong as an ox, weak as a child. Feeling rather smug, I considered myself different; tougher than these landlubbers.

After saying goodbye to Karla and promising to meet her again, I decided to find Lex and ask him to play a board game with me in the children's room. As I staggered through a doorway, I almost collided with Jack-the-lad, who had his arm around the waist of a giggly girl of about seventeen. 'Watch your step, little boy, or you'll fall over,' she remarked.

Jack-the-lad had a grin on his face, but I had the presence of mind to reply, 'You won't have to worry about falling on *your* face, with that lanky boyfriend to hold onto.'

She gave me a withering look, as if to say, 'And who do you think you are, you cheeky upstart?'

Jack-the-lad shot me a conciliatory glance, then said, 'Don't concern yourself with this smart aleck, my lovely. He's only my little brother and not worth bothering about.'

Meanwhile, Bill was bedridden in the infirmary and our parents were worried about him. Lex and I were also concerned, but figured that sooner or later he would get better. And he did.

The weather remained unrepentant but at last we saw land, much as the explorer Frederick de Houtman would have seen it from a distance in 1619. The view included Rottnest Island, named by another Dutch explorer, Willem de Vlamingh, in 1696. The native quokkas were apparently mistaken for giant rats. 'Rotte' is the seventeenth-century spelling of the Dutch word for rats, which is different from the modern spelling, 'ratten'. Like other Dutch explorers, de Houtman gave up on this vast western land as useless and barren. Interestingly, he died in Alkmaar, in 1627.

Exhausted after our trans-Indian-Ocean ordeal, we breathed a sigh of relief when we reached Fremantle. It was a sunny day with a light, fresh breeze, and the townscape looked quite different from Alkmaar; not much high-rise, but solid sandstone buildings pleasing to the eye. Watching the ship manoeuvre towards the docks, guided by plucky tugboats, I felt grateful we had made it to the other side of the world.

Situated not far from the harbour, the town seemed spacious, with an air of lightheartedness. Looking down at the wharf, I saw men wearing shorts and blue singlets, despite the nippy weather. What strange attire for workmen! They were yelling to one another, but I couldn't understand a word they were saying, thus confirming Karla's assessment of Australian English. Even the Arabs sounded more comprehensible.

The wharfies kept shouting and issuing commands, sounding as if they had swallowed a swordfish. They strode across the tarmac, fag in hand, and having secured the ship's rope to the bollards, turned towards the stern, yelling, 'She'll be right, mate!' whatever that meant. The derricks at the rear of the ship were now brought into action to shift the cargo onto the wharf. How many passengers were to disembark, I hadn't the faintest idea. Father and Mother were busy completing immigration forms.

We must have stayed in Fremantle for a day at least, because once again the oldies traipsed off – to nearby Perth for a good look at the new country. We were allowed to leave the ship, but only to the Fremantle shopping centre. I recall the main street as a long row of squat buildings and double-storey, nineteenth-century shops. The wrought iron on the balconies of their second floor was a work of art, and although some of the lacework was rusty, most was neatly painted in black, white or grey, or even burgundy, each building with its own intricate pattern. We particularly appreciated the beauty and grandeur of the hotels, with their ornate verandahs and large leadlight windows showing pictures of colourful bearded characters drinking lager and smoking pipes.

The streets were wide, with pavements under cover, something puzzling to us, as Dutch streets were narrower and rarely covered. Later, I realized the heavy downpours and stinging sun justified this sensible precaution. We read the names of shops and tried to make sense of the advertising material on the shopfronts. Lex kept looking into some known as 'milk bars', and took a great deal of interest in the sweets and food available.

The prominent hotels, the sturdy banks, and other impressive grey-brown edifices, certainly left their mark on me. I didn't know what they did in those buildings, but whoever built them knew what they were doing. It wasn't till much later that I learnt that Fremantle was a rather special place in terms of its architecture. For a small town, it valued its colonial heritage far more than many other and larger Australian cities.

We didn't understand the language, yet felt comfortable because *Auwstraliers* looked similar to us, although perhaps a bit shorter and heavier. They seemed a relaxed lot, standing on street corners and outside pubs nattering away. There was something comical about these people, and *Auwstraliers* obviously took beer drinking seriously, judging by the large crowds outside the pubs. Must have something to do with the climate...

Father and Mother, apparently, were quite taken by Perth, although they thought the shops left a great deal to be desired: old-fashioned clothing, a limited range of food items, and not many restaurants – for all the hardship in Holland, the shops and eateries recovered quickly in the larger cities. Perth was beautiful, with its curved boulevards and waterways, but when compared to Amsterdam, rather staid and socially insipid, or so it seemed to Father. 'The grid design of the main streets and the oodles of open spaces are probably a bit like American towns,' he mused. 'There's so much room, you can run and jump without touching anyone. You can breathe here, but there isn't much of a social life. Let's hope Melbourne is more exciting.' None of us realized that at the time, Australia was still in the grip of wowsers. For all the easygoing habits of Australians in the 1950s, there was still a puritanical streak that dented enjoyment.

The last leg of the journey took about four days, and despite the turbulent crossing of the Great Australian Bight, didn't upset us because by now we were inured to the wildness of the ocean. All the talk was about what Melbourne would be like. How would it compare with Alkmaar, or Amsterdam? Would it be a bigger version of Fremantle? I decided to ask Karla; she might know.

Karla was sitting with her parents in the main lounge, which also doubled for nightly entertainment. Since they were strangers, I didn't particularly want to approach her folks, and, being professional people, were probably rather serious, so just walked past them. Afterwards, I caught her attention and made signs to come over. She left her table and joined me on the other side of the room.

'Hello, Henri! What do you want?'

I looked around and whispered, 'I'm a bit reluctant to talk to your parents. I just wanted to ask you something.'

Karla wasn't offended and said, 'Don't worry about my parents, they aren't that strict and are easy to talk to. What do you want to ask me?'

'We'll be parting soon, once we get to Melbourne. Do you know much about this city? I'd love to know,' I implored.

'Well, no, not really,' she answered rather disappointingly. 'Apparently it's a lot bigger than Perth or Fremantle and has many migrants living there. Our friends said that once you get used to the people and learn their ways, they're very friendly and helpful. But what Melbourne actually looks like, I have no idea. Don't worry about it. The people in Fremantle looked pretty normal, even if they *did* wear strange clothes... I'm more interested in meeting girls my own age.'

My interest was geographical, hers personal. I thought that perhaps this revealed something about the difference between boys and girls, but supposed one ought not to take such stereotyping too far.

The ship had become a second home and we quickly adjusted to the cuisine, which was mainly Italian. I enjoyed the grand gestures of the crew and had become attached to Knobby, often meeting up with him on the front deck; he always managed to find time to engage with us. Melbourne was now to be our point of separation, the beginning of a whole new way of life, which felt both a little frightening and exhilarating.

The weather was cool and overcast as we entered a large bay through a narrow gap between the headlands. On either side we saw scattered buildings, but couldn't get a measure of where the ship was heading. As the bay widened we saw a low-lying mountain to our right – Arthur's Seat – and a few sharply delineated mountains in the distance to our left – the You Yangs.

After about an hour, we became aware of a cluster of low buildings to the north. It was only when we came closer that the city of Melbourne began to take shape. Apart from church spires, from a distance, Melbourne in 1952 seemed rather flat. All very unimpressive when compared to Sydney, as I discovered much later; but I didn't know Sydney then and during the journey had no basis for comparison, other than Port Said, Aden and Fremantle. A scattering of factories, built from bluestone or red brick, loomed in front of us. To the right we saw double-storeyed white villas surrounded by well-kept gardens. The esplanade went on forever, fronted by a continuous beach. Only a few people were walking on the footpath, probably because it was winter. Not many cars or buses were to be seen, either. Altogether, Melbourne looked a bit grim.

The ship slowly drifted to a long pier protruding from the land like a welcoming finger. As the *Fairsea* gauged its bulk against the pier, people thronged the quayside, no doubt friends and relatives of our passengers, plus curious onlookers. What drew my attention was the long train on the other side. Who, or what, was the train waiting for?

Lex waved to the crowd and said, 'I reckon we'll be on that train. It's too long for only a few people.' He was right, but it would take quite some time to disembark.

Amsterdam had given us a foretaste of the bureaucratic agony of emigration: long queues, detailed forms and endless instructions. Always waiting. As youngsters we were bored witless by the snail-like process: Father and Mother did all the work, while I punched Lex amicably in the solar plexus. Our tired suitcases served as chairs while we waited for our surname to be called.

The *Fairsea* was our last link with Holland and I felt both nostalgic and bereft...but only a little. Earlier, when I searched for Knobby, I found him on the upper deck painting the lifeboats. He hugged me, amid tears, and said, '*Ah, mio piccolo amico. Forse, un giorno, ci rivedremo.*'[84] As I stared into his eyes, I realized for the first time how vulnerable he was, and also realized he had shifted his affections, normally reserved for his family, onto us. Despite the language barrier, I understood him and shared his emotional attachment. I would probably never see him again.

At last we made our way down the gangway and were ushered through the crowd onto the train. The carriages were blue and looked comfortable. As we meandered through the crowd, the locals pointed to our clothing, as though we had just arrived from the upper reaches of the Amazon. The sight of fair-skinned children with conspicuous blond hair wearing such peculiar clothing and carrying battered suitcases drew comments: we wore plus-fours, or 'apple catchers' as they were better known, and which were very fashionable in Holland, together with heavy Bata shoes that also seemed out of place.

'Must be reffos,' an angular man muttered to his wife.

'I don't think so, dear,' replied the better-informed spouse. 'They're new migrants from northern Europe.'

---

[84] 'Ah, my little friend. Perhaps one day we'll meet again.'

By the Scruff of the Neck

We couldn't understand them. Nor did we particularly care! Our eyes were on the carriages, hoping to find a window seat. Karla was nowhere to be seen and presumably was being met by her friends.

In 1952, locomotives were a mixture of diesel-electric and steam. Ours was steam-driven and seemed rather old-fashioned when compared to the trains in Holland. Having made ourselves comfortable, we waited impatiently for action. We had been given hard-boiled eggs to eat and thin slices of bread called 'sandwiches'. We studied them and thought them paltry when compared to our chunks of bread, thick as textbooks and filled with jam or dried liver. These slivers had lettuce, carrot, and some yellow mush called 'mayonnaise'.

At last there was a grunt as the long train snaked its way out of Station Pier. The rhythm of the train calmed me as I hoed into the surprisingly tasty sandwiches; although the eggs were white-green and hard as bullets. I persevered, but John and Bill hurled theirs through the window, out into the open spaces. 'Who do these *Auwstraliers* think we are? Starving desperados?' hollered John in disgust.

As the train clickety-clacked its way into the suburbs, I became a prince ensconced on a green leather throne, looking down upon urban scenes created by unknown tradesmen and architects. Occasionally, tall chimneys popped up unexpectedly while we wended our way through long rows of houses and factories. Advertising painted on sooty brick walls and almost washed away by grit and rain, promoted Robur Tea or Bisto Gravy, brands unfamiliar to me.

Cobbled-together wooden houses with red corrugated iron roofs and flowerpot chimneys, and attached to scruffy backyards, flitted past, some displaying washing lines or a Hills Hoist, others, patches of lawn with furious dogs arcing up against broken fences; and, here and there, cats slinking or sunning themselves. Sometimes I caught a glimpse of someone chopping wood for the winter fires or children playing in alleys, bouncing balls off walls.

Dutch houses were usually made of brick and were clean and tidy. Here, the hotchpotch of dwellings and lean-tos were intriguing in their casualness. They wouldn't be tolerated back home... Nevertheless, I was attracted by all this architectural anarchy and wanted to meet the locals. Eventually, when the train began to nudge open spaces, the landscape changed. The train also seemed to go faster.

'This is a lot quicker than the boat and much more fun!' exclaimed Lex enthusiastically.

I ignored him; I was studying the rolling hills, the grey-green vegetation and the vast tracts of land. I thought again of Holland. Our 'clog' country was flat, with arteries of water spreading throughout the land. The soil was rich and moist, Holland being the delta of the Rhine and blessed with ample rainfall. Despite its small size, there was considerable space for lush grass, supporting placid Friesians. In contrast, the cattle in this land were black, brown, white, mousy-grey, or even red and white. It was quite something to get used to: why the mainly uniform black and white in Holland and the variations here?

In neat, almost miniaturized Holland, clusters of red-tiled houses surrounded by leafy poplars and beeches dotted the countryside, while in the middle of an old village, a church spire pointed directly to God. Not much had changed for centuries and the atmosphere was one of routine and comfort. Dutch farmhouses were large and imposing, like many of their owners. In winter, the ditches and canals froze over and the fields lay quietly beneath a thick blanket of snow. The livestock, part of the family, were kept indoors during the cold weather, and brutal winds from the east and north turned people into mummies as they fought their way home from work, or other only-the-most-necessary outings. Like old men, the birch and elm trees bent double, conjuring up the shivering scenes of Vlaminck and Van Gogh.

The old adage, "God created the earth but the Dutch created Holland", refers to the ancient battles of reclamation, yet also to the incessant contest with the elements, which cause so much hardship: the flooding of the land and the drownings. Dutch landscape and its watery surrounds are character-building, making the Dutch a tough, sceptical lot. Trial and error is seared into the Dutch psyche. They have needed to outwit their tricky environment for centuries and have largely succeeded...

The changing scenery interrupted my thoughts. The train had settled into a steady rhythm as it sped towards its destination: Bonegilla, in Northern Victoria. The long journey that followed has stayed in my memory like a snag in a river. I don't know why exactly; maybe the shock of being on firm land once more and the adventure of going on a fast-moving train into the wilderness. To borrow an American term, travelling through the Australian landscape seemed almost as if we were 'greenhorns', setting foot in the frontier for the very first time: I was still fired up by Karl May and thought the Australian countryside would be little different from the Wild West. How wrong I was! The trees, lighting and overall landscape were quite unlike what I imagined America to be. The weather too was softer, there was more fragrance in the air, and it wasn't so numbingly cold as in Holland; or, I suspected, in America.

Flatness becomes a state of mind; to see land take off vertically was a wholly new experience for me. The new contours I saw included unusual shapes and colours: a shifting mosaic of rust-brown, ochre, green, and the pale golden yellow of wheat. Clumps of trees hugged bare hillsides, with their isolated rocks and tiny creeks. The trees had narrow, pointed leaves and strangely-coloured trunks. Set back from the railway line, farmhouses were bordered by either these gums, privet hedges, or cypresses, serving as windbreaks. What did they do on those farms? Were there any children of my age? The houses appeared so far away and lonely, although I enjoyed the swagger of cattle ambling along a ridge or hunkering down near a fence. Here and there, sheep clung to the grey-green side of a hill like in a pointillist painting. What a contrast to measured Holland!

Being so young, I couldn't articulate these impressions, yet experienced them nonetheless. Australians who haven't travelled abroad perhaps take their country for granted, but Northern Europeans are often bowled over by the different coloration, the fierce light, the dryness, the isolation. Northern climes are darker, closer, and wetter somehow, people seeming to mesh more easily, perhaps because of close proximity and shared history.

Even as a child one instinctively adapted to the seasons: trees shed leaves in autumn and birds flew southwards. This continent was different. To the Dutch immigrant, eucalypts such as stringy barks and ghost gums, illustrated vegetation gone mad, while strange pouched animals, gentle and cuddly, inhabited this severe landscape; severe, that is, by European standards. As I sat inside the carriage, snugly and warm, my heart thumping in unison with the clackety-clack of the train, I didn't know what to make of this new land, but as soon as I got the chance, I was determined to climb the nearest hill and form an idea.

My reverie was broken by a prod from Lex, who pointed to a young couple on horseback galloping alongside the train. The young woman was dressed in jodhpurs and a white shirt while her companion wore a flaming-red shirt pushed into a tight pair of dark pants. Both wore cowboy hats.

'Look at them go! I'm surprised they don't fall off!' Lex exclaimed.

The horses' hooves kicked up the dust and the man whooped and lifted his hat, as if to welcome us. I placed the striking duo into some cowboy movie I had seen just before we left. The man was Roy Rogers or John Wayne and the woman, Susan Haywood, with whom, by nine years of age, I had already fallen in love. My romantic inclination at that stage was, of course, a mere overlay to adventure. Girls were all right, but not the 'real thing'. Shooting outlaws or corralling rustlers was the whole point in life, the idea of kissing girls repugnant. True, girls smelt different and behaved themselves better than boys, but still came second best when action, bravado and conquest were called for.

Sexist stereotyping was rather rampant in those days, and to me, girls just looked sweet and innocent; mere window-dressing to more exciting events. My exploration of Liesbet had been an adventure, of course, but of a different sort; something beyond my control: it had just happened.

The happy couple we were watching managed to beat the train for a short burst, then swung away, pelting up a nearby hill. We followed the two figures till they were obscured by trees, quickly disappearing from view.

'When we get a farm,' Bill declared solemnly, 'I'm gonna buy a horse and a rifle to shoot rabbits. We'll never starve.'

'You can't even shoot, *or* ride a horse!' said Lex, laughing. 'Anyway, you don't need to ride a horse to shoot rabbits. You have to be very quiet and hide behind a tree so they can't see you.' He was being his practical self and felt obliged to correct his brother.

Bill ignored Lex's advice and said emphatically, 'Don't you worry, ya fat lard, I'll learn to ride and shoot and show ya! You need a horse to cover distance. Rabbits don't live next door!' Bill had a point and Lex remained silent.

The hills near Wodonga became more prominent and sinewy as we entered the final stretch of our journey. We pulled up alongside a long platform and were met by a row of buses ready to take us to the Bonegilla Army Camp, more euphemistically rendered as the Bonegilla Reception and Training Centre. The buzz of anticipation, made even more agreeable by the good cheer of the immigrant horde, helped us enter the buses in good spirits, despite our long journey. Everything seemed well organized. We were hungry, though, it being late afternoon.

Although Prime Minister Menzies was in power at the time, we were Arthur Calwell's[85] children. It was he who advocated mass immigration and the belief that through assimilation, migrants would become ideal Australians, especially the children – whatever that 'ideal' might be. He has been proven right, but in my view underestimated the lingering cultural ties to one's native country. Both are compatible however. Multiculturalism is now the preferred social approach, though predicated on certain givens, like the rule of law, democratic pluralism, learning the language, respecting individual rights, and a broad acceptance of the host country's values.

Upon arrival at Bonegilla, we were allotted a hut divided into two cubicles: not enough room to swing cats or possums, the latter abounding in the trees nearby. Farts reverberated within the small confines. We slept on metal army beds and saw ourselves as heroes in Karl May's novels, who were used to roughing it.

Modesty was forgotten as seven of us lived cheek by jowl. But we were happy. The huts were essentially used for sleeping, people preferring the

---

[85] Member of the Federal House of Representatives from 1940 to 1972, Minister for Immigration in the government of Ben Chifley from 1945 to 1949, and leader of the Australian Labor Party from 1960 to 1967.

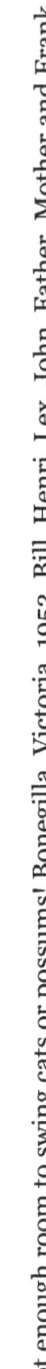

Not enough room to swing cats or possums! Bonegilla, Victoria, 1952. Bill, Henri, Lex, John, Father, Mother and Frank.

large mess hall to socialize in, or otherwise they went outside, exploring the natural surroundings of the nearby Hume Weir.

I can't recall our first meal on that late afternoon when we arrived, but generally the food was pretty dull. Plenty of bread and spuds! Still, as hunger is the best sauce, our stomachs weren't fussy, although eating cold chops for breakfast was weird and certainly novel. At the ages of ten and nine respectively, Lex and I were already rostered for spud peeling duty; our reward, hot cocoa. Once the routine was established, accompanied by jokes or a singsong, I didn't mind the chore. Once a week wasn't onerous and allowed oodles of time to do as we wished. Church attendance, however, remained obligatory and Lex and I once more became choirboys.

Our parents continued to heed Twain's advice, so no school. At that stage Father probably assumed we wouldn't be there long enough. He was right, but like many other immigrants, our friends the Kogers lingered in Bonegilla for a long time.

The mornings were bitingly cold, with a whitely glaring sun hanging unhelpfully in a clear blue sky. No hot water either. We took perfunctory showers or simply slapped cold water over ourselves, before racing back to the hut to put on warm clothing. Then breakfast. The cooks were locals, or remnants of the displaced persons brigade, who stayed on at Bonegilla because, in 1952, there was a recession and little work available. Nevertheless, these and other men from the camp sometimes walked or hitchhiked to Wodonga and Albury, some fifteen kilometres away on the New South Wales-Victoria state border, looking for work.

After breakfast, we usually met up with the Koger boys and various other kids to play a game of soccer, talk about future plans, or indulge in chitchat.

'I hope the soccer pitch is free; I'm busting for a good game,' said one.

'When we leave this joint, my family wants to move back to a big city. More to do!' said another.

'Noticed how *many* there are in this camp?' observed a short lad with skinny legs. 'Most speak another language. Wonder where they're from?'

We never met for long; we were too restless, and also drawn to the Hume Weir, next door to the camp. The weir became a magnet for immigrants. Some grown-ups continued their habits of fishing and strolling. Others were apt to reflect on their move to a strange new land as they dilly-dallied along the foreshore. Our parents discouraged us from going there because of possible danger, but how does a parent stop a kid from licking an ice-cream, so to speak? Jack-the-lad, in the meantime, was busy wooing the migrant girls, while whippersnappers like us were keen to re-enact the adventures of Huckleberry Finn, or pretend to be Ironfist or Winnetou from May's novels.

'They won't know what we're up to,' said Lex, after suggesting we visit the weir to see what it had to offer. 'Pa isn't around and doesn't really worry much, and Ma's too busy with other people. She can't be bothered anyway, so let's go!'

Father, in fact, was looking for work and gained a temporary job killing rabbits. Rabbit was as popular as chicken, the fur a by-product used for clothing and hats. The farmer who employed Father, and also Mr Koger, referred to them as "penny ha'penny", Father being tall and Mr Koger very short.

One afternoon, much too hot for that time of year, and with no swimming pool around, we decided to go for a swim in the weir. We had no swimming trunks, so opted for our underdaks. All were enjoying the coolness of the water, splashing one another, as boys do, when Bill spotted a blueish wooden dinghy.

'Hey, what's that boat doing upside down, over there?' he asked nobody in particular. 'All right you dumbheads, get out of the water and let's have a look!'

We duly got out of the water and ran to the tub, a few hundred metres away, and inspected it. The boat's blistery paint didn't worry us; we were more interested to see if there were any holes, or whether it was so rotten as to be useless. Lex tapped the wood and found it sturdy, but discovered a few small holes the size of pennies.

'Well, that's it then. Can't sail with holes,' Bill pronounced emphatically.

'Wait a minute,' said Lex. 'I remember seeing a few workers mending the road yesterday. I wonder if they're still there.'

Bill and John Koger decided to try their luck and returned half an hour later with a kero tin full of bitumen. The workmen were easygoing chaps and despite our funny English didn't mind giving tar to the foreign kids. No questions asked as they leant on their shovels.

Lex found a flat piece of hardwood to dip in the tar and proceeded to plug the holes, saying, 'Let it dry for an hour or so and we should be right.'

We continued our swimming, occasionally checking whether the bitumen had hardened. After lunch back at the camp, we returned to the boat. The tar was almost hard, so Lex pronounced it seaworthy. We turned the boat over and found the interior in reasonable condition, including the seats. Six of us pushed the boat into the water. With a final strong shove, our gallcon gripped the water and, buffeted by tiny ripples, sailed like a swan. We named her the *Batavia* and all tumbled in, with Bill at the front. He told us to be careful, to prevent it rocking. We had fashioned a few oars from some planks and timidly made our way around the snags and blanched trees sticking up from the water. It couldn't be deep, but even so, deep enough to cover our heads.

We soon made distance, the boat gently swaying away from the shore. Elated, we began to sing an old ditty: 'Rubadub, rubadub, who's in the pub to kill the giant spider?' We were moving further from the shore, quite unconcerned since all of us could swim, although not long distances. Bill suggested we row to a promontory about two kilometres away. We were moving steadily when Lex noticed the boat was taking on water. At first we attributed this to our wet legs and soaked underpants, but as the water level rose, Lex yelled, 'Damn, we've sprung a leak! One of the plugs didn't hold.'

Even so, he didn't seem too worried and added, 'We'll have to keep bailing and hope we reach land before she sinks.'

As a precaution, Bill had nicked two empty soup cans from the mess kitchen and these came in very handy during the next half-hour. I must admit, we did become rather nervous though as we took turns bailing, and looked to Bill for guidance. He kept yelling to scoop faster. We were still about a kilometre away from shore and the wind was changing; the clear blue sky had given way to bruising clouds. As I looked up, I saw screeching cockatoos tree-hopping their way to shore. How I wished to be a bird...

We were in a pickle and had to work faster. My arms began to ache and the tedium of scooping was starting to irritate me. 'Keep going; we're still too far away,' urged Bill. The water was rising more rapidly now, as other holes had come unstuck. We were too impatient and should have waited till the next day... But then again, other kids might have taken our boat in the meantime. Anyway, all these thoughts came too late and we began to panic.

It became a race between the rising water, the clouds about to release their burden, and the distance to shore. Soon, light showers began and the temperature dropped, which helped energize our efforts. We were making headway and could make out people along the fringe of the weir.

'Try not to rock the boat or the holes'll get bigger!' Robbie Koger shouted.

We needed to remain calm, scoop frantically, and avoid unnecessary movement; not an easy thing to do. As we neared the promontory we noticed people waving to us: to warn us or to say hello? Either way, their gestures were meaningless, although a couple of the men had entered the water, indicating help was nearby. However, we weren't about to rely on them, so redoubled our efforts while Bill reassured us: 'Almost there; we can almost swim from here.'

At last we jumped out, confident of feeling sand beneath our feet, and made for the shore. As we did, our grand vessel gurgled and gave up the ghost, slowly sinking. Exhausted, we paddled and waded our way to the rocky outcrop of the headland. Just when we reached dry ground, the heavens bucketed down, as if to remind us that water can be a dangerous thing. We were shaking and laughing at the same time.

'Shit, that was close,' I said. 'I'm not going sailing again.'

The men in the water smiled and one of them replied, 'Next time, get a metal boat, they're much safer.'

'Thanks for looking out for us,' replied Bill, 'but we couldn't find such a boat.'

Despite being exhausted, we were sort of pleased with our adventure, and after letting the adrenalin abate a bit, dawdled home to our hut: the overcrowded hut had become home in a very short space of time. We realized we had been lucky, but also that we had been very foolish. Still, we conquered the Hume Weir! No use gnashing teeth over something that has passed. We would be more careful next time.

Conversation around the mess table that evening bounced around, ranging from the what-ifs to the should'ves. The whole block had heard of our ordeal and depending upon who you talked to, we were considered either fools or heroes.

Mother scolded Bill, while Father was annoyed by the sloppy preparation. 'What idiot goes out in a leaking boat before checking the plugs properly? And how come six of you got in? Too many for a small dinghy! And, always stick to the coastline if you're not sure. You're all mad.'

He was right, of course, but we didn't take much notice. After all, we survived!

Most of the migrants were keen to make money on the side, but Bonegilla wasn't a good place to do this. Aside from the recession, there wasn't much work in either the camp or around Albury-Wodonga: Father and John Koger senior were lucky to be working for the local farmer. Blessed are the rabbits for some...

The seasons changed, yet the vegetation changed little, until the acacias sprang into flower in midwinter. Wattle, like a brassy showgirl, exploded in the bush, dominating throughout the country, with the sweetness of the blooms wafting in the air. Someone came up with the idea of picking and selling wattle flowers to the workers returning from Albury and the nearby farms. Wattle abounded, was easy to pick and climbing a delightful challenge.

The best possie was the front boom-gates, where I had become chummy with the elderly security guard. He was easy to talk to and took a fatherly interest in the migrants. At first, the day labourers smiled and ignored us, until the security guard pointed out that Thursday was pay day. We either charged a ha'penny or a penny, depending on the size of the bunch. We didn't realize that wattle wilts quickly and nor did those who bought the flowers. Father was proud of us when we handed over the copper coins. It never occurred to us to keep the money for ourselves, aware of the dire straits our parents were in. Family came first and personal gain second.

On sunny days we worked the many huts covering the large grounds of Bonegilla, hoping for a decent haul. Many migrants were single males and hence emotionally adrift. It was common for the lonely Polish and Italian bachelors to ask us in for a glass of water. Some of them showed us their black and white or sepia photos of families and girlfriends back home. We never felt uncomfortable or threatened. They were pleased to have company and amused us with their animated gestures.

'Comma inside and I show ya photos of my Papa anna Mamma anna *famiglia.*'

'Hey, blondie boy, you gooda football player?'

The questions were basic and predictable. 'Yes, mister, I am a champion.'

One of them tickled my skull as I left for the next hut, then laughed. 'So, little boy, remembra the e... Roma backwards is *amore.*'

I didn't quite understand the joke but laughed anyway.

It was courageous to leave one's home, family and friends and start again in a new land. Father and Mother were in their early forties when we emigrated. Quite old really! At least we were a cohesive family.

Father once spent time giving comfort to a young Dutchman in tears because of loneliness and uncertain prospects. Another time, I was embarrassed to observe a man clutching a picture of his wife and kids, blubbering. Adults shouldn't cry. I felt sorry for him, nonetheless. Father talked to him for a long time too, and I still remember Father telling us about a suicide due to the man's inability to cope with this new and harsh country. Little has changed for the more recent influx of single refugees.

One day, Father gathered the family around the card table, the heart of our tiny room, to inform us that a very important person wanted to see us. We donned our best clothes, combed our hair and polished our only boots, then waited impatiently for this lofty personage to arrive.

After an hour or so, the priest appeared, accompanied by a man with a very long nose and wearing a brown overcoat and grey hat. We were asked to come outside and line up in order of height, like queuing for a school photograph. What a strange request... Mother took an instant dislike to the man, but we went along with the task, tittering and shoving.

We followed the eyes of this Cyrano de Bergerac,[86] who looked on impassively.

'Well, isn't this a healthy-looking family,' began our priest. He was all smiles and continued, 'This is Mr Melville,[87] who has come all the way from Tasmania to find work for you on his farm, so he'd like to get to know you a little better.'

Mr Melville coughed and his enormous nose shook in the process. 'Welcome, g...good to make yer acquaintance!' he said, and began walking back and forth, appraising us like cattle at a country fair. He argy-bargied with Father on the side, nodded his approval, then turned to our priest, who was talking to Mother, and stammered 'Th...they'll do! We'll leave the day after tomorrow.'

We had passed a test of some kind, known only to the grown-ups, and quickly dispersed to let our mates know we'd be leaving Bonegilla for some island to the south. In a flash, everything had changed and a strange tingle in my stomach told me a new adventure lay ahead. Even now, whenever I leave a place, a hotel, or even a tent, I develop this odd sensation of regret, nostalgia even, as if I were a little afraid of leaving somewhere secure, or of leaving something of myself behind – *la petite mort*,[88] although it has nothing to do with sex.

The return to Melbourne seemed more prosaic and familiar now. We were becoming used to this new country, although the rain drumming against the split windows of the train prevented us from seeing the countryside properly. We were so bedazzled the first time that we couldn't get enough of the scenery, but now turned to our books and conversation, bragging and quibbling over trivia. It wasn't then apparent to us that the Australian Government had assisted Mr Melville by subsidising the cost of our travel; which must have been the case – far too expensive otherwise.

We stayed in the Victoria Hotel in Little Collins Street and slept in a huge double bed, easily swallowing up we three younger brothers. For breakfast, we were served cornflakes and scrambled eggs, a novel experience for us, and favourites ever since. During the day, we annoyed the hotel workers by running up and down the stairs and overusing the Otis lifts, clanking the cast-iron concertinaed doors.

'I bet I can beat you to the next floor by running up the stairs!' said Lex. 'You have to wait for my signal.' The lift won every time.

---

[86] Cyrano de Bergerac, 1619–55, French dramatist and duellist. He had a large nose which people would travel from miles around to see.

[87] Not his real name.

[88] 'la petite mort' – the little death – is an idiom and euphemism for orgasm, but can also be used to describe poignant, melancholic experiences.

Not being used to hotels, the swankiness of the carpet and the wooden panelling on the walls made us feel important. In its own late-nineteenth-century style, the place reminded me of Hotel Krasnapolsky.

The following day we boarded a red double-decker bus and immediately raced to the top to view the changing streetscape. As we inched our way up Sydney Road to Essendon Airport, some of the buildings reminded me of Fremantle, with their decorative wrought iron lace and covered walkways. What a life! No school on the horizon, flying in an aeroplane for the very first time, and new foods to savour. What else could a nine-year-old ask for?

An old Douglas aeroplane flew us to Tasmania, the 'Apple Isle'. We were a little nervous, except for Flozzie, who clapped his hands in delight as the plane shook its way into the sky. Though tired, the excitement eased the tension and airsickness of the journey. Poor Lex, though, was in agony with earache as we thumped across Bass Strait. The formidable pine crate, brought from Holland, would be sent to Hobart to be collected later. Meanwhile, our trusty suitcases were hurled onto the back of a truck once we landed, and as the second-youngest, I was fortunate to share the cabin with Flozzie and Mother. Mother looked unhappy sitting next to the gruff Mr Melville, who Father had anointed as 'Nose' Melville.

It was chilly and dank this time of year and when dusk set in the bush took on a sinister look. What type of animals could be lurking there? When the headlights came on, wallabies hopped alongside us, as if guiding us to our new destination, their dark silhouettes a welcome distraction. The winding road and potholes, from Hobart through to Dunalley, Eaglehawk Neck, Koonya, and finally, Premaydena, made the journey seem longer than today, while the bends in the road made Mother ill. I enjoyed the rough ride, the cabin shaking with each thud over the long stretches of corrugation: in the early 1950s, most roads around the Tasman Peninsula were unsealed.

At last Nose Melville drove up a short track to reveal a white-timbered house with a small verandah enclosed by flywire screens. On either side of the brick steps leading to the front door were white pillars, neatly cemented over to give them bulk and a semblance of chic. The house was nothing like the one we had left behind in Newportslane.

Still, home is where the heart is and as we explored the green-painted rooms we thought the house seemed big and comfortable enough for the seven of us, especially after our cramped quarters in Bonegilla. We were all dog-tired though and once Nose Melville had unloaded our baggage, he left us to ourselves. He had bought a few necessary items for us, such as linen and blankets, a radio and kitchenware; which was just as well

A white-timbered house….with white pillars. Premaydena, Tasmania, 1952. 'Anna', Henri, Frank and Lex.

because the pine container never arrived: on further consideration, Father thought it best to keep it in storage for the time being. He and John planned to visit Stephens, the storage company in Hobart, to take out the essentials, including Mother's beloved green oil cookers, hoping that in time the rest could be forwarded. First, though, our parents wanted to check out the lie of the land. It turned out that our new home was a few miles from Saltwater River. Mother thought she had reached the end of the earth and cried the whole week.

Much later, it transpired that someone, probably a wharfie, had stolen some of our family heirlooms, including a valuable edition of the nineteenth-century *Catholic Illustration*, a collector's item. It puzzled Father, who said, 'The dills can't even read Dutch; what use is it to them?' He also suspected we weren't the only ones fleeced. 'Bloody convicts; haven't kicked the habit!' He remained philosophical, however, and took it in his stride, but Mother was far more upset. 'Herman, did we do the right thing coming here? How are we to survive in this jungle?'

The day after our arrival, we reconnoitred the area, the term 'neighbourhood' hardly being applicable to our isolated dwelling. We had been warned to stay away from the shed next to the house – dynamite was stored there. Nose Melville had secured it with a lock, but the flimsy wooden doors could easily be overcome. Father pointed out we could all be killed if the dynamite was disturbed, so we left well alone. Nose Melville eventually removed it.

There were other sheds and outhouses used for shearing and storage. Lex and I thought we had found a magical playground. Old handsaws, ripsaws, wedges, rabbit traps, thick ropes, pitchforks, shovels and chains were left casually on floors or strapped to walls in a haphazard way. Nose Melville wasn't fussy, it seemed, and assumed the equipment wouldn't be stolen because it belonged to the farm. For that matter, what would we do with it anyway?

Exploring the paddocks, we discovered rusty bits of farm machinery, discarded water tanks, and sheep. Sheep were a novelty! We chased them, all to no avail. They just looked stupid and stared haughtily at us, as if to say, 'Silly boys, you wouldn't know your arse from your elbow, so leave us alone.'

Behind the sheds and potato paddocks a dirt track wound into the forbidding bush. Though nervous that natives could be hiding in the scrub, or even the rarely sighted Tasmanian tiger, our curiosity overcame our fears and we ventured on till we reached a billabong. A few old tyres bobbed against some water cress, while frogs were croaking a hallelujah chorus. What a racket! It's incredible to think now just how pig-ignorant we were about Tasmania.

A few days after we entered the mixed-farming world of Nose Melville, we younger ones were enrolled at Nubeena Consolidated, or Area,

School. The school was a shock to our system. We metamorphosed from urban sophisticates to rural yobbos.

Before long, our family were invited to the Melville's, where I met Tom[89] for the first time. We sized one another up from a distance. Tom was about my age but bigger-boned. His dishevelled straw-blond hair and round face made him look friendly enough. His younger sister gawked at us as if we had just arrived from another planet. To be honest, our plus-fours, fair complexion and poor English would understandably have disturbed her quite a bit.

Mrs Melville was a neat, compact woman, who showed a great deal of interest in our circumstances. A little younger than Mother, she spoke well and, even to an undiscerning boy like me, I could tell she was elegantly dressed. Her easy manner and husky voice were reassuring as she passed a plate of Anzac biscuits around the table. What did she see in her boorish husband?... This judgement being more intuitive than objective!

'So, Mrs Licht, tell me about your boat trip and life in that migrant camp.' We left the women to talk, even if Mother found it frustrating expressing herself in clumsy English. Tom showed me his Hornby train set and we soon became good mates.

Tom's house, built on a bleak hill overlooking the valley towards Norfolk Bay, was a good two country miles from Skeggs' general store, which guarded the Nubeena-Premaydena junction. I usually stopped by the Melville's after the bus dropped us off from school, and every Friday, before going anywhere, we went into the store to thumb through our favourite comics, then bought the most violent, along with a sticky bun, and skylarked homewards. Mrs Skeggs didn't seem to mind us and our antics. On the way, we mocked the kookaburras, tossed stones at the crows and hurled each other's school bag into the blackberries. Apart from the usual chores, we were free to do as we wished for two whole days!

Homework unheard of, we mucked around for a while before it was time for me to go home to help around the house. Mrs Melville's chips tasted wonderful and I was reluctant to leave, especially when it was cold. Frequently I stayed too long; the wood fire, hissing and crackling, so cosy and seductive.

Sometimes Tom and I sprawled out on the linoleum-covered floor reading the latest Phantom comic, just bought from the general store. We let our bums rip as The Phantom, alias 'The Ghost Who Walks', mangled some cropped-haired Neanderthal with his lethal fist. The Phantom was a sublime role model for young boys wishing to be changed from runts into supermen. I loved the Phantom's skull imprint that he left on his

---

[89] Not his real name.

opponent. We wore his trademark ring like a married couple; the comics, treasured trophies! We even cultivated Phantom-speak to impress our mates at school. Quite pathetic really! Yet in those slower, pre-television days the imaginary excitement of these stereotypes was a godsend to boys like us.

In 1952, the Tasman Peninsula was not so different from a hundred years earlier, except for the motor car and the gift of electricity. But I wasn't aware of that then – as a nine-year-old you generally aren't, preferring to be distracted and to live in a cocoon of wonder. This wonder, sometimes stemmed by fear or boredom, kept bubbling up like a fresh mountain stream.

My world, shared with my brothers, was sealed off from my parents. Parents were aliens most of the time. They seemed a necessary appendage to our daily lives, but were in many ways invisible. Food and clothing materialized by association. Mother, querulous as ever, would scream at us, reminding us of sacrifices, rarely understood, and of how lucky we were to have such wonderful parents. However, her emotional barrage never had the impact she hoped for: we were too busy with other far more interesting matters.

I learnt little at Nubeena Consolidated, though. My true teacher was Tom. He taught me the words associated with the bush and our school subjects, since my inability to understand the nasal English of either teachers or pupils caused me to fret and suffer. It was Tom who taught me the gist of expressions such as 'tough as leather boots', 'not the full quid', 'Buckley's chance', and 'a brass razoo'. He also taught me how to use a 303 rifle, fish in the local creeks and billabongs, swing an axe and saw through fat logs – pulling not pushing – all bread-and-butter activities on the Tasman.

Save for Miss Prendergast, who took pains to explain things and to spend a little extra time with the immigrants, I learnt more from Tom Melville than the cranky teachers, who refused to empathize with the migrant kids. We had to adjust to the Aussie way or be damned. Recent immigrants have the advantage of better resources, well-trained language teachers, and the most important virtue of all, compassion; though, sadly, not yet shown by everyone. Even so, our treatment was an innocent cruelty and perhaps inadvertently added flavour to our lives. The dry seeds of antipathy yielded unexpected fruits: the determination and tenacity not to be beaten by the 'enemy'. We'd show them!

How Father, John and Bill fared as farmhands still remains a mystery. Nose Melville had aspirations and saw migrant workers as cheap labour, also hiring another family, the Nuttrees,[90] who arrived later. The Dutch had a reputation as hard workers and were quickly hired by more enterprising farmers around the country. The pay, however, was paltry and we ran up a monthly bill with Skeggs, the general store owner. For us, it was subsistence farming.

Melville's income came mainly from apples, so the spraying of orchards with chemicals and pesticides wouldn't have done Father or my elder brothers much good either. Melville made his own wooden boxes for the produce and also grew mixed vegetables for his and our family, although we had to do our own potato digging. The source of the rest of his income was more tenuous and experimental, and included cray fishing.

Father was a cheese maker by trade and commercial traveller, yet quickly adapted to his new work environment. He had no choice. Mother, meanwhile, kept the home fires burning by baking bread, cakes and other delicacies, but she was lonely and loathed the place. The arrival of the Nuttrees and contact with a lonely Dutchman up the road helped a little.

'This will hurt me more than it will hurt you!' Not bloody likely, I thought. The Headmaster straightened his lapels before he twanged my bum with his favourite bamboo reed.

Whereas the intensity of pain is forgotten moments after its infliction, and although the sensation lingers for a time, the injustice of it all lasts a lifetime. In Holland, a heavy oak geography pointer was commonly employed to mete out punishment, the thud shuddering through the body when the rod landed on the buttocks. Not nice! Girls were exempt, though, for reasons of propriety.

Nevertheless, this bamboo performance was more personal. My new Headmaster owned a quiver of bamboo reeds. Each reed, in his estimation, had a different role to play depending on the nature of the misdeed, an assessment arrived at through criteria peculiar to himself. Swearing called for a finger-thick reed administered with a moderately hefty swipe. Insolence went up the scale, so a thinner, nastier reed was applied with greater enthusiasm, and after his exertions a few drops of sweat would form on his pallid forehead. However, my offence was on a grander scale and required a more considered response.

Headmaster Jethroe[91] was a measured man. He had a high-pitched voice and always wore the same suit, even when the temperature exceeded eighty-five degrees. To me, he seemed prematurely old, and his

---

[90] Not their real name.
[91] Not his real name.

PREMAYDENA
Phone 8   Dec 12th 1952

M T Licht

Bought of

BERT SKEGGS
General Storekeeper and Cartage Contractor

Bushells—the Tea of Flavor

10	lbs Sugar	7	8½
4	butter	16	10
2	dripping	2	6
2	brown sugar	1	7
2	white sugar	1	7
2	doz eggs	18	6
3	jam	7	3½
3	Corn Flakes	8	6
7	W.R. flour	4	11
1	Golden Syrup	4	9½
2	lbs biscuits	6	1½
1	nescafe	4	6½
1	Black Nugget	1	1
4	oz tobacco	8	5½
1	tin Peas	3	1½
	Freight	1	0
	£	4 5	6½

Skeggs' account for groceries. Premaydena, Tasmania, 1952.

baldness, thin face, and brown, double-breasted suit made him look menacing. His military bearing suggested action in some theatre of war...or conceivably he had taken part in the Rum Rebellion and was over one hundred and forty years old! I had little to do with him until committing my heinous crime, in what I regarded as a very just cause.

Tasmania, as probably elsewhere in Australia, was quickly recovering from the devastation of war, and one item deemed essential to the restoration of the nation was milk. Milk then wasn't your namby-pamby range of light and fat-free milk we have today. Oh no! Although most certainly pasteurized, milk in those days was full-bodied, with a proud head of cream. It was a meal in itself. Moreover, the milk was provided free to school children, in pints, not like the penny-pinching midget bottles of later years. We were issued a bottle each at morning break and, for us at least, it was a luxury to look forward to each morning. Some affluent students added exotic flavours, like caramel or raspberry. Sometimes, but rarely for migrant kids, we were rewarded with a second bottle in the afternoon, if we had been exemplary in class, as adjudged by our teacher. It never occurred to us that there could be bottles left over because some of the students were either allergic to milk or hated it; we understood absenteeism to be explanation.

During the break, I usually met Tom near the cattle yard, next-door to the school, where we sat on the greyed gum railings, guzzling our milk. The wintry days attacked us with Antarctic blasts from the south or nose-numbing gales from the west. It often rained and if the weather was too nasty, we fraternized in the large shed beside the stockyard. The shed also served as a boxing ring for the boys, disputes settled the old-fashioned way.

'I suppose you want a kick o' the footy?' Tom asked, in his easy manner.

Soccer wasn't known here, but I assumed it was just a variant of the universal game. How wrong I was! I was handed an egg-shaped leather ball and looked at it intently. A different kind of skill was required to handle this monstrosity... Tom and a few of his mates took up positions at opposite ends of the schoolyard then kicked the ball in an elliptical trajectory and jumped to catch it. Whoever caught it was given what was quaintly called a 'mark'. I watched the contest closely and when one of the boys slewed the ball off his foot in my direction, I did what any soccer player would have done and headed the ball. The nature of the contact itself didn't bother me, knowing perfectly well how to angle my forehead correctly. Unfortunately, it was the lacing on the ball that made the contact, and the tingling pain, not unlike an errant tattooist putting in the needle, nearly knocked me out. I didn't let on, but the lads stared at me in disbelief, expecting me to collapse on the spot.

'Are you all right?' yelled Tom from the other side of the schoolyard.

'I all right! That what we do with sport balls,' I replied boastfully. This act of bravery impressed the boys, and as they wandered back to the classroom, Tom gave me a grin and a clap on my back. 'Shit! That would've split m'head. You must have a concrete skull!'

A certain respect grew out of this incident and very slowly I mastered the drop kick and learnt how to take a mark.

A few weeks later, one blustery day, with branches crashing onto the roof of the classroom, followed by sheets of rain falling every which way, we huddled together at lunchtime on the narrow verandah overlooking the centre playground. Lex was nowhere to be seen but Flozzie was trying to get past some of the boys to enter the classroom and reach his desk, though without much success. With his long, curly blond hair flying in all directions, he cut a comical figure.

Being a placid boy, unsure and cautious, Flozzie was always keen to please. 'Hey, boy,' he implored gently, addressing the ginger-haired son of the postmaster, 'you please...move over for me?'

The boy swung around and snarled, 'Fuck off, you little wog! I'm not shifting for you,' and to make his point shoved Flozzie into an awkwardly placed metal cupboard standing alongside the wall. Flozzie hit the back of his head against the metal handle and bit his tongue. He screamed and yelled, 'Why you do that?!'

His tongue was bleeding profusely, and quite uncharacteristically, if understandably, Flozzie attacked the surly lad, who was twice his size. Everyone's attention turned to the boys. Some shouted words of encouragement to the bigger of the two: 'Get the little Dutch bastard!' and 'Smash the migrant shit! We'll help you.' There wasn't a teacher within cooee.

I hadn't noticed Flozzie and was about to take a bite out of my fat sandwich when I heard the commotion at the other end of the verandah. When I moved closer to take a look, to my surprise I saw my brother being held tightly while the postmaster's pride and joy got stuck into him.

Without a moment's hesitation I looked around and, spotting a crate of leftover milk, grabbed the nearest bottle then rushed in to clock the aggressor. A glass pint of milk is a weighty weapon and the thud sounded awful. Blood immediately began to ooze freely from his skull, the two reds intermingling creatively. The onlookers went quiet as the boy collapsed onto the timber floor.

After the momentary satisfaction of having saved my brother from a severe thrashing had washed over me, I realized I was in deep trouble; the shock and awe of my deed had stunned the crowd and I instantly opted for escape. Grabbing Flozzie by the hand, I bawled, 'Let's get out of here!' Fortunately, by this time Flozzie's tongue had stopped bleeding. Meanwhile, everybody focused on the victim as he was carried away to the Headmaster's office, sick bays not yet having been invented.

By the Scruff of the Neck

Flozzie was about four years younger than me and his short legs took off, pumping like pistons. I jumped the cattle yard fence while he slipped between the railings, then we ran for the short-cut to the dirt road, heading to Premaydena. We barrelled along, hoping to quickly put a fair distance between the school and us. Clump! Clump! Clump! Our heavy boots bowling along as fast as possible.

The Headmaster, having assessed the situation, spoke to two strong lads from the eighth grade, they being the most senior boys in the school. About fourteen, and built like thugs from a Phantom comic, they were given the task of bringing us back. We were about a mile from the school when, looking over my shoulder, I espied the two. They didn't seem in any particular hurry...probably grateful to be out of the classroom...and took their time in overtaking us, about half a mile further on. Flozzie had run out of puff by then and I obviously couldn't leave him. However, I looked towards home with mixed feelings. Father wouldn't be too impressed and might give me a hiding, whereas Mother would verbally castigate me but also act as a protective barrier if Father lost his cool.

By this time, the miserable wind had died down and the rain had eased. I heard a deep voice yelling, 'Okay, you little shits, you've gone far enough. Stop yer running! Come back quietly or we'll thump ya! Ya unnerstand?'

I didn't know about Flozzie, but I knew the game was up. In my poor English I shot back at them, 'He hurted my little brother; that why I hitted him.'

The lads chuckled and one of them said, 'Yeah, sure, you little clog wog! But you don't hit anyone over the head with a bottle. Heavy glass bottles hurt!' At least he seemed to have an inkling of my point of view. As it turned out, the same couldn't be said for our Headmaster.

The boys pushed us into the main schoolroom, where the Headmaster was teaching sums. The room had a high ceiling and just below where it met the white-timbered walls, a row of small windows let in the afternoon sunlight. Each top window had a long cord tied to a cleat far below. It was a large room, brewing with the odours of sweaty boys and sweet-smiling girls. This older class combined two grades and was the largest in the school.

Flozzie was sent back to his own class and left untouched, while I was commanded to step forward in front of everyone. I felt weak-kneed and naked as thirty pairs of eyes bored into me. I looked up at the tiny windows, momentarily watching the swaying branches of a giant gum tree. How I wished I could be a roaming magpie, free to fly away! Instead, I was nailed to this floor awaiting execution. I didn't bow my head, as you were supposed to; I kept looking up, hoping for a miracle.

The Headmaster now played his part. He stood up, walked to his quiver of reeds, didn't hesitate, and selected a very thin, almost dainty specimen which he swished through the air like a jockey's crop, then motioned me forward. He thwacked the desk loudly as an overture to the main event.

The school was abuzz with the incident but no one was prepared to defend me, seeing as how the injured lad had to be carted off to the doctor. So here I was, a young boy in funny trousers, perspiring, quaking in his oversized boots, and held up to ridicule in front of tough boys and serious girls. *Hurry up and get it over with!* Somehow I kept my bearing; whatever happened I wasn't going to blubber and give them the satisfaction of seeing me cringe.

I was ordered to lean over an empty desk, now vacated for the punishment ritual. The thin-voiced skull addressed the class: 'This terrible boy has attacked an innocent lad and put him in hospital. The suffering, not to mention the cost and anguish – this last word unfamiliar to me – have needlessly burdened the boy's parents. Let this be a lesson to you all. Don't take matters into your own hands!'

After this homily, he forced me down hard over the desk and with one hand on my back for extra leverage, raised his bamboo stick and in quick succession worked on my derriere with diligence. Waves of prickly pain surged through my body, the short interval between each wallop an eternity. *When will he stop?* After a dozen or so strokes, he stood back, while I waited for something else to happen.

The initial sensation was one of numbness but it didn't take long for the hurt to reveal itself. It was as if a porcupine had done a backflip onto my bum! I was tempted to run around the room like a headless chook, rubbing my rump. But that would only amuse the class. I gingerly stood up and though red in the face with anger and embarrassment, looked straight into the Headmaster's eyes. He turned around and ordered me back to class.

I limped back like a rodeo rider given the heave-ho. As I waddled into the room, the whole class stared at me. The teacher pointed to a back seat, where I sat on my hands to spread the soreness.

After school, Tom raced up to me as we boarded the old Bedford bus and kept asking stupid questions. 'Did it hurt?'

'Nah, like feathers touching my bum.'

'You shouldn't've clobbered him with a milk bottle, ya clown!'

'But Flozzie was hurted!'

'You should've just jumped on top of the bastard and hauled him off.' Tom was just sparring with me; enjoying himself at my expense.

'Yeah, his friends then kill me. I must help Flozzie or he go to hospital.'

Tom gave me a friendly punch and grinned. 'Yeah, I reckon you're right, but I wouldn't've had the guts to do it.'

When some girls tittered and pointed at me, I rather enjoyed being the centre of attention, but my mind was preparing itself for Father's reaction...if he found out. As we got off the bus, Lex, already informed about the saga, advised me to say nothing.

Mother had been visiting a neighbour and was chatting away merrily about some recipes she'd been given. For us, food was fuel and the intricacies of baking were like obscure code. We weren't all that interested, and since my rear end was still recovering, Mother's harmless banter was about as welcome as a headache. I fell onto my bed, placed my hands behind my head and began to worry about Father, then shifted to what I was going to do on the weekend.

That evening, as we attacked our tucker with the usual vigour, I stayed silent.

'You're quiet tonight,' observed John. 'Lost your tongue, or did something happen to you?'

I just nodded, then sighed and said, 'No! I'm just tired, that's all. Nothing to worry about!'

Father was recounting his experiences of the day: dragging the heavy hoses for orchard spraying, warding off the wind-blown rain, watching the antics of the cattle dogs, and the like. But as he spoke, his eyes wandered to each of his sons 'Well, nosy parker, you were in trouble today weren't you?' he remarked. Parents being parents, at least the discerning ones, have an uncanny ability to fathom the unfathomable when it comes to their kids.

I was stunned. How did he know? We didn't have a telephone, so who told him? It couldn't have been Lex... Flozzie was fingering his soup noodles and hadn't noticed the change in the verbal landscape, but stupid me gave away a clue. 'Nah... What do you *mean*, Pa... Trouble?'

Father, being a salesman, could read his customers like a wise owl. My defensiveness betrayed guilt. He knew it and I felt it. 'Okay, Pikfin – my Dutch nickname – out with it! What did you do? And don't lie to me.'

I'm hopeless at lying and soon confessed, offering minimum details and putting myself in the most favourable light possible. In a spirited manner, Flozzie backed me up: 'But Pa, if Herrie hadn't hit him I would've been *dead*!'

A trifle over the top but it did the trick, especially as the deed appealed to the machismo of the older brothers.

'Well! We'll see what happens from the school end,' said Father, 'but you're not off the hook yet, my little man.' As far as he was concerned, the matter was on hold pending further developments, not least the matter of any possible costs.

Despite these provisos, I was immensely relieved.

Mother saw it differently. 'You could have killed the poor boy! What would his mother think?' The father didn't rate a mention; the

Headmaster was simply doing his job, albeit a little heavy-handedly; and she completely ignored the reason for my action.

The 1950s were light-years away from the present. Authority was God back then, swift punishment the norm – which, amongst other things, saved time and intellectual effort.

As it turned out, nothing much further happened. The Headmaster walked past me as if nothing had occurred, but I did notice some silly girls following me around. Carrot-head came back to school wearing spectacular bandages, soon defaced by rude inscriptions and scrawled signatures. He had toned down somewhat and for the next few weeks at least, an aura of peace and tranquillity descended on the school. The whole matter faded like the morning mist over Norfolk Bay. Instead, our activities at lunchtime were given over to exploring the treacherous cliff face on the other side of the stockyards.

We were warned about the dangers of walking too close to the edge of the cliff – even worse, to avoid the test of nerves involving the narrow ledge two yards down from the top. The rocky ledge was about five yards across, a mere eight inches wide, and had a good ten yard drop to the growling sea below. Whether it was windy or calm, the green waves smashing their white manes onto the rocks below were enough to send shivers up my spine. I hated heights, though didn't mind climbing trees so much because there were at least branches to hang onto. Lex, by contrast, more courageous than me, thrived on nerve-racking feats. He adapted to the bush like a native. Crossing torrential creeks, stomping on venomous snakes, aiming a shanghai at birds and hitting them with unerring precision, were all par for the course. If something should be done, then it had to be done, regardless of the consequences. Lex always took charge.

Amongst boys, cowardice, or being 'yellow', was the unpardonable sin. You might rattle in your boots or cack your pants, but you never refused an order from the gang leader, unless it was clearly absurd or you decided to challenge them, just for the sake of it.

One sunny winter's day five of us headed to the cliffs, wanting to be away from the other students and any prying teachers, and hoping to find a cosy place to have lunch. Girls were outlawed, and anyway, didn't seem particularly interested in tagging along. We shared our rude jokes and stories with pleasure. After polishing off our grub, we were going to the beach west of the school to explore the rock pools. The quickest way was via the accursed ledge, and since Lex was the leader, we were compelled to follow.

By the Scruff of the Neck

'Last one across is a donkey's arse!' was enough to spur us on even more. Young Timmy Robbins, the one who said this, was always full of beans. 'Ya wanna see me lizards? Come over on Satedee. Me parents'll be in Hobart and I'll cook ya some chips! You wanna see me footy cards! Why don't we...' and on he usually went.

I had learnt from earlier times that crossing the ledge was best done by slowly shuffling along, while facing the cliff's calcified veins, and searching for protruding roots or rocks to grab hold of, never looking down. I followed Lex, involuntarily farting due to sheer terror. I made it!

Alas, Timmy froze halfway and began to totter, his teeth chattering like a polar explorer. 'I'm...um...stuck,' he managed to get out. I hadn't heard of epilepsy, but in hindsight that's what it was. His whole body shook. We all assumed it was blind panic and if something wasn't done he would lose his balance and skydive to a watery grave.

Without hesitation, Lex edged back and cradled him. 'Hang on tight, Timmy! Don't look down! Give me your hand!'

We thought Timmy was beyond help, given his state, but somehow he lifted his hand and placed it in Lex's.

'Now just follow me...slowly. Nothing will happen!'

Both inched their way to safety and when they reached the other side, Timmy, still convulsing and looking decidedly wan, lay there, staring at the sky as if God had intervened. Lex instinctively covered him with his black jacket...and then we waited. Definitely no rock pools now!

After about ten minutes, with all of us standing around watching, glum and silent, Timmy opened his eyes. Staring at us, he exclaimed, 'Shit! I thought I was gunna die!' It was time to go back to class, and just before we snuck back into the schoolyard, Lex said to Timmy, 'Well, you little turd, you're not coming with *us* again!'

While all the brothers were good at arithmetic, thanks to the thorough Dutch education system, our English was at first poor, but rapidly improved. My favourite subject was Nature Study, which I believe has bifurcated into more highfalutin' disciplines like biology and geography. Nature Study combined visuals and fieldwork, and it was the latter that really appealed. The clean air, the scents of the bush and sense of freedom took a strange hold of me. Our teacher, Miss Prendergast, was short, pretty and very caring. Neatly dressed in a green skirt and white blouse, she was a wonderful reader, her cadences caressing our ears. She was intelligent, too, calm and very aware of her students' strengths and weaknesses, as any decent teacher should be. Most Wednesday afternoons, weather permitting, Miss Prenders, as we called her, took us into the bush, a leisurely ten-minute walk from the school. She would survey the scene, making sure not to visit the same location twice, then say something like, 'Well, my little doves, I think that hill over there will do, don't you?'

'Yes Miss, of course Miss, a terrific spot Miss!' we all yelled. No dissent or equivocation; we were far too aware of how fortunate we all were, enjoying ourselves in the bosom of Mother Nature. It was also an age of post-war innocence, with the impatient rancour of today's students fortunately absent.

We parked ourselves anywhere we liked and were instructed to perform two tasks: to do a drawing, either in pencil or charcoal, and to find specimens to use for our talk to the class. By specimens, Miss Prenders meant insects, lizards, birds' eggs or rare rocks. The drawing soothed the savage beast within, while the scurrying and netting gave vent to our energies.

It took only about five minutes for Timmy Robbins to be bitten by a bull ant. He swore, then danced a corroboree around Miss Prenders, who pacified and mollycoddled him. The rest of us just ignored all these goings on, preferring to pursue our fantasies and individual lines of enquiry.

I was hopeless at drawing and the butt of everyone's joke. 'Geez, is that supposed to be a tree; it looks more like a flash of lightning' or 'How come that rock is bigger than the tree behind it, when it should be the other way around?' I didn't take much notice, just made another miserable attempt.

Searching for insects was more to my liking. I hid in the dry wheat-coloured grass and pushed my nose close to the ground, hoping by some miracle to enter the busy world of tiny ants zooming along in pursuit of some morsel twice their size. The tiny insects front-loaded their booty into the communal headquarters, then returned for another load. I loved the loamy smell of the soil, the growth at the bottom of trees, the tall green stalks from where a solitary grasshopper jumped over me. I now became Gulliver, tracing the hidden paths of tiny creatures going about their business and enjoying themselves. My huge head poked into a world where it didn't belong.

I am constantly amazed at the variety and depth of the Australian bush. There are few places on earth like it. The minty tang of the eucalypts, the acid smell of ants, the sweetness of ethereal insects wafting by...all bestowing a sense of euphoria as the sun beat down on our young bodies and time stood still.

These were the sensuous days of self-indulgence and at times my heart still aches for the beauty and wondrous secrets this new land offered me. You can have your paradise in the afterlife; like a sailor shipwrecked on a perfect island, I'll remain *here* forever...

By the Scruff of the Neck

When young, we are closest to this illusion and can best afford to kid ourselves: as Carl Sagan put it, "We are like butterflies who flutter for a day and think it is forever."

Spring's sounds and smells kept me spellbound like a new piece of music, but back inside the classroom, the tense atmosphere made me decidedly unhappy.

A travelling Methodist preacher came once a fortnight to tell us stories from the Bible. As Catholics, we were suspicious of other God interpreters. This man, however, entertained us by sticking biblical cut-outs on a felt board, where the holy characters clung determinedly, never falling, as if by divine intervention.

The problem was that the minister spoke too quickly and I couldn't follow him. As a result, I lost interest and my mind began to wander. After each story, we were told to rest our heads on the desk, close our eyes and pray with him. I couldn't understand the words, and opened my eyes ever so slightly to find out whether everybody else was praying. To my surprise, they were...or pretended to.

I was sitting next to fat Kev Richards, whose eyes were dutifully shut. Just to alleviate the boredom, I opened my pencil case, took out my compass and stuck the sharp point into his rear end, his large bum an irresistible target. A bullish roar broke the solemn silence and everyone sat up, popeyed, then stared at fat Kev.

The minister quickly summed up the situation and I was banned from religious instruction. I now shared an empty classroom with a Jewish boy who had also been removed, but for quite different reasons. We were allowed to play draughts.

School holidays were a gift from the government and everyone, including the teachers, was unusually cheerful in the final week of the winter term.

'Now tell me, Henri, what are you going to do during the holidays?' asked Miss Prenders. Most students when asked either responded with a 'Dunno, Miss' or 'We're goin' to the Hobart Show, Miss.'

When I was asked, I hesitated, then replied, 'I'm goin' to shoot rabbits and wallabies, and...do some fishing...and just before we come back to school, I'm goin' ta kill myself 'cos I hate this place.'

The whole class gasped in astonishment, except for Miss Prenders, who said, very quietly, 'Will anyone be there to watch?'

Feeling a bit silly, I muttered, 'I dunno, Miss!'

On the way home, Tom and I punched each other on the bus, too excited to act normally. A whole fortnight of freedom, no school and oceans of time! We couldn't believe it. The catchcry became, 'Explore! Explore! Explore!' What else matters to young boys with gallons of energy? Apart from food, of course!

Lying in bed drowning in warmth, the late winter storms resisting the arrival of spring, I savoured my precious atoll, removed from the rest of the family. It was Saturday morning, the first day of the holidays. I had finished reading the most recent Phantom comic, to do with smuggling guns into the Congo, and felt like a break from my hero. I browsed through some of my favourite Dutch Westerns – a self-contradiction, I know – the indefatigable Eagle Eye or White Feather doing their best to amuse me, but I just couldn't concentrate.

As the sun skipped onto my bed, the kitchen radio announced a new champion by the name of Marjorie Jackson, winning gold for Australia in a place called Helsinki. A funny name that, I thought. Athletes sinking in hell! Twigs scratching the corrugated roof interrupted my thoughts, which were further shattered by Lex jumping onto my bed – we all had separate beds for the first time. He hit me over the head with his socks.

'Hey! Why don't we go over the road and follow the track to the jetty? I'm bored witless just hanging around here,' he said, after a final flick.

'Yeah! Good idea!' I replied. 'And if it isn't very interesting we can come back to the empty water tank and turn it into a cubby-hole. Waddya reckon?'

Lex nodded and grinned. I pulled on my new gumboots, bought from Skeggs at considerable expense to my parents, and after some toast and rice bubbles was raring to go. Lex was flexing his shanghai at a butcher bird. As the frightened bird took off, we saw the Nuttrees coming over the bridge. They lived just past Tom's place, in a pale brick house right on the main road. The Nuttrees were younger immigrants and loved talking to our parents about food and shopping in the old country, and inevitably the War. They were a family of nine, large families being fairly common amongst the Dutch. Post-war optimism and perhaps the relentless advice by the Catholic Church to go forth and multiply, may have had something to do with it. Many Dutch immigrants came from the Catholic South.

The Nuttrees had three daughters, the middle one our age and named Anna, plus four boys, who seemed very young to us and rather indistinguishable. Anna[92] was a tall strapping girl, but gentle in manner. She wore a ponytail and simple blue dress and enjoyed playing with us.

---

[92] Not her real name.

We tolerated her, but made no concessions. Whether climbing trees, riding stupid rams, throwing a fishing line or rowing a boat, if she couldn't do it we just let her be. She was a real trier, though.

Some of our female cousins in Holland were, by contrast, painful: they refused to dig for worms before going fishing, wouldn't dream of helping to find timber for cubbies, never shared their scooters, and became prissy when dealing with bodily matters. We thought most girls a bloody nuisance!

Not so with Anna, who made herself part of the gang. Anna was no shrinking violet, either. She happily squatted behind trees to irrigate the bush, taking her time. We may have experienced latent sexual curiosity, I suppose, but being so young, and occupied with more tangible matters like negotiating a slippery log across a creek, it didn't register much: *Sigmund* had yet more work to do.

The day was windy and overcast, but warm, as spring showed her better side. We crossed the dirt road and ambled a few hundred yards up the hill, then turned immediately right onto a narrow track parallel to an embankment on our left. The track was flanked by thick bush either side and fronds of bracken leant over the edge of the embankment, which, after a few minutes walk, rose even higher to form a long strip of blue-black rock, seeping water of iridescent colours, like an oil stain.

Amazed, Anna exclaimed, 'I'd love to do a painting of these rocks!'

Such a response left us in awe; there was more to her than met the eye. Some time later, a solitary neighbour called Old Ced told us that this tongue of land facing Norfolk Bay was riddled with ores such as copper, iron and bauxite, as well as black coal. We didn't fully understand the geological complexity of Old Ced's learned talks, but gathered that the Tasman peninsula had much more to offer than bush, beasts and sadistic headmasters. Old Ced also knew a great deal about the Tasman's history, including that of the former convict settlements at Port Arthur and Plunkett Point.[93]

Our mood was buoyant; we whistled and played the fool, not taking our eyes off the patchwork beauty of the ever-changing bush. High above the majestic gums, standing sentinel in the dense green undergrowth, soared peregrine falcons, gliding on the upward thermals, scouring for prey.

We screwed up our eyes against the sun, which at last showed itself, and watched these lords of the sky biding their time, before hurtling downwards at jet speed to seize an unsuspecting rabbit or lizard. Our voices, echoing in the green valley below, ceased as the birds regrouped for another attempt.

---

[93] Port Arthur, Tasmania's main penal colony, was founded in 1830. The Plunkett Point coal mines were discovered in 1833 and mined by convicts.

I sauntered along looking up at the canopy, wondering what it would be like to cruise over this terrain of trees, grass and sea and then propel oneself like a dive-bomber onto the enemy below. But falcons aren't human and they were just after food, glorious food!

Black currawongs emitted their haunting cries, resonant of times past, then, as they ceased, silence reigned, until, here and there, small wattlebirds could be heard, scattered amongst the trees, their peculiar creak-squeak calls startling the listener. A bush symphony! The raw convicts would have been transfixed by the strange sounds of this extraordinary land, previously unknown to northern men, yet known intimately for aeons by its southern dwellers.

The orchestra persisted until we reached the shores of the bay. Then, suddenly, the lapping of water reached our ears. We had almost reached our goal. The track wound its way to the rocky waterfront, where seagulls and terns squawked and preened themselves, at low tide searching for nourishment in the rock pools hidden within the seaweed.

After the darkness of the bush it was as if a giant veil had lifted and we cast our eyes towards Dunalley, gazing out over the calm sheet of water where seagrasses flip-flopped in the tidal currents. To our right was a short, rickety jetty, with gulls perching on its rails like uniformed soldiers lining up for inspection. We scrambled across the rocks to get to it, then sat down, dangling our feet over the edge. Time evaporated as the sun licked our bare legs and browned faces. Surrounded by trees and the many birds standing and fussing nearby, the serenity of the bay affected us strongly. We said nothing for a long time. The birds, dancing and squabbling like kids, strutted along the rotting wooden rail, watching us. I wanted to hold on to this natural world.

Not far from the jetty, in the hollow below Premaydena Point, Old Ced staked out his crayfish pots, usually in the late arvo, because, during the night, the restless crays could be attacked by giant sea lice and eaten alive. He emptied the pots before dawn and had been doing this work on and off since his return from the Great War. In 1952 this part of Norfolk Bay yielded large and plentiful crayfish. They were taken to the Dunalley fishing port and sold to the wealthy on the mainland or exported overseas.

According to Old Ced, who, a long time ago, had lived with the natives on the Gove Peninsula in the Northern Territory, the indigenous hunters of Australia had been trapping and devouring crays for thousands of years. A certain aboriginal woman named Krubi was renowned as a wonder woman. It was claimed that she was absolved from other tribal duties so she could devote her skills to catching the prized crays. After the Great War, when he made his home in Tasmania, Old Ced made good use of the knowledge gained from the natives living around the Gulf of Carpentaria.

By the Scruff of the Neck

Although Ced, as a young man brimming with ideas, had loved the Gove Peninsula and the Gulf, the spirited person he once was never returned from that pernicious war. His decampment to France, where he lost mates at Fromelles,[94] changed him forever, and soon others viewed him differently, too. Before the war he had been talkative, expressive, and eager to engage with people, but since that nightmare, though always civil, he had little to say. Now, he preferred his own company and womenfolk rarely crossed his life. Old soldiers don't like to talk about what they've seen and experienced. They know too much...

One afternoon, after I'd left Tom's house, I dawdled along the main road, absentmindedly kicking a can, until I reached the top of the hill and took a breather, before walking down to the bridge near our place. By the edge of the creek stood a mysterious house, dark and low, covered with brambles. At the northern side stood a few neglected rose bushes. Some of the weatherboards had come loose and the rusty roof added to its air of neglect. Once, the house had been painted green, but time had exposed the boards, so only shreds of paint were now left near the eaves.

It was quite common after the War for houses to stand empty. Soldiers didn't always return, forcing the missus and kids to go to the cities or move in with better placed family members. As kids we just ignored this particular house and quickly walked past, although I always felt ill at ease. It was as though someone was staring at me from behind closed curtains. Nevertheless, one day my curiosity got the better of me. My fists were clammy as I approached, and once outside, I stood there awhile, sizing up the place, before mustering enough courage to kick back the broken front gate then walk closer to the front window. It was covered up, so I crept warily along the cracked path at the side and made my way to the rear of the house. There, my heart rate shot up and I held my breath as I saw a huge vegetable garden: silverbeet, potatoes, rhubarb and carrots, all planted in neatly raised beds of soil. Someone lived here!

Towards the back of the garden, in an open shed, I noticed an old car, and nearby stood a huge aviary containing blue-winged rosellas and other parrots, wrens, quails darting in and out of logs, and even some golden whistlers kept in a smaller aviary within the giant one. What a surprise!

I leant against the back wall of the house soaking up the scene, bewitched, when a voice roared, 'Whaddya want?!' I froze on the spot, my

---

[94] The Battle of Fromelles on the 19th to 20th of July 1916 was the first occasion during which the First Australian Imperial Force saw action on the Western Front. The battle is widely regarded as a disaster for the Allies, historians estimating that 5,500 Australians and 2,000 British troops were killed or wounded.

knees almost giving way, then turned around to see a thin old man standing within the frame of the back door, his arms folded. A shadow hid his face.

I didn't know what to say; I just stood there! After an agonizingly long pause, the old man took a step forward and I saw a craggy face with small eyes glinting in the afternoon sun. He studied me closely. 'I've been watchin ya. You're the migrant kid from up the road.' I slowly nodded and out of the blue the old man began to laugh. What a strange man! He laughed for a long time, while I treaded water, feeling extremely uncomfortable.

'I've been watchin you kids each mornin, wonderin where ya all come from, wearin those daggy clothes.'

I felt a little more relaxed now. 'From Holland! We come from Nederland.'

'Ah! Tulip heads, eh! Well! Come in for a cuppa an' I'll show ya sumthin.'

With a certain amount of trepidation, I followed him, not knowing whether he would murder me, or harm me some other way.

A smell of rancid oil hit me as the flywire door snapped shut behind us. The rear lean-to had an old wooden table covered with newspapers and plants. We passed through a sitting room, containing flaky leather chairs, a small, wobbly table, and some interesting paintings of nature scenes hanging on the walls. At the front of the house another door opened onto a brightly lit enclosed verandah, hidden from the main road by a row of young cypresses. After the brief tour, we returned to the sitting room. Above the glossy, tiled fireplace was a mantelpiece and some books. Against the wall opposite were two glass cabinets filled with wonders of the deep.

'I've been fishin here now for nigh on fifty years, with the exception of the First War and me adventures up north. As yer can see, there're some surprises here.'

'Th...thanks for showing me!' I stammered.

He sat down, then remained silent for a while, staring out the window. 'Me name's Cedric. What's yours?'

'Henri... Henri Licht,' I replied reluctantly, never fond of admitting to my name, for some peculiar reason.

Cedric got up and wandered off to fetch something. I took the opportunity to study the collection of shells, molluscs, anemones, dried cuttlefish, crayfish claws of gigantic proportions, kelp, and oddly blanched driftwood, all adorning his glass cabinets. I had never seen such a variety of sea items in one place and lingered longest over the massive shark teeth, laughing at me, it seemed. In Ced, Neptune was still alive.

When he returned, he shoved a cup of milky tea into my hands and sat down again. He had wanted me to admire his collection. 'Bring yer brother next Satedee and I'll teach yer how to row. 'Bout nine in the mornin... Drink yer tea and then yer'd better be off!' Cedric was quick to the point.

After telling my parents about Cedric's offer, Father thought it a great idea. 'Might learn a bit! Remember to stay in the middle of the dinghy, though!'

Mother muttered something about drowning, but was ignored. Our shared excitement overrode her objections.

On the Saturday, Lex and I took only two minutes to reach old Ced's house. We knocked on the door and he emerged from the side garden, telling us to take it easy. We dutifully followed him, waved to Mother and Flozzie as we passed, and made our way to the now familiar jetty. Father and the older brothers were already at work: they only had Sundays off.

When the old man met Lex, he introduced himself as Cedric, although we called him Ced to his face, which he didn't seem to mind, and 'Old Ced' behind his back. He had already collected his crays that morning and told us to row a fair distance from shore into the bay. Apart from wanting to teach us how to row, he indicated, by stretching his arms out wide, that the further out from the coast, the better the view of the coastline.

'It's all 'bout rhythm and resistance,' he said. 'Move yer arms evenly and don't crunch the tholepins!'

At first we both made complete fools of ourselves, but slowly tamed the oars and began to get the hang of it. Lex adapted more quickly. The steel dinghy bobbed on the small waves as we took some respite from the heavy rowing.

'If ya sail past Deer Point towards Ironstone Point yer'd pass the Coal Mines, where the worst convicts were sent in 1834. It's a bewdiful area 'round Lime Bay. I often used ta fish there 'fore the Second War, but it's too far to row now. I'll take youse there one of these days...usin' the outboard. Well worth the visit.'

We knew from school that this part of Tasmania was dripping with history. The way Old Ced described the various aspects of the gruesome peninsula, now covered up by the passage of time and the innocence of the thick bush, made it take on a new reality. He told us Tasmanian tigers once roamed the gullies in considerable numbers, too, until just about all of them were killed by stupid white folk.

'If yer lucky,' he said, 'the Tasmanian tiger might still pay youse a visit.' Old Ced winked, then, poking some Erinmore tobacco into his pipe, he began to relax and to find his true vocation: filling up the empty skulls sharing his dinghy.

'It stands to reason, dunnit? Jus' look around ya! Trees everywhere, and like what's below this dinghy, full of surprises. The last Tiger was s'posed to have died in 1936...but I don't believe he was the last one. Jus' take a good look as far as ya can see, past the hills and through the gullies. Few, if any, bushmen 'ave ever been in there. Ya can't tell me the tiger's just disappeared into thin air! The blackfellas knew about 'em and stayed away. Nah, the tiger's a *very* shy animal... Easy to get away from the white fella! As for that mangy thylacine in the Hobart zoo just before the War...a fancy word for the tiger if yer must know...they jus' let it starve to death. Ya can't rely on that bit of bulldust. Nah, I reckon there are still tigers lurkin in there.'

As the little rings of smoke corkscrewed upwards from his pipe, he kept pointing to various spots on the coastline, giving us their history, their relevance to fishing and to early convict life. At times he fell silent and became reflective. Who were we to interrupt him? Then, as we looked at one another, I asked him, 'How come you know so much, Ced?'

He shrugged his shoulders, as if he didn't care to answer, then changed his mind. However, most of what he said escaped us, partly because of the language, but largely because we were stone ignorant.

'Well, I've lived 'ere most of me life and when me sister Ada died of the Spanish 'fluenza after the First War, the folks shifted to Hobart, but I came back here. I some'ow feel this part of the world belongs to me. Ya see, me great grandfather was a former inmate at Port Arthur; I should say Point Puer, actually. He came out as a boy... So, me dear tulip heads, convict blood runs through me veins and I don't mind a bit.' Old Ced seemed pleased with himself now that he had found a captive audience. Lex and I vowed to read more about the Tasman Peninsula when we returned to school. After all, it wasn't every day one went rowing with an old salt, especially one who had criminal connections with the past.

On Sunday, Father and Mother wanted us to stay with them. There being no church nearby, we prayed together in the small living room. Around the dinner table we asked Father questions about the Tasman, but he admitted to having little knowledge of the place. As an antidote to our disappointment, he lifted our spirits by telling us that Nose Melville had proposed to take us all to the Coal Mines next Saturday. A few yearlings roaming around some leased land there had to be carted back to his farm. The older boys would help with the rounding up, while the younger ones could do some rabbiting; the latter suggestion coming from Tom. Mother didn't want to go, preferring instead to visit the Nuttrees.

We were now in the middle of the holidays and already becoming aware that time was running out, but were still determined to convert the large, empty water tank into our retreat. Anna helped us with items such as stools for seating and a large log for a table, covered with a discarded tablecloth. Flozzie and I fetched some discarded lino from one of the outhouses. We'd be right at home! The idea was to make a few sandwiches, pour some cordial into an empty milk bottle and have a picnic inside the tank. Mother even gave us a tin of homemade biscuits.

We first rolled the tank onto a flat spot. When it was righted, we made ladders for either side from straight gum saplings tied with rope. Apart from an open manhole at the top, the rest of the tank was sealed, although a few small bullet holes allowed for fresh air once we were inside.

Lex found a square piece of timber large enough to cover the entrance hole and when everything was ready, we descended into our den. Lex and I went first, followed by a giggling Flozzie, and finally, Anna. Anna was wearing a rather short dress and, seemingly oblivious of her gender, straddled the tank, exposing her firm thighs and white knickers. I glanced at Lex, but his eyes were fixed on Anna's female attributes. He sat down on one of the stools, sighing heavily and saying nothing. *Sigmund* was at last peeking around the corner.

When it began to rain, Lex closed the manhole and lit two candles, which cast grotesque figures on the round walls. We sat there for a while and told a few stories, then, as the bursts of rain increased, fell silent, the downpour strangling our words. The cosiness of the tank made us feel secure and reflective. After half an hour the rain stopped and the air became warmer. Anna broke the silence by saying, 'Can I come with you to the Coal Mines next week? I won't be a pest and maybe I could be of some use.'

'You'll have to ask your folks first, though I reckon Nose Melville won't mind,' said Lex. 'I'll check it out with Father and see how we go.'

The last Saturday of the holidays promised to be a day to remember. At ten o'clock, Melville hooted the horn of his red International truck and we all jumped aboard. Anna was allowed to come and had put on some long pants for the occasion.

We passed a few homesteads, crossed the bridge at Saltwater River and headed for the Coal Mines. Just before Nose Melville dropped us off, he insisted we be back at the gate leading to Lime Bay by four o'clock.

Tom was familiar with the area and took the lead. 'Before we explore the mines,' he said in a businesslike manner, 'I'll show you a way of catching rabbits.' With no traps, we were completely mystified.

We made our way through thick scrub and after several minutes reached an opening where there were numerous green knolls, smooth as billiard tables, covering old coal shafts and the remnants of buildings. The grass was kept short by grazing wallabies and rabbits. Plots of strong-smelling jonquils gave a festive touch to the overall bleakness of the convict ruins.

'If you walk around the edge of the mounds, you'll see rabbit holes,' said Tom. 'Find the largest and that'll be the best entry to the warren.

We'll plug all the remaining holes first.' He gave us each a bundle of newspapers then instructed us to scrunch the sheets into tight balls and use them to plug the holes. Clearly, he had done this before.

'If there are any young ones, give 'em to Charlie; he loves 'em.' Charlie barked furiously, his tail wagging in anticipation, and probably alerted the rabbits below as he watched Tom open up the tunnel with a shovel. Near the centre, the tunnel dipped and Tom stopped. He chuckled to himself as he reached deep into the warren and plucked out a large rabbit. Its frantic kicking came to an abrupt end when Tom stretched its neck. It went limp. We were horrified, but didn't say anything, respecting his expertise. 'That'll be our tucker for the next few days,' he announced, with a grin.

Soon after, Tom pulled out the remaining bunnies and threw them to the dog. 'I know you think I'm cruel, but you got to remember they ruin the paddocks. Rabbits are a bloody curse! Normally I'd bring the ferrets. It's much quicker, but I wanted to show you how easy it is.'

Despite our squeamishness, we were impressed, and followed Tom to the next clearing, where Lex only found young rabbits, or kits, as they're sometimes called. Charlie had a feast day. After a few more sallies we lost interest and decided to follow Tom to the Coal Mines.

As a group of wide-eyed kids exploring the beautiful grounds of this hideous convict outstation, our imaginations were fired up. Tom knew all the tracks that followed the old main roads connecting the various hubs of the convict colony. Later, in the 1960s, the tourist dollar prompted the Tasmanian government to do something about protecting the area.

For us, the Coal Mines became a playing field unknown to most tourists and concealing far more than the rubble initially revealed. The sights were truly extraordinary. Situated on a hill overlooking Norfolk Bay, and facing towards the heavily forested Forestier Peninsula, the once solid-brick military buildings looked out across the dazzling aqua water, frequented by a wide array of seabirds: 'prime real estate', as it's referred to now.

Gardens with flowers grown from English seeds once adorned the exterior of the military barracks. Anna whispered to me that she could see the small women of the settlement plucking the flowers grown by convict gardeners. They strung daisies or daffodils from a Wordsworthian garden into garlands for their beautiful children. Fifteen acres of land, would you believe, were under cultivation, testifying to self-sufficiency of a sophisticated order.

Who were these people who carved out such a civilized niche in the wilderness? Colonial British souls to be sure, with surprise in their eyes and hearts stirring, just like ours. As for the convicts, well...they suffered.

Tom gave us a sober commentary. 'They used to dig up to three hundred tons of coal a week, and just further towards the main shaft, you can still see the pick marks on the stone walls of the big northern quarry.' He pointed upwards and we followed the direction of his finger, open-jawed.

It was eerie to think that a whole community of up to four hundred and fifty people lived here in close proximity but under vastly different circumstances, now almost erased by time and neglect. A few graves in a cemetery may offer a glimpse of earlier generations, but it's the physical outlines of once thriving dwellings and human activity that breathe life into the past. And what of the shafts and tunnels themselves, where the convicts laboured and suffered under such great duress?

Tom led us to the main coal shaft at the top of the hill. This location, once cleared, overlooked the entire settlement, but had now returned to its natural state, judging from the spindly trees and scrub that had sprung up since its closure many years ago. The absence of completed edifices or well-defined groundwork somehow made the historical connection more fluid. Much was left to the imagination, of which, as youngsters, we had plenty.

Next, Tom took us down the old wooden railway which led to the jetty, where the stumps of wooden pillars covered with barnacles could still be seen, just below the water. On the way, as we laughed and amused ourselves, he stopped to reveal sunken grass-covered holes, once deep shafts. I looked down the inclined plane from on high, towards the coal jetty, while the others jumped about, inspecting remnants of the shafts. Standing still in the silence, I thought I could hear the groaning of tired convicts working the winches and see the loaded wagons descend as empty ones came up the incline. What did the convicts have to look forward to apart from food and sleep, with the same routine eked out each day in sweat and sorrow?

The afternoon grew darker. Tom had proved to be a great guide, but it was time to head back and let the ghosts of the settlement play in our minds. Each of us took stock of this little-known place, the cries of children and mutterings of prisoners echoing in our ears.

When we followed the adit[95] sites, climbing down the main shaft, then inspected the solitary cells, afterwards wading into the crystal clear waters off the old jetties, we seemed closer in time to the original inmates than now, over sixty years hence, when artificiality has, to a marked degree, taken over.

Old Ced's umbilical link to his convict heritage kept reminding me of how recent these events were. *Oma* and *Opa* Goudsblom, born in 1879, were only forty or so years distant from them. The convicts were immigrants of sorts, just as we were, but without our luck to have arrived over a hundred years later.

---

[95] An almost horizontal entrance to a mine.

Old Ced knew more than he let on. What happened here can never be properly recorded, just as, even now, we can never truly understand the lives of others in far distant lands; despite the pervasive swoop of the camera and the internet.

The truck was already waiting for us when we arrived at our agreed meeting point, drizzling rain now sprinkling our coats. The bellowing of beasts confirmed new company. 'You took yer time!' Nose Melville grumbled, as he revved the engine.

'Aw, Dad, there was so much to see and we forgot the time,' Tom replied easily, not at all worried by his father's tone.

Earlier, Melville had anchored some iron railings onto the sides of the tray and we all joined the cattle for the ride back, stroking them, smelling their shit with earthy pleasure. Safety wasn't a concern in the 1950s; you just rode the bumps and hung on for dear life. Charlie seemed happy as he jumped onto the backs of the nervous heifers...

The Saturday had indeed been special. Lex began to sing and Anna joined him. The wind took wing, the bush smells strengthened and the truck skidded and shuddered its way across the ruts. As the late afternoon air turned chilly and even wetter, my heady thoughts were accompanied by hunger pangs. I wondered what Mother was cooking for tea. Lex pointed to his mouth. Great stomachs think alike! Meanwhile, Anna looked dreamily into the last of the sunset, narrowed by swollen clouds signalling more rain.

Old Ced was pleased with himself, having planted his spring crops. He visited now and again, showering us with lettuces, spinach or silverbeet, carried inside a beer box. Strawberries, rabbits, and best of all, crayfish, were also typical gifts. Father particularly loved the spinach and crays. We were introduced to the art of boiling and shelling crayfish and their armour reminded me of armadillos.

In exchange, Father provided old Ced with homemade cheese, compliments of our Jersey cow. Knowing all about cheese, Father made his own equipment. We took turns thumping the cream into curds and finally into a blob, leaving the finishing touches to him. The barter economy was alive and well.

Each weekend was different. Depending on the time of year, we also dug up spuds, chopped wood, and helped with the rounding up of cattle or sheep, even when it rained. The smell of dead sheep and lambs killed by dogs, crows, disease, or when caught in a wire fence, was as strong as the lingering smell of abattoirs on a hot day. The maggots had a feast day, squirming over one another inside the swollen carcasses.

By the Scruff of the Neck

Sometimes we trudged to Koonya, where a visiting priest from Hobart said Mass and heard Confession. I usually had a great deal to confess, including swearing for having to walk the three miles to attend the dreary service. There were a few visits to Port Arthur as well, where a number of the buildings were now overgrown by ivy. It was haunting but forbidding, and we preferred the historic mines at Saltwater River. Other times we played in the paddocks, visited Ced, or played soldiers. We enjoyed climbing the pine trees at the back of the woolsheds too, the aromatic resin sticking to our hands. Baboon-like, we clambered to the top, where we were able to survey the area from an immense height. In colder weather, the late afternoon chill eventually forced us inside to read or play games.

One late winter's day, I had again been too long at Tom's house. Time had gotten away from me. Dinner was at six o'clock sharp, lateness taboo, and punishable by chores such as washing up. I looked up at the mantel clock and, triggered into action, thanked Mrs Melville for her kindness and left. It was a twenty-minute walk down the hill through long, dry grass, then across the creek and uphill to our place. I had only a quarter of an hour. Tom accompanied me part of the way.

Nearing the creek, we instinctively headed for the log serving as bridge. It was getting dark as the sun slunk away over the horizon and I tripped across what I took to be a leather belt. Tom was a fair way behind me. Who would drop a good belt here in thick grass, I wondered. I picked it up and wound it around my waist, quite pleased with the unexpected gift. By this time, Tom had caught up with me and as I was about to tell him about the find, the belt began to wriggle.

Tom shouted, 'It's a bloody snake, ya fool... Drop it! Chuck it away!'

I couldn't tell who was the most flummoxed, Tom, me, or the snake. I hurled it into the air, expecting to be chased and bitten there and then, dying a horrible death, not even having had time to say goodbye to everyone. I didn't know then that the cold evening had rendered the snake sluggish and not in the least interested in exerting itself. Tom took off back to his place and I bolted like a greyhound to ours.

When I raced into the kitchen, I saw the table hadn't even been set. It transpired that Father had had a fall while spraying the apple orchards. He was all right though; just a few bruised ribs. My snake story would have to wait...

In early spring we ran to the woolsheds to watch the shearers, while the bleating orchestra deposited their little brown marbles all over the oiled shed floor. Sometimes we helped lift a sheep into position, its hooded eyes looking at us like an indignant old madam. We offered to sweep the floor, covered with fleecy bits, bloodied dags, and the ball-bearings of shit. Meanwhile, Flozzie buzzed around the shed like a blowfly, yelling his heart out. He was about six and the clattering atmosphere must have got to him. Perhaps he identified with the sheep...

I sometimes attempted to wrestle a sheep, and always lost. The shearers were good-natured and enjoyed a laugh. For a wager with an old shearer called Murphy, I even rode a ram. Murphy thought I was a dickhead for even trying. As I grabbed the animal by its swirly horns, it just shook its remarkably strong head and easily repelled me. So, instead, I crept up from behind and managed to jump onto its back to straddle it. The deal was to last ten seconds, but Murphy laughed his head off when I cleaned the deck. The ram simply bucked and twisted, and within five seconds I was flat on my back, listening to it bleating victory.

The day I turned ten, John returned from Hobart with a blue-chromed canon that shot wooden bullets, a gem that stayed with us for years in mint condition until it finally succumbed to rust and neglect. We had already bought plastic soldiers, representing the three branches of the armed forces, and an array of cowboys and indians, either from the local store or during visits to Hobart. These were placed around our bedroom ready to be sent skywards by our wooden bullets.

We were rarely idle, though, but the most despised task, avoided to the point of murder or serious bribery, was digging holes every fortnight for the burial of the family poo. The holes were dug some fifty yards away from the back of the house. Fortunately, the soil was soft because of plentiful rain...and the rampant fertilising by our digestive systems; I never remembered the location of the last hole dug.

On Saturdays we chopped kindling for our shower, while on Sundays, after visiting neighbours or vice versa, we often played soccer in the front garden. Everyone joined in except Mother. The garden consisted of apple trees grown in rows on either side of the dirt footpath, and only near the house could be seen red and pink geraniums. The widest space between the fruit trees became the pitch and two trees at opposite ends were selected as goal posts. The laughter, threats and cries of 'Goal!' reverberated throughout the valley, while the birds looked on in amazement, ruffling their feathers, then flying off with a shriek when things got too much for them.

One particular Saturday, Mother nearly fainted when she entered the laundry at the back of the house. Rushing out, she yelled, 'Herman, Herman, a beast, a beast!'

Mother was rarely precise about animals; or cars, for that matter. We all emerged from our nooks, wanting to know the nature of this beast, responsible for almost frightening Mother to death. She was given a chair, her heaving bosom testifying to her ordeal. Meanwhile, Bill found a sturdy stick then cautiously entered the monster's den. He peered around the door and spotted a creature curled up in the concrete wash trough. It was a beautiful ringtail possum, which, once disturbed, lifted its head and stared at my brother with its sad, dark eyes, large as saucers, as if to say, 'Would you kindly piss off! I'm trying to sleep.' He prodded the animal, which took off faster than a cornered rat.

The 1950s was a decade of 'Get on with it, don't whinge, or you'll be whacked!', a crude yet wholesome injunction which oiled the machine of family life. We weren't fussed, but Mother was, up to a point. She bemoaned her lot by throwing tantrums and complaining to Father, who felt somewhat guilty, but powerless. Mother always grumbled about being tired, of how hard she worked, of never-ending cooking, of being queasy at the end of the month, of not being appreciated. It was her oblique way of saying she hated the house. We largely ignored her, not being mature enough to understand her misery. Even so, we tried to make it up to her by offering to do menial tasks. We would fart around polishing the brass ornaments so typical of Dutch households; wash the dishes, sloppily, flicking one another with the tea-towels; sweep the rooms superficially; make the beds in a slovenly fashion, and nick off as soon as we could. It certainly must have been hard for her...

Father's worries and interests lay elsewhere. Putting grub in front of his brood was one thing, but craving cultural nourishment was quite another. We wound up the beautiful wooden gramophone, 'His Master's Voice', either left behind by the previous occupants – Italians, we were told – or perhaps it belonged to Nose Melville. The gramophone's heavy silver arm bobbed around on the 78s as if floating on water. Father reclined in his chair, in his socks, smoking a pipe or puffing an exquisitely cut Ritmeester. He would sigh as the voices of Tauber, Gigli or Björling filled the still Tasman air. There were about ten shellac 78s, all in excellent condition. We weren't to disturb him, except when the hallowed tenors of the day began to improvise from soprano to drunken bass because the gramophone had been wound up either too much or not enough.

With our work for the morning taken care of, one lazy Saturday afternoon, Mother baked a cake, rich in butter, cocoa and cinnamon, topped with cream and Ced's own strawberries. This treat, plus a bunch of daffodils, was to be taken to Ced in appreciation of his vegetables and crayfish. Lex and I were entrusted with the task. We carried the items in a cardboard box and caught up with Ced hoeing his vegie patch.

'Thanks very much and tell yer folks it wasn't necessary. Anyway, I've just bought some cordial; would ya like some?' Silly question! We followed him to the sitting room, again admiring his maritime collection, which had expanded of late: rainbow-coloured sea dragons, a variety of corals and sponges, a monster whalebone, and some dolphin teeth. Where did he find them all?

The cordial disappeared in a few seconds, and when we were about to leave, Ced said, 'You Dutchies are good lads but I reckon yer wastin yer time stayin in this neck of the woods.' What did he mean exactly? As if sensing our confusion he made a forthright observation: 'Mr Melville's usin' yer family for his own benefit. He couldn't give a *stuff* about ya. Mrs Melville is all right and so are the kids, but I've never taken to *him*. I don't trust Melville at all.'

Lex and I couldn't fathom why Old Ced had given us his opinion. As youngsters, we weren't used to such adult honesty, although our parents didn't generally conceal their worries from us. As a family we needed to understand the state of play, even if we younger ones didn't always comprehend the finer points. We were aware, however, that money was hard to come by and we weren't making much progress. Perhaps Ced wished to avoid upsetting our parents and hoped we would spill his beans around the dinner table?

This duly happened, but no one seemed overly surprised by Old Ced's revelations. 'Ced is right,' said Father. 'Mother and I have been tossing up whether to stay till next year or leave sooner. The problem is work. No good burning your bridges, even if we *are* being done over by Melville. At least we aren't starving and still have our pine container. Where to go, that's the question.'

This time Mother totally let go. 'I've always despised this place! I don't like the people around here and Melville gives me the creeps. He never sticks to his promises... We aren't getting *anywhere* and if this goes on I'll go mad! My days are so empty... I want to go back to Holland!'

John agreed. 'No girls, no dancing, no pictures. What the *fuck* are we doing here?'

Mother rebuked him for swearing, but for once didn't fuss too much, being more in tune with *his* sentiments than Father's.

John had already visited Hobart a few times, with the aim of finding work and, of course, girls. Dalliances with the local girls increased his desire to get out of this 'hellhole', as he saw it. Hobart became more and more attractive as he made his frequent return trips there on Sundays, his one day off. Jack-the-lad could be a charmer and butter wouldn't melt in his mouth in the right company. On occasions, he'd even played tennis with Mrs Melville and some of her friends, thoroughly enjoying himself, being a competent player and surrounded by nice women. Nevertheless, he was becoming desperate.

Bill, getting stronger and wiser by the day, had already worked out that there couldn't be much of a future here, given the poverty all around.

'Skeggsie reckons there's worse to come,' he said, 'especially here in Tasmania. We're better off going back to Melbourne.'

I understood my family's frustration and wished to help, but didn't know how. Lex and I were happy in our bush setting, but resented school. We were arithmetically streets ahead, yet inhibited by poor language skills.

It was fast approaching the end of the final term and Christmas wasn't far away. We were rehearsing for the annual nativity play, to be performed on the evening before school closed. Parents were encouraged to attend. Flozzie had been chosen as a young shepherd, driving everyone nuts with questions about the star of Bethlehem, the size of the crib, the proximity to the baby Jesus, and how to bow to the audience.

Our parents were conscientious and were given a lift to Nubeena by Mrs Melville, who was to help with the refreshments. Before the evening's entertainment, Miss Prenders wanted a quiet word with Father and Mother. 'Mr and Mrs Licht, I'm delighted to make your acquaintance at last. Your boys are making good progress, but Henri is a trifle difficult. He's too restless and disruptive, although he's good with figures. Lex is better behaved and a fine student. Frank seems a bit lost, though he's very sweet.'

Father and Mother were self-conscious about their language shortcomings and though they understood Miss Prenders, didn't say anything in reply.

In her pleasant way, she continued, 'The Tasman must be a bit of a shock to you, coming from Holland. My folks come from Launceston and regard this part of Tasmania as a bit of a backwater...er...rather remote. Do you understand what I'm trying to say?'

Mother deferred to Father, only because his English was better. He shifted in his seat, wiped his mouth nervously, and said, 'Thank you very much. Yes...yes...I know. It is hard for my family. What do you think we should do?'

Miss Prenders calmly met Father's eyes. 'I regard you and your wife as very brave in coming here. If I may be honest with you, I would suggest you move back to a large city, or at least a much bigger place, for more opportunities. I believe you are city folk – you'd be better off in a town.'

This was music to Mother's ears, but Father saw complications. 'You can't just land in a town without money and say, here we are, please, someone help.' He knew from bitter experience that God only helped those who helped themselves. He had to think things through.

Soon afterwards, Lex and I sang *Silent Night* in Dutch, and I was even allowed to play carols on my harmonica, drawing praise from the small audience. It was as if we wanted the locals to know we immigrant kids had talent and that they were missing out if they didn't realise it. For once, I enjoyed the school atmosphere.

*

Father was a cautious man and kept his cards close to his chest. On the *Fairsea* he had befriended a pastry chef, Ben van Hulst,[96] who seemed a congenial chap and they got on splendidly. They played *klaverjas* – a popular Dutch card game – and engaged in tittle-tattle. Van Hulst had been promised a job and a house in Traralgon, Victoria, and had given Father his new address. During the first few months after our arrival in this new land, both families wrote to one another, to keep in touch and to swap information about *Auwstralië*.

At the time, Father had sounded out Van Hulst about jobs and was told that Traralgon was a town in the Latrobe Valley, which was named after Victoria's first Lieutenant-Governor, Charles La Trobe. Van Hulst informed Father that the area was primarily industrial, and the source of Melbourne's electricity, so work might be available since the State Electricity Commission was expanding to cater for an increasing population. However, since then, the recession had put a brake on construction and employment – 1952–53 wasn't a good time to be looking for work.

In the meantime, once the spraying of the orchards was completed and the shearers had moved on, there wasn't much work left for any of us. Nose Melville, being shifty but pragmatic, must have realized that while we were good workers, we weren't farmers, which meant he had quite possibly chosen the wrong family. Fate, therefore, intervened. To put it politely, our services were no longer required, but Melville couldn't just dump us on our ear. Once hired, if immigrants lost their jobs through no fault of their own, their employer was obliged to find them work elsewhere; at least, those whose passage had been subsidized by the federal government. What to do? He gave Father an address in the Huon Valley, just south of Hobart. A timber company wanted workers to fell the famed Huon pine, a type of wood renowned for its hardness and used extensively for shipbuilding, housing and furniture. Melville calculated that if we rejected the work, it was no longer his responsibility: it was our choice, not his. He omitted to tell us that conditions there were worse than on the early squatter runs. The Huon valley, despite its scenic beauty, can be extremely wet and cold during winter. In 1952 it was certainly inhospitable.

The decision, however, was made. Father asked Bert Skeggs to help us shift. We hadn't accumulated much in the Tasman, but enough to require a small truck…which was necessary anyway, since there were seven of us. The pine crate was to remain in storage.

---

[96] Not his real name.

By the Scruff of the Neck

It was a good time to move. School had finished, it was summer, and the older members of the family had had enough of this primitive way of life. On the morning we left, it was cold and windy, not at all summery. Nevertheless, while Mother was ecstatic, though also vengeful, Father looked apprehensively to the future and thought it best just to cut his losses.

Nose Melville came around, supposedly to say goodbye, but more likely to make sure we hadn't nicked anything of value. We didn't have room for large items anyway, and were, for instance, too honest to take the old gramophone player, even though we would have liked to. When she saw Melville, Mother fumed. She thought we had been duped and made to suffer; in her mind, he was another Seyss-Inquart.

I loved her performance. Her eyes rolled menacingly as she hurled her deep-throated stream of abuse at him. 'You are the devil! You are a bloodsucker and I'll report you to the government for stealing from us.' She was referring to the pittance paid each fortnight for the long hours put in by Father and the older boys and wouldn't let up: 'You *fielt* – you scoundrel! You won't get away with this!'

Although tempted to stop and listen, the rest of us got on with it, loading the truck with boxes and our familiar suitcases, dusted off for yet another journey. I still hear her voice, though, trembling with anger and speaking in a hybrid of Dutch and English: '*Ik krijg je wel, hufter!* You *sekreet*! You *duivel!*[97] How can you walk here? You must shame yourself.'

Melville paced up and down the driveway, overseeing his domain, trying to ignore the virago cursing him. Mother even took out her brownie camera and tried to take a snapshot of the villain. However, each time she had him in focus he put up either his hand or notebook in an attempt to deprive her of her prize.

I still have a photo of him holding up his hand to cover his face – and thereby his sizeable hooter. Upon reflection, if he had nothing to hide, why the subterfuge?

Father paused to watch the charade, quietly enjoying himself: Mother was right, but wasting her time. Great theatre though, vintage Mother; a fond farewell! Now, for the unknown journey! We said goodbye to Old Ced the day before and took down his postal address, hoping to write to him one day. This never eventuated and I wonder now what befell this kind old man, who had shown the positive side of the Aussie character. We also said our goodbyes to the Nuttrees, especially Anna, and stayed in touch with them for a long time. As far as we know, they never left Tasmania.

---

[97] 'I'll get you, lout! You bastard! You devil!'

Nose Melville remained in our collective consciousness as the callous Australian, the exploiter and user. But generalizations betray lazy thinking. No country has a monopoly on vice or virtue.

The three-hour trip to the Huon was a *via dolorosa*. Mother and Flozzie were in the cabin of the truck, while I foolishly chose to sit on the back with my brothers and Father. The Ford may have been moving slowly due to the ruts and potholes, but moved fast enough to intensify the bitter southerly snapping at our faces. We crawled towards the front and centre of the tray to be shielded by the cabin. The luggage got in the way and despite our attempts to hide in the hollows of the tarpaulin covering our belongings, the wind always found a way of whipping us. *God* it was cold!

'If that wind doesn't stop, my knackers'll drop off!' Lex shouted.

Plagued by the vicious wind and the juddering of the truck, it was impossible to snooze. The journey was the most frenzied of my entire life, reinforcing both our despondency and our concerns. It wasn't until we reached Hobart around midday that the wind gave up and the sun triumphed. The sheer relief, as well as the warmth, revived my body: we had reached civilization again! The old buildings, like sedate Victorian ladies, sat comfortably in this harsh environment. We took the chance to refuel: not take-aways, just plain sandwiches. Then, having sorted ourselves out, we turned south, towards our final destination.

Tall trees, winding roads, desolation! We loved the scenery, yet harboured misgivings. Were we about to jump from the frying pan into the fire? Tasmania must be one of the most beautiful islands on earth and may well have charmed the early settlers, but it can also seem like the remotest place on the planet. As townies we looked for any sign of houses and congenial habitation.

It took an hour to reach the Huon hamlet, set in thick bush, where we followed a narrow track until it reached a clearing. Around the periphery were a dozen white makeshift wooden huts for the timber workers. This was to be our new abode! To us, the place felt even more isolated than Premaydena, less habitable, and far more depressing.

Father looked at Skeggsie and Skeggsie looked at Mother. Lost for words, the boys appeared almost comatose. No longer safe in Premaydena, cut adrift from a relatively comfortable home... I saw the collapse of expectations in everyone's faces. This camp was for tough, single men, not families!

Mother eventually managed to say, 'Herman, this is the *end* of the world. I *am not* staying here!'

Even Skeggsie, a hardened local, couldn't believe his eyes. 'Fuck me dead, pardon my French. What a dump!'

There was nothing to redeem it. Quagmires fronted many of the huts, the result of cars doing wheelies trying to escape the bog. The dwellings were only fractionally larger than our hut in Bonegilla. No gardens, no shops within a bull's roar and no evidence of women to soften the harshness. The ugly uniformity reminded me of a prison farm. This was a giant step backwards. Later, as an adult, having travelled in eastern Kentucky and witnessed the poverty of the hillbillies, as portrayed in mining documentaries and the film *Deliverance*, the camp reminded me of those tiny, forlorn, American townships dotting the Appalachian mountains.

We all looked at Father. 'Hm, not quite what I expected. Bloody Melville! He's sent us on a wild goose chase. Well, let's not panic. I'll have to talk to the overseer and politely tell him to stick this god-forsaken place up his arse.'

Fortunately, Father and Mother had a crash-landing plan. They hadn't trusted Melville and just prior to our departure took the precaution of resuming written contact with their friend, Van Hulst. The idea was to phone him from Hobart, tell him our plans had been dashed, and ask if we could come over to Traralgon for a few days, until work and accommodation were found. Pending confirmation, we would stay in a dosshouse near the Hobart city centre. At this point, it has to be remembered that my folks knew next to nothing about either the geography or the overall economic conditions of Australia.

'Father knows best,' we all thought, and with a sigh of relief, clambered back onto the truck. He explained to the timber boss, as best he could, that the setting was unsuitable for his family. No grudges; both men shook hands and that was that.

Upon returning to Hobart, Bert Skeggs was thanked for his help and paid his due. 'Drop us a note to let us know how you get on,' he said, waving goodbye.

We were dead tired from the long trip, so after some fish and chips, went to bed early. The family, for some obscure reason, was split up. Lex and I shared a room with a Chinaman, who was discreet and courteous. A quiet man, he slept most of the time and minded his own business. What was he doing here, I wondered?

My parents, in the meantime, needed to make some quick decisions. On the very night we arrived, Father contacted Van Hulst, who, luckily, had a phone, not available to everyone in the 1950s. Since he worked as a chef, perhaps he needed to be available to his boss and customers... He had no objections to us coming over.

The following morning, while we remained in the rooming house, John and Bill helped find the airline office. Father booked a flight with

Trans-Australia Airlines, more commonly referred to as 'TAA'. He was told at the airline office that a daily bus service, called the Latrobe Valley Bus Lines, left Flinders Street, Melbourne, for Gippsland at around six o'clock in the evening. Traralgon was the last stop. It all seemed relatively straightforward. By now we had surrendered to fate, or *manana*: Father would come up with a solution.

These arrangements, however, depended on reasonable English, which still eluded Father. John had been the quickest to master the new language, and therefore did most of the negotiating. Bill, wanting to be part of the action, served as backup. Mother stayed with us, awaiting the return of the men. We looked forward to our plane trip and leaving the island: to our minds, Tasmania was associated with hardship and backwardness.

On the return journey to Melbourne, Lex carried on again with earache. The aeroplane banked crazily as we eventually circled Essendon; one moment we saw red roofs, the next, limitless sky. The shuddering of the plane didn't help my nerves, and when we at last landed, like the Pope, I felt inclined to bend down to kiss the tarmac.

Some of our belongings were sent by ship to Melbourne and kept in temporary storage, to be collected once we were established in the Latrobe Valley. The pine crate would be shipped later. Nonetheless, we were burdened once again with suitcases and hand luggage. Yet although we were tired and drained by the constant travelling, we knew it was pointless to complain. We stayed at the YMCA hostel just off St Kilda Road near Princes Bridge, opposite the Trocadero Ballroom. Thanks to the vision and generosity of George Williams,[98] many a skint person, Australian-born and immigrant alike, has found temporary reprieve in this practical Christian institution.

We had plenty of time before catching the bus the following day, so explored the city centre. Mother was now in her element, and John, upbeat about the future. Lex was especially taken with Flinders Street Station and reckoned it was bigger than Amsterdam's Central Station. Comparisons jumped easily from our young mouths.

Melbourne was austere and prudish during the 1950s, primarily due to its religious culture and relative poverty. Yet, I have always found the city easy to move about in, comforting in its architecture, and with some delightful surprises. The street grid was easy to follow and landmarks such as Flinders Street Station, Saint Paul's Cathedral, the Town Hall, Public Library and old Museum, reflected a rich architectural heritage and immense charm. All very welcoming after our frontier existence! We soon discovered a Dutch restaurant called *Joliette* in Swanston Street, specialising mainly in Indonesian cuisine, and even a 1628 Rembrandt in

---

[98] George Williams founded the Young Men's Christian Association in England during the 1840s. Melbourne's YMCA began in 1853.

the National Gallery of Victoria: *Two Old Men Disputing*. We greatly appreciated the Dutch connection.

The bus driver was a laconic chap but helpful: 'Just leave it; I'll stow it.' He was used to sorting suitcases and seemed to enjoy his job. We made for the back seats and were surprised by how few passengers were onboard. The late afternoon sun, shining through the thick haze of car emissions, bathed the Melbourne streetscape in a golden glow. We loved travelling down St Kilda Road, taking in the beautiful gardens. In some respects, the central part of Melbourne hasn't changed much over the past sixty years, notably the botanic gardens and the parkland around the Shrine of Remembrance. Hurtling down Dandenong Road, we enjoyed the art deco mansions, the trams in the middle of the median strip, the plane trees, and the sense of entrenched wealth within this small stretch of Melbourne. After Caulfield, the houses, while robust, were smaller and less impressive. Once we passed through the city of Dandenong, we entered the countryside. The distance between Traralgon and Melbourne seemed huge in the 1950s but today takes only a couple of hours drive.

Even as the dull grey bus made its steady way to Gippsland, I felt we were leaving a city behind with which I was already beginning to form an ineluctable bond: I would one day return. Despite my newly found love of the Australian bush, and my treasured memories of the Alkmaar Wood, I had inherited Mother's passion for city life. I knew from John, too, that because of the many immigrant communities established there since the Second World War, Melbourne boasted a vibrant soccer culture.

Gippsland is a lush part of Victoria and looked more inviting than Tasmania. The varied scenery held me for a long time, the hills and the railway line beside the Princes Highway a pleasant diversion. My focus on the tracks was lost at times, my eyes wandering off to discover a small cemetery or a tiny church on the side of a hill. It occurred to me, even then, that the idyllic setting of the graves was wasted on those buried there. It is the living who perpetuate the myth of immortality by burying them on the slope of a hill overlooking wonderful vistas, as if, somehow, they could still see! Resting in peace, a secondary consideration...

By the time we reached the regional town of Warragul, it was getting dark and we grew silent. We passed wooden and metal sheds; herds of cows waiting to be milked; a vast mountain range in the distance; silos shooting up like silver canisters, incongruous in their bush setting; steel windmills in the middle of nowhere, and endless fences.

The next major town was Moe, in the Latrobe Valley. It struck me as unusual. With the aid of dimly lit streetlights, a new architecture emerged: square houses with corrugated iron roofs and made of either wood, fibro-cement sheeting, or stucco, situated on hills and divided by wide streets. The uniformity was soulless and bespoke poverty. The only distinct variation was the pastel colours of the houses: blue, pink, yellow, green and mauve. Ironically, Moe, which we pronounced as a long, single vowel, means 'tired' in Dutch.

This type of housing, in its varying cohorts of bland architecture that echoed the coalmining towns of Wales and Northern England, can be found throughout the Valley. The Housing Commission of Victoria and the State Electricity Commission, both government agencies, were responsible for building these cheap, small, functional houses as a response to industrial development in the region. As we later discovered, Moe, Newborough and Morwell were unfortunate enough to be counted amongst the dreariest towns in Victoria...no disrespect intended; after all, we lived in the Valley for six years. The township of Yallourn, not far from Moe, at least had character, with a fine town centre. Eventually, however, Yallourn, to the dismay of its five thousand residents, would be demolished to make way for new coal fields.

Traralgon, due to its rural history, had less of the ugliness of the former three towns, instead enjoying a pleasant, privately-built residential sector. It isn't surprising that the town won out in the development stakes. The more diversified economy, relative flatness of the land, and better aesthetic ambience, as in its wide shopping streets, attractive older buildings, and nearby river, have saved Traralgon from unsightliness. A large, stinking paper mill at Maryvale, halfway between Morwell and Traralgon, plus cement works near the Princes Highway, employed many people and fortunately didn't impinge on the overall character of the town.

At last we arrived at the bus terminal. We thanked the driver and hailed a taxi at the stand opposite the bus station. For some reason, weariness perhaps, one of the doors hadn't been properly closed, and as we swerved around a corner, it shot open, almost causing Flozzie to fall out. This was a time well before compulsory seat belts. Flozzie began to whimper but Mother soothed him with alluring promises: 'We'll soon be there and maybe some lovely food is waiting for you.'

It wasn't far and we soon knocked on the front door of a white weatherboard. Mr van Hulst opened the door and with a welcoming handshake, invited us in. Later, in the morning light, we noticed the house had little appeal, with its dry front garden and no flowers of any type.

Since there was so little room for the seven of us, the boys were allocated the linoleum floor in the living room for sleeping. Our parents were given a small room at the back. Not a relaxing start to our brief stay. At least we didn't have to worry about school, thank goodness, since it was still the end-of-year holidays.

Mrs van Hulst was a large beefy woman with small dark eyes. She appeared distant and watched us closely. While Mr van Hulst worked nightshift and seemed a likeable fellow, his wife resented us being there. I now wonder how he persuaded her to agree to the arrangement. They had two boys, the elder a year younger than me. It became apparent that Mrs van Hulst was determined to protect and promote her boys. Understandable... up to a point! We were aware of the favouritism but didn't let it bother us, although Mother began to resent Mrs van Hulst because of her stinginess and lack of humour. When Christmas arrived, we received nothing, while her lads were given presents. Still, Mr van Hulst managed to bring home some lovely Dutch cakes and a large fruit loaf baked in the Dutch manner, full of ginger, raisins and almonds, and covered in icing sugar. This was our Christmas treat.

From Mr van Hulst's subservience and eagerness to avoid conflict, Father deduced that the wife had the stronger will, but managed to get along well with them both. To be fair to Mother and Mrs van Hulst, eleven people in a small house isn't conducive to harmony.

We enjoyed being in a big town again, even though the weather was becoming warmer and more oppressive. The house wasn't far from the commercial centre and the Gippsland train could be seen going by every day. I loved watching the huge yellow and blue diesel shoot past, sounding its electric horn, loud enough to wake the dead. To amuse ourselves, we collected millions of matchsticks to make trays and the like. Wastage was not in our lexicon. Scrap wood, for example, could be burnt, used to build tree houses, seesaws and billycarts, or for artistic expression. Even so, Lex managed to pick up a huge splinter that required medical attention. On wet afternoons, once the rain stopped, we made mud cakes to keep the creative spirit going. Most of our time, though, was spent wandering around the shopping centre, admiring the toys, bicycles and household goods, all very much out of our reach financially. Meanwhile, Bill took up smoking.

We stayed with the Van Hulsts for about a fortnight, broke and desperate for a change in fortune. We younger ones nibbled at adult conversation and realized we were trapped in Traralgon. Father and the older boys left home early in the morning to look for work and attend to the business of searching for a house or flat, only to return empty-handed. Generally, flats were a recent phenomenon in rural Australia: single men boarded, while immigrant families shared a house or remained in camps.

Then, at last, Father brought home the good news that we had been promised a commission house in Morwell, whether by ballot, which was a standard way of allocation, special pleading, or sheer good luck, we didn't know, but we were all ecstatic to be moving from the tense Van Hulst home. At last! A house of our own, even if not 'a room of one's own'. Home is a metaphor for liberation, room to move and conviviality – on one's own terms.

When first introduced in 1938, Commission house construction was regarded as a 'war on slums'. Most of these houses were built in Melbourne, but spread to the country post-war to accommodate returning soldiers and waves of immigrants. For us they were a godsend, particularly since house rental was subsidized by the government. This was at least one monkey off Father's back. Now for the vital one: work, any work!

The shift to Morwell, about nine miles closer to Melbourne, took a few extra days since the house wasn't quite ready for occupants. It didn't matter much, but being young and impatient, we wanted to move that very day. No more sleeping on the floor, avoiding the critical eye of Mrs Van Hulst, or eating food prepared by someone else. Eventually, a truck was hired to carry our goods and chattels to Morwell. Ben Van Hulst was ever helpful and drove some of us in his old jalopy. It was a bright afternoon as we chugged merrily along the Princes Highway. Our former misgivings about the future gave way to the pleasure of looking forward to a new town, a large backyard and our own shared rooms. It turned out that the Morwell yard was at least five times bigger than our handkerchief plot in Alkmaar. Unimaginable and invaluable! Our Tasmanian surrounds had been too rough and remote to be called a backyard, not that Lex and I minded.

'I'm going to make a billycart,' insisted Lex, grinning enthusiastically.

'Well, I want to grow vegetables,' I replied.

Jack-the-lad saw Morwell as a launching pad for female conquests, while Bill had his eye on a horse. Flozzie saw potential for pushing dinky toys and plastic soldiers through the dirt.

Father had a few ideas of his own, like building a chicken run, a vegie garden and a shed. Mother just wanted some flowers and took a shine to geraniums; a genus I detest because of its smell and vulgarity, like a rouged tart. Father promised her dahlias and flowering shrubs, which were far more romantic.

All these simple dreams took time to realize, but for us that early time heralded possibilities undreamt of back in Holland, or in Tasmania for that matter. In the meantime, the family went berserk exploring the new rooms; exploration perhaps a rather inflated term given the size and modesty of the house.

By the Scruff of the Neck

'That's my corner,' stated Lex.

'We need to buy some cupboards to hang our clothes,' remarked John.

'What's the best spot for my bed?' asked Bill.

'We need to find beds first,' replied Father, in his droll Mokum accent.

'And some pillows too!' Mother added.

We were prepared to sleep in one room, if need be. This was *our* house now and everything would fall into place once Father found work.

Outside, the weatherboard was soft pink, the paint still fresh, while inside, the house had amenities unfamiliar to us, like a proper bathroom with a bathtub, a first for us. We fed kindling into a silver-coloured burner that didn't take long to heat up. The living room had an open fire and behind the back door, but still under cover and part of the house, was a laundry with a wood-fired copper for the washing. Opposite, we found a chain-pulling flush toilet. Unheard of! No more digging to bury the poo. Fantastic! The rear porch divided these small back rooms and there was an inbuilt cupboard in the small passageway, which pleased Mother, who was concerned about her linen. We had acquired a palace!

The newness was something we weren't used to. The house in Tasmania, built in the 1920s, had poor facilities, and our home in Holland was old by Australian standards, with an outside can toilet and tiny kitchen. We were now in the lap of luxury.

In other respects, we roughed it for the first few weeks, until eventually a semblance of order emerged. John and Bill shared the middle room. Lex, Flozzie and I were given the rear bedroom, while our parents occupied the front, overlooking the garden and street. For the first few days we slept on the floor again.

Morwell's Commission dwellings were spread across a number of hills, which made some of the roads very steep. The older part of the town, near the shops and town hall, which also served as a picture theatre, was flat and easy to negotiate. Our house, in Butters Street, was at the top of a ridge and while more easily accessible from Maryvale Road in the west, the forty-minute climb from the shops to the south was exhausting.

Because of the uniformity of the houses it took a while to memorize the streets, their contours and lengths. The first few weeks became a navigational chess game – a few streets forward, two streets back. We walked everywhere, always with an eye on shortcuts.

Father and Mother walked to the township, looking for cheap bedding. Used and new beds of various sizes were delivered and we must either have had sufficient money for mattresses or else they were paid off on credit, a clever system to trap the unwary and debt-prone. Other second-hand furniture was bought in stages, and until the pine crate arrived, our heavy coats served as blankets; which was convenient enough since it was summer, which meant the coats were only used occasionally during the daytime.

At long last, though, the pine crate arrived, with its precious cargo of furniture and blankets. It had been so long that I had forgotten what was inside. Once emptied, Father initially used it as a toolshed, then converted it to a woodshed.

The iceman cometh! Morwell, like most sizeable towns, had an ice works. During the 1950s, home delivery by the iceman was as common as the milkman and bread man. It was a miserable job, though. Icemen had to use their picks or hooks to transfer dripping blocks from the coolroom to the truck for delivery, then hoist the block onto their shoulder, cushioned by sackcloth, to put it into the top of an ice chest. It was heavy wet work and poorly paid. But beggars can't be choosers. Father and the older boys were determined not to be beggars, so at first grabbed whatever came their way. Icemen they became, albeit for a very short time.

Bill was the first to leave this onerous occupation, having found work as a farmhand in Orbost, East Gippsland. It fitted with his desire to become a farmer. However, the sharefarmer, surprise, surprise, exploited him! Bill also felt like a shag on a rock in that remote part of Victoria. He missed his family, felt vulnerable, lonely, and was doing filthy work for which he was underpaid. He already knew how to milk, for example, having been taught by *Opa* Goudsblom, and he learnt little. Putting family before himself, he nonetheless managed to save enough to buy Father a silver smoking stand. He was only fifteen.

Smoking stands were popular during the '40s and '50s, since nearly everyone smoked and the idea of having an ashtray next to the sofa while reading or listening to the radio was the height of modernity. Father was rapt. Bill also bought presents for Mother. He was very generous by nature and remained so throughout his life.

Jack-the-lad, never one for uncomfortable work, soon followed Bill's departure and found a job in Yallourn. Father laboured on with ice deliveries until he slipped and injured himself. An authority on cheese, he sought employment with Kraft in Melbourne, but they laughed at his Dutch certificates and continued churning out cheese that looked and tasted like soap – commercial ignorance of the parochial kind, well known to other immigrants.

In 1953, two construction companies, Thompson, and Johns and Waygood, were commissioned to construct a new powerplant in Yallourn: 'C' station. The demand for electricity was growing rapidly and the regional towns took off like rockets, including Morwell. The companies were looking for riggers and almost overnight, Father and

John, despite their inexperience, were employed as such. Bill returned home from Orbost, finding work with the Gas and Fuel Corporation of Victoria. As a maintenance worker, he learnt how to paint, a trade he was to ply for the rest of his life, as well as farming, the one complementing the other.

Soon afterwards, Father, quite a bit older than his fellow riggers, was made storeman, a promotion of sorts and certainly a lot easier than walking the girders. The workers liked him because he was efficient, affable and funny. Immigrants and Aussies mingled easily, despite the language barrier.

While every workplace has its pilferers and slackers, most workers were honest and industrious. Regular work not only created security but self-respect. The men regarded themselves as privileged working on the power stations, knowing they were contributing to something Victoria needed. The dangers of working there, however, weren't properly understood by the workmen of the day. Some walked around with radioactive isotopic fuel rods in their pockets. Others worked nonchalantly with asbestos: Jack-the-lad succumbed to mesothelioma at the age of 69 as a result. Health and Safety regulations were primitive and many men and some women paid a heavy price for this ignorance.

Mother liked Morwell, mainly because she could jawbone to her heart's content with other Dutch immigrants. We became friendly with the Zwart family, who lived a minute's walk into Angus Street, off Butters Street. Mr Zwart was a plasterer, loved a cigar, and like Mr Brown from Newportslane, did his utmost to off-load the rearing of his tribe onto his wife, a most gracious and sensitive woman who bore the brunt of family mishaps – a not infrequent phenomenon. There were seven children. She made most of the decisions and kept the dynamics of family life under reasonable control. She was a saint, he a very lucky man.

Mother and Mrs Zwart became inseparable in those early days and usually shopped together. Because of the language barrier, they couldn't always make themselves understood. On one occasion both wanted to try some rump steak, an expensive delicacy. The butcher was patient but confused, so, to get the message across, Mother, with her inimitable audacity, turned around and slapped her own generous rump. The butcher fell about laughing.

Mrs Zwart, God bless her, left difficult public matters to Mother, who wasn't shy in coming forward and who would use any method to make her point or win an argument. It was she who advised a Dutchman organizing a Dutch float in a multicultural parade to put away his penis, which had protruded, accidentally or deliberately, from his costume.

While both women were embarrassed, Mother, for the sake of decency, set him straight.

Our lifestyle was beginning to take shape for the better. When Mother found employment house cleaning for Dr Alan Crook, he and his wife treated her as part of the family. Mother spoke to them as equals, which they appreciated, and when they shifted to the Dandenong Ranges, on the outskirts of Melbourne, we sometimes visited them.

The twin engines of our household were work and education, which we automatically internalized. Work was regarded as the natural way out of hardship. While we hated the dirtiest tasks, such as chopping wood in the rain, plucking chickens, or washing mountains of dishes, it was an implicit injunction never to shirk a job or leave a task unfinished. Because we were poor, our attitudes were shaped by the needs of the day – saving for a rainy day, only spending what one could afford, diligence and restraint.

Reserved only for Sundays, religion had little influence on our daily lives. We were spurred on by a sense of moral obligation and an appreciation of what was considered best for the family's common good. If one of us proved uncooperative, Father would simply say, 'Oh, you don't want to do it? Well then, forget about eating.'

Our parents didn't have to nag much. Father and Mother, in different ways, set the example by always looking for savings, working hard themselves, finding means of getting ahead, and improving our lot in any way they could. They did it by sheer slog – no commercial adventurism or taking risks – possibly a legacy of the War and the Depression. Father and Mother both left school around the age of twelve and had to rely on application and common sense. They believed in doing the hard yards, having neither the wiles nor the education to embark on grandiose schemes, as some immigrants did.

If anything, Mother was more cavalier and sanguine than Father. He erred on the side of caution and worried more than Mother, who mainly fretted over her boys, yet was prepared to stick her neck out when confronting authority, for instance, or asking for a bank loan. Her future daughters-in-law often became frustrated by her selective memory and tendency to manipulate, yet admired her gusto.

John and Bill had been more deeply affected by the War than we younger ones and had their own views on life. Jack-the-lad was driven by opportunism, a hedonistic streak, and a healthy ego. Bill, by contrast, became a slave to hard yakka, partly to prove a point to a world that hadn't been particularly nice to him as a youngster, and partly to pursue his dream of farming, of making something of himself. Bill had cunning in him that made him understand business better than his family. He was also prepared to take risks, a quality inherited to some extent from Mother.

By the Scruff of the Neck

With perhaps the exception of Jack-the-lad, none of our family were particularly acquisitive. Yes, it was nice to own material goods, but it was more important to appreciate people, forge relationships, contribute to familial interaction, show one's feelings, do something worthwhile, create or make things; and celebrate events such as naturalization, anniversaries, promotions, passing examinations, making a good purchase, and so on. It was the process of life that mattered, the enduring texture of daily living.

In February 1953, we began school in Morwell, and walked the two miles to the Sacred Heart Primary School, founded in 1884 by the Josephites, the order set up by Sister Mary McKillop. We didn't know the history, of course. In the early 1950s, the school was bursting at the seams, due to the influx of immigrants. In 1956, for example, the school peaked at around six hundred students, which was large for a country primary school. The current enrolment is around one hundred. I mention this to show how busy and impenetrable the school seemed to children like us during that time.

The Sacred Heart Primary School had a strange setup. Grades three and four, like five and six, were combined due to lack of teachers. Class sizes were so huge one could become lost in the multitude. Added to this impediment was the fact that many of the migrant kids couldn't speak English, so were regarded as a bit of a nuisance.

I was put into grade four, so lost one and a half years, partly due to the differing school calendars in Holland and Australia, and partly as a result of the clowns in Tasmania having already thought a lower grade would benefit me because of the language hurdle. To some extent, this explained my boredom and antisocial behaviour while attending Nubeena Consolidated School in Tasmania.

Lex was put into grade five and Flozzie in the prep class. Flozzie fell between two stools, as they say. He hadn't received a good educational grounding in Holland, being too young, and found reading difficult. He sat at the back, where he was generally ignored. In 1954 he switched to Saint Vincent's, on the hill in Rowell Street, because it had just been opened and was quite close to home. The classes were too large, though, and the nuns poorly trained, with Flozzie their unwitting victim.

Although the nuns forgot Flozzie, over time, his reports revealed the opposite to what one might have expected from our knowledge of him at home: they were positively glowing. How this could be, none of us quite fathomed. We now know that being gentle, dreamy, and considerate made him an ideal student, his conduct impeccable. From the nuns' point of view, out of sight meant out of mind. Pity he learnt bugger all! Our parents, however, were too respectful to query his lack of progress: nuns were sacrosanct.

Even Flozzie eventually worked out he was wasting his time, so he wagged. He left for school at the usual time, but never arrived. The nuns, fraught with having to teach hordes, didn't even notice. Apparently he kept himself amused in the Robertson Street Reserve, playing about with dinky toys and bits of wood. I don't blame him. He kept it up for a while, then one day made the mistake of returning home too early. Father and Mother worried of course, but didn't know what to do.

For Lex and I, Sacred Heart wasn't very sacred when it came to discipline, which was imposed indiscriminately. Apart from breaches of rules, such as talking out of turn in class, lateness, cheating and the like, not knowing one's times-tables or spelling meant instant punishment. No allowance was made for the language barrier. You learnt fast, cheated cleverly, or were punished relentlessly.

One mad nun went apoplectic at the flimsiest of transgressions and happily hit pupils across the face with her thick strap. Spite, maybe, at having been forced to become a nun by overzealous parents? *Sigmund, you know the answer: unhealthy repression, what else?* But who knows! She had a moustache and was damned ugly, and all I'm sure of is that she scared the shit out of everyone.

Arithmetic didn't pose a problem, but I dreaded the daily spelling list. Phonics – phonetics and meanings – escaped me at this stage, so misspelling was common, resulting in the inevitable strap. I soon grew cunning though and sat next to the best speller, a lanky girl with glasses. Maybe she was sorry for me; possibly she had a crush on me – it may not have occurred to her that I might cheat. I took the risk and became wily in copying from her, deliberately making the odd mistake to avoid attracting too much attention. I also began to exercise my reasonably good memory. At best, pain produces mixed results and not always negatively.

Certain shards of memory in particular stand out from my time at Sacred Heart. The first was teaching the parish priest's cockatoo to swear. Whenever there was Mass, we walked from the school, past the convent and the presbytery, to the church. This was a common occurrence, presumably because our spiritual requirements were so great. Still, it meant no classes.

As the line of students crawled its way to church, it was frequently held up to allow for shunting into the correct pew: girls, one side, boys the other. It gave us ample time to train the cocky in the vernacular. We hoped Father O'Reilly, the parish priest, would enjoy an earful! Sadly, we never found out, but were more than happy to hear the vulgarisms repeated each time we went to Mass.

'Who's a pretty bastard then? Fuck O'Reilly, Fuck O'Reilly.'

By the Scruff of the Neck

For some unknown reason, Lex and I were recruited to make a pavement for the nuns. Lex must have shown aptitude for this task; he was frequently pulled out of class to do handiwork of some type or another. A great education nonetheless! We also joined the choir, since the nuns quickly noticed our tuneful singing: some of the Aussie kids sounded woeful.

As choirboys, we were allowed to leave before the rest of the class. One day, as we leant over the balustrade of the choir loft, some wag suggested dropping hymnbooks on the heads of the students entering the church. As the file emerged below, they copped it.

Unfortunately, we hadn't reckoned on the mad nun rushing forward. She looked up and backtracked, then raced up the stairs as fast as her habit would allow, screaming like a fishwife: 'How dare you! In God's house! You are as bold as brass...bold as brass. You'll be sorry! You won't get away with this.' She unfurled her weapon and attacked us on the buttocks, legs and shoulders.

It was a perverse spectacle, but I suppose she was doing the same as Jesus did when evicting moneylenders from the temple. We covered our bodies as best we could, while ringing in my ears was the wonderful phrase "bold as brass", a phrase I still use on occasions. At least I'd learnt something...

Another memory is more delicate. Having strong voices meant Lex and I were usually placed near the front, perhaps to drown out the awful singing of some of the other students. One crisp morning, the choir was augmented for a special occasion. A number of new girls were put at the back, at the top of three tiers, no doubt to give more strength to the singing. In between hymns, I turned around to squiz at the newcomers. One girl was exceptionally pretty and wearing an unusually short tunic. I accidentally looked up and espied firm thighs, which rather flummoxed me. Each time we stopped singing I took a furtive glance at her face. Dark wavy hair, finely chiselled chin, full lips and lustrous brown eyes I went weak at the knees.

The juxtaposition of angelic features and sensuous flesh gave me a guilty thrill. This imprint has stayed with me into adulthood. It was the innocence of her face rather than any physical quality that entranced me, as if her face didn't quite belong to the rest of her. Even so, the bare thighs represented sexuality in its simplest form. The moment was something ineffable, pure, yet somehow sullied.

This sensation repeated itself with other girls. Forgive me, Father, for I have sinned. Yet again!

*

School was best outside class time. We usually arrived early. At the back of the playground, cypresses, planted at the beginning of the twentieth century, now served as a windbreak. They had long, thick branches, some almost parallel to the ground, and were ideal for climbing and walking on. We supported ourselves by hanging onto the limbs above, just like our simian ancestors. We did this regularly, even going to the very top to overlook Morwell. The wonderful, astringent smell of the foliage soon became enmeshed with my roaming amongst these trees.

During breaks, we played hoppo-bumpo and other games. The migrant kids kept to themselves on the whole but were often challenged by the local lads. There were Poles, Maltese, Germans, Ukrainians, Italians and Dutch. Initially, each nationality stayed within its own circle. One lunchtime a big Aussie kid began to pick on me; I was afraid of him and tried to avoid his pushing and shoving. The bullying continued, until one day I'd had enough. I wasn't going to tell my parents, though, or Lex, who would've had a go. This was my problem.

The time came when I was singled out yet again by the Aussie boy, who thought he had me. He pushed me off the tree stump where I was devouring my big Dutch sandwiches and sat on top of me. He weighed a ton! So, what to do? I had little choice but to be inventive. My fear evaporated, anger took over, and with my free right arm I grabbed him by the knackers, squeezing them like oranges. As he screamed, I managed to wriggle out from underneath him, then stood up and got stuck into him. Though not particularly strong, I was quick, and punched him in the face. It turned out he was weak as dishwater and ran away. He never picked on me again.

Later, I became friends with a Ukrainian boy, who was disfigured. He was quite a bit older and lived with his mother in Holmes Road. There was no father. The back of his hands had been burnt and despite skin grafts, they were still ugly to look at. Another quaint legacy of the War... He could, however, hide a sixpence in a pocket of skin! We were all gobsmacked by this magical feat. Ironically, my Ukrainian mate lived on the same road as many of his former tormentors, the Germans. One hot summer's day, when the air was motionless and nothing moved except me, I rode into Holmes Road to collect empty beer bottles and earn a little money. A number of the Germans were stripped to the waist, leaning on their shovels and chin-wagging in their own language. Their houses were built in the German style: solid brick with barn-like roofs. I collected my cargo, then was shocked to see swastikas tattooed under their armpits. Later, I mentioned this around the dinner table.

'Bloody Nazis – it's not difficult to fool Australians,' stated John, with a grimace.

'We don't really know what they did during the War,' said Father even-handedly.

By the Scruff of the Neck

'Why are they all living in Holmes Road?' asked Bill.
'Should we report them to the police?' Mother sounded worried.
We didn't pursue it; immigration coughed up strange bedfellows.

By the second year, I felt more comfortable with school and began to make other friends. Most of the Aussie kids were easy-going and generous. They offered to share their flavouring for milk, as well as their lollies and cakes, and even gave me football cards. Usually, as long as you adopted values such as fairness, modesty and respect, kicked the footy well, played cricket and weren't a sook, you were easily accepted.

Morwell became a marvellous town for games and adventure. Our house, on the northern fringe of the town as it was in 1953, was the last street before paddocks and swathes of long grass; many more houses and roads were to be built during the next six years. Given the simplicity of our lives, with only the ghost of Karl May now hovering in the background, we usually looked for excitement outside the house. Only when it was teeming down did we stay indoors.

There were many places to visit. The most alluring was the bush, a fifteen-minute walk across rolling paddocks. Half an hour east of our place was the Water Hole Creek, simply referred to as 'the Creek'. The narrow stream purled across rocks and fallen trees, making crossing a doddle. Walls of blackberries loomed either side, in late summer enticing us to stand midstream to pick the luscious fruit. Our fishing ventures weren't a great success; only the odd eel, yabbie or trout. The Creek was also a favoured location for tiger snakes. Our first killing of a snake prompted us to leave it on the front porch of a recently occupied house, then knock on the door, scarper, and watch from afar.

There was also the tip, full of treasures, such as pram wheels, bits of timber, carpet cast-offs, crooked nails, screws, springs, boxes, steel rods, axles, and the like. Everything could be used. We questioned the wastefulness of people, but thanked our lucky stars for such a cornucopia of discarded riches. As for the smell, that went with the territory.

Our next-door neighbours were the Browns, part indigenous, part Anglo-Saxon. All four boys were ideal playmates. They excelled at marbles, shanghai accuracy, comic swaps, pranks – such as the snake incident – and climbing trees. What more could one ask for in a neighbour? Despite financial hardship, they managed to have the first television in the street. It was common to have fifteen or so kids sitting, or rather lolling, on the linoleum watching the Mouseketeers and the Road Runner on a tiny black-and-white screen. Better than the picture theatre! You couldn't beat entertainment at home. Mrs Brown, a wonderful woman, sometimes gave us bread with dripping, which we regarded as rather ordinary, but enjoyed all the same. No one misbehaved, or if you did, you were told to leave.

Saturday afternoon was the time for adventure. 'Coming to the bush this arvo?' Lex would ask Billy Brown. Lex had been given a slug gun and a Bowie knife for his birthday: Ironfist, Karl May's fictional hero, quickly resurfaced.

'After I've fed the chooks...' he drawled, as they stood either side of the fence separating our properties. 'Mum wants me to polish some shoes, too. Bloody Les always gets off. I'll join youse later down at the dam.' Five or six of us moseyed over to the bush, armed with knives, slingshots, a bit of rope that might come in handy, and some 'Niggerboy' liquorice or broken biscuits for sustenance. We took our time, taking pot shots at magpies swooping past. Sometimes we stopped at the dam for a leak. Once we found a tyre floating in the middle and coaxed it ashore. Inside, Lex discovered a ten-shilling note, a fortune. Other times, we found eels inside tyres. It was an easy life and full of surprises.

The bush, just off Maryvale Road, was a maze of little tracks, with wider ones on the periphery. The vague aim was to explore the area that finished near Derham's Hill, which was a dismal collection of small white houses plonked in the middle of nowhere and set up during the '40s and '50s for immigrants working at the Maryvale paper mill and Yallourn's power stations. It could easily have been a village spirited in from outer space, inhabited by aliens. It didn't survive long and was demolished in the early '60s. Or perhaps it vanished into some intergalactic backwater... It certainly deserved to be swallowed up by a black hole.

The eastern side of the bush went downhill, trailing off into swamps and paddocks, which were frequently flooded, creating new attractions: frogs, snakes, lizards, ferns and clumps of tea trees, good for hiding in. On the northern edge, heading towards the paper mill, quarries, gouged by earth-moving equipment and heavy rain, left caves and gullies ideal for playing cowboys and indians, cops and robbers, or pirates, depending on our whim. The sandstone terrain resembled a lunar landscape.

I was a little afraid of the bush at first, not knowing how big it was, what monsters might lurk there or how to find my way around. In the company of others I grew more confident and after a few weeks it became a second home. We crawled through bracken and large ferns, and selected trees for building huts or hiding places. Once Lex had chosen the most suitable, we hammered strips of wood against the trunks for easier climbing, but later cottoned on to the idea of securing a rope ladder, which could be pulled up. Planks were nailed across sturdy branches and the platforms covered with carpet carted from the tip, a few kilometres away. Tin sheets were then nailed and wedged above us, in case of rain. Tarzan, here we come!

By the Scruff of the Neck

Alongside possums, birds, goannas and the odd stray wallaby, the bush was ours. But this was about to change.

Our neighbourhood gang was centred on Butters and Angus streets, with a few kids from Maryvale Road. In the four years we played in the bush, we never encountered a forestry or council worker forbidding what we were doing, and in the beginning we didn't have much competition, either. On weekends, dreamy lovers used the bush for exploration of a different kind, although they stayed near the perimeter and didn't intrude on our territory. Sometimes equestrians visited but stuck to the wide tracks. The real threat came from new gangs.

As Morwell grew, more gangs emerged, usually formed on the basis of neighbourhoods, not usually ethnicity. Every gang wanted control of the bush, which was big enough to accommodate just about everyone, but some wanted to dominate. Clashes were inevitable; macho instincts sought out stoushes. One of our lads was caught by another gang and tied to a tree. They pulled down his pants and attached a brick to his testicles, which sorely tested his vocal cords. The cruelty and psychology were later to remind me of Jack and Roger from *Lord Of The Flies*, by William Golding: unhindered by adults, some of the boys in this story went native and reverted to tribalism, resulting in horrible acts. At the time, we hadn't heard of Golding, but understood cruelty.

Fortunately for their victim, we, although spread out, were aware of the interlopers and homed in on his screams. We made sure not to approach the stricken lad all together, in case of an ambush. Two of us untied the brick and ropes, while the rest waited in the bushes. Whether the poor boy's manhood had been permanently damaged wasn't apparent, but we took him home rather slowly, the boy's face ghastly pale and grimacing in pain. Still, he did better than Simon or Piggy in Golding's novel.

Full-on fights were rare, since the bush allowed a quick retreat. Once under cover, it was difficult to locate anyone, unless betrayed or not well enough hidden. Gangs came and went, but we stayed, and after a year ventured further away, to the hamlet of Tyers and to the Latrobe River: by this time we had acquired our first bikes and could move further afield.

We skinny-dipped in the Latrobe River and traced the Tyers with the aim of finding pools for swimming and fishing. It never occurred to us to be careful in case of currents, or to worry about hitting rocks as we dived unconcernedly into the cool water. Our parents rarely knew what we were up to, nor took much notice, unless one of us returned with a deep cut requiring attention, or with fish, or even the occasional rabbit. Our parents had more than enough to keep them busy without chasing after us.

*

Morwell was an immigrant town, an industrial hub and full of single men, many of whom lived in barracks on the hill near the Morwell open-cut. Alcohol consumption was the usual way of coping with life and work. Beer, not wine. Morwell, at this time, seemed to be floating on beer, and in my estimation outboozed the capital.

As we grew older and more responsible, we were expected to pull our weight. It didn't take long for us to discover money was to be made from collecting beer bottles, as well as selling wood. Flozzie eventually helped with the beer bottles too.

I don't know where Father got the idea of becoming a wood merchant. Maybe from someone at work... Or perhaps from watching others in this occupation? It certainly made sense, and since Morwell could be freezing in winter, I suspect the high cost of wood spurred him on to find his own supply.

This was the era of open fires, bar radiators being too expensive and domestic air conditioners an invention of the future. Many families during the fifties also relied on kerosene heaters. They were efficient, but since heat remained localised, not particularly effective, and also, the vapours caused headaches. In the middle of winter, before and after school, we all huddled near the kero heater in the kitchen, bums facing the heat, postponing going outside for as long as possible. Whenever I now encounter the smell of kerosene, which is rare, the heady smell pulls me back to our Morwell kitchen and all its associated memories.

Judging from the piles in driveways, Father knew most households burnt lots of firewood, and it seemed that fuel merchants couldn't keep up. He wanted a slice of the action, at a competitive price. Our backyard was large enough to cope with stacks of wood.

'If I can get a reasonably-priced sawing machine and a reliable truck, we can make some dough,' he said, as we hoed into the evening meal. 'I'll ask around and look at the *Morwell Advertiser* for wood-cutting machinery.'

Shortly thereafter, Father got the wood bug: a strange affliction! As a newly-made wood fetishist he couldn't drive past a piece lying by the side of the road without collecting it, or at least assessing its usefulness. *We thought he was mad.*

When he bought his first motor car in 1955, a lemon-coloured FJ Holden, he felt richer than Onassis and put it to good use. Whenever we made a trip to Inverloch, a favourite destination, or Lakes Entrance, likewise, he would herb along contentedly, his head held slightly to one side. One day, when all of a sudden he applied the brakes, we were all thrown about, seatbelts being non-existent in those days, and wondered what had possessed him. A simple explanation: he had spotted a log of wood. He did a quick u-turn, and like a desperate lover, pulled up next to it, then straightaway opened the boot, lest a kangaroo or other mortal stole his trophy. The log was chucked in and off we went, Father smiling in satisfaction.

Another time, when returning home from Yallourn, Father and John passed through the small, now defunct, town of Morwell Bridge, once a thriving stagecoach stop on the road east to Sale. A few houses and a second-hand car yard were the only remnants of this former bustling township. Like Yallourn, it too was destined to be swallowed up by the coalfields, and by the early 1960s ceased to exist.

However, an old six-cylinder, green Bedford truck caught Father's eye and after some serious haggling, he bought it cheaply, because it was unroadworthy. The brakes were suspect, the differential of dubious merit and the gearbox was apt to make strange noises. It was, without doubt, a lemon, except for one virtue: an indestructible engine. Later, Father got a few mechanic mates to give it the once-over and they pronounced it driveable, but only just.

The police were fairly easygoing, aware of the endemic poverty in Morwell. They understandably bent the law on minor matters, so turned a blind eye to Father's vehicle – or perhaps simply couldn't be bothered to check it – leaving us to get on with it. Ah, the days of bureaucratic non-interference. Alas, no more!

Soon after, Father spotted a sawing machine for sale in the *Advertiser*. It was in a place called Erica, about twenty miles north of Moe and a few miles from the former gold mining town of Walhalla. The older boys, including Lex, squeezed into the cabin of the Bedford, and off they all went. Eventually, the sturdy and clumsy sawing behemoth was rolled onto the back of the truck, secured with rope and brought home. The machine had been built in South Melbourne and was kerosene-driven, with a single piston. Once ignited with petrol, it switched to kerosene, a comparatively cheap fuel. The magneto wasn't always cooperative though, especially in the wet, so on many occasions endured being roundly cursed.

Father was almost ready for business: only a few other crucial matters needed to be resolved. Australian hardwood makes for excellent heat, red gum the most sought after, but where would the firewood come from and how was the wood to be cut into manageable lengths for the sawing machine to handle, before being sorted? Also, how to find customers? Father relied on leg-work, word of mouth and dollops of good luck.

The bush around Maryvale Road and the nearby town of Yinnar all fell within the confines of either coalfields or farming land, some of which was later sold to developers for housing. The area around Derham's Hill, between Morwell and Traralgon, later lost its old timber forests, to be replaced by seemingly endless miles of *Pinus radiata* plantations. This common species of pine is excellent for pulp and grows quickly, but sadly, destroys native habitat. Thus, a mixed blessing!

We, however, didn't need to worry about this modern intrusion, as there were plenty of eucalypts to be found in those days. Father searched around, spoke to people, listened to old-timers and studied the lie of the land in our vicinity. Amongst others, he made contact with an old cow cocky called Charlie Paint, who owned considerable tracts of virgin bush recently flattened to make room for his cattle. Huge caterpillar tractors with heavy chains and a big iron ball in the middle took on the bush in spring, the best time for felling, the soil being moist and the surface dry, which meant trees fell over easily. After the trees were pushed into heaps, they were set on fire, with the aim of reducing the size of the piles. The root systems, entangled with soil, stones and whatnot, took longer to burn. Father persuaded Charlie to let him take away the burnt trees. Charlie was an easygoing bloke who saw the advantage of having trees removed so agreed to let us do it. Talk about symbiosis! Charlie's paddocks were just up the road, too.

The matter resolved, Father bought a couple of two-man saws to cut logs and tree limbs to lengths of about six feet. We had already been introduced to this laborious art form in Tasmania. When enough lengths had been cut, we stacked them and began the arduous task of sawing them into one-foot blocks, using the sawing machine, which we positioned in the paddocks to cut up the wood on the spot. We then loaded the Bedford to the gunnels and took the firewood to our customers. Sometimes the truck got bogged, and when the Bedford eventually carked it, Father bought a trailer, painted it orange, and the FJ Holden was pressed into service.

Father soon bought two huge circular saws, which required regular sharpening. The machine was incredibly noisy, with its fanbelt clapping along at a phenomenal speed. Except for Flozzie, we were all expected to help. In the five years of wood carting, Bill and Lex did the bulk of the sawing. Jack-the-lad helped too, but only on occasions: he regarded the work as interfering with his social life. He had recently bought a black Morris Oxford and was proud as punch, offering Lex and me sixpence to clean it, which we did, grudgingly.

Lex excelled at wood splitting and at thirteen could handle an axe like a seasoned woodchopper. He also became an expert on the sawing machine, diagnosing the faulty combustion and eliminating the magneto problems. It was an impressive sight to see him swing the iron bench into the saw as he enjoyed cutting the six-foot lengths into blocks. He was a natural and his technical bent was undoubtedly shaped by his experience with this work. The noise was overwhelming, though, with no earmuffs and with the whole contraption vibrating like an unsteady washing machine. Once, Lex cut a log and discovered a snake and its hatchlings.

Father got the wood bug. Paddock near Morwell, 1957.
Bill, Henri, Father and Mother.

Another time, he unwittingly cut a snake in half as it tried to crawl out of a log onto the wood bench.

'Hey, Pa, how many more logs to go?' Lex would shout above the din.

'Oh, another six, and we'll call it a day... Herrie, get off your arse and lift the other end.'

We hadn't heard of health and safety; too intent on making a living. Those times are unimaginable in the Australia of today.

We were skinny, muscular and fit, our language work-centred, with few words wasted. The fuel business honed our work ethic and gave us much satisfaction. We learnt to use wedges like experts, looking for the cracks in the wood, then placing the wedges at strategic points as we moved along the split. There was something satisfying in seeing a log come apart, large binding splinters hanging on tenaciously.

Father began with deliveries to neighbours and acquaintances and the word soon got around. He charged two pounds a ton and it didn't take long to build up customers. To begin with, the wood may have been burnt on the outside, but it was pristine on the inside. People occasionally complained about the soot, so it was Father's aim to find unburnt wood, provided it was dry and easily accessible. Green timber was strictly out. Customers just wouldn't accept it and complained if even a little moisture was evident.

Past Yinnar, towards Delburn or Boolarra, the thick forests were a goldmine for our wood business. The density of the bush meant many trees were felled and uprooted by wind, fire or lightning, or simply succumbed to old age. The natural cycles of birth and decay were unforgiving, as they were meant to be.

We often spotted snakes emerging from hollow logs, goannas climbing trees, rosellas chatting and flirting in pairs, or eyeing us disinterestedly. Blue tongue lizards were a common sight in spring, while mosquitoes and flies were a constant menace. What I remember most hauntingly, however, was the overwhelming silence, a sense of timelessness, the bush having been there for aeons, ignored by man, or at least, in harmony with the indigenous clans. The coal onslaught, however, undid centuries of growth and beauty in only a few juggernaut months.

While no animus is intended, our family, and some of the other Dutch families, were a study in contrasts. Our parents were good immigrants, in that they adjusted quickly and creatively to their new locations. For the few disgruntled migrants, the sky was always bluer back in the land of their birth, so they returned. Others went back and forth because they couldn't make up their minds. As will o' the wisp wanderers, this caused rootlessness and discontent, and stymied progress: they had little time to shape their lives.

Our family soon made friends with the fellow Dutchies who were also carving out their futures. The cultural ties, as with so many other nationalities, meant frequent visits and exchanges. Morwell had a considerable Dutch community, of varied backgrounds. The older members had all been affected or scarred by the War and appreciated the freedom and ease of Australia. A few of them came here after 1949, when Indonesia became independent. They may have been Dutch by nationality, yet couldn't adjust to Holland, their place of birth, because of its atrocious weather and severe economic constraints. Moreover, before the War, they were spoilt by their colonial way of life, with servants, chauffeurs, plentiful and exotic food, ongoing festivities, and privileged, class exclusiveness. Australia, then, was preferable to post-war Holland and they migrated in droves, although their values and social habits remained firmly colonial. Some had been Captains or Chief Mates in the Dutch Merchant Navy, others had managed plantations. Quite a few were well-educated, but for a while lost this advantage in their new country. Some were skilled tradesmen, as well as excellent soccer players, adding to the mix of Morwell society. Father and Mother associated with many of them, being of similar age and mind.

The ex-colonials still believed in the good life of pre-war Indonesia. I can recall the magnificent Indonesian artefacts and intricate furniture some of them owned. They spoke Bahasa and displayed the aplomb of seigneurs used to authority and fiefdoms, and despite being good Calvinists, stuck to gin and cigars as the perquisites of leisured living. To enter their commission homes felt like a mis-en-scène in an Australian comedy. Dutch knick-knacks of the Delftware-blue variety, as well as shiny copper, mingled awkwardly with Javanese and Sumatran wood carvings, rugs, masks and drawings, all artfully arranged next to ornate objets d'art, some designed as musical chairs or glory boxes. The exquisite oriental furnishings also contrasted strangely with sets of miniature clogs on the mantelpiece, or elaborate gilt-framed oil paintings of some northern scene by an obscure artist, who, nevertheless, knew his trade. These vast collections of ornaments, all placed within the ordinary houses of the land of kangaroos and koalas...many with the ubiquitous three ducks flying up the wall. Someone must have made a fortune out of those ducks!

The bourgeois Dutch interiors differed markedly from the sparse décor of the Aussie homes. I got to know the interiors of houses because it was my job to take wood and kerosene orders and to collect beer and lemonade bottles. I was often asked to come inside: 'Come in, little fella, and help yourself. It's boiling today; I'll fetch ya a drink... What a

'Come in, little fella, and help yourself.' Morwell, Victoria, 1956. Frank, friend, and Henri.

delightful boy you are. Yer folks must be ever so proud of you... All right, Snowy, just go through the kitchen; you'll find them in the laundry.'

It wasn't uncommon to be met by naked toddlers, gaping at me, mouths fringed with vegemite and snot oozing onto the lino or wooden floor. Sometimes the homes were filthy, faeces smeared across the wall like a Jackson Pollock. While *our* family hygiene wasn't always commendable, I recoiled from the stench, the grubbiness, and the indifference, which was in an entirely different league. The occupants obviously didn't give a damn, but they couldn't live without their grog.

Today, rampant alcoholism has morphed into, or has been boosted by, drugs and gambling. Vice will always find its way, like water its level.

I recall a woman up the road who kept her horse inside. She had dismantled the walls and the horse, a docile creature that loved to nuzzle, followed her everywhere, defecating on the bare boards. The woman was very kind though, and in addition to a good haul of beer bottles, she offered me sweets, or, on a hot day, an ice block. I enjoyed visiting her, too focused on the task of collecting bottles to pass judgement. Anyway, her devotion to the horse was far more interesting than the squalor.

Father and Mother were magnets for single Dutchmen. Not only did they enjoy Dutch cuisine, but adored listening to Father's humorous anecdotes from the old country. Mother became their earth mother, attending to their emotional needs and stomachs. They missed their family and were more than happy to adopt us as surrogates.

One of these was Toon Vendel, a handsome, gentle giant from Texel, the largest island north of our province in Holland. I often sat on the back of his motorbike enjoying the thrill of zooming through the Strzelecki Ranges near Thorpdale, swerving around corners, his broad back shielding me from the wind.

Toon grew to love Father and often helped with the wood sawing. On occasions his elder brother, Cor, joined him. To observe these men was something else! Their biceps, taut as power cables, pulled the long saw as if yanking at a piece of string. In no time they had built a huge pile of six-foot logs for our disposal. Whenever they turned up, the stacks of wood grew exponentially. A good Dutch meal is all they wanted, preferably with plenty of spuds, followed by a card game and good conversation.

I remember Toon taking mild issue with Mother and me over the word 'too'. As an adverb meaning 'in excess', he deemed it 'bad', as in 'too good', 'too much' or 'too beautiful'. Since the Dutch word 'te' means 'too', he argued that wherever this adverb preceded a word or modified a verb, it had a negative connotation. Unfortunately, there are exceptions to this sweeping observation. As an assertive fourteen-year-old and rather

Toon, a gentle giant from the island of Texel, Holland. Centre, Aunty Anne, Oma to her right. *The Dyke*, 1955

obnoxious at times, showing indecent triumphalism whenever outsmarting someone, I pointed out that words like 'tevreden' – being satisfied – or 'tekeergaan' – to carry on, to make a fuss – didn't denote excess. Mother sided with me, yet despite being outflanked, Toon stuck to his guns, yet never lost his temper or swore in protest. He was placid and good-natured and took things in his stride. In hindsight, though, the thrust of his point was valid.

At one time, he wrote a passionate letter to a fraulein who was looking for a suitor in Australia. He even sailed back to Europe to meet her; Hamburg as I recall. *En passant*, he dropped in to see *Oma* Goudsblom, Uncle John and Aunty Anne, their first contact with someone who could give them direct news of us. Sadly, the love of Toon's life turned out to be a shyster, who happily took his money for the journey back to Australia, then eloped with someone else. As he described it, 'I waited for her at Port Melbourne with a bunch of flowers, only to discover she had nicked off with another fellow.' I wonder how many other single male migrants were duped in this way?

Tragically, he died in a motorbike accident aged twenty-six. On a drizzly morning, on the way to work, his bike slipped from underneath him at the turn-off from the Princes Highway into Yallourn. I grieved for a very long time and couldn't understand why God would take Toon, my special friend, at such a young age. For many years afterwards, on weekends, I still expected to hear the sound of his motorbike, and sixty years later I still visit his grave in the Haunted Hills cemetery near the old site of Yallourn.

Bill also lost close mates in motorbike accidents, one decapitated by a wood truck. As a result, none of us took up motorcycling. Around this time, John and Bill were in a neighbour's car one day when a toddler ran out in front of them and was hit. The little boy died at the scene, leaving a lingering impression on them both, and, of course, on the rest of the family when they told us about it. For these reasons, I came to associate Morwell with tragedies.

The guardian of the wood empire was our mongrel Micky, given to us by the Stewart family as a pup. The Stewarts were a large, boisterous lot living at the bottom of our street. Micky was a terrier, part Scottish, part Australian and Fox, plus vestiges of other breeds: it was hard to tell. He was jet black and as he grew older, limped on three legs, either the result of dog fights or arthritis. He was agile, though, game as Ned Kelly and irascible. Micky was particularly close to Lex, following him everywhere. He was adorable, snuggling up and wagging his tail, ears pointing back, wriggling his sleek body in excitement and affection, all the while hoping for a belly scratch. He howled at the moon for something to do, sang in unison with neighbouring mutts and crooned strange melodies to us all. Like most dogs, he loved rolling around in dirt and dung. He was also an excellent swimmer. In summer you could hear him snapping at flies like a clapperboard, or ferociously searching his coat for fleas: he and Bill's Alsatian may well have been the cause of the flea plagues around our house!

Morwell, like most country towns, had its swag of dogs chasing whatever took their fancy, usually trucks, cars, bikes, cats and, of course, other dogs. Dog fights and attacks on humans were common, doctors and vets kept busy with ripped flesh, twisted limbs and bloody snouts. Micky loved a fight and often won, but on the odd occasion was mangled by a stronger or nastier cur. However, he usually knew when to leave well enough alone, especially after a blistering mauling by a tomcat. He loved going out with us and stood on the back of the truck, right at the edge, barking furiously at any pack of dogs giving chase. He knew they couldn't touch him and felt like a regal warrior, totally in control of the situation. Unfortunately, one day Father swerved around a corner too fast and Micky fell off. He was immediately set upon by the baying horde and if we hadn't stopped to come to his rescue, Micky may well have been digging up bones in dog heaven. As soon as he was safe, he snapped at his attackers, shook himself, and jumped back onto the truck as if nothing had happened, quickly resuming his yapping. He could never give up and once even attacked a snake, which hastily slithered away, having met its match.

To this day we still don't know what happened to Micky after he eventually disappeared. I suspect he was either killed by a vehicle or taken to the vet to be put down. This occurred just before our departure for Melbourne in 1958: our parents were always coy on the subject.

Morwell was booming in the 1950s and there was money to be made in the Latrobe Valley. Our lot soon improved markedly and our parents even put down a deposit on a block of land, something formerly only within reach of the wealthy, as far as we were concerned. Owning private property! We had become 'landed gentry', or so we liked to think of ourselves; although the land actually belonged to the bank holding our mortgage.

Jack-the-lad bought not only a car, albeit second-hand, but a new suit. Bill, in turn, sported a new maize-coloured jacket, purchased Californian Poppy to grease his coif, and launched into rock'n'roll like a madman. He was an excellent dancer, exhibited great flair and had the gift of the gab, so soon had girlfriends on either arm. No slouch, our Bill! When he acquired a De Soto sedan, with chrome trimmings that almost seemed to smile at us, he went up in my estimation.

As well as the car, Bill also bought a horse called Bess, a tall brown-black mare of calm temperament. Bill turned out to be an excellent rider and later even broke in horses. Lex was given an old pony on which we learnt to ride. Morwell was in fact obsessed with horses, as well as scrambling bikes, football, soccer and netball. Tennis was for the wealthy and the more refined. Given the size and relative dullness of Morwell, I suppose these sports kept young people out of trouble.

Both Jack-the-lad and Bill often attended local dances, held in church halls, at the town hall, and at the Karma Hall.[99] Girls marooned on one side and boys on the other, promoted a weekly stampede of suitors once the music began. Desirable boys and girls were quickly selected, like specials in a supermarket. 'Wallflowers', as they were called, wilted and suffered inwardly, both boys and girls. What a cruel convention!

Still very Dutch in both accent and manner, with his formal bearing and immigrant status, Jack-the-lad, despite his good looks, was often met with a curt 'No thanks!' when he asked for a dance, a slur he sarcastically invoked for the rest of his days. On the other hand, Italians, Maltese and Greeks *really* copped it, their swarthy looks being interpreted as signs of evil intent. Australia was very much in the arms of racial bigotry, and to some extent, still is.

We younger ones used to sneak into the town hall when it was used as a cinema for matinees. I loved the serials, always ending in cliffhangers to suck you in for the main feature, like *Treasure Island* or the *Tarzan* series.

Later, in 1957 and '58, we went to the Maya picture theatre in Buckley Street[100] with our parents. After working our rear ends off stacking wood and bottles, we showered, combed our hair – Lex already captive to the charm of Brylcreem – and drove off in the FJ Holden for our weekly entertainment. They were the days of innocent expectations. The recently built Morwell drive-in, however, allowed for passion in comfort: for others, that is... Our elder brothers usually took responsibility for us younger ones: John for scenic trips, Bill, when it came to the drive-ins. He was a wiz at smuggling us in, the ushers either sympathetic or not too bright. We would slowly share a Mars Bar between the three of us while we watched the film. Girls, however, took priority over us for the drive-in.

*

---

[99] Built in 1948, the Karma Hall was destroyed by fire on the 5th February 2005. It served as cinema, dance hall, and venue for wedding receptions.

[100] The Maya picture theatre opened in April 1956 and closed in May 1962.

Bill was an excellent horseman. Morwell, Victoria, 1954. Frank, Lex, Henri and Bill.

While Jack-the-lad and Bill drove around in their cars, Lex and I built billycarts. Morwell was ideal for billycart racing. The steep roads and footpaths made for exhilarating descents...and accidents.

Morwell Council held annual billycart races. Some of the boys relied on their fathers to build the carts, in my view a form of cheating. I loved my bulky box, its sides clad with tin sheets, but knew it wasn't made for speed. Lex, on the other hand, approached a race from a technical and mechanical point of view. Whether he won or not was of secondary importance. He built his cart aerodynamically, ergonomically and aesthetically. The aim was to be the fastest through best design. He took a minimalist approach: large wheels at the back, smaller ones at the front, a strong yet light timber frame, tri-ply to close it in, and finally, a small, soft cushion for his back. Weight was a crucial factor, while the angle of the cart pointed downwards to maximise speed. He trialled it, tinkered with it, oiled the axles endlessly, and was finally ready for the big day. Lex's cart was engineered like a greyhound, mine a bullmastiff.

The event took place at the top of Tobruk Street, where proud parents lined the steep descent towards the state school. Half of Morwell must have been there. *Our* parents were doing something else, so we turned up unaccompanied and expecting stiff competition. Lex won easily and I finished somewhere in the middle. I can't remember the prize, but Lex repeated this feat two years in a row. It augured well for his future career as draughtsman and mechanical engineer.

Just after the Melbourne Olympic Games of 1956, which we attended for the soccer and the closing ceremony, Morwell, caught up in the feverish aftermath, and Australia having won thirteen gold medals, built its own Olympic-sized swimming pool. We therefore no longer needed to travel to the Yallourn pool, which, in its large natural setting, was far more attractive, but more difficult to get to.

We learnt to dive from the high diving boards, completed our 'Herald' swimming certificate in no time, ogled girls from a distance, narcissistically inspected our first pubic hairs in the changing rooms, dived into the pool with burgeoning erections, and monstered people with 'bombs' and 'bellywhackers'.

I recall Les Brown, our next-door neighbour, taking a few moments to study my anatomy while we were showering in the change room at the baths. When he noticed a healthy growth of pubics, he admiringly said, 'Shit, Lichtie, you *are* coming on!' Les was two years younger and still bald down there. I was chuffed and felt rather superior, adolescent hubris pumping up self-esteem.

Lex and I were growing up fast, but I never quite connected with the more clownish antics of my peers. I loved sport, but work and study came first. At one stage, we had collected over a thousand beer bottles – Victoria, Melbourne, Fosters and Abbotsford were the well-known brands. Ah, the smell of hoppy dregs...

Our first purchase with the money we'd earned was a toaster for our parents, followed by a small green and white Malvern Star bicycle, to be shared. This bicycle, plus an attached trolley, replaced the heavy wooden billycart I had pushed up Butters Street, seemingly forever. The trolley, though it carried fewer bottles in the one swoop, was a great time saver.

From 1956 onwards, others tried to muscle into our rounds, especially the snooty 'Poms' next door. They even tried to start their own wood business, which must have been too hard for them because they soon gave up. We had established a close rapport with our clients and resented competition; though strictly speaking, anyone had a right to our clientele – it was a voluntary arrangement, after all. Nevertheless, shades of the liquor wars in Chicago emerged, with Lex as Al Capone. He clocked the lad next door for having stolen beer bottles promised to us by one of our regulars, and a Dutch bus driver boarding in a house diagonally across from us took great delight in urging Lex to punch the shit out of our irritating neighbours.

The turf wars escalated when another Dutch family wanted a slice of our patch. With determination, loyalty from our customers, a bit of heavy handling, and early intervention, we saw them off. 'If you come near our streets again, we'll kneecap ya!' Lex threatened. Capone and Dutch Schultz[101] would have approved. As for the characters in *Bugsy Malone*, mere amateurs!

Morwell, despite its larrikin image, was, in truth, big and tolerant enough to accommodate other aspiring bottle collectors, even if the rough and tumble for easy pickings did at times result in violent behaviour. We weren't easily intimidated though, having made friends with most of the boys in our neighbourhood. Fortunately, the adults had their own concerns and left us alone. Despite it being in many ways a dreary time, the beauty of the '50s was its freedom of movement – the absence of adult interference. Morwell, like Lex and me, was changing rapidly. It was neither rural nor urban, but essentially industrial, yet allowed for a large canvas of activity, particularly given its walkable size. We loved hiding underneath the newly-built commission houses, which, due to the steep slopes, had stumps at one end almost as high as the houses themselves. When older, we lured girls there, but otherwise used these places to hide from other boys, or just for a stickybeak, but never wrecked anything, having learnt the value of a roof over one's head. Tall,

---

[101] Dutch Schultz – Arthur Flegenheimer, 1901–35. Like Al Capone, 1899–1947, he was a notorious mobster of the 1920s. Of German-Jewish origin, he was born in the Bronx.

narrow trenches dug for sewerage connections became our catacombs, twisting and turning, the caramel soil, cool and moist in summer. When the workmen went home, or on the weekend, we explored, pretending to be archaeologists and playing hide-and-seek, revelling in the newness of it all.

Away from the towns, the Valley is beautiful and full of surprises, like nearby waterfalls, thick forests, rolling hills and prolific birdlife. On turning fourteen, I bought my own bike, chestnut-red and navy-blue, and spent days exploring the countryside, as I had done back in Holland. As ever I was addicted to Mother Nature, her dazzling treasures inexhaustible: huge gnarled gum trees, tiger snakes and brown dozing near the creek, wallabies scratching in the undergrowth, demented kookaburras cackling at jokes only they knew, elusive black cockatoos in the canopy, silent streams and mossy logs providing habitats for a myriad of shy creatures, all with the majestic blue of the Baw Baw plateau in the background. During spring and early summer, the Valley became my Eden.

By this time, I had also joined a mouth organ club, as I promised myself on the *Fairsea*. It seemed quite a few Dutch boys played this working-class instrument. We met weekly at a Dutch musician's house and practised slavishly. Some played huge bass-harmonicas, others, mouth organs of varying sizes. We became well known around the Valley and even had a uniform – black pants and a golden skivvy.

In 1957 I was given a Hohner chromatic harmonica for my fifteenth birthday, a wonderful if expensive instrument. Soon afterwards, our club featured on the radio, 3UL in Warragul, now 3GG, and appeared at civic functions and multicultural festivities. I even entered a few competitions and did reasonably well. It was all small beer, but intensely satisfying.

Meanwhile, Flozzie took his first communion. God took a temporary back seat for Lex and me, but we sang in the choir on Sundays, and when Mother worked for Dr Crook, a keen music lover, I was invited to sing in Haydn's *Creation*. So began my own love affair with classical music. On Sundays, at two o'clock, Father and I listened to a radio program called *Famous Tenors*, sponsored by a chemist from Korumburra. Jussi Björling, one of the leading operatic singers of the time, filled the void exquisitely and I regarded him as the greatest tenor ever, even surpassing the great Caruso, who, admittedly, was disadvantaged by inferior recording. Even today, Björling sends shivers up my spine.

That same year, 1957, Lex and I made some extra mullah picking beans, near the Gas and Fuel plant. The backbreaking work, however, yielded little money. It took ages to fill a bag and the employers knew it. During this hot weather, we used our lunch breaks to swim naked in the run-off channels, in company with the Koori boys and girls who had travelled from Lake Tyers to do seasonal work. Unselfconsciously, we

I was given a *Hohner* harmonica. Mouth organ club, Warragul, Victoria, 1957. Henri centre-right.

jumped into the water together, paddling happily and enjoying their company; their easy laughter and relaxed manner making them great playmates. It was a miracle we didn't get sick from the polluted run-off, though. Perhaps our immune systems, having been thoroughly tested by the immigration process, Bonegilla, Tasmania, and the local tip, provided us with panzer antibodies... Aside from colds, cuts and bruises, we rarely got sick.

During summer, Bill Brown, Lex and I also worked for a Dutch farmer, Buurman, gathering hay, the wood business being idle at that time of year. We turned the hay into bales, tied with wire we had to poke through a machine; fiddly and very tiring. In the scorching sun, we hated this job. Bill chucked it in after a few days, but Lex and I kept going. The Buurmans had a brown Ford Prefect ute, a 1954 model, sometimes referred to as the 'skinny one', in which we travelled to their farm, magpies carolling our welcome. The early morning sun gave the countryside a tranquil beauty, with the odd cow here and there, head down, glued to its pasture, and no doubt enjoying the coolness of this time of day, which I also loved.

We also collected hay from another of Buurman's paddocks, on the Maryvale Road. A few years later the land was sold to the Education Department and in 1959 became the site of Morwell Technical School.

Lex and I enjoyed the work as we sat on a red, horse-drawn hay rake, the clawing hoops sometimes annoying us, however, by jumping up too soon and startling us; fortunately, the placid chestnut mare remained biddable and unconcerned. We soon became used to the machine and learnt to lift, let go, and clamp down at the right time. Since the task wasn't particularly tiring, inhaling the sweet fragrance of the freshly cut hay out in the open air, I thought that, in addition to the modest lucre, this was "the best of all possible worlds".[102]

During our final year in Morwell, Father used his Bedford to transport a local farmer's hay bales; a little extra money for honest work. The loads were so high he needed to drive slowly to prevent the bales from toppling. Even so, we sat on top, overlooking the bonnet and the paddocks abutting the Water Hole Creek, the danger never entering our minds.

My last Morwell job was as a petrol pump attendant. I was expected to mollycoddle the customers, fill up the tanks, keep the garage floor tidy, collect the used oil removed by the mechanic when he serviced the cars and then deposit it into a forty-four-gallon drum at the back, and do whatever else was demanded of me by the boss. I hated the job because I ran out of things to do. Boredom is a killer of productive work...

*

---

[102] To borrow from Voltaire's character, Pangloss, in his tale *Candide ou l'Optimisme*, published in 1759.

Our large backyard was a study in enterprise. Because of the Depression and the War, many immigrants, and some Australians too, converted their yards into vegetable patches; Mediterranean and other migrants often carried on the traditions of their forebears in doing so. It was common to see row upon row of climbing beans, carrots, broad beans, silverbeet, pumpkin, cucumber, brussel sprouts, snow peas, leeks, lettuces and tomatoes in both the front and back yards. All were sensibly spaced and staked. The miniature market gardens could supply a family for much of the year. Not only did the vegies taste better, they saved money. I grew my first crop in 1955, a tiny patch squeezed between a wall of bottles and the big pine crate. I was ecstatic when the first cress-shaped leaves of radish broke through the soil, soon followed by beans and a couple of lettuce shoots. Our front garden, for some reason, was ignored and looked quite barren, except for some irritating geraniums that Mother had insisted on, as well as a few other desiccated flowers. Father was too busy to plant much, although he always intended to, and Mother wasn't a gardener, staying largely indoors.

Initially for jingoistic reasons, we attached an iron flag holder to the front weatherboards, though in the end never used it. After sixty years or so, we think it's still there; a tribute to utter pointlessness. Father also found time to build a chicken run in the backyard, but it was a slapdash affair and the chooks often got out, quickly heading for the vegie patch, picking off the most tender leaves and hunting for worms. The chooks varied between White Leghorns, Rhode Island Reds, and Bantams. Father claimed bantam eggs, while smaller, tasted better. When the chooks grew old and stopped laying, they finished up in the pot. He hated killing them and left the job to Bill, who had no qualms in wringing their necks or belting their heads against the timber railing outside the back door until lifeless. Quite gruesome really!

However, chooks are good for the soul as well as for the stomach. We loved our silly chooks, and as a youngster tip-toeing through the pen collecting eggs, I felt like a thief. I still find chook noises soothing, emblematic of a reliable food supply; and remarkably reassuring when having a pleasant bog on a Saturday morning. Hens make distinct sounds: when being chased, when laying eggs, while being wooed by roosters or pecking and scratching at feed, and 'brawking', my term for brooding. With their dopey eyes and emphatic struts, the stentorian urgh-a-urgh-a-urgh of a self-opinionated rooster and the contented urrrs of the hens capture the wonderful ordinariness of life, together with a sense of optimism. Perhaps the constant laying of eggs suggests perseverance and pluckiness...

Our backyard also became a private playground, where we younger ones were allowed to build tiny gravel roads for our Boomerang trucks and dinky toys, swings, and cubbies. Old, bent nails from discarded planks were straightened, timber was retrieved from the tip to be used for construction, and old carpet found its way onto dirt floors. We thoroughly enjoyed the process of building and making, afterwards adopting the domestic accoutrements of our parents: tables, benches and plastic plates. Our instincts were those of cave dwellers, providing shelter and warmth. We also became imaginary truck, taxi and ambulance drivers, transported earth from one end of the yard to the other, fixed billycarts and helped weed the garden.

A bird's eye view saw the backyard divided up between woodpiles; rows of empty beer bottles; a large kerosene drum; a pine crate full of kindling and tools; a huge rusty sawing machine; a Bedford truck, backed into place, followed by an FJ Holden; a middle area devoted to vegetables; a chook pen at the back; two cubbies attached to the right-hand fence, and little dirt tracks everywhere. Finally, just below the back steps, lying peacefully on the ground, was Micky, half-asleep, smiling and grunting, dreaming of bones and brawls, then suddenly snapping at another fly, which quickly met its fate.

Dividing the vegie patch was a long T-shaped clothes line, with short crossbeams at either end that could be raised and lowered like semaphores; Hills hoists were out of our league. Working on power stations, cutting wood, digging the soil, and attracting dirty motes floating through the air from both the coalfields and the paper mill, meant filthy clothing, while the attendant noxious smells were just another routine aspect of life in Morwell. Mother spent hours boiling work clothes in the copper, then wringing them through her Dutch contraption and, finally, trying to dry them as best she could in winter or when it rained: no modern washing machines or driers... Afterwards, she ironed and folded for more hours. It must have been a nightmare, yet she did it on a regular basis with relatively little complaint and we hardly noticed.

I finished grade six in 1955 and my parents needed to consider what to do next, although the Sisters of Saint Joseph made a valiant attempt to keep me at the Sacred Heart primary school for another two years, in grades seven and eight: I was studying piano and French at the time and the nuns thought I would benefit by remaining with them. Father and Mother, however, had different ideas. Lex had already moved to Yallourn Technical School and was thriving. The solid brick art deco design of the school was atypical and Lex loved the place. As an aside, why didn't the

Education Department build similar schools throughout Victoria? Other States were architecturally far more sensitive.[103]

Since the Latrobe Valley was growing in population and industrial development, and because many European migrants in the Valley were Catholic, having come mainly from Catholic countries, the church hierarchy committed itself to harvesting the minds and souls of its younger members, mine included. Monsignor O'Mara, parish priest of Traralgon, in conjunction with Bishop Ryan of Sale, deemed it desirable to establish a Catholic secondary college for boys in Traralgon. Consequently, a Mr Simon Stoddart donated ten acres to the Marist Fathers, and before long, their Provincial, Father Jim Harcombe, who died in 2009 aged ninety-six, gave his blessing to the founding of Saint Paul's. The school opened in 1956.

Returning from Lakes Entrance one summer afternoon, my parents made a slight detour to the recently built college in Grey Street. They must have heard about the Marists from the pulpit at the Sacred Heart Church in Morwell: a good Catholic education fitted in with their religious values. A number of my friends from Sacred Heart had already enrolled and so it seemed a natural progression for me to also enrol in this new educational asset for the Valley. I was accepted as a student at a reduced rate because of our low income and still have the payment card. The weekly fee was 10/6, or ten shillings and sixpence, a considerable sum for my folks nonetheless.

Enrolling at Saint Paul's felt like a privilege. Here I was, an immigrant lad bamboozled by well-intentioned nuns, allowed to attend a freshly minted school run by a religious order I had never heard of. The fact it was a boys' school didn't matter, coming from a male household. The freshness and novelty of the place struck me as a good opportunity to improve myself. I look back to this brief but formative period, when, as an eager young boy, I wanted to please everyone: the teachers, fellow students and my family. Besides, my parents forking out all that money meant I'd better not disappoint them!

Saint Paul's began with ninety-two students across three forms, guaranteeing close contact with the Fathers. The Fathers had high expectations, but alas, the Valley, then as now, was a community of generally lower socio-economic status. That is not to say there weren't able students or many well-paid, highly educated professional people, but overall, the academic profile at St Paul's, at least, remained somewhat mediocre.

---

[103] Victoria's highly attractive red and hawthorn-brick schools were mainly built before the Second World War. Because of the upsurge in migration during the 1950s, the Victorian Government usually built relatively inexpensive, unattractive, Light Timber Construction, or Chicken Coop, schools between 1954 and 1977. The private school system on the other hand usually built architecturally designed brick edifices.

By the Scruff of the Neck

ST. PAUL'S COLLEGE GROUP

'Religion' was a very weighty matter. Traralgon, Victoria, 1956. Henri: second row from front, eighth from left.

Founded in France by Father Jean Claude Colin in 1816, the Marist Fathers, of the Society of Mary, were a missionary and teaching order. They did considerable evangelical work in Oceania, in the West Pacific; in particular, New Zealand, Tonga, Kiribati, Fiji and Samoa. A few of the teachers at Saint Paul's arrived in Traralgon after working as missionaries in Tonga.

The Marist Fathers were housed in a cream brick building on the premises. I remember visiting the house at various times. Outside the back door was a stack of empty beer bottles. I don't wish to criticize them whatsoever; it must have been tough on the priests in that early period, having so much to manage and consider: new buildings, the curriculum, enrolments, staffing, and getting along with the local clergy. They were hardworking men from New South Wales, with a strong rugby and rural background, and who can begrudge them a few ales on a hot dusty day? Some of them were also heavy smokers.

Christian doctrine at Saint Paul's was instilled at a more sophisticated level than my basic 'spiritual' development in Holland. Leaving aside other subjects, 'religion' was a very weighty matter. As a youngster in Holland and Australia, I unequivocally accepted whatever the priests, brothers, lay-teachers and nuns told me. A kind of mindless subservience, if you like. Perhaps understandable, given the era and our particular background. Father and Mother rarely questioned their own beliefs and enjoined us to do the same. They accepted the basic theological framework of the Church and ran with it. On the other hand, they weren't overly pious and resented holy joe-ery, even though they endorsed the guilt trip.

At Saint Paul's we attended mass regularly, sometimes followed by confession, were always on the receiving end of advice and hortatory sermons, thanked God for everything, yet didn't always fully understand what we experienced or were told. Religion ruled from before school until after, with prayers before lessons and in between, and at the end of the school day. On Fridays, the school routine was briefly pushed aside when we were allowed to buy chips from a van...if we could afford it. On occasions, too, the Fathers showed films, usually at the end of term: *Great Expectations* and *Whisky Galore*, for instance. Such pleasures, however, were rare.

At one point, we were visited by Chanel College from Geelong[104] to share experiences: I expect theirs were similar to ours. Church dignitaries too came and went, and we were supposed to be impressed. Archbishop Carboni, Rome's Apostolic Delegate to Australia from 1953 to '59, was the most eminent cleric to visit Saint Paul's. However, the only famous

---

[104] The college closed in 1998.

person I really remember was Lindsay Hassett, the elegant, diminutive cricketer.

The Catholic ethos of the 1950s was heavily influenced by Archbishop Mannix, a highly politicized Irish cleric who had the ear of such luminaries as John Wren, Joe Lyons, James Scullin and Arthur Calwell. He was bitterly opposed to conscription in the First World War and a fervent Irish nationalist. He supported B. A. Santamaria during 'The Split',[105] although Cardinal Gilroy[106] did not. Not having any degree of political awareness at the time, I had no knowledge of the tremendous rupture in the Labor movement that occurred during 1955. The Catholic Church, including our teachers, were fiercely anti-communist, essentially because it was regarded as a heathen or atheistic ideology. However, although my religious doctrine teacher, Father Cox, did rail against communism, I can't recall the other priests ranting and raving against Karl Marx to any marked degree.

Father Jim Cox, a terrier in his defence of the Church, was an engaging man. He applied the school motto, *Certa Certamen Fidei* – 'Fight the Fight of the Faith' – rather vigorously. He sat on a desk in the front row and took us through a series of booklets on the sacraments. The sacraments and their explanations were printed in large capital letters, just in case we didn't get it. He waged war on Protestants and atheists, claiming confidently, 'I can prove them wrong, anytime.' We were most impressed with his swagger and considered him a polemical champion. Islam wasn't on the horizon in Traralgon in 1957, but would have been peremptorily dismissed by Coxie as being false.

A thin, highly-strung man, Father Cox was a fine pianist and always on the run, with his fair, curly hair bobbing up and down as he went. Like Saint Paul, he was a religious zealot, but managed to make his Christian doctrine classes come alive; I was very fond of him. He died in 1976 from a heart attack, in Malaysia. It was rumoured he left the Church to become a Buddhist. Somewhat ironic if true!

I should stress that in describing my teachers of the time, I don't intend any harm, but can only state my impressions and recollections through the tricky lens of distant memory, something already spoken about as unreliable and possibly dangerous. No doubt I may also be

---

[105] In 1955, the Australian Labor Party split into the left-leaning ALP and the right-wing, Catholic-dominated, Democratic Labor Party, led by B. A. Santamaria. Whether Dr Evatt, the communists, or Catholics, were responsible for 'The Split' remains a topic of debate.
Note: Herbert Vere Evatt, 1894–1965, was an Australian statesman, judge and author who played an important part in establishing the United Nations.

[106] Cardinal Norman Gilroy, 1896–1977, the first Australian-born cardinal, was head of the Catholic church at the time of 'The Split'.

guilty of misremembering or selectivity, but hope that others still alive from this time can fill in the gaps or correct me.

Little is known about these priests: when and where they were born, what kind of education they received, their qualifications, the history of their earlier careers, their likes, dislikes and idiosyncrasies. It now seems these men in their black cassocks, while unquestionably devoted to their calling, were relative strangers. Certainly to me! As young boys we judged them superficially, not knowingly. How could we? Like distant spirits, they arrived in Traralgon, became tangible for a few, slow years, then disappeared without trace; not just because my family and I shifted to Melbourne, but also because they were moved along far too quickly. It's as if they had fallen off a cliff or entered Doctor Who's *Tardis* to fly to some obscure destination. The Marist Fathers had all left by 1962, allegedly because of differences between them and the Bishop of Sale, Patrick Lyons,[107] and were succeeded by the Marist Brothers.[108] More's the pity, for the Fathers were, overall, a positive influence in the Valley.

The strap-happy culture of Saint Paul's undoubtedly mirrored those in Catholic schools elsewhere in Australia at the time. No one enjoyed the strap but everyone took it in his stride as a natural part of discipline. The Marists walked up and down the aisles lazily swinging their leather, stopping here and there to strap someone for talking, disruption, or more insidiously, for not remembering their Latin or French vocabulary; or perhaps for not having completed homework.

Father McMillan was an exception. A dark, handsome chap, who caused women to swoon during Sunday Mass, he was always good-spirited. If someone erred, he took the culprit into the corridor and pretended to strap him, then warned the boy not to breathe a word to the others: he was a big fellow and would strike a stack of books instead, with such force that the class was totally convinced the victim had been permanently maimed. A genuinely lovely man, Father McMillan left Saint Paul's far too soon.

Father Sid Mitchell, later rector of Saint John's 'Woodlawn', Lismore, was solid, ginger-haired and methodical, and given the lofty title of 'Prefect of Studies'. I liked him, but in hindsight didn't regard him as a great teacher. He knew his science and maths but couldn't explain himself clearly. Sitting near the back of the newly constructed tiered science room, I tried to remember and understand the properties of chemicals, as well as various scientists' experimental results and their discoveries, but found the process onerous. For example, Father Mitchell had a habit of speaking slowly and describing an experiment only once,

---

[107] *Latrobe Valley Express*, 16th October 2006, p.11

[108] Priests are ordained and may celebrate the sacraments of the Church, give sermons and teach. Brothers are members of a religious order, taking the vows of poverty, chastity and obedience and are usually teachers.

using his fat fingers for emphasis. He was reluctant to repeat himself, or give reasons for the experiments. Scientific laws and procedures were plucked from thin air, so it seemed to me, and given to us as something self-evident. He seemed unable or unwilling to provide context. Most of us simply couldn't digest his lessons. He did the same in mathematics. As a result, many did poorly in these subjects for the Proficiency Certificate – form three, or year nine – and were afterwards accused of laziness. Unfortunately, Father Mitchell didn't have the knack of entering the callow minds of his charges. He also seemed a little bored with it all...but I don't bear him any animosity.

Father Michael O' Grady[109] was a different kettle of fish entirely. There may have been all kinds of reasons why he was disliked, though not necessarily by everyone, and I should be careful in what I say, but from my perspective, truth must out. I had him as a teacher for History and English and as sports master.

In one instance, while he was in the preparatory annexe at the back of the science room, which was also the storeroom for footballs and soccer balls, I knocked on the door, wanting to collect a soccer ball, but as I didn't get a response, entered the annexe.

'Did you knock, before you came in?' he asked.

'Yes, Father, I knocked on the science room door,' I replied.

'Yes, yes, but did you knock on *this* door?' he asked insistently, meaning the annexe door.

'No, Father, I didn't.'

He then produced the strap and gave me six of the best.

Like my ordeal in Tasmania, I was more hurt by the unfairness than the punishment itself, even though this time at least a semblance of justification was given. I was in fact strapped on many occasions; simply *de rigueur*. But there was a mean streak in Father Michael O' Grady. He was unpredictable, his wrath feared, and his sullen moods to be avoided. Nor was he a particularly good teacher. We read *The Merchant of Venice* in class, some of the boys strangling Shakespeare execrably. He could have done a number of things, such as ask a few *good* readers to act, as best they could, the various rôles, *he* taking on the most difficult; *Shylock* comes to mind. Or he could have asked the boys to read the play first, by themselves, preferably at home, and then attempt to read it aloud in class. Films and recordings were also available, which could have been used as excellent teaching tools, but they weren't. Father O'Grady didn't even discuss the play in detail or explain Shakespeare's language. The characters never left the page and we died of boredom.

As for history, I wondered about his knowledge, even then. Aside from the Catholic bias, he didn't exhibit much grasp of historical argument or

---

[109] Not his real name.

moment. His lessons were turgid and he looked surly, as if he didn't want to be there. This also applied to his role as Marist priest, I suspect. I believe he has since left the congregation, and if he is still alive, I hope he is happier now than when I knew him.

Father Lynch taught me history in 1958. I remember him as a gentle, sensitive soul, but his teaching left me unimpressed. Like Sid Mitchell, he too has passed on. The standout character, in my view, was Father Harry Davis. He was loathed by some, certainly respected and feared, and admired by others. I belong to the last group. He reminded me of a pugnacious frog due to his bulging eyes, beer belly and bellicosity. He was also a heavy smoker and an entertaining raconteur.

Father Davis was rector at Saint Paul's until he moved to Burnie, in Tasmania, where he was also rector. He died in 1973. Though their personalities were quite different, Father Davis was to have a similar impact on me to that of Barry Jones, the 1960s quiz champion and later, parliamentarian: I had Barry as a teacher when I attended Dandenong High School after we moved to Melbourne. Father Davis was dynamic, righteous, humorous at times – *"Les(lie) Miserables is a great actor"* – a splendid orator, relentless and tough, but under certain circumstances, generous and kind. One time I had a tooth abscess that hurt like hell. A boy hit me, for some reason I can't remember; a rather uncommon event, since violence or bullying, though present, was actively frowned upon. Pus and blood shot out of my mouth and I thought I was going to faint; I can vividly recall the pain. Father Davis put me into his Holden and drove me home to Morwell so that Mother could take me to the doctor. All the while he regaled me with stories of his past.

If my memory serves me right, he came from a country town somewhere in northern New South Wales, from a large family, mainly sisters, and went to school barefoot. Not significant perhaps, but nonetheless revealing. Poverty was clearly evident in his early life. He had a prodigious memory and could reel off quotations from Julius Caesar, Napoleon, Churchill, and others. I think in a whimsical way Father Davis had a Napoleonic complex. Was it mere habit to keep his hand inside his soutane, just like the little Corsican did, but inside his uniform?

Some of his favourite quotes were, "It takes extraordinary men to keep ordinary men ordinary", and "A throne is only a bench covered with velvet". He quoted Cicero and the medieval philosophers, and recounted stories from Tacitus and Ovid. I still have his list of famous Latin sayings, mostly to do with religion, but also some from Caesar and Scipio on virtue, military strategy, wisdom, and the like.

Father Davis didn't suffer fools and used the strap as much as his pen. For all that, he wasn't devious or vicious and one could sense his desire to lift up his students to higher matters. I see myself, a skinny blond boy standing next to his desk reciting declensions and conjugations, petrified I might get them wrong; if so a quick belt on the hand, and then told to continue.

Morwell was soccer and football mad during the 1950s. One time, on the bus to Traralgon, a few boys asked me which team I 'barracked' for. I hadn't a clue what the word meant,[110] so just replied, 'I prefer soccer, if you don't mind.' The enthusiasm of the boys in declaring their club allegiance did rub off, though, and I wanted to be included in their banter. One morning, Melbourne having beaten Collingwood, I said fervently, 'I support Melbourne.' Essendon, Melbourne and Collingwood were the great teams of the fifties.

'You must be joking,' replied Rob Munro, a mate at the time. 'Melbourne is for the toffs...the rich... You'll have to support someone else.'

I thought about this and asked, 'Who should I barrack for then?'

A passionate discussion about the relative merits of various football teams ensued. Rob reasoned, 'Collingwood is an Irish-Catholic side and belongs to us,' meaning our faith and cultural heritage.

This wasn't entirely clear to me, but having tribal instincts, I saw the merit of Rob's point and became an ardent Collingwood fan from then on. Historically, clubs like Collingwood and Richmond represented the working class, but this didn't dawn on me till much later. At the time, the fact that Collingwood was considered a Catholic club sealed it.

Australian Rules football was, of course, the dominant code and gradually grew on me to the point of fanaticism, yet I could never understand the petty rivalry that existed between the two games. They are entirely compatible and I adore both, although I preferred to play soccer. Even so, Aussie Rules is, in my view, the grander spectacle. Jack-the-lad hated it and always referred to Aussie Rules as aerial ping-pong. 'How can you like a game with a ball shaped like an egg?' he asked petulantly, yet never watched an Aussie football game in his life.

Bill became a goalie for the Morwell soccer team, the *Rangers*, later named *Pegasus*, while Jack-the-lad briefly played as an outside right. Being younger, I entered the game a little later, while Lex had other interests. Before joining any team, I had been encouraged by Manfred

---

[110] According to *The Concise Australian National Dictionary*, in 1878 'barrickin' meant to jeer or mock, or, as in costermonger Cockney, it meant 'gibberish; a jumble of words'. The most likely theory, however, is that the term 'barrack', as listed in *The English Dialect Dictionary*, came from Northern Ireland, meaning 'to brag, to be boastful of one's fighting powers'.

Kaminsky, an older neighbourhood friend and excellent soccer player himself, who told me later it was my dribbling that impressed him.

From 1956 onwards, I played junior soccer for the Dutch building company, *Werkspoor,* responsible for the new Gas and Fuel station. The club was simply called *Werkspoor.* Father, a soccer enthusiast, let me play on Saturdays and Sundays, provided I helped with chores first, and nor was it to interfere with homework. Pain before pleasure!

Because the Latrobe Valley was an immigrant stronghold, the standard of soccer was relatively high. The *Werkspoor* guernsey was blocked red-and-white, just like those worn by the Alkmaar Boys, Father's beloved team of the '30s and '40s. How could he not encourage his son's talent?

Sport became an obsession, and Saint Paul's excelled at football, producing some fine league footballers; Bernie Quinlan, for example. I became school soccer captain and thoroughly enjoyed the freedom of Wednesday afternoons, letting all the pent-up frustrations of the classroom go into the ball.

One of the driving forces of the local soccer scene was a crazy Czech, who owned a driving school. He was passionate, devious and unhinged. Whenever his side scored a goal, he would either kiss the ground or rush onto the field and kiss the scorer, his arms outstretched, his portly body and pale flabby face shaking with delight. He was a charmer; or should I say, bullshit artist. Lex and I briefly worked for him, washing cars. We never got paid. I soon learnt not to judge people by their appearance or manner. Rogues come in all kinds of guises, immigrants no exception.

One cold Saturday morning I sauntered to the nearby state school to be collected by our coach, clunky boots slung over shoulder. Ted Heineman, a Dutchman who lived a few streets away and who was a soccer fanatic, became my soccer mentor and drove us to all our games in the Valley: four soccer boys, all arms and legs, squeezed into his baby Austin, or Austin 30. He came from an educated family in Holland, wrote for the *Dutch-Australian Weekly,* and reminded me of Uncle John Goudsblom. He was single at the time, marrying late, yet still managed to father a large family. He was a rather nervous man, but precise, as well as enthusiastic and caring.

Werkspoor played against the other towns in the Valley and won two championships. During our last year in Morwell, 1958, three of us were selected as the best players from the Latrobe Valley and were to be tested on the old Hakoah[111] grounds. We were to compete against the foremost

---

[111] Founded in 1927, Melbourne's Hakoah sports club had a predominantly Jewish supporter base and became one of the first successful non-Anglo-Celtic sports clubs, laying the foundation for other migrant-run clubs after WWII. It eventually merged with South Melbourne's Victorian League reserve side during the 1980s.

Clunky boots slung over shoulder. Werkspoor junior soccer club. Henri: middle row, second from right. Morwell, 1957.

Victorian players. The aim was to select the best squad to represent the State.

Having inherited a flighty disposition from my parents, I felt nervous and exhausted before the round-robin tournament, organized by the soccer administration, especially after our long trip from the Valley. I didn't play very well and wasn't selected for the State squad.

A year later, however, after shifting to Melbourne, I received more incisive coaching, became stronger and quicker, so grew in confidence. I then played for Dandenong and was selected for the Melbourne Metropolitan team and the All-High-Schools' side as an outside left: I played with and against Billy Vojtek, who was playing for Essendon at the time but who was also selected for the Melbourne Metropolitan team. Vojtek, a Croatian, finished up representing Australia during the 1960s and '70s.

Having been selected for the Melbourne Metropolitan team virtually ensured my selection for the under-sixteen State side. Unfortunately, in a practice match – Victoria against New South Wales – their goalkeeper kicked me in the solar plexus, rupturing my spleen. The coach wasn't at first overly concerned, advising me to have a hot bath and all would be well. Serendipitously, during my paper round I fainted, collapsing right in front of a doctor, by the surname of James.

Flozzie, doing the paper round with me, sounded the alarm. Apparently the sac around my ripped spleen was leaking, but as with the earlier diphtheria episode, I survived, and now share my organ loss with former prime minister Bob Hawke's grandson, David Dillon, a rugby football victim. Soccer, let it be known, can be just as dangerous as other football codes.

While visiting me in Dandenong hospital, Father deflected his anxiety by wittily observing, 'Weeds don't perish,' which is a Dutch saying and backhanded compliment. Once I recovered, I continued to play soccer for leisure, but as furthering my education became increasingly important, my sports career fizzled to an end.

I excelled in languages and the humanities, not so in the sciences, and did well in Christian doctrine. Fear worked some of the time but enquiry and curiosity worked better. We applied ourselves and weren't allowed to dream, as I sometimes did, looking at pictures of women picking tea in India or some peasant picking cocoa beans in another land...

With the pervasive stink of the Maryvale paper mill in my nostrils, I looked up from my dull geography book and out the window, trying to reconcile the verdant vista towards Baw Baw with a desert scene from the Sahara of a woman drawing water in an oasis. I was determined to visit these places one day and discover the world anew. The grainy black and white prints were my escape route from the tense atmosphere of the classroom.

My reveries were abruptly broken: 'Henri Licht, you are not paying attention!' Wrong, actually, I was, but not to what was being demanded of me.

I read somewhere that Alexander Pope, the shrivelled little hunchback poet, wrote that all he wanted from his masters was to be left alone: he endeavoured to sit at the back of his class on a wooden bench, hoping to avoid scrutiny. At times, I shared his desire for anonymity, but this was virtually impossible under the frenetic vigilance of the Fathers. Even looking out the window could be dangerous, if caught!

For much of the time, the impact of authority and indoctrination made learning an uncomfortable experience. Saint Francis Xavier's well-worn adage, "Give me a child until he is seven and I will give you the man", may well be true. The Fathers, however, had a much longer time to work on my character. My teachers were of course genuine in their beliefs and times were vastly different from now, but it took me a very long time to whittle down their influence. In a sense I have never broken their shackles, including having a near nervous breakdown in my matriculation year, which was, in my view, largely determined by the existential dread of the world shaped by my experiences at Saint Paul's.

The hold over me was more psychological than punitive. The Church relied heavily on 'guilt' and 'fear' to steer people's behaviour. The sops were absolution, forgiveness, penance, and the slick gift of 'grace'. Many years later, at a reunion, a few of my fellow students expressed such a degree of hatred for Saint Paul's that I was completely taken aback. In hindsight, I suppose, if you weren't academically interested or able, the tedious talk and chalk, nervous recitations, and incessant strapping, would have turned most students against learning; some just marked time and left as soon as their parents permitted. Yet by and large, Saint Paul's worked for me, although only in an academic sense: the religious world created by the Fathers kept me anxious and fearful for an inordinate length of time. When I attended Dandenong High School, from 1959 onwards, I discovered there were other ways of instilling knowledge, and certainly not by the use of the strap or humiliation.

After seeing Fred Schepisi's film *The Devil's Playground*, John Gordon, a non-Catholic friend of mine, asked a Catholic mate of his, who had been taught by the Christian Brothers, 'Tell me, Mick, was it really as bad as all that?' To which Mick replied, 'No, no, no! Far worse.'

*

One Sunday, in my matriculation year, during high Mass in Saint Mary's, Dandenong, the congregation was warned not to vote for the Australian Labor Party because they were deemed to be Communist bedfellows. I stood up in front of the faithful and told the priest, 'You have no right to tell people how to vote, Father.' I left the Church that day, never to return. My parents were mortified. Aged seventeen, it was the beginning of my extrication from the religious clutches of the Church. At the time, however, I needed to turn to someone...or somewhere...for support. I even consulted a priest from the Church of Saint Francis, on the corner of Lonsdale and Elizabeth Streets in the city, yet found him wanting, indeed frivolous, in his answers to my earnest questions.

My studying philosophy at Monash University can be directly attributed to the implosion of my religious beliefs. Philosophy, in its broadest sense, opened a new door and I entered a conceptual world that called religion and its postulates very much into question. I suffered for it for some time, as I said earlier. The whole edifice of belief came tumbling down in a relatively short period of time, once I learnt how to apply the blowtorch of rational thinking and scientific method to the nature of religious belief. Bertrand Russell and John Hospers[112] were the torchbearers of my conversion.

Looking back to my early secondary schooling, the teaching of Christian doctrine at Saint Paul's was like entering a world of make-belief, a cathedral of ideas made of balsawood. There were so many assumptions and blind assertions to refute, like lifting scales from one's eyes: creationism, transubstantiation, confession, papal infallibility, immaculate conception, Mariolatry,[113] original sin, heaven and hell, purgatory and limbo. All were scuttled in time. In my first year of university, I questioned everything to do with religion, notwithstanding guilt and doubt stalking me like cold-war spies.

However, when I disclosed to a close friend of mine, Michael Walsh, another escapee from the Church, that at Saint Paul's I was never interfered with, he wryly observed, 'That's probably because you weren't pretty enough.'

I don't wish to defend my looks, but this was untrue. The more important point was that in my case and, as far as I could tell, in that of the other students at Saint Paul's, what I said happened to be true: during my time at St Paul's, there was not one skerrick of evidence that the Fathers were guilty of any transgressions. Scurrilous gossip is a staple of student communities: I would most likely have found out if anything was amiss. Also, for example, when Father Davis drove me home to

---

[112] John Hospers, 1918–2011, was an American philosopher and politician. In 1972 he became the first presidential candidate of the Libertarian Party, and was the only minor party candidate to receive an electoral vote in that year's election.

[113] Excessive veneration or worship of the Virgin Mary.

Morwell he had ample opportunity to sexually interfere. Instead, if he were alive today, he would be horrified by the recent paedophilia sagas exposed in the tabloids.

The rot in our particular branch of the Catholic Church set in much later. It emerged that the most notorious paedophile at Saint Paul's was the Marist Brother Gerard McNamara, who taught there decades after I left. In various other branches, as the 2013 Royal Commission into child abuse within the Catholic Church revealed, the issue was detected much earlier, but hushed up.

In 2006, while attending a celebratory Mass to commemorate fifty years since the founding of Saint Paul's, an elderly gentleman stood up with a placard condemning the Church for its persistent cover-up of paedophiles. Neither the bishop nor the congregation knew what to do. Instead, I was bemused to see the Catholic hierarchy of the Sale diocese cringe and suggested to the school counsellor sitting next to me to just let the man be and get on with the service: I admired the man's guts. Inwardly, I thought to myself, 'Ah, "As ye sow so shall ye reap",' the author none other than Saint Paul (Galatians 6:7).

The philosophical underpinnings of Catholic belief derive substantially from Saint Augustine and Saint Thomas Aquinas. Medieval scholars, such as Saint Anselm of Canterbury, Duns Scotus and William of Ockham,[114] contributed specific doctrines related to proofs for the existence of God, the idea of the Immaculate Conception as formulated by Scotus, and variants of the now largely discredited ontological argument, the non-separation of existence and essence – a concept opposed by existentialists such as Jean-Paul Sartre (1905–80), who asserted that existence preceded essence. They were men of sound intellect; their ideas, however, controversial and challengeable.

On the fideist[115] side, biblical scholars ever since Saint Paul were busy combing through the New Testament looking for evidence for the seven holy sacraments that were formalized during the reign of the Byzantine

---

[114] Saint Augustine, Bishop of Hippo, 354–430, early-Christian theologian; Saint Thomas Aquinas, 1225–74, Dominican friar, foremost medieval philosopher and theologian; Saint Anselm, 1033–1109, Benedictine monk, Archbishop of Canterbury, an eminent scholar and theologian; Duns Scotus, John Duns, 1265–1308, important philosopher of the High Middle Ages; William of Ockham 1288–1347, Franciscan friar, distinguished philosopher and theologian.

[115] In questions of religion, reliance on faith alone, rather than scientific reasoning or philosophy.

Emperor, Michael Palaiologus[116] when he converted to Catholicism in 1274. The Catholic Church is obsessed with sacraments, principally the Eucharist. The theological force of the sacraments allows for tight control or power to be exercised by the Catholic hierarchy. Personally, I believe the hunt for sacramental justification in the Gospels is overdone; but don't wish to get into a theological scrape over this...

I became aware that apart from problems of critical explanation, the compilation of the Bible had a chequered and obscure history. It was only at the request of Ptolemy II Philadelphus (288–47 BC) of Egypt that the sources of the Bible were systematized by seventy specially chosen Jewish scholars, who translated the text into Greek, forming the Septuagint,[117] which in turn became the basis for the modern Bible. The Bible consists of many books, many different styles, and many little-known Prophets. Much of ancient Judaic law and the writings and words of the Prophets was lost and had to be rediscovered by Hebrew and Hellenic scholars. Therefore, what precise influence did Philo of Alexandria[118] and Seneca the Younger,[119] for instance, have on early Christian tradition, practice and morality, as distinct from the elusive Jesus Christ?

Moreover, translating from Hebrew, Aramaic and Greek allows for error and muddled interpretation. Not being a biblical scholar, I will leave this for others to substantiate, although an example may suffice: the technical terms *homoousios*, of one essence, and *homoiousios*, of similar but not of the same essence, confused interpretation of the trinity for centuries. Were Christ and the Holy Spirit commensurate with God the Father in terms of divine essence, or were they of lesser status? This question was raised at the Council of Nicaea in 325 AD and became known as the Arian Controversy. The debate caused great bitterness and long-lasting feuds. Edward Gibbon[120] observed that Christianity was nearly split by the smallest letter in the Greek alphabet, the letter 'i'. To base Catholic theology on such rickety foundations was to ask for trouble. Martin Luther revisited this controversy many centuries later and came

---

[116] Michael VIII Palaiologus, 1223–82, Byzantine Emperor. For Catholics, the seven sacraments – Baptism, Confirmation, Eucharist, Penance, Holy Orders, Matrimony and Extreme Unction – are all imbued with the spirit of Christ and are crucial rites of passage.

[117] This Greek version of the Hebrew Scriptures contains both a translation of the Hebrew and additional and variant material. It was regarded as the standard form of the Old Testament by the early Christian Church and is still canonical in the Eastern Orthodox Church. The Septuagint is symbolized by the Roman numerals LXX.

[118] 20 BC–c. 50 AD, a Hellenistic Jewish philosopher who lived in Alexandria, Egypt, during the Roman Empire.

[119] c. 4 BC–AD 65, a Roman stoic philosopher, statesman and dramatist with close ties to the early Christian Church.

[120] 1737–94, an English historian and Member of Parliament. His most important work, *The History of the Decline and Fall of the Roman Empire,* is known for the quality and irony of its prose, its use of primary sources, and its open criticism of organised religion.

up with his own view of divinity and the meaning of the Eucharist. The same process, but even more distilled, applies to Islam. The ambiguity concerning the alleged illiteracy of Muhammad doesn't help authenticity, either. The use of Muhammad's *hadiths* by Sunni, Shiite, Salafi and Abadi scholars also pose innumerable problems – dogmatism and fundamentalism implicit dangers: don't question, because the alleged word of God, or Allah, and cognates thereof, is way above your understanding... Yet if all religions claim the 'truth', whether Abrahamic, Hindu, Buddhist, animist, or whatever else, then self-contradiction clearly arises.

I'm dwelling on these matters to illustrate the kind of questioning I pursued at university, shaped to a significant extent by my experiences at Saint Paul's. Nevertheless, lingering doubts remained, similar to the trajectory described in Tolstoy's *A Confession*. Those not brought up in a religious world cannot perhaps appreciate the daily anguish and aching self-doubt suffered by those of confused faith. One is lulled into the belief that a theocratic cosmos and its Pythagorean balms of music, art, ritual, and architecture are all part of God's design; and given our fickle will and 'sinful' temptations, one is constantly admonished to be morally upright, be up to scratch spiritually and avoid becoming the plaything of the devil.

Catholicism has a long and profound history and can't be easily discounted. Its hold is such that by rejecting its tenets one is made to feel an outsider, or indeed, the jetsam and flotsam of a blind universe, and to rub it in, an apostate. The same might be said in varying degrees about the whole spectrum of Christian sects. I found it puzzling how friends, intelligent fellow students, scholars, scientists, and indeed my own family members, retained the 'faith', or a 'faith', regularly attended mass or other church services and prayed ardently. How could they? This puzzlement lingers with me still.

My going against the grain may have all kinds of explanations, but the one inescapable cause was harassment and oppression by the Church. For others, alcohol, drugs, gambling or power become their affliction; apathy also a tragic and constant factor. Yet, in a strange kind of way, I am grateful to have travelled the path I did. In my case, quaint as it may seem, religion was both nemesis and liberation.

Those who have avoided religion through non-exposure, indifference or argued rejection may be fortunate in having escaped its negative effects. But whether morality preceded religion as something innate or as something learnt, religion has been an inextricable part of culture and history over many centuries and has played a crucial role in shaping a sense of morality. This is not to say, of course, that ethics can't be taught rationally. But judging from man's not infrequent irrational behaviour, reason has its limitations. William James[121] points out in *The Varieties of Religious Experience* that the need for religion is as much an emotional and psychological matter as a quest for 'truth' by analytical means. Sigmund Freud on the other hand is rather dismissive on the origin of religion. In his publications *The Future of an Illusion* and *Civilization and its Discontents*, he sees it simply as delusional, or as a suppressed longing for either a father, guidance, or security; a primitive neurosis. After his fascinating demolition, he leaves little solace, however, maintaining that people often prefer opiates of the mind, in whatever form, to the 'truth'.

While still living in Morwell, I spent many nights sweating in fear for having disobeyed God. Tossing and turning, I was determined to improve my moral scorecard, as well as my school reports. While the latter inexplicably improved, sexual urges, however, threatened the former. In form one, or year seven, in response to biological prompts, my close classmate Scotty Egan and I decided to look up rude words in the dictionary; we were shielded from further temptations by our parents and the times we lived in. I looked up the word 'adultery' and thought it a pretty good naughty word. I didn't fully understand it, but having lusted after some well-developed girls from Traralgon High School who shared our bus, I peeked down the unbuttoned shirt of a fulsome girl one sultry afternoon. Aside from warm sensations running riot in my groin area, I knew at once I had committed a sin, to my mind a kind of adultery. What I had allowed my eyes to see was clearly wicked.

The next week, in subdued tones, I confessed to Father O'Reilly, our parish priest: 'Forgive me, Father, for I have sinned. Last week I committed adultery on the bus.'

A stunned silence, followed by a guffaw, followed by loud laughter, followed by an enlightened rebuke in his Irish brogue: 'You canna have committed adultery, you little devil; you aren't wed. C'mon, what did you do and be quick about it; I have others to attend to.'

After completing my penance, I scurried from the confessional in embarrassment and vowed to be more careful next time when consulting a dictionary.

*

---

[121] 1842–1910, an American philosopher and psychologist who was also trained as a physician. James wrote widely on many topics, including epistemology, education, metaphysics, psychology, religion and mysticism.

By the Scruff of the Neck

On Queen Elizabeth the Second's visit to Traralgon in 1954, I won a prize for a badly written Dutch composition in her honour. We were ecstatic to see the young monarch waving at us from the back of the train and reciprocated with Aussie flags, still acknowledging England's hold over her colony. Many immigrants embraced the Queen as head of our Federation, while others were hostile, coming from more republican backgrounds. Some Dutch migrants simply transferred their allegiance from Queen Juliana of Holland to Elizabeth the Second. Our family followed suit, but from age fifteen I became an enthusiastic republican.

Towards the end of 1958, Father, Mother, Flozzie and I were naturalized; or 'neutralized', as Mother called it. The ceremony took place in the town hall and was conducted by the mayor of Morwell, Councillor A. L. Hare. We took the whole affair very seriously, as it meant we had to forego our Dutch citizenship and embrace an Anglo-Celtic culture, with links to Britain and its monarchy. Historically, the Dutch weren't always enamoured of things English, the Second World War being an exception, but Father adored *Auwstralië* and could see only the positive side. Mother equivocated, but eventually fell into line. Flozzie and I, being under sixteen, didn't have much choice. In time, the older brothers swore their own allegiance to Australia and the Queen.

While most of Britain's former colonies embraced full independence with patriotic fervour, Australians, in their sentimental way, still cling to the monarchy, which never fails to astound me. Australians in general remain stubbornly conservative on certain matters, such as euthanasia, exempting religious organizations from paying taxes, religious education in state schools, prison reform, and this perennial issue of our formal ties to Britain.[122] Perhaps it has, amongst other reasons, something to do with the attitude, 'If it ain't broke why fix it?' However, the dismissal in 1975 of the Labor Prime Minister, Gough Whitlam, by the Governor-General of the time, Sir John Kerr, which was in principle sanctioned by the British Crown, led to great controversy over the role of the Governor and the legitimacy of such an act.

Furthermore, if between twenty and twenty-five percent of the population come from non-British backgrounds[123] and culturally have little or no connection with the British Queen, the relevance of such a monarch is diminishing. As the number of immigrants from a wide range of cultures increases over time, the British monarchy will

---

[122] The Fairfax Nielsen poll of April 2014 on the monarchy found republicanism to be at its lowest point in twenty-two years: 51 percent did not want any change to the current position, while only 42 percent backed becoming a republic. The recent visit by British Royals, William and Kate, may quite possibly have helped the monarchist cause.

[123] Australian Bureau of Statistics – Report number 4102.0: *Australian Social Trends*, 2014. Report number 2071.0: *Cultural Diversity in Australia. Reflecting a Nation: Stories from the 2011 Census.* Report number 2070.0: *A Picture of the Nation – Second Generation Australians*, 2006

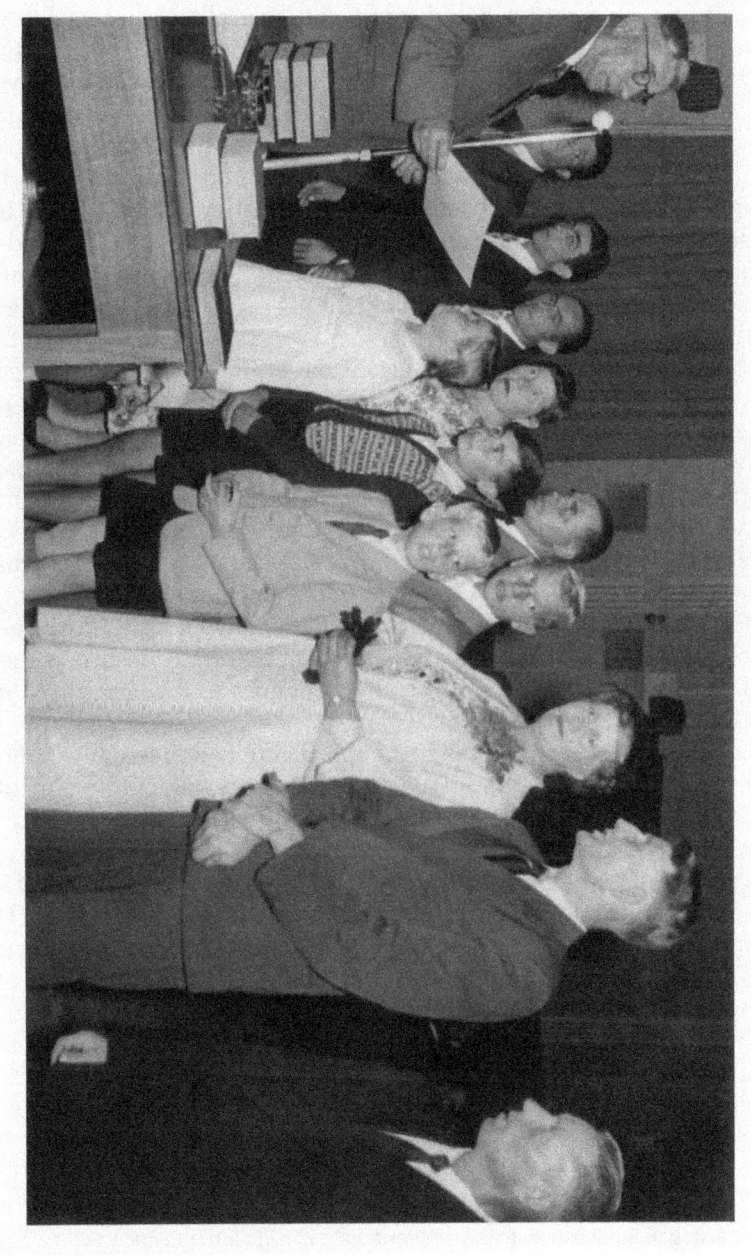

The family being naturalized. Morwell Town Hall, 1958. Frank and Henri watching Father, with Mother next to him.

correspondingly seem more and more anachronistic. For example, the combined Chinese and Indian immigrant population now exceeds those arriving from New Zealand.[124] It is just a question of time. Indeed, according to a report based upon the Australian census of 2006, the Anglo-Celtic element of the population is expected to drop to sixty-two percent by 2025.[125] The crucial question, however, is how many Anglo-Celts, which includes Irish, Scots and the Welsh, are in fact pro-monarchy? Or, for that matter, how many of our other immigrants or indigenous citizens? At this stage, it is hard to tell. Even so, while the issue of republicanism continues to fester, it is bound to raise its head again in the future. Presumably, we are mature enough to stand on our own flexible constitutional feet and to democratically elect our own head of state, or abolish the position altogether. This doesn't mean we should jettison our heritage and constitution.

Historically, monarchies encapsulated the idea of privilege, land ownership by an elite, colonialism and wealth, symbolised by palaces, perks and pageantry. After all, the origin of royalty derives in part from conquests by robber barons, earls and the like, the victors transformed into royalty, the trappings legitimizing what was initially theft of property and subjugation of the conquered. The principles of conquest and hegemony are common to chieftains, nobles, petty kings and rulers. In the end monarchy is based on the principle of 'might is right', irrespective of other absolutist stratagems, such as 'the Divine right of Kings'. There are of course many other reasons that can be adduced, such as the desire of people to be protected from their enemies and competitors; nothing original here...

The link between my religious upbringing and monarchism, however, is the concept of unexamined authority; that is, taking these institutions for granted. Whether a celestial puppeteer, a bully-despot, or an enlightened figurehead, people often persist in either self-laceration in pronouncing their unworthiness before these dubious entities, or idolizing them to the point of blindly following their edicts. Perhaps *Sigmund* was right in explaining our fears and rationalizations in terms of irrational forces. Some may find monarchism rational, and in some countries, even useful, but in this modern age, its once despotic and elitist hold over human beings may ultimately be irrational and in many cases, grossly anti-democratic. Monarchies are usually also very expensive to maintain, notwithstanding the compensation of the tourist dollar.

---

[124] Australian Bureau of Statistics – *Migration, Australia 2011–12 and 2012–13*, 2013

[125] *Approaching Transnationalisms: Studies on Transnational Societies, Multicultural Contacts, and Imaginings of Home* B. Yeoh, M. Charney, T. Kiong, 2003, Kluwer Academic Publishers: Dordrecht, Netherlands p.108

*

During the spring and summer of my last two years in Morwell, I often cycled the nine miles to Traralgon and back. No gears! I was dangerously fit. I loved the subtle changes in the countryside and balmy weather; though fresh air wasn't always forthcoming in the Valley.

Sometimes I took the Maryvale Road, locally referred to as the Paper Mill Road, stopping at the bridge to inspect the twenty or so dead snakes draped over the railings by the local snake catcher. Cicadas assailed my ears like a platoon of umpires all blowing their whistles at the same time.

Occasionally, I took the flat Princes Highway past the golf course and when battling a headwind, cursed myself for having misread the weather forecast. In those days, the traffic was sparser and not as threatening; nor were people as abusive as today, so I always felt perfectly safe riding my bike. Of a late afternoon, I was glad to see the brightly coloured commission houses welcoming me home, even though the steep roads of this last stretch made cycling so difficult.

The long rides gave me time to think. There was a growing sense that the Latrobe Valley had served its purpose. For some time, too, Father had hinted at the idea of moving to Melbourne. He wanted a change from the power station and the wood business. My parents also wanted to be closer to John and Bill, who, by 1958, had already moved to Melbourne.

The sheer energy and restlessness of youth allows for improvisation, usually up the ladder of optimism. I thought I had done a lot, although in fact very little, and thanked my sensible parents for having allowed me to express myself in novel ways, but it was time for new horizons. I was changing faster than I realized; adolescence, that morass of bizarre impulses, had seized me by the scruff of the neck and thrown me into the unknown.

My family, too, were changing, with an eye on new prospects. Jack-the-lad married after he left home; in Melbourne, Bill was trying his luck in the painting business, while Lex had completed his Intermediate, or year ten, at Yallourn Tech and wanted to be a draughtsman. By 1958, I had passed the Proficiency Certificate, or year nine. Flozzie meanwhile had run his unfruitful course at Saint Vincent's and needed help.

Mother, always agitated, was torn between her love for the two older boys, now gone, and the needs of her younger ones, who, she thought, might want to remain in the Latrobe Valley. Her hand was agreeably forced when Bill persuaded Father to join his painting lark and move to Melbourne. Bill had rented a few rooms in Williams Road, Toorak. The irony of living in an area surrounded by wealth and privilege didn't go unnoticed. For about six months or so, Father travelled between Morwell and Melbourne, but only on weekends. Both worked hard as painters and soon found plenty of clients.

By the Scruff of the Neck

At last we decided to chance our luck in the city I had always wanted to live in. The time was right and our parents realized Melbourne had more to offer than the Valley: we had outgrown Morwell. Lex and I were academically bright enough to make a better fist of the future by living in the capital, while I also dreamt of joining a large soccer club, where the competition might be more challenging and rewarding.

"There was movement at the station" and decisions to be made! We sold the block of land in Morwell and used the money as a deposit for a new home in Noble Park, or 'Nobbly Park', as I called it. A similar sense of excitement overcame us as when we moved from Traralgon six years earlier. This time, though, the house would be truly ours; eventually anyway, although as for most Australians at the time, and indeed today, houses really belonged to mortgage companies and banks.

We left Morwell at the beginning of January 1959, Father, Mother and Flozzie in the FJ, I in the removalist van. Lex was already in Melbourne by this time. I had been instructed to help the removalists with the shifting when we reached Noble Park, so sat in the middle, between the men. The truck stopped at the Beaconsfield Pub, where we had a counter lunch, my very first. It was a stinking hot day, but I loved every minute of it. The men were friendly and helpful and treated me as an equal: I felt like one of them. There was much to look forward to: acquiring my own room, attending a new school, making friends and assessing soccer options. As it turned out, I didn't have a room to myself for two years, having instead to share with a loud-snoring boarder. The room looked out onto the backyard, which abutted open grassland; which in turn meant there were no neighbours beyond the back fence. You beauty! We used the field as a soccer and cricket pitch.

Joan Court, Noble Park, just off the Princes Highway, was to become our parents' last house. Noble Park represented the outer suburbs in the 1950s, on par with Pakenham today. The backyard was of similar size to Butters Street, while the house was a little bigger, but nothing like the 'mansions' of today, where much of the space seems wasted. I sometimes joke to my friends, young and old, that many modern houses could easily accommodate at least twenty Vietnamese, Indians, Afghanis, Sudanese, or, as in our day, Italians, Croatians or Greeks...or indeed, Dutchies. It's a joke that often doesn't register too well. They look at me as if to say, from under which rock did I crawl? Huge houses seem to be the norm today, a bit like current rates of obesity, I daresay.

By the time we moved to Melbourne, Jack-the-lad was living in Malvern, and had become a father. Bill was still in Toorak. He moved back home briefly, then married soon afterwards, only to return to the Valley for a short time, where he bought a farm near Thorpdale. He eventually sold it and moved to Tasmania, remaining there for the rest of his life, a very happy man.

Flozzie briefly attended Dandenong Technical School, then transferred to Saint John's, Dandenong, where he remained until old enough to gain an apprenticeship in plastering: an earlier attempt at panel beating having soon been abandoned.

Melbourne rapidly became my oyster; work and education, as ever, the twin engines propelling me forward. There was so much to do! I attended a school quite different from Saint Paul's: aside from girls, Dandenong High School had much more to offer, as I discovered in due course. At sixteen I also became a glass washer at the Springvale Hotel, which had a wild reputation and, during this heyday of six o'clock closing, claimed to be the second busiest pub in Melbourne. I was soon promoted to barman and worked there for seven years. I could handle a 'pluto' [126] faster than Wyatt Earp his gun!

There was something final about leaving Morwell, as if we had all suddenly grown up; or, as Spike Milligan put it, "Children don't grow up, they disappear."

I have come to associate Morwell with self-expression, hard work and nostalgia for a testing period of my life. There was something unrelenting about the place; there was always something that needed doing. Perhaps it should have been called Lesswell or Downwell, then we could have relaxed more, and yet it exercised a more profound grip on my psyche than any other place we lived. For all its trials and niggles, the town provided us with the scaffolding for a rewarding life. 'Poverty keeps one respectable,' Father used to say. It also sharpens one's life skills, makes one appreciate the smaller things in life, and teaches one never to take anything for granted.

To illustrate my point, when the Bedford truck in which Lex and I learnt to drive in our early teens died from metal fatigue, it was left to rust in one of the nearby paddocks. It became a family monument. Around it, new roads and houses mushroomed, but the cabin stayed there for another forty years or so, as if to thumb its nose at time. My two grown-up sons still remember the green cabin as a memorial to our youth. For years, whenever we visited Morwell from Melbourne, we did our obligatory run to our former commission house and fondled the Bedford like a long lost lover, still sitting there determinedly, hail, rain or shine. Speaking of which, since the climate was wet and cold in winter, and stinking hot in summer, I have also come to associate pouring rain, gusty weather and heat waves with Morwell!

---

[126] A 'pluto' is a beer tap shaped like a gun, attached to a hose, which is connected to a keg, and is used to fill beer glasses.

By the Scruff of the Neck

*

One broiling Sunday, during the first weekend after we arrived, I decided to explore Dandenong, hoping to locate a soccer pitch. The shops were familiar to me, since I'd passed through Dandenong many times on trips to Melbourne; however, they had taken on a new complexion. The gateway to Gippsland was now my new neighbourhood, Melbourne's central city area being too far away. At first the area wasn't much to rave about, admittedly, yet was varied enough to make it vaguely interesting.

Sweating gallons and needing water, I placed my bike against a rubbish bin and went into a milk bar to ask for an Adam's ale, which was cheerfully offered. I also bought a sausage roll. George de George, the Greek proprietor, was an affable fellow and his milk bar became a popular watering hole from then onwards.

I cycled through the wide stretch of the town centre, passed the town hall, was mystified by the military huts on the other side of the creek, noticed the swimming pool, and headed into Dandenong Park for a breather. No soccer pitch to be seen. I found a shady spot beneath a gum tree and sat down to catch my breath. Slowly, peace descended: a pale blue sky; warm, dry grass; leaves rustling intermittently, like strings of milk bottle tops, the sun scattering furtively through the foliage. Nature had its own rhythm and was clearly not interested in me. I relaxed completely, breathing in the scent of eucalypts and yellowing grass. I liked Dandenong. The distant roar of a motorbike, followed by the swish of cars, suggested constant movement, people always in a hurry. Cars and motorbikes, just as the earlier horse and buggies, seemed to have been around for a very long time, giving me both a sense of pleasant familiarity and of connection with the community around me.

A few pesky ants were racing off with a tiny crumb from my sausage roll. I followed their trail for a while, then heard the drone of an aeroplane and looked up, trying to match sound with location. I spotted a silver dot sliding westward, probably on its way to Essendon Airport and wondered who was up there, speculating that they might be businessmen, returning tourists, or even new immigrants from goodness knows where.

The oppressive afternoon heat began to abate as the breeze became stronger. It was time to go home. Humming *Tom Dooley*, I got on my bike, ignored my rumbling stomach, which wanted more than the snack I'd eaten, and cycled on, looking forward to a hearty meal of grilled fish and Hussar salad.

Father and Mother settled comfortably into their brand spanking new house. Father soon replicated his Morwell backyard, but without the wood business and huge pine crate. A vegetable garden, plus the novelty of a fig tree, were quickly established. He enjoyed Noble Park and loved going to McEwan's in Dandenong. McEwan's was a hardware store and supermarket, with a bottle shop, a forerunner of the changes in retail shopping. The one-stop shopping model appealed to Father. 'I'm just going to Maceewe to buy some sherry,' he'd bellow to Mother.

Mother adored shopping in Dandenong, with far more choice than Morwell. Living nearer the city, she was also closer to her married sons. With much clucking and fussing, becoming a grandmother reawakened her maternal instincts. Most families experience this, of course. The women in our family saw beauty and family features everywhere, the men sleeping walnuts and shitty nappies. Even so, Father adored his grandkids and they him. I was hauled to maternity wards and expected to admire the little prunes and their proud mothers, yet found all this focus on breeding tedious and overdone. All too humdrum! But then, aged sixteen, I had other things on my mind. Nevertheless, whenever a baby arrived, and they kept coming like new generations of chooks, I asked Father, 'A boy or a girl?' He either curved his index finger downward to indicate a boy, or muttered, 'A coffee bean.'

'Dandenong' is indigenous for 'lofty mountains', which are its backdrop. It had been a market town since the late 1880s, a town of crossroads and radial destinations. The cattle yards eventually shifted to the south of the town and ceased to exist altogether in 1998.

Dandenong is now an industrial hub and regional centre for modern services. Houses, flats and units were, and still are, relatively cheap, and work may be found in the factories and other facilities along the Princes Highway towards Hallam and beyond, as well as along the Dandenong-Frankston Road in the 'industrial parks': an ironic self-contradiction in terms.

The area soon became a magnet for immigrants. More than many others, it is a suburb of transience, or displacement, but just as in earlier days we brought habits and customs from the old country, so newer immigrants bring their cultures with them. Even today, while living in the Dandenong Ranges, I enjoy shopping at Dandenong Market, which, just as in the '50s and '60s, is a microcosm of the outside world, with its vibrant mix of nationalities. 'Spot the Aussie', meaning Anglo-Celt, is a favourite pastime of mine, as well as studying the faces and mannerisms of our newest migrants.

There are few other places in Melbourne where one can find in a single spot so many churches, temples, mosques, shops and restaurants reflecting the many cultures, both local and foreign, that make up the Dandenong community. Even the Uighurs have left their mark, with their exquisite cuisine. Afghani, Hazaras, Sudanese, Indian, Chinese, Bosnian,

Iranian and Sri Lankan communities have sprouted up, seeming to co-exist peacefully; at least for the time being. I often wonder how many people from the more affluent suburbs of Melbourne have ever visited the area and appreciated its ambience? In this sense, I regard Noble Park, Keysborough and Dingley as offshoots of the Dandenong area – Springvale is different, being strongly Vietnamese influenced, while Clayton's immigrant population is so high due in part to its overseas students studying at Monash University.

There is something tentative about Dandenong, as if it's a sorting house for migrants and the less well-paid, perhaps waiting for the next generation to break away, to mingle with other immigrants, indigenous Australians and the Anglo-Celts, eventually to shape a unique Australian identity not predominantly based on British culture.

As when one listens to Stravinsky's *The Rite of Spring*[127] for the first time, or studies the fibre artefacts of the Tjanpi desert weavers in the Northern Territory, Australia's identity is forever evolving and capable of being both surprising and surprised. A sense of rejuvenation is ever-present and to some extent, peculiar to this country.

Australia is big enough in size and small enough in population to experiment with all these differing cultures, provided each sticks to the ground rules. Perhaps our unique, multicultural society can become the prototype of an entirely reassembled *Brave New World*, deflating that of Huxley's dark, ironic creation?

---

[127] *The Rite of Spring* by Igor Stravinsky caused outrage and a near riot when it was first performed in 1913: the shock of the new. It took some getting used to, with its visceral rhythms and odd orchestration, yet today it is considered a popular work in the modern repertoire. By analogy, Australia's non-Anglo-Celtic immigrants have at times both shocked and confounded other Australians, until understood and culturally internalized by the population in general. So, just as music and art can initially be disconcerting, the assimilation, or co-existence, of immigrants can at first be challenging to the host culture.

www.ingramcontent.com/pod-product-compliance
Lightning Source LLC
Chambersburg PA
CBHW022107150426
43195CB00008B/299